Television and Youth Culture

Education, Psychoanalysis, and Social Transformation

Series Editors:
jan jagodzinski, University of Alberta
Mark Bracher, Kent State University

The purpose of this series is to develop and disseminate psychoanalytic knowledge that can help educators in their pursuit of three core functions of education. These functions are:

1) facilitating student learning;
2) fostering students' personal development; and
3) promoting prosocial attitudes, habits, and behaviors in students (i.e., those opposed to violence, substance abuse, racism, sexism, homophobia, etc.).

Psychoanalysis can help educators realize these aims of education by providing them with important insights into:

1) the emotional and cognitive capacities that are necessary for students to be able to learn, develop, and engage in prosocial behavior;
2) the motivations that drive such learning, development, and behaviors; and
3) the motivations that produce antisocial behaviors as well as resistance to learning and development.

Such understanding can enable educators to develop pedagogical strategies and techniques to help students overcome psychological impediments to learning and development, either by identifying and removing the impediments or by helping students develop the ability to overcome them. Moreover, by offering an understanding of the motivations that cause some of our most severe social problems—including crime, violence, substance abuse, prejudice, and inequality—together with knowledge of how such motivations can be altered, books in this series will contribute to the reduction and prevention of such problems, a task that education is increasingly being called upon to assume.

Radical Pedagogy: Identity, Generativity, and Social Transformation
By Mark Bracher

Teaching the Rhetoric of Resistance: The Popular Holocaust and Social Change in a Post 9/11 World
By Robert Samuels

Television and Youth Culture: Televised Paranoia
By jan jagodzinksi

Television and Youth Culture

Televised Paranoia

jan jagodzinski

palgrave
macmillan

First published in 2008 by PALGRAVE MACMILLAN® in the United States –
a division of St. Martin's Press LLC, 175 Fifth Avenue, New York, NY 10010.

Where this book is distributed in the UK, Europe and the rest of the world,
this is by Palgrave Macmillan, a division of Macmillan Publishers Limited,
registered in England, company number 785998, of Houndmills,
Basingstoke, Hampshire RG21 6XS.

Palgrave Macmillan is the global academic imprint of the above companies
and has companies and representatives throughout the world.

Palgrave® and Macmillan® are registered trademarks in the United States,
the United Kingdom, Europe and other countries.

ISBN-13: 978-1-4039-7808-0 (paper back)
ISBN-10: 1-4039-7808-5 (paper back)

ISBN-13: 978-1-4039-7648-2 (hardcover)
ISBN-10: 1-4039-7648-1 (hardcover)

Library of Congress Cataloging-in-Publication Data is available from the
Library of Congress.

A catalogue record of the book is available from the British Library.

Design by Macmillan Publishing Solutions

First edition: December 2008

10 9 8 7 6 5 4 3 2 1

Printed in the United States of America.

in loving memory of my father

Michał Jagodziński
(1923–2006)

who was unable to see this book's completion

Contents

Acknowledgments

I have a number of people to thank for making this book possible. I would first like to thank Gayle Gorman for the special edition of the cover. Her choice of the "still" from the television series *Freaks and Geeks* is just perfect. I would also like to thank Brad Smilanich for the generous use of his extensive DVD library. At the beginning of this project he gave me first-season starter sets on a number of television series that I ended up viewing. It was Brad who put me on to *Freaks and Geeks*. And, to Mark Bracher, my friend and coeditor of the *Education, Psychoanalysis, Social Transformation* book series. His support and commentary are always welcome. Lastly, I would like to thank the staff of Macmillan Publishing Solutions for the amazing detail and care that they took with my text. I appreciated their amazing eye for detail and feel for the language. Without a thorough edit, this text would never have reached the shape that it is in.

Introduction: Youth Living in Paranoiac Times

Is psychoanalysis a successful paranoia because it claims to have the last word in every discussion, the decisive explanation to every interpretation, the universal key to opening and closing every problem? Or might its success and inability to laugh at itself result instead from the need to invade all existence for all time?

(François Roustang, "How Do You Make a Paranoiac Laugh?")

This is the third book in a trilogy that began with *Youth Fantasies* (2004), which was followed by *Music in Youth Culture* (2005). In those first two books, a Lacanian psychoanalytic framework was put to use to theorize the complexity of youth, interrogated to some extent by Gilles Deleuze and Felix Guattari's (sometimes cited as D+G, but I am not consistent) challenge to Jacques Lacan's dominant position. I took popular media culture seriously, exploring films, the Internet, video games, and a particular selection of music (gangsta rap, Nü metal, grunge, grrrl culture, techno) to identify what I took to be post-Oedipal developments in youth where postadolescence has been culturally extended to blur clear-cut distinctions of adulthood brought about by the global sociohistorical changes wrought by capitalism and its accompanying teletechnologies.

Television and Youth Culture: Televised Paranoia is a slight departure in the sense that the media of concentration is television—more specifically, televised youth series whose ubiquitous and seemingly innocuous programming constantly invades our homes and daily lives. Those who are expecting the usual ethnographic study of youth, complete with transcripts and analysis, will be disappointed. The fictional narratives that emerge in these televised serials, as well as the fictional narratives that emerge in research, especially arts-based research where the imaginary is forwarded, do not escape their fantasy frames. In some forms of arts-based research, the overbloated ego of autobiography only seems to produce a fantasy frame and little else. My intent is to rethink the representation of youth on television along psychoanalytic lines. Deleuze and Guattari come more to the fore in my continued attempts to find a transpositional space between them and Lacan to help theorize the becoming of youthful identities in postmodern times. In a nutshell, I argue that the Lacanian Real can be enriched through Deleuze's "transcendental empiricism" as that infinitely potential field of virtual potentialities from which reality is actualized. The psychic Real is the topological site of becoming. Further, the bifurcation that is so often made between Lacan, as offering a "negative" articulation of desire as informed by lack (*manque*), and Deleuze and Guattari, as champions of its "positive" articulations, is, in my analysis, misleading. This hardened division has developed by ignoring Lacan's late works and Deleuze and Guattari's own admiration for Lacan. In this sense, Slavoj Žižek's continuing articulations of Lacan are as much "post" Lacanian as Deleuze and Guattari, in that his oeuvre is marked by a shift to the psychic register of the Real. In chapter 2, the term I use for this unlikely hybrid of thought is "self-refleXion," where the capitalized X stands for a graphically sighted meeting place that recognizes the heterogeneity of both forms of desire as negation and affirmation, psychoanalysis and schizo-analysis, which can be respectfully queered as post-*Oedipal* and *post*-Oedipal. It should be pointed out that affirmation for Lacan precedes negation at the level of the unconscious. It is not ontologically primitive as it is in G. W. Friedrich Hegel, but remains an effect. Lack emerges only when the two systems come together—nature and culture.[1]

Deleuzian developments speak to image and time, both of which are crucial to theorizing the "flow" of television and the "forever becoming" of youth; his theorizations on "becoming" seem singularly apt when identifying a process that has some nebulous starting point (tweens, teens) and a nebulous ending (adulthood). Generational analysis, as argued in *Youth Fantasies*, is perfectly suitable for categorical market research. Generally speaking, this "smooth" space is continually undergoing paedomorphic transformation on both ends of the continuum. Infants are expected to learn more, while adults are expected to maintain their flexible, youthful selves to keep up to changing technologies. Deleuzian "becoming" is a suitable trope for a "never-aging" youth; it has its dangers, since, as in my previous books, I take postmodern morphing identities to be precisely the capitalist subject of performative production that ties in so well with neoliberal notions of "possessed subjectivity"—possessed, as Arthur Kroker (1992) once put it, by virtual reality that has made material at the molecular level seem malleable and manipulable into any desired form.[2] What are we to make, for instance, of Deleuze and Guattari's (1983, 290) life—force materialism with its claims of reducing the unconscious to the structures of the genetic DNA code? How much of Deleuzian antihumanistic thought falls into reductive biologism? If difference is constantly being reterritorialized by the capitalist marketplace by managing and targeting identities, then it becomes extremely difficult to point to where difference and its multiple live up to the promise of releasing revolutionary transformative schizophrenic desire.[3] When does subjugation lead to subjectification on an individual or social level? These questions impact my discussion of television paranoia.

The Paranoia of the Posthuman

I have chosen the term *undercover* as a descriptor to allude to a number of developments that have emerged in this post-Oedipal paedomorphic period of human development, the key of which is the continual uncertainty and anxiety that clouds the institutions of the family and schools as they continue to decenter the boundaries that once corralled "youth" as typified by biological and psychological developmental theories. As the boomer generation progressively becomes older, retires, and begins to loose touch with popular culture that once sustained it, youthful vitality through health and exercise becomes a megaenterprise, and the nostalgia for youth is sure to linger. Who would think that the prune figures of Mick Jagger and Keith Richards would still be doing concert tours! Or, that a never-ending parade of Elvis Presley imitators would just keep endlessly rockin' along? Youth, extended and pulled in both directions, has become a socioeconomic category that is studied for the success of the marketplace.

It should be no surprise that the actors in the televised series that I discuss are much "older" than their scripted ages (Banks 2004). This is to be expected, since the target audience is not only teens but now extends to "young" adults. Transgenerational media have become the standard. As argued in my previous two books, youth is no longer a developmental or age-related category. Mary Bucholtz (2002) puts this succinctly: "Youth foregrounds age not as trajectory, but as identity, where identity is intended to invoke neither the familiar psychological formulation of adolescence as a prolonged 'search for identity,' nor the rigid and essentialized concept that has been the target of a great deal of recent critique. Rather, identity is agentive, flexible, and ever-changing—but no more for youth than for people of any age" (525).

Identities shift rather than evolve. Issues surrounding them abound to a point where a new form of agoraphobia has emerged in the "phantom public space" where consensus and rationality is sought under the cover of nostalgia; open public spaces are claimed to be unlivable and feared because they are riddled by alterity "caused" by identity politics (Deutsche 1996, 269–327). With no "safe" public zones left (as if they were there to begin with), these agoraphobes become paranoid from the fear of being stared at by an unknowable Other that is no longer identifiable by a confirming gaze (in the Lacanian sense) on them. Such agoraphobia is shaped by what might be termed an *alien invasion*, haunted by a phantom of alienation.[4] As Homi Bhabha (1994) once wrote, "Hybridity represents that ambivalent 'turn' of the discriminated subject into the terrifying, exorbitant object of paranoid classification—a disturbing questioning of the images and presences of authority" (113). This same anxiety is extended to the Internet. "The info-paranoid responds to the current 'public' infrastructure of the Internet by creating private (that is, secret) spaces or cloaks, within which they hope to be invisible" (Chun 2006, 249). Paranoia, as will be developed, is very much part of our televised culture.

Being *undercover* also suggests wearing a mask, a mask that is a simulacrum, which repeats a familiar image but assumes another identity to cover up hidden intentions. The television series *Alias* is an obvious paranoid narrative in this sense. Sydney Bristow (Jennifer Garner), a double agent, is always in danger of being found out that she is working for the "Man," but which one—for the CIA operation or its double, the SD-6? Who does her father, Jack, a double agent "truly" represent in her unconscious? Deleuze and Guattari (1987) maintain that "We fall into a false alternative if we say that you either imitate or you are. What is real is the becoming itself, the block of becoming, not the supposedly fixed terms through which that which becomes passes" (*TP*, 238). This makes Sydney's identity of "becoming" even more elusive. We have a case of "beyond" good and evil, raising the specter of Nietzsche's "powers of the false," where Sydney has become a demonic double that puts to doubt the good–bad opposition of clandestine government activities. I would maintain that this dilemma is precisely what lies at the heart of the generalized paranoia experienced by the East and the West in the contemporary globalized conflict: the moral Law that defends the public Good in the name of Freedom and Democracy and its possibly inherent rottenness can no longer be sustained with any assured confidence.[5] As Eric L. Santner (1996) succinctly put it on the closing page of his study of Judge Schreber's paranoia, the crisis of post-Enlightenment modernity's symbolic order, its central paradox, is that the autonomy of the individual is constantly undermined and betrayed by the Law that is meant to preserve it. Like Sydney, who is a *double* agent, we are caught in a *double* bind of the superego: "Do as I say: don't do as I say, for the law is this—there is no law!"

Undercover also alludes to that part of the Self that remains unconscious, a Real self in Lacan's terms, governed on the molecular level by its topological intensities in Deleuze's sense, which I will later develop as a form of self-refleXion, where the "X" will refer to this unknowable core that is formed through *bodily affect*. Youth become alien and monstrous in their excesses, beyond containment. Identity becomes continually riddled by the anxiety caused by not fitting in, explored as "freaks" and "geeks" in the context of this book, and by the television series of the same name in chapters 5 and 6. The postmodern period is marked by paranoia, a public crisis in epistemology when it comes to truth claims and the status of knowledge. The postindustrial, post–cold war, post-Marxist, global capitalist societies have produced a perpetual crisis over what is considered to be "real," and over just how the "reality" of the symbolic order is to be determined and authorized. Traditional liberal notions of citizenship, individuality, and agency decentered by postmodernity have been shored up by the spread of a surrealistic global "war" on terrorism, as spearheaded by the George W. Bush administration, that emerged from the epicenter of 9/11. Referring to what happened simply by its date suggests that we "have no concept and no meaning available to us to name in any other way this 'thing' that has just happened, this supposed 'event'" (Derrida 2003, 86). Patrick O'Donnell's (2000) brilliant study of cultural paranoia in the United States, published a year before the attacks on the Twin Towers (note the rhetoric—not the World Trade Center), has as its main title *Latent Destinies*. This is surely right on the mark when it comes to this traumatic event. "The consequences of such constructed destinies [George W. Bush's war on terror, his Christian crusade to rid the world of evil] are inevitably forged in the aftermath of the event itself, but as if the event, its latency, always possessed this meaning and was always being prepared for by history itself" (20). Each time a terrorist attack occurs or is thwarted, the fantasy narrative of Bush's destiny becomes reconfirmed. His National Security Strategy of preemptive action ends up being an "autoimmunitary logic" in Derrida's (2003) terms, "producing, reproducing, and regenerating the very thing [terrorism] it seeks to disarm" (99). For Osama bin Laden the outcome of this inconceivable event became a sign that Allah was indeed behind his own destiny to slay the Evil Western Empire and to rid the world of its decadence, decay, and corruption. But Bush's grace period of superpatriotism, as Michael Parenti (2004) called it, has waned for many, while Al Qaeda continues to garner a never-ending stream of suicidal martyrs for the Cause. The supply of youth for recruitment camps on both sides is in constant demand. The U.S. military is disproportionately represented by young minority and lower-income men and women who have joined for the benefit of government-paid college tuition, or because they are searching for a stable career, or for authority structures that are missing for them (Berlowitz and Lang 2003). So, whether it is through conscription in some countries (e.g., Israel), the lure of patriotic duty, or merely the call to visit "exotic" lands to find excitement and to escape dull, meaningless jobs, war once more beckons youth, but there is a vast difference in the level of commitment between a regular soldier's duty and the willing desire to commit suicide for a Cause, as history, time and again, has shown.

As developed in *Youth Fantasies* and *Music in Youth Culture*, the breakdown of traditional forms of Oedipal authority continue to be worked out through various televised fantasies and series, where youth play central roles.[6] This post-Oedipal climate emerges from a sense of alienation from our "species being" as questions of origins on both "bookends" of what it means to be "human"— animal and Artificial Intelligence (AI)—have become increasingly more open to debate and questioning, pushing science fiction in new directions in terms of what is true or false, real or a simulacrum, confusing fact with fiction in a society of spin. Such a paranoiac decentering has led to a return of fundamentalism to quell the panic, but this only intensifies lived reality further. The posthuman is gripped by our relationship to Nature and animals on the one end and our technological inventions on the other, as mediated by and through the limits of language—that is, our capacity to retain a semblance of cognitive rationality—an ontological state of existence as to what is fantasmatically framed to be the state of "reality" made possible through the anchoring of signifiers. But this, too, is out of our control as machines talk to one another through languages we invent, but few know. There is a wide and growing global gap between those who write software and wetware programs and those who simply use them, in terms of both their approach to what technology promises and the shift toward cognition as imaging processes made possible by the computer as a prosthetic device. The ill-defined and nebulous term *neurosis of yesteryear* has been displaced and dispersed into the psychic conditions of hysteria, perversity, obsession, and paranoia, which identify more adequately the tensions between the ego's Imaginary and the questionable symbolic order of global capitalism and the nation state.

The posthuman ethos is defined by an attempt to overcome the division between our species being and nature. One direction is to rethink the symbiosis along the lines of becoming-animal,[7] to think of the body as a multiple so that its potential for difference, for becoming-other, can break the categories that define it by forming new assemblages and, hence, different body affects. On the other side of the ledger, technologies extend our symbolic universe, harnessing the "body without organs"—that undifferentiated as yet to be stratified mass of flow—into a system of differentiated zones by extending the capacity and capability of each organ through various multiplier effects made possible by increasingly intelligent machines, machines that are acquiring a specific pseudohuman ontology all of their own.[8] So while the former bookend can be characterized as organically "machinic" in Deleuze and Guattari's sense—as an assemblage of one node hooking and unhooking onto another in a constant breakup of flow—the latter bookend can be characterized as inorganically "mechanical," with electronic circuits that continue exponentially to become more and more hypercomplex, striving constantly to become organically machinic but never completely achieving such a fantasmatic goal. This would ultimately mean the possibility of cloning humans, eradicating disease through technological medical wizardry, and, of course, eliminating the boundary that sets AI apart from the human—the stuff of science fiction (SF) (*Star Trek*'s Data, The Borg, *Blade Runner,* and my favorite—*Battlestar Galactica*[9]). Bioinformatics or "wet computing" has already begun to blur any easy distinctions between the two (Malik 2002).

The enfoldment of these two bookend problematics on top of one another, not as a dialectical resolution, but as two disjunctive and separate symbiotic, posthuman developments that trouble identity, present the paradoxes of postmetaphysical thought. The dialectic between matter and mind as once played out between materialist and idealist philosophies has been deconstructed into what Jean François Lyotard (1971, 39) characterized as a "diadeictic." No longer is such a relationship dialectical, but it takes on a heterogeneous coexistence; or put in another context, a "third culture" has emerged where science and the humanities have collapsed into one another as developed by "the new humanists" who have embraced the oxymoron of spiritual materialism (Brockman 1995, 2003).[10] The Deleuzian paradigm also shakes itself loose from the subject-object dichotomy and describes an action of one element on another in an act of never-ending becoming, where the interchange that takes place need not be primarily filial. The concept of the "desiring machine" as developed in *Anti-Oedipus* is meant to startle and surpass the distinction between the technical and the organic, between mechanism and vitalism.

This backdrop of posthuman developments adds to the general paranoia manifested in numerous scenarios of the machine taking over (from *The Matrix* to *Battlestar Galactica*) or in cases of genetic experimentation leading to such horrific scenarios as Francis Lawrence's *I Am Legend* (2007), where most of the human population has become rabid, turned into animals, thanks to a cancer cure that has gone wrong, causing a global plague to spread. There is nothing to indicate that Homo sapiens as a species might eventually vanish like so many other species have in the past. The paranoia of the cyberpunk genre has emerged to quell and deal with such anxiety. *Smallville* and *Buffy*, for example, are two series that obviously address these anxieties from opposing points of view: the former from a position of a transcendental savior with a "destiny," and the latter from a transcendent empiricism, dealing with the ethical conditions of everyday existence.

Youth in postindustrial societies are faced with the task of mastering digitalized technologies and becoming media savvy to the screen cultures that now shape their lives, if they are to stave off the anxieties of living in such an uncertain world.

The decentered global network of global capitalism has become impossible to grasp. It has become "unmappable" (Jameson 1999) in any conventional sense. Conspiracy and contingency theories, as two ideological perceptions, have arisen to counter one another from coming to terms with the trauma of the social symptoms—the loss of authority—that are indicative of a troubled world defined by a global ecological disaster and the euphemism posited as the "war on terrorism." Conspiracy theories answer to this loss of authority by positing an "invisible Master" who is behind the public Master, keeping things under control (Žižek 1996). Authority is restored, as is the support of power now transferred to clandestine state agencies, iconically represented in the past by the Central Intelligence Agency (CIA). Contingency theories also prop up the authority of the status quo by dismissing conspiracy theories as being paranoid, and by maintaining that chance, the random event, and accident largely determine history—all those unintended consequences that emerge are not in our control. The capitalist system is taken to be basically harmonious and sound. Social symptoms such as school killings, torture during the war in Iraq, the clandestine activities of right-wing militia groups (anthrax scare), or periodic stock market crashes are simply the result of aberrations in the system—the work of a "few bad apples," "screwed-up kids," or greedy chief executive officers (CEOs). Complexity theory has arisen to help with the "chaos" of contingency, ideologically supporting global capitalism's market economy as the best possible managerial system. Complexity theory, too, has its "invisible Master"—the not so blind workings of global capitalism. As Fredric Jameson (1991, 1992) has argued, conspiracy theory becomes an imaginative way to coordinate a map of the world, to live with the anxieties in it by still identifying someone in charge; whereas contingency theories claim that no such mapping is possible. We should accept such uncertainty and the anxiety it produces, because the possibility of another future outside that of capitalism seems impossible and foreclosed. Both ideological positions form a self-referential loop of pessimism-optimism, resulting in a form of political paralysis.

Between Post-Oedipus & Anti-Oedipus

With all this in mind, it seems that the descriptor "post-Oedipal" serves this book much better than the Deleuzian and Guattarian anti-Oedipal ruse.When it comes to authorial loss that now accompanies global geopolitics, a youthful population swings between cynicism and kynicism—*Borat* being the latest incarnation of the later expression. According to the Foucauldian thesis, as is so well-known and argued by many, authority in its visible Oedipal sense has never been entirely "lost"; rather, it has become hidden and decentered (homologous to Lucien Goldmann's [1964] "hidden God" of Deist empirical nineteenth-century science) into the myriad micromanagement techniques of power so that it seems that no One is in charge. Yet the deauthorized controls of the surveillance society (remote surveillance cameras and techniques, testing, certifications, examinations, and even Web Cam Whores) have inverted the "eye" of the panopticon—the pornographic society of control is meant to keep people OUT rather then IN through encrypted passwords that allow access. We now live in the machinic assemblage of a synopticon: no longer do the few watch the many; rather, the many watch the few—namely, the celebrities and the fodder of "regular" bodies that continuously appear on reality television programs. Michael Hardt and Antonio Negri (2000) once held out hope that globalized anticapitalist youth movements would create a groundswell of change. Naomi Klein (2001) still does, as she attempts to document every scrap of global resistance. However, the post-Oedipal Father has disappeared, leaving all youth *orphans*—the Father has left home, gone to "war," or remains unknown, missing or dismissive of his son or daughter; the Mother is dead, run off with another man, died of a disease (cancer most often), or has become a superegoic replacement for the missing father of her children, or she may be simply ignorant of her daughter's struggles, as the Buffy narrative makes evident, confused by the excesses of youth.

It should not be surprising, therefore, how often the idea of the orphan, both literal and metaphorical, emerges in the televised narratives discussed. Harry Potter has lots of company. Clark and Lana in *Smallville* are both literal orphans—their biological parents are completely missing, while the relationship of Lex to Lyle Luther is obviously paranoid. The three aliens in *Roswell* are orphans. They don't know where they came from or who their parents were. They miraculously emerge from sleeping pods already six years old, quoting the infamous *Invasion of the Body Snatchers,* a film released in 1956 that was not even the film Don Siegel originally made and intended to show (Siegel, 1993)! In the metaphorical sense, only Dawson Leery in *Dawson's Creek* escapes from being an orphan (although his father dies in season five). As for the other characters, Jen Lindley is estranged from both parents; Joey Potter's mother is dead, while her father remains in jail throughout most of the six seasons; Pacey Witter has a rocky relationship with his father and older brother; Jack and Andie McPhee have a hellish relationship with their father, while their mother is estranged. In *Freaks and Geeks* , the parents come across as silly but concerned, as sweet bozos who can no longer quite comprehend the struggle of their two children—Lindsay and brother Sam. As orphans of the post-Oedipal era, their filial loyalties are in question—suspended. Their abject, abandoned, and orphaned position in society has been compensated most often by way of a *gift*—Harry Potter has his magic, while the mutant *X-Men*, the *Fantastic Four*, and *Spiderman*, the adolescents of the new era, are all freaks of nature. (I discuss this in chapter 10.) Whether it is the special gifts of the *Roswell* youth, the fledging powers of Superman as a teenager, or Buffy's ability to slay vampires, these special gifts enable them to compensate for their loss of place in the symbolic order. The once overdetermined Oedipal phallic structure has always been historically specific. Being orphaned begins to denote a queer kinship structure, as demonstrated in *The Seed of Chucky*—as Judith Halberstam (2006) put it; reproduction has become transbiological. With their genetic powers, the mutant children in the *X-Men* series stir fear and trembling in the "happy home," while Chucky terrorizes the dollhouse.

Is this a post- or anti-Oedipal development? Deleuze and Guattari go through great theoretical pains to entirely discredit Oedipus and the filial drama that accompanies Oedipalization. The "anti" descriptor is more in keeping with a complete rejection of Sigmund Freud's Oedipal drama. D+G want to mark Oedipus's disappearance once and for all. Their antipsychoanalytic stance is to take psychosis rather than neurosis as their point of departure. Psychosis is taken to be "outside" the realm of psychoanalysis—incurable and, hence, untreatable. They maintain that capitalism engenders psychosis and schizophrenia by reducing the human (meaning and belief-systems) to quantifiable calculations of the marketplace: the reduction of the human that has been levied by left-minded critics ever since Karl Marx. Schizoanalysis is their way of coming to terms with this process and transforming it.

The postmodern transition of capital has been toward a credit and debt economy where "xenomoney" is floating and incontrovertible to anything outside itself—signifying only itself—money as simulacrum.[11] In such a volatile system, what is unclear is whether schizophrenia—as unlimited semiosis that the global form of capitalism fosters, where meanings and beliefs are unhinged to sell new products and open up new niches—results in paranoia as a conservative force (as argued by O'Donnell 2000, for instance) in order to restore lost identities and centerings. Or whether the paranoia that I speak of is precisely the way to resist the fall into psychosis and schizophrenia resulting from the unremitting instability of existence, the way to resist the rottenness of authority without falling into a disabling psychosis. Is such paranoia simply a disjunctive process that complements the more radical schizo process they develop? I find this a dilemma, a tension that is further explored in the next chapter, since it has consequences for the way I interpret the television series that I explore, especially *Buffy* and *Smallville*.

For Deleuze and Guattari, schizophrenia supplants paranoia when it comes to the current capitalist development, although not entirely. They do point out (*A-O*, 260–61) that "progress" of capitalism produces an oscillation between paranoia and schizophrenia. Capitalism is disjunctively torn in two directions at once (*A-O*, 76). Paranoia is taken to first emerge in a despotic system where meaning is permanently fixed and stable, issuing from a supreme authority, whereas schizophrenia emerges as a result of the frenetic speed of change in postindustrial societies. These are two distinct forms of libidinal psychic investment, although capitalism's (paranoiac) reterritorializations are said to be an ambivalent cultural holdover when it comes to trying to free market forces for power and expansion. It could be said, for example, that the nation state is a paranoiac detriment to the schizophrenic deterritorialization of global capital when it comes to free trade. They make this tensional divide quite clear in both volumes: *Anti-Oedipus* (366–67) and *A Thousand Plateaus* (120–122). Paranoia is implicated with Oedipus as a molar development characteristic of subjugated groups where identity is categorical (e.g., the agoraphobes mentioned earlier)—it is hardly revolutionary; whereas schizophrenic libidinal investment is molecular—the subject group is revolutionary. This is not an either/or nor a binary relationship, but a conjunctive heterogeneous one—an "included disjunction." It would be fair to say that both elements will be found in the televised series that I examine—paranoid and schizo. In some, the schizophrenic process enables an "escape" or "line of flight" to happen; at other times, the paranoia blocks the passages. *Roswell* and *Smallville* are more paranoid, while *Buffy* is more schizo.

There is a subtle (if perhaps impossible) difference maintained between the psychiatric sense of the schizo and the revolutionary schizophrenic process. It seems that the psychiatric notion of the schizo is minimally posited as the take-off point for the schizophrenic process that would consciously carry out the "escape" from capitalist servitude that the psychotic schizophrenic has already demonstrated by disavowing the social order. His or her psychosis is the ultimate refusal, which requires a strategic schizo process that then brings this tendency to fruition by breaking the flows. In *A Thousand Plateaus* (119–24), they discuss the psychiatry of the twentieth-century approach to paranoia, which is presented as a regime of "interpretive delusion." They contrast this with a "passional, postsignifying subjective regime" where interpretation appears vacuous. These two types, again, are presented disjunctively. The former regime is said to evolve insidiously, organized by a hidden center influenced by endogenous forces. So it's an "inside" form of madness, so to speak, which then radiates out by "circular irradiation in all directions." The latter is defined by an external occurrence, more emotional than ideational, more as an effort or action than as imagination—"active delusion" as opposed to "ideational delusion." "[I]t operates *by the linear and temporal succession of finite proceedings, rather than by the simultaneity of circles in unlimited expansion*" (120, original emphasis).

These two types of delusions strike at the heart of the psychiatric dilemma: "suspected of mistaking the sane for mad [first type] and the mad for sane [second type]" (ibid.). Freud's Judge Schreber is an example of the second type: he seems completely mad but didn't appear so—he was able to function socially depending on which organizational "circle" he found himself operating in, and on how far or how close it was to his hidden psychotic center. The first type might be called "truly" mad, since the sane person suddenly commits a mad, unexplainable act. Psychiatry reveals this double image: "seemingly mad without being it, then being it without seeming it" (*TP,*121). However, psychoanalysis operates on another level: in dreaming we seem to be mad (e.g., we may dream of killing and violence), but we don't actually act out our dreams in everyday life. That was "only" a dream. Psychoanalysis attempts to grasp the relationship between the two. The psychotic, however, cannot distinguish between the imaginary and the symbolic registers—s/he lives in the Real, and hence, again for Deleuze and Guattari, this is where psychoanalysis ends. These distinctions, as shall be shown, are particularly apt for my discussion of *Buffy* and *Smallville* in what I hope is a surprising way.

Deleuze and Guattari attempt to extract the revolutionary potential from this distinction by maintaining that those who are ideationally delusionary tend to be bourgeois paranoiacs who maintain the status quo, while the passional or subjective and postsignifying tend to be the proletariat who wreak havoc on the social order through their mad, subjective actions in linear, localized forays. In this second regime they maintain that "*a sign or packet of signs detaches away from the irradiating circular network*" (121, original emphasis) and that a map of such a delusion may provide the coordinates for an escape—for a way out, for a linear flight out. This movement is an *authoritarian subjectivity* that is postsignifying and therefore noninterpretable, and quite distinct from the despotic paranoiac-signifying regime. So, D+G say, "Unlike the seer, the prophet interprets nothing: *his delusion is active rather than ideational or imaginative*" (124, original emphasis). In brief, passionate delusion becomes a form of revelation; unquestioning belief in the coordinates laid forth rather than in some signifying assurance that can be deciphered. But can such a disjunctive (or inclusive disjunction) distinction be sustained? A Lacanian would say no; the burst of passionate madness becomes a "sign" from the Real, first as "non-sense," which then will eventually postsignify as a form of latent destiny. This happens also in the first regime as written memoirs where the story's line of flight is revealed, the difference being that it remains confined to the individual and is not seriously taken up within a societal line of flight; that is, there are many false prophets before the true prophet is found.

James Hillman's (1988) analysis of paranoia becomes interesting in this regard. He maintains that a clear distinction between a theological revelation and psychiatric delusion cannot be maintained. The three cases he examines, Anton Boisen, John Perceval, and Judge Schreber, all of whom left memoirs, would fit well with D+G's first regime. However, it is unclear just when a packet of signs detaches away into a line of flight—an escape is then followed toward a new beginning, universalizing the experience. Joan of Arc was obviously psychotic (or at least Luc Besson's 1999 film *The Messenger* presents her this way), yet she was earnestly embraced by Charles VII and supported by the Catholic Church of France. The mystical and ecstatic writings of Teresa of Ávila (Saint Teresa), whose masochistic pain/ecstasy became a point of contention between Lacan and Luce Irigaray,[12] led a life that was precariously balanced between accusations of diabolical possession—ready to be burnt at the stake by her accusers when her writings concerning her sexual intercourse with God and her ambitions of founding more Carmelite nunneries strayed "too far" from Church doctrine and it's influence—and her outright devotion to the Church and its Fathers through confession, asceticism, and torturous self-repentance. St. Teresa's hysteria, as both Lacan and Irigaray would maintain, is another way to shake up the patriarchal order by developing an opposing Imaginary (through her hallucinations of what she heard and saw) accompanied by a body of invented signifiers (her delusionary thought put to ink).

Hillman jokes: If one goes alone to the top of a mountain to wait for an alien spaceship that will emerge from behind a comet, then one is certain to be paranoid. But, should someone else join that person (*Roswell*, the television series would be an example), then there is the beginning of a cult. With enough money and backing, this could become an organized religion—and lead to the tragedy of a Jonestown or a Heaven's Gate. For Hillman all delusion is revelatory and all revelation is delusional, confounding the disjunctive synthesis through a deconstructive move. In religion, madness is endemic because religion requires it, which is ultimately supported by an irrational belief that the hidden Deity is the very voice of Truth. There is no veil to lift, for the veils themselves are delusional. This discussion points to the w(*hole*) in the Symbolic Order, which is why Lacan's concept of the Real continues to be so useful as the void of non-sense, for (transpositionally) it is the site[13] of ecstasy and the Deleuzian "plane of consistency"—the "burning, living center of matter" as Deleuze and Guattari (*A-O*, 19) would have it. It is the inherent tension between paranoia and schizophrenia that seems to constitute Žižek's (1993) claim that the capitalist's ambivalent Superego demands that we "Enjoy!" where there seems to be choice "without a choice" in the myriad ways the system appears open on one level only to be closed on another. Žižek jokes about the way we have "fat-free" foods that enable us to buy and eat twice as much and to feel good about avoiding the trans-fat threat, but then end up multiplying our caloric intake through overconsumption, not to mention divesting ourselves of our savings. At the same time, the speed of change, the geopolitics of global affairs, distrust in leadership, and corporate scandals (e.g., Tyco, Enron, WorldCom) produce a paranoia that cannot be so easily dismissed as simply a psychical remnant of capitalism's past social oppression, as D+G maintain. This is paranoia returned with a heightened vengeance. As Andy Grove (1996), the chief executive officer (CEO) of Inter-Tel succinctly says in his book of the same title, "only the paranoid survive." Organizational psychologists, like Stanford's Roderick Kramer (2004), push the concepts of "prudent paranoia" and "strategic paranoia" to ensure company survival.

Nevertheless, paranoia as a vehicle of resistance that questions authority, as developed in this book, does bear many similarities to schizoanalysis, as it will be articulated in the next chapter before various televised series are explored. The delirium of complete psychosis, the dividing line that is never made entirely clear in D+G's two books, however, proves to be useful as a narrative device. "Madness need not be all breakdown. It may also be a breakthrough" (A-O, 131). However, the question that always remains is, when?[14] It is to their credit that they do question the disjunctive synthesis between paranoia and schizophrenia. As they write, "It is true that we run up against all kinds of problems concerning these distinctions [between paranoia and schizophrenia]. In what sense does the schizoid investment constitute, to the same extent as the other one, a real investment of the sociohistorical field and not a simple utopia? In what sense are the lines of escape collective, positive, and creative? What is the relationship between the two unconscious poles, and what is their relationship with the preconscious investments of interest?" (A-O, 367).

I take self-refleXion, developed in chapter 2, as one possible way of answering D+G's uncertainty regarding narratives that take such a form, narratives where paranoid psychosis and early schizophrenia are indistinguishable, emerging as paranoid schizophrenia in the imaginary figures that will be encountered in some of the televised series, especially Buffy and Smallville. Sometimes the term paraphrenia has been used to denote late schizophrenia where there is a working integration with the symbolic order; in other words, there is less subjective destitution, since the narratives discussed insist that a "'cover'" be maintained so that their alien nature is not exposed. Could this be yet another inflection of being "undercover?" Such talk, however, misses the point, since madness inside of thought can only be evoked through fiction.

In a nutshell, this book is divided into four sections. Part I, "Theoretical Considerations," has two chapters that address the theoretical backdrop of the five television series directed at youth that I have chosen to examine. Chapter 1, "Madness and Paranoia," is a theoretical exploration of paranoia and schizophrenia, which speaks directly to chapters 7 through 11, which form Parts III and IV. *Buffy*'s two chapters form Part III, "The Real Paranoia," while *Roswell* and *Smallville* form Part IV, "Televised Paranoiac Spaces." Chapter 2, "From Self-Reflexion to Self-RefleXion," the second chapter in Part I, "Theoretical Considerations," provides theoretical context for *Dawson's Creek* and *Freaks and Geeks,* chapters 3 through 6 of Part II, "Self-RefleXive Narcissism and Alienation."

Part I

Theoretical Considerations

I

Madness and Paranoia

The Vicissitudes of the Schreber Case

In *Anti-Oedipus* Deleuze and Guattari interpret the paranoia of Judge Schreber as an exhibition of a storehouse of protofascist fantasies. They criticize Freud for neglecting to take into account the ideological social context in his analysis of Schreber's paranoia. Although they are sympathetic to the transgressiveness of Schreber's delusions, they do not make him out to be an exemplary case of schizo-analytic practice, which was subversive and resistant to the fascist regime of Nationalist Socialism. Franz Kafka is given exemplary credit for such literary prac-tice. Yet, as Santner (1996) humorously notes in his study of Schreber, "one should not, as they say, try this at home" (144), meaning that the price Schreber paid to come to terms with the fascism of his time was high; it cost him his mental health. For Santner, it was precisely Schreber's identification with his symptom as a *refusal* of the symbolic power and authority of fascism when he was writing his *Memoirs* that enabled him to stave off psychological death. While Santner makes his own evaluation of Freud's interpretation of Schreber (see chapter 2) and examines the myriad of Oedipal connections, he is much more generous in his study in regarding the way Schreber resisted fascism through his paranoia than Deleuze and Guattari are. For all intents and purposes, Schreber's *Memoirs* are a form of schizo writing in Deleuze and Guattari's terms. "What ultimately saved Schreber from psychological death, at least for a short while, was no doubt his residual need and capacity to *communicate and transfer* his 'discoveries,' to inau-gurate a new *tradition* constructed out of and upon the inconsistencies and impasses of the one he had known and which he had been called upon to repre-sent" (Santner, 2006, 144, original emphasis).

When exactly then *is* schizoanalysis deemed *non*-pathological, as a "line of flight" in response to symbolic authority that reveals its obscenity? Being "mad" certainly suggests an intense experience that goes beyond the Imaginary, skewed to hallucinations as to what is seen and heard, and beyond symbolic thought skewed to the point of delirium. This intense experience pinpoints the molecular "schizzes and flows" that Deleuze and Guattari refer to as transformative poten-tials. Yet, there *is* madness, and then there is *madness* that remains silent, unable to be rendered into language. Where there is no imaginary form of outward expression, there can be no "talking," "writing," or "arting" cure. For Jacques Lacan in his S III *Psychosis*, this second, "true" madness is the loss of the unconscious signifier, Freud's *einziger Zug*, the unary trait as "an insignia of the Other" (Lacan 2002, 253) that keeps the subject invested in the symbolic order. Lacan later reworked this as the *sinthome*—one's symptom as a quilting point that gives consistency to the subject by knotting the three registers. This is precisely where the subject begins to "fade" (*aphanisis*), eventually becoming totally unraveled. In his S XXIII, *Sinthome*, 1975–76, written about the same time as *Anti-Oedipus*, Lacan argues that James Joyce's writing was a way to stave off his own psychosis— the "foreclosure" of the-Name-of-the-Father—by "naming" himself. It could be argued that the Freudian Oedipal concept continues to haunt the *sinthome*, which has now become post-Oedipal in its formulation, although not entirely anti- Oedipal. That possibility rests with the potential of the posthuman queering the symbolic order.

Post-Oedipal Concerns

This problematic question of Oedipalization bears on the television series discussed, because their plots are so obviously post-Oedipal. Perhaps the answer to this question hinges on the difference between whether the adjectival descriptor used is anti- or post- when it comes to Oedipalization.[1] Deleuze and Guattari's account aims at a form of liberal capitalism that institutes the nuclear family where there is an internalization of a subservience and identification with the superegoic Law. Capitalism in its postforms has obviously decentered this nucleus to blur the distinct public/private sites of production and consumption. The invasion of television into the private space of the home in the 1950s was just the beginning of such a breakdown. In their book *Kafka* (1986, 9–15), the existence of Oedipal motifs is granted, but their concern is with a "line of flight" that leads to becoming-other from the blockage of the forces of Oedipalization. "The question of the father isn't how to become free in relation to him (an Oedipal question) but how to find a path there where he [the father] didn't find any" (10). If this is what they term *schizoanalysis*, then post-Oedipalization is a much better descriptor for the televised series that I discuss, where it is precisely the nuclear family and the authority of the Law as represented by Big Daddy capitalism that is so obviously questioned. In *Smallville*, Lex Luther is caught in an Oedipal struggle that "blocks" his line of flight. To be "free" would require the outright death of his father, Lionel. But, that would also mean there would be no restraint on his desire.

This is a master-slave relationship in which jealousies abound. At first, Lex may *seem* to be neurotically afraid of becoming like Lionel: evil. But as Deleuze and Guattari say, "it's not Oedipus that produces neurosis; it is neurosis—*that is, a desire that is already submissive and searching to communicate its submission*—that produces Oedipus" (10, original emphasis). Lex wants his Father to love him, but he knows it's too late. He thus loathes him and makes him his adversary. This is not neurotic behavior, but a perversely paranoid "game" between them, a game that exhibits a re-Oedipalization as much as a de-Oedipalization as various escape routes are repeatedly tried throughout the various episodes. Lex is always initiating a diabolical plot against his father, just as Lionel plots against him. Their paranoia is that of capitalism itself. The alliteration of the letter *l* produces a surplus of *subtle* and *minute* differences between them that keeps the game going. This alliteration is extended to Lois Lane, Lucy Lane, Lana Lang, and the mermaid Lori Lemaris, forming an "L-assemblage" that has the specific affective impact of a tightly intertwined ball of intrigue—a shrinking feeling of confinement. It is a further pun on Superman's family name—El. Viewers are positioned as always, wondering whether Lex is to be trusted or not. Is his kindness to the Kents simply an undercover game, or is he truly sincere? Is Lionel as evil as he seems, or is he just demonstrating good business acumen? The trauma between father and son stems from Lionel's repressed accusation that Lex had strangled his baby brother, Julian. It was, however, his mother, suffering from postpartum depression, who smothered the baby in his crib, an act—not unlike that of Medea—aimed at destroying Lionel Luther's desire to have yet another son, a child she never wanted, and to put a stop to the competition Lionel was cultivating between his two sons. Furthermore, there is another half brother in the Luther family closet, Lucas (another "L"), the child of an illegitimate relationship Lionel had with a secretary.

Then there is Clark Kent's line of flight away from his biological father, Jor-El, through his adopted father, Jonathan Clark's "becoming-human" as his way out from the bind of his superpowers parallels Lex's desire to "becoming-alien" so that he can supercede his Father. The nuclear family appears to be "boringly dead" when compared to these televised plots. Post-Oedipal plots, on the other hand, are always proliferating, revealing new aspects of Oedipalization as deterritorialization.[2] In each and every episode of *any* series discussed here—life is *cracked*. In Lacan's terms, the Real always intrudes into the symbolically organized reality so that a possible becoming-other can take place. This I would call self-refleXion, a concept I develop in the next chapter.[3]

Deleuze and Guattari dismiss Freud's limited analysis of Schreber as being too heavily focused on the familial situation, and maintain that economic and political influences were ignored. Their analysis thus becomes anti- rather than post-Oedipal, since they become preoccupied with finding a way to discredit Freud. This criticism may well be leveled at Freud, but Lacan had long moved on to articulating the Real when *Anti-Oedipus* first appeared in print. Lacan's (S III, *Psychoses*, 319–21) analysis of the Schreber case never reduces the Oedipal complex to simply a mommy-daddy-me triangle as Deleuze and Guattari so mockingly accuse Freud of doing. "What is it that makes the Freudian conception of the Oedipus complex cohere, it is not a question of a father-mother triangle, but of a triangle (father)-phallus-mother-child" (320). Of course, it is the phallus that concerns Lacan. Without the signifier of "being-a-father," Schreber remains paranoid—stuck in the Real, unable to move into the Symbolic.[4] Schreber is mad, yet appears sane only in the sense that his *Memoirs* keep him that way. This is a different "madness" than the one Sandra Gilbert and Susan Gubar (1979) explore in their study of nineteenth-century women writers for whom the madness of their women characters is a metaphorical representation of their own repressed anger at and rebellion against being confined within restricted gender categories by the Symbolic order. The fantasy of madness allows them to stave off their anxiety.

Jerry Aline Flieger (2000) craftily points out that Freud was more Deleuzian than Deleuze had acknowledged; that Freud pointed out Schreber's situation as a member of Germany's discriminated-against Jewish minority and that his identity as a paraphrenic man-"woman" was a way to escape fascistic masculinity. She maintains that Santner is able to utilize both Oedipal explanations and ideological social conditions to account for Schreber's paranoia as "a creative (unconscious) solution to fascistic conditions, as well as a symptom of a personal crisis of legitimation" (50). I would further support Flieger's (2005, especially chapter 4) superb, humorous, and clever efforts to show just how disingenuous Deleuze and Guattari's efforts were when criticizing the straw figure of Freud that they had erected. That said, as Flieger also contends, there is much promise for an enriched position when Deleuze and Guattari are juxtaposed with Lacan, and this is also the path that I follow in this book when theorizing television paranoia. Flieger rhetorically shows that the Freudian Oedipus triangle, which is problematized by Lacan to reveal an implied fourth term—the fantasy phallus, reflecting the fantasmatic Father as all-powerful that has become "limp"[5]—is not unlike a Deleuzian desiring machine that is being refigured by the next generation and that is not an agent of repression. Post-Oedipalization would refer to the new circuitry that emerges when phallic power becomes more and more difficult to sustain, as hilariously depicted by Žižek's (1999) take on Viagra as the miracle drug that props up the masculine mystique—namely, to cover up a man's inability to achieve an erection at will. There is now no excuse *not* to enjoy sex. Castration should more accurately be called "wounding, separation, frustration, recognition, socialization, maturation, accommodation, even diversion" (Flieger 2005, 108). Such descriptors point to the identity struggles of youth who have been "orphaned" and abandoned, left to face the anxieties of the age when choice falls on their neoliberal shoulders.

Post 9/11 Paranoia

If the Harry Potter books speak to a generation of preteens who are facing their uncertain world through magic, these televised youth series do the same for adolescents and young adults. Castration anxiety has only increased for youth today. In my two earlier books, my argument was that perversion (*père version*)—when it came to boyz/bois/boys—and hysteria—when it came to gurlz/girls/grrls—helped to explain youthful transgressions in the media, with the occasional fall into psychosis (e.g., Kurt Cobain; high school shootings). However, it is schizophrenic paranoia in its narrative forms that I maintain is most obvious when it comes to televised youth and some key series such as *Buffy, The Vampire Slayer, Smallville,* and *Roswell.* While perversion is a specific way to call authority to task by manipulating it to set limits to *jouissance,* and while hysteria is a refusal to accept what is offered as the symbolic order of authority by manipulating and refusing it,[6] paranoia appears to be more prevalent in a historical moment when leadership is not to be distrusted, since time and time again it shows itself to be corrupt.[7] Literature, film, television—the media in general cannot escape this *Weltanschauung* (world view). When Steven Spielberg, the quintessential director of American fantasy films, offers us the vision of aliens as "sleeper cells" in *War of the Worlds* (2005), the penetration of paranoia seems complete. Paranoiac behavior is driven by inadequate information, which is then combined with an obsession with needing to know or with conjuring up an explanation, no matter how magical and seemingly illogical.

In Seminar XI (1979, *Four Fundamentals*), Lacan says that at the basis of paranoia, which nevertheless seems "to be animated by belief, there reigns the phenomenon of the *Unglauben*. This is not the *not believing in it*, but the absence of one of the terms of belief, of the term in which is designated the division of the subject" (238, original emphasis). What makes this absence of belief so apparent in dividing the subject in postmodernity is the blurring of *fact with fiction*. Just what is to be believed by our representatives who uphold the symbolic Law, or by the journalists who are trusted to report the "truth" when media-savvy recipients are quite aware of the rhetorical constructions of media "spin"? As Flieger (2005) puts it, "the paranoid looks *so* awry at reality that she or he sees that the symbolic Other, the guarantor of meaning, does not 'really' exist" (82, original emphasis). "Her 'know-it-all' perspective disturbs the uniformity of the 'normal' field of view, precisely because her paranoia contains *more* than 'a little piece of the [R]eal' for her, the alien object . . . becomes dominant, as it expands to determine, skew, and resituate the psychotic field of vision, outside of symbolic consensus" (82, original emphasis). Just as perversity should not be understood in its usual colloquial terms, paranoia should also *not* be dismissed so quickly as a pathology; rather, it may well be a healthy way to retain skepticism, as a symptomatic condition of postmodernity, a position sustained by Slavoj Žižek (1991) and Fredric Jameson (1992) as a desire to locate oneself spatially in the social confusion inherent in the postmodern condition.

When discussing *Dawson's Creek* in chapters 3 and 4, I maintain that the hyper-self-reflexivity of dialogue between the characters is precisely a healing narrative that tries to come to terms with "the real illness, the breakdown of the symbolic universe, the end of the world, the breakdown of the [R]eal, reality barrier" (Žižek 1991, 19) that youth encounter so much in their lives. *Dawson's Creek* does not appear at first to be a paranoid melodrama of any sort. It is, however, the unique speech acts between its principal characters that stave off the uncertain future that all the characters face. *Dawson's Creek* illustrates Lacan's general claim that human knowledge is *necessarily* paranoid, insofar as it requires projecting one's own view on the outside world and identifying with the views of others through fantasy. Or, as Paul Smith (1988) put it, "In paranoia, the libido is turned upon the ego itself so that, in a loose sense, the paranoiac's object-choice is his/her own ego" (95). Knowledge becomes an intersubjective "duel" that must be deciphered, since one's subject position is always informed through the Other, making it always relative, perceived, and interactive. The subject receives his or her message from others always in an *inverted form*. "All human knowledge stems from the *dialectic of jealousy*, which is a primordial manifestation of communication" (Lacan S III, Psychoses 39, added emphasis), a form of "fundamental transitivism"; that is, a form of inverted speech where the subject attributes to the other what comes from him- or herself, just the opposite of subjective identification. *Dawson's Creek* is riddled with such exchanges of jealousy between Pace and Dawson, Joey and Jen; *but* they are staged to undo and defuse these jelousies. Given that there is an inherent uncertainty in all acts of intersubjective communication, this underscores the fact that paranoia is very much a part of everyday life, especially when trust has been lost. Yet, *Dawson's Creek* is an extraordinary anomaly in the way it represses paranoia through the various triangulated friendships and love interests that become established only to be resignified into new relationships at a later time. In chapter 4, I specifically question the hyper-self-reflexivity of *Dawson's Creek*, wondering why the unconscious has been erased through self-therapeutic dialogue.

There is a fine line between a "healthy" paranoid response and a "prophylactic" one. In the age of fiber-optic technology, the latter characterizes the national security initiative when it comes to information processing; a search for seemingly irrelevant terms that can generate possible plots of terrorist activity or ways to prevent hacking into secured archived zones of digitally stored information. Such a logic of "prevention" leads to such (paranoid) initiatives as racial profiling where key terms generate the composite profile of a possible intruder. Exemplifying CIA terrorist paranoia was the case of Steve Kurtz, the cofounder of the radical performance cell known as Critical Art Ensemble, who was arrested for biological terrorism on the grounds that he had bought vaccine over the Internet illegally (Hirsch, 2005). The issuing of national identity (ID) cards, the new iris check recognition stations at border crossings, and the installation of face-recognition technologies at airports for non-U.S. citizens fall in line under this paranoid prophylactic logic. Inhuman technologies become the new master signifiers of a failsafe system to achieve the pretense of security. Instrumentalized hypervision now supplants human vision, which paradoxically is said to be blind or inaccurate.

The paranoid structure emerges when there is a *"lack* of belief in the symbolic order and in the Other as its guarantor, the site of the Law" (Flieger 2005, 84). Lacan (S III, *Psychoses*) explains this through his "distinction between the Other with a big O, that is, the Other insofar as it is *not* known, and the other with a small *o*, that is, the other who is me, the source of all knowledge. . . . It's in this gap, it's in the angle opened up between these two relations, that the entire dialectic of delusion has to be situated" (40). This gap between the other and the Other has widened to such a point to where the distrust of authority has affected all walks of life on the global planet—leading to the obvious manifestations of cynicism, conspiracy theories, and the return to postmodern twists of fundamentalism.[8]

This also means that the *small other takes on a new dimension* in such a climate of paranoia. Subjectivity as formulated by Beck, Giddens, and Lash's (1994) general thesis of self-reflexion needs attention, as I discuss in the next chapter. The climate of paranoia that manifests itself on television can be understood only against the broader backdrop of a delusional democracy spearheaded by the

George W. Bush administration "that builds on a mandate for open-ended war justified by the unfathomably deep sense of injury, a conviction that the entire life of the world would not be enough to compensate for 9/11" (Apter 2006, 369).[9] Bush's "war" against terrorism that fills the vacancy left by the end of the Cold War has stained the *aura* that America once had as a model of liberal democracy in the world. A crisis of "symbolic investiture" into his leadership has generated an uncomfortable parallel to Freud's famous Judge Schreber's paranoia, which stemmed from his aversion to his own symbolic investiture in a "prefascistic" court of law that emerged in league with National Socialism (Santner 1996).

Emily Apter identifies the way the paranoia has been created by the Bush administration through media spin, which creates a climate of distrust—what she refers to as "oneworldedness." "In this scheme, what we are told *is* connected [weapons of mass destruction in Iraq and the links to al-Queda, the global network of jihadists who mask themselves as ordinary citizens, the worldwide political conspiracy that masquerades as a religious sect] *is* rivaled by what we are asked to believe is *not* connected: there is apparently *no* link between oil and the Iraq invasion, *no* coincidence between electioneering politics and war, *no* cause-effect relationship between the media-hyped epistemology of insecurity and the abrogation of civil liberties, *no* common thread of sadism between Iraq and U.S. treatment of prisoners at Abu Ghraib" (369, original emphasis).[10] The gap between the small and big O presents a catch-22 situation, but it is not foreclosed (*Verwerfung*) as it is in psychosis. The-Name-of-the-Father is recognized, but viewed with suspicion and skepticism. Hence, this is again why post-Oedipal remains a more convincing descriptor than anti-Oedipal does in this climate of distrust. Paranoia is unlike psychosis, where the big Other turns into the little other as the ego becomes the replica of the psychotic self, where language no longer maintains its dialectical nature, and where there is no discernable relationship between the signifier and the signified, no ability to create metaphor or achieve a metaperspective on language (see Lacan, S III, *Psychoses*, 14, 268). It is not a matter of the failure to distinguish between the real and the imagined; paranoia is rather the failure to accept the imagined *as* real. The ensuing disillusionment is brought about by the failure of authority to convince, to show that it has the answers that satisfy the impossibility of a final answer, which is why teleology and utopianism have become questionable concepts. As Apter maintains, such a "logic of nonconnectivity condemns *you* as a paranoid if you suspect that the cause of the war is less than solid, and doubts *your* credibility if you fail to see that only when it comes to terrorism are all the dots connected" (369). Equally important is her insight into the way "oneworldness" has assimilated bipolar systems into one template: "communism and capitalism, democracy and terrorism, totalitarianism and religion, cults and family values" (378).

There are, however, differences of interpretation as to when paranoia falls into a "sick" psychosis rather than a "healthy" skepticism. For the former possibility, the small "o" can manifest itself as a "god" complex reinforcing "unipolar thought, specifically, a model of oneness as allness. If God is another name for intellectual unipolarity, the paranoid theorist will be God by devising a system of omniscience capable of binding everything into coherence, thereby rendering discrepant orders of signs mutually intelligible or pantranslatable" (Apter 2006, 371). This speaks to the holism that has gripped the ecological discourses where everything is connected to everything else, leaving us with nothing. *Smallville*, discussed in chapters 10 and 11, is obviously a paranoid narrative where Clark Kent is struggling with a "god complex" sent to him courtesy of his big Other (his father Jor-El), which is only a voice inside his head projected from a spacecraft that he destroys. Yet, the series struggles with Kent's rejection of the voice of his biological father, which reappears as a "nowhere" place, the place of the Real, represented as a complex of icy structures and crystals, The Fortress of Solitude, nestled somewhere in the incomprehensible stretches of desolate polar ice.

The paranoid figures who assure and guarantee us the symbolic order are not to be believed; however, to look at them from *too* skewed a perspective creates a danger of psychosis. What is left is only an awry look (an indirect discourse), which for Žižek (1991) prevents us from sliding into psychosis. Such a reading of paranoia is epistemic. It deflects the gaze "to see the alien presence (the death drive, the skull[11]) that inhabits human existence. . . . For psychoanalysis, then, it is precisely the play of the inhuman with the human, the savage identification with the alien Other/Rival, which constitutes the human, grounding taboo (Freud), producing the divided subject (Lacan)" (Flieger 2005, 87). This positive vector of projective identification with what "looks back" at us, makes us "*reasonably* paranoid" (ibid.) and enables a mechanism of introjection and identification to constitute the subject. The alien and the inhuman can be encountered through a projection of the self into the "place of the other as truly Other." This happens often in the series *Roswell*—for example, when Liz Parker falls in love with the alien Max Evans.

How then is this awry look staged in the televised narratives to be examined? As Flieger puts it, "only a skewed vision may provide resistance to the all-seeing monitor in the sky. Projective identification is the field of insight, rather than oversight" (87). It is essentially the Real as a *blind and contingent* automaton that needs to be faced and not recuperated again by contingency theories where this unknown dimension becomes managed chaos—contingency as complex regularity within parameters of uncertainty. On the other side of the ledger, the paranoid believes that the "Other of the Other" exists, which sustains conspiracy theories of a Master puppeteer pulling all the strings. To look awry as a form of self-refleXivity is discussed in the next chapter. Perhaps what is needed is to cope with strangeness—the alien within and without, a difficult proposition.[12] The Real as covered by a hypervisible floating sign, which, when debunked and displaced, exposes the big Other as "refracted into others. The too-public eye in the sky that haunts paranoid discourse becomes a sighted private 'I'" (Flieger, 88).

Televised Simulacra

Postmodern kynicism, as practiced by descendants of Diogenes like Michael Moore, Borat, Jean Baudrillard, and Slavoj Žižek, presents a challenge to the dividing line between fact and fiction, original and its copy, high and low theory, historical (elite) memory and ahistorical (popular) memory, and so on, through clever argumentation and buffoonery that mask a brilliant wit—the "gay science" of affirmative laughter as Deleuze and Guattari say of Kafka, who is "mad." (In French, the word *folie* carries the connotation of madness and gaiety of spirit.) It is the practice of a particular "cheekiness" (*Frechheit*), as Sloterdijk (1983, 203) called it, where a self-refleXive parodic style emerges that is decidedly non-Platonic, but empirically grounded to the earth. *Dawson's Creek*, for example, presents a hyper self-refleXive style that raises the question of whether its ironic and satirical form enables a savvy cynical viewer merely to passively confirm the absurdity of reality without the compulsion to change it, in line with such narratives as *The Simpsons*, *The Family Man*, and *South Park*, or whether it has cynical potential. "Kynical reason culminates in the knowledge—decried as nihilism—that we must snub the grand goals" (194). It is along these lines that paranoiac knowledge emerges through a practice of producing simulacrum—as similitude or simulation—to further the interests of kynicism in a climate of terrorism where attempts to reinstate transcendental truths of Christian and Islamic fundamentalism, both given their updated postmodern spins,[13] are hard at work to restore the grand narrative of authority where those in charge of the moral Good of the New Social Order are clearly identified.

An anti-authoritarian paranoiac stance becomes acutely evident in the repetitive searialization of the television series, which turns out to be the perfect form of simulacrum, where a form of youthful identity is performed through a succession of fantasies that are founded on temporal simultaneity and synchronicity. The serialized episodes discussed—*Dawson's Creek*, *Geeks and Freaks*, *Buffy*, *Roswell*, and *Smallville*—are self-contained, synchronic, intense repetitions each week, made even more so through the DVD boxed sets that are now available. Each season is characterized by what D+G (1987, 260–61) call a *haecceity*, whereby the youthful bodies presented seem to be organized "on a plane of consistency" defined by a specific cartography. "*[A] body is defined only by a longitude and latitude*: in other words the sum total of the material elements belonging to it under given relations of movement and rest, speed and slowness (longitude); the sum total of the intensive affects it is capable of at a given power or degree of potential (latitude). Nothing but affects and local movements, different speeds" (original emphasis, 260). The assemblage of these series is purposely limited and their movement confined. Each weekly episode is shot within a sustainable cartography. Clark Kent is confined, by and large, to the farm, the school (mainly to the location of the *Torch*, the school newspaper), a cave, Lex's mansion, and, once in a while, to Metropolis (Luther's corporation). In *Dawson's Creek*, confinement is to the restaurant in downtown Capeside, Capeside High School, the yacht club, the homes of Dawson and Jen's grandmother, and later to the dorm life at Worthington University in Boston. *Buffy* is confined to the ironic sounds and sights of Sunnydale, California, to Sunnydale High School, and later to the University of California Sunnydale, while *Freaks and Geeks* takes place at McKinley High School, from 1980 to 1981, in Chippewa, Michigan. The *Roswell* series is self-explanatory. Here the confinement to the infamous city in New Mexico and to Roswell High School is complete.[14]

The sets of characters repeat, over and over again, their foibles for ethical gains. Living in such "small," confined places, they are always being observed and monitored. The local sheriff "knows" Clark Kent very well already, as he always seems to be present wherever trouble occurs. The paranoia of the Symbolic Order that encloses them is always felt. The Roswell threesome is always paranoid with the fear of being found out by the sheriff, Jim Valenti, who is always "suspicious." He eventually is let in on their secret. Clark is always paranoid (like Sydney Bristow in *Alias*) about being "discovered," while Jason and Jen, as outsiders to the Symbolic order of Capeside, have to "face"—in self-refleXion—their undercover life: Jason, his closeted homosexuality, and Jen, her "godlessness" as a "pleasure" seeker—she loves promiscuous sex. The coupling of these various characters throughout the series presents different flows and affects for viewing pleasure. The concept of haecceity as "a mode of individuation . . . very different from that of a person, subject, thing, or substance" (Deleuze and Guattari, 1987, 261) addresses directly the "agency panic" (Melley, 2000) in an age of paranoia where the grand narrative of classical liberalism is breaking down, for the haecceitic assemblage has agency shared through connections. The objects of passionate attachment are given "voice" in such an assemblage, for example Dawson's love of film, Clark's attachment to the farm, and the alien paraphernalia in *Roswell*. Questions of freedom and control are no longer answerable simply according to a theory of an autonomous subject, nor are they resolved by structuralism as its theoretical opposite. Self-refleXion will be my attempt to develop a particular hybrid direction that borrows from Lacan, Deleuze, and Guattari. It is neither performative (Butler) nor critical theory orientated (Adorno), but combines virtual affect (Deleuze) and the Lacan Real as the "site" of struggle—the virtual Real. At least that is its aim.

The Power of the Simulacrum

I end this chapter with a brief discussion of the simulacrum. This seems appropriate, since the television narratives I discuss can be thought of as time-images where Euclidean space and chronometric time are subverted. Parallel worlds are presented most often in *Smallville*, *Buffy*, and *Roswell*, but even in *Dawson's Creek*, which appears straightforward in its presentation of time and movement has irrational gaps between its episodes. They are all, in this sense, narratives that have a falsifying capacity, and they are all examples of simulacrum. Simulacrum as the simple collapse of narrative into searlialization has had two influential postmodern interpretations: the first Baudrillardian and the second Deleuzian (Durham, 1998, 7–17). Jean Baudrillard's by now classic definition of the simulacrum of mass culture is as follows: "Simulation is the situation created by any system of signs when it becomes sophisticated enough, autonomous enough, to abolish its own referent and to replace it with itself" (cited in Smith, 2003, 70; Baudrillard, 1991). Such a definition remains caught up in the claim that hyperreality places us in an order of pure signs at an infinite distance from the "referent" or "real object" that would serve as the ground or point of origin. Without the ground of the empirical "real," society is launched into a virtual reality that circles around an empty center of signs. An accusation of nihilism can be levied. By dismissing the original, we are left with the question of whether there was any material reality to begin with, from which we broke free—or whether there was only the simulation of reality from the start. Baudrillard's (1983) famous "precession of simulacra" (the era of an original, to the counterfeit, to the mechanical copy, to simulacra of the "third order" where the copy replaces the original), which follows the trajectory of the Enlightenment, could also be read through Žižek's (1994) notion of the "vanishing mediator," each phase of the simulacra mediating changes to the free flow of capitalism itself, ending with the current phase of xenomoney. The notion is not so easy to dismiss—the stock market floats on such an assumption.

The second is a Deleuzian interpretation of simulacrum, which for me has affinities with Lacan's notion of the Real. Deleuze's virtuality treats the unconscious as the proliferation of identity through simulated differences in dreams and artistic productions as forwarded by the "powers of the false." Deleuze (1990) rethinks the simulacrum toward another trajectory in his often-cited essay "Plato and the Simulacrum," which was further applied and refined by Michel Foucault's (1983) discussion of René Magritte's famous painting *Ceci ne pas une Pipe* (*This is not a Pipe*). As Foucault explains, the simulacrum is a form of *similitude* and *not* resemblance. This produces a paradox that scrambles the hierarchy between original and copy. The last is made first and the first is made last so that the identity of the original seems suspended within and between its repetitions. The series that is developed has neither beginning nor end; it can be followed in one direction as easily as in another. Hence, each televised series often begins with a "pilot" that seeds the story line, but it always begins in medias res. The episodes that follow are its simulacra that retain the trace of this "original." The arcs that are developed pick up previous plot lines in ways that can confuse and surprise the viewer. A character who one thought was dead is brought back to life, and so on.

The new technology of television *only* produces simulacrum. As Wendy H. K. Chun (2006) reminds us, "Fiber-optic telecommunications cables, double-coated glass tubes stretched to tiny threads, *do not allow for vision*. Unlike medical fiber optics, they do not simply allow for a more penetrating view. The 'picture' we see on our screen is generated: there is no guarantee that the image we receive is a pixel-by-pixel representation of a previously recorded original" (249, added emphasis). She goes on to reiterate the posthuman aspects of this new media. Computer-mediated communications always have an inhuman element about them, as machines talk to one another through iterative electronic traces that are not always humanly understood. This engenders a hyperrepresentationalism where the simulacrum plays the role of an "exclusive disjunctive synthesis" rather than an "inclusive disjunctive synthesis." (One wonders how different this is from Lacan's own use of the logic of equivocity ("both and yet neither"), which I discuss in chapter 6.) This distinction, as developed by Deleuze and Guattari in *Anti-Oedipus* (1983, 75), can be understood in the way face-recognition technology exemplifies the former and not the latter. Seeing, knowing, and believing are intertwined flawlessly by *inhumanly* bypassing any forms of rationalization and deduction: "a terrorist is a terrorist not because he looks like one, nor because he carries certain weapons, nor because of past crimes, but because s/he can be positively matched *to an already existing picture*" (Chun, 263, added emphasis). Here the original and the simulacrum come together to reterritorialize difference into a closed circuit of a closed system. It is a form of inscription where the body is reduced to a numerical series through a computerized program that "reads" eigenvectors (called eigenfaces). That's "exclusive disjunctive synthesis."

Rather than quelling the paranoia associated with terrorism, control mechanisms like face-recognition technology actually increase it (Katti, 2002). "Inclusive disjunctive synthesis" on the other hand keeps difference open through the recognition of faces that exist "outside" facial data banks—the +1 element that enables the system to remain open, since human thought cannot be exhausted and archived. As Lacan (S XI, *Four Fundamentals*) would have it, the impossible gap that is created between *seeing and being seen* is where this difference lies—the very blind spot of face-recognition technologies.[15]

Unlike Baudrillard, Deleuze is unwilling to throw out the referent (the original), but maintains that a repetition may produce a productive difference; only such difference enables a becoming, a movement into another possibility. This is not unlike Lyotard's concept of "diadeictic" mentioned earlier, where there is no dialectical synthesis, only a difference formed in becoming. This surplus of difference, its latent signification, is theorized through Friedrich Nietzsche's "eternal return" and the "powers of the false." Such a return as a repetition with its effect as a "will to power" attempts to subvert the world of "truth" and representation as propped up by authority (e.g., God, the Self, the Symbolic Order) so that it appears questionable, shaken, and unfounded—a series of marks and/or fables.

Each episode in the televised series discussed has this odd sense of renewing the accepted question and the truth it holds. On one level, this Eternal Return of the repetitive simulacrum can become a "non-exit," a nihilistic repetition of an empty self-identity, but on another level, it can also be a liberating event, a way to escape the proclaimed truth of the Symbolic Order, offering another line of flight. Through the creation of the false—as an image or mask—the potential for transformation emerges. This staging of the possibility of becoming other than oneself comes, I argue, at a heightened sense of paranoia and, in some cases (e.g., *Buffy* and *Smallville*), schizophrenia. This is illustrated throughout in *Dawson's Creek* as each character learns about the other by playing roles that have already been occupied by friends, thus forming a self-reflexive repetition. The love-triangles are where this Eternal Return in its repetitive modes of simulacra occurs. The experience of the repetition of the simulacrum as the masked return of difference is where Deleuze and Lacan come together in what I hope makes sense as the virtual Real.

2

From Self-Reflexion to Self-RefleXion: Acknowledging the Inhuman

The various television series examined in this book require a rethinking of both narrative structure and the subject as theorized in the space between Lacan and Deleuze. In this chapter, I want to argue for a richer, more nuanced understanding of subjectivity that develops by attending to *both* a Deleuzian and a Lacanian understanding of the subject. Some broad assumptions are made that claim that there are many transpositional concepts between these two systems of thought that coalesced after the French publication of *Anti-Oedipus* in 1972, when Lacan placed more and more emphasis on the psychic register of the Real. This took place about the time of S XX (*Encore*) in 1973, although Slavoj Žižek (1999a, 29–31) sometimes maintains that the break between the "standard" and "late" Lacan occurs as early as S VII, the *Ethics* seminar of 1959–60. Rather than concentrating on the discursive functions as developed in S XVII (*Envers*), also the year he *rejected Freud's fixation on Oedipus*, Lacan begins to further explore the unchained floating signifier outside the Symbolic Order that is charged with *jouissance*, which he eventually names *le sinthome*. This is a point at which the fundamental life of an individual's singularity is constituted. However, it is neither a symptom in the traditional sense as constituting the truth of desire coded within the symbolic order, nor is it a fantasy that fills the gap in the symbolic, generating belief and making it tolerable to live with uncertainty. Neither is this formulation a *lack* that is a site of an undecidable and ambiguous location within a system. Rather, this psychic kernel as *sinthome* is "life" itself, pure immanence as theorized in Deleuze's last essay (2001), the ultimate ground of one's being, a *singularity* that is a radical excess, a nomadic *virtual* difference that Lacan asks us to identify with and accept. It is thus outside of psychoanalysis proper, heading in the direction of schizophrenia. If Deleuze and Guattari chose Kafka as their *Exemplar*, Lacan chose James Joyce. As argued earlier, the dividing line between psychotic and schizophrenic remains contestatory. For me, Lacan and Deleuze come together in the *virtual Real*—the X of self-refleXion, as I hope can be intuitively shown.

The information society, or designer society as I would prefer to call it, under global capitalism has forced social scientists to rethink the subject—to update the liberal paradigm to its present, neoliberal form. This has generally developed under the umbrella term *poststructuralism*, often hailed as a radical turn where identity and power grasped through linguistic discourses has produced a decentered and cynical subject ripe for multiple modes of niche consumption and ideological disavowal (Žižek 1989, 21). Multiculturalism, for example, could be managed through an anthropological discourse that enabled discrete articulations of each culture before "hybridity" proved to ruin its premises. Yet, even the nuances of hybridity could be categorized before too long. DNAPrint Genomics is able to analyze a person's DNA to determine the exact percentage of the person's Indo-European, sub-Saharan, East Asian, and Native American heritage and then assign him or her to categories such as white, black, East Asian, Native American, or mixed race, reminiscent of eugenic experiments at the turn of the twentieth century. In contrast, in an attempt to confuse easy signs of demarcation, the Mongrel Collective (www.mongrelx.org) constructs identities that prove to have no definitive allegiance to race and ethnicity along color lines, trying to confuse any easy signs of demarcation, closer to the D+G's sense of "becoming-animal" in their orientation where identification plays on a moment of co-recognition at an existential level, thus failing to be considered purebred.

The poststructuralist psyche seems ideally suited to maintaining itself within a capitalist information society (designer society) where flows and the emergence of complex systems such as the stock market require stochastic mathematics to deal with the impending uncertainties. Late postindustrial capital is being slowly left behind. We no longer sell our labor to quasi-paternalistic businesses. The hyperflexible job market insists that we now sell ourselves as the product to businesses and consumers in a general market through Web pages and designer vitae—as "immaterial labour" in Michael Hardt and Antonio Negri's (2000) terms. The neoliberalist subject has morphed into complexity, and it is precisely the new sciences of complexity and enactivism (Varela, Thompson, and Rosch 1991)—which slide easily into various humanist ecological theories, such as deep ecology, ecofeminism, sustainable economy, social ecology, and so on—that enable a globalized vision of capitalism to sustain itself. These developments usher in a new biologism that, at one end of the spectrum, falls dangerously close into to becoming a renewed eugenic movement, a neo-Darwinism with no soul where DNA mapping and the new explosion of epigenetic research has skewed the promises of the Human Genome Project. Now it has been discovered that environmental factors can affect genes; while on the other end there is a New Age ecological spiritualism, a holism whereby everything is connected to everything through various embedded layers.

In these accounts, cognition triumphs as new forms of rationalization, perhaps best exemplified by the initial philosophical direction marked by Daniel Dennett (1991), come to the fore. How far should Humberto Maturana and Francisco Valera (1980) be followed into updating the paradigm of evolution as an autopoetic system characterized by "satisficing" (a suboptimal solution that is taken to be satisfactory)? Do their theories apply equally to Homo sapiens? Should culture be swallowed up by this new biologism of complexity? Is there not something "more" about our species Being that sets us apart, gives us a specificity in terms of encephalization from other species? Did not the emergence of anthropology, admittedly from racial roots in the nineteenth century, argue that it is not *adaptation* but minimal *modification* that specifically characterizes our species? Our species is an active shaper of its psyche (the flows of desiring production) and environment through language and technology, which includes writing, abstract symbolization, and our relationship to machines. Or, has this now come to be perceived as the worst kind of conceit, simply an overbloated misrecognition, for certainly we are not in total control of this modification process, what Norbert Elias once called the "civilizing process"?

Between the biological influences of Nature and the determinisms of Culture lie Freud's speculations regarding the drives (*Tiebe*), the primary process of creativity and secondary processes of signification that mediate the two in an unconscious complex. This is the realm of the *inhuman*. It creates monsters and aliens outside our control through both negative and affirmative desire. In this sense I treat psychoanalysis as the complexity theory of philosophical anthropology specific to Homo sapiens. On the one side, the technologies of culture provide inhuman prosthetic machines. And, on the other side is the inhuman voice with its music. When embodied, the voice is able to coalesce the drives into the human symbolic order. Disembodied, the voice becomes a viral infestation of psychosis, inverting the drives. This space of in-betweenness, as the gap between Nature and Culture, forms the *inhuman* X in self-refleXivity.

What is needed is a link between metapsychology and social theory to grasp the emancipatory potential of freeing up the internal compulsions of culture, especially when the superego within designer capitalism demands so loudly that we enjoy! Freud's basic insight that reason must be understood dialectically as *repressed desire*—as that which emerges in and through the demands of the primary drives (the demands of the id) on the one hand and the demands of the superego (society) on the other—helps overcome a strictly cognitive orientation. It is a dialectic marked by repression and rebellion, a return of the repressed in various prohibitionary forms of which youth are the primary suspects and bearers. Psychoanalysis in its Lacanian and Deleuzian forms provides such a possibility by attempting to "(un)ground" desire at both the molecular and molar levels via the fantasy structures generated by the human ego as the seat of consciousness. Grasped psychoanalytically, these televised youth narratives offer some insight into what is being desired in the context of the contradictions that have emerged in a designer information and consumerist society such as ours.

From Self-Reflection to Self-Reflexion

In contrast to cognitive approaches, here an effort is made to develop the necessity to turn to an unconscious self that is informed by self-refleXion, where the X marks the spot for unconscious molecular subjectivity of the affective inhuman. Lacan's unconscious *Je* becomes informed by Deleuzian virtuality of time that impacts the potentialities of actualization. The theoretical shift from self-reflection to self-reflexion is well established in the literature. It is often associated with the sociological writings of Ulrich Beck (1992) and Scott Lash (1990; Lash and Friedman 1992) as the transition from industrial to informational modernity, from the logic of structures to the logic of flows (Castells 1989), and the indeterminacy of risk and risk-taking concerning those flows, often referred to as the coexistence of "simple (or first) modernity" and "reflexive (or second) modernization."

Jürgen Habermas (1978 chapters 10–12) and Anthony Giddens (1991), who have also used the term *self-reflexion*, are associated more with postindustrialization or late modernism (especially Giddens) as "reflective modernization" rather than with information (designer) society. Habermasian self-reflexive social theory, with its emphasis on hidden self-interests, placed a high value on the structure of agency and emancipatory politics. The starting point of psychoanalysis for Habermas was the experience of resistance that stands in the way of free and public communication of repressed contents. Self-reflexion leads to understanding these repressed symbolic structures as a form of enlightened cognition or *remembering* where psychoanalysis becomes a variant of depth-hermeneutics. Memory and its vicissitudes are more suited to the self-refleXivity of the unconscious where the signifier fails.

Unfortunately, the Habermasian position still maintains that language discloses *logos* and makes it present. The presumption is that a metalanguage is still possible, which constitutes the Being of all beings. Logocentric metaphysics in this case continues to function positively as presence, disclosure, and understanding. Derrida's critique has made such a position untenable. It is not radical enough for Lacan, Guattari, and Žižek, for whom language functions negatively as lack, dissimulation, and alienation; nor is it tenable for Deleuze for whom minoritarian affirmative language generates forceful performative concepts that are able to intervene empirically to escape institutional molar confinement.

Psychoanalytic knowledge as "truth" is theorized negatively, not positively, for language is the expression and the movement of desire. Desire forms the metaphysics of "nonbeing," of the drive to "be"—as Freud's "death drive" that is beyond the "pleasure principle." It is the will to survive, to live. This is a perpetual alienation of the unconscious "I" within the imaginary "me" (ego) so as to be recognized by the symbolic order, often referred to as the big Other. Nonbeing is therefore equated with Freud's death drive. It is a "positive transformative principle," a form of becoming for both Deleuze and Lacan. One need only look at the paradoxes that surround G. W. Bush's disavowal of the tragedy that has unfolded in Iraq to confirm such a proposition. He believes that history will vindicate him no matter what happens, no matter what the "will" of the American people might be. He seems oblivious to the possibility that his administration may well be approaching the oxymoronic line of "democratic dictatorship." Bush's *jouissance* now supplants that of the nation, forming a growing disconnect between them. Such a fantasy is riddled with Oedipal transferences in his refusal (one imagines) to listen to and receive advice from the one person closest to him who has had firsthand experience of a Gulf war—his father. In every respect he is a "lame duck" president, no longer responsive to the electorate, yet in terms of his "death drive," he continues on. There is no turning back.

It becomes a moot point as to whether desire as lack should be naïvely interpreted as desiring something because one does not have it. This is certainly Imaginary desire, but Real desire in the Lacanian sense is every bit as productive as desire theorized by Deleuze and Guattari. Daniel W. Smith (2004, 641) pinpoints this when he quotes Deleuze and Guattari's *Anti-Oedipus* (1983) text: "The objective being of desire is the Real in and of itself" (*A-O*, 27).[1] Smith makes the point that *Anti-Oedipus* is a theory of the Real and that *Anti-Oedipus* contains no negative comments about Lacan. "The true difference in nature is not between the Symbolic and the Imaginary, but between the Real machinic element, which constitutes desiring-production, and the structural whole of the Imaginary and the Symbolic, which merely forms a myth and its variants" (*A-O*, 83). There is agreement that Lacan oscillated between two poles of desire: the first, as it related to *objet a* as a productive desiring machine; the second, as it related to the big Other—a signifier introducing a certain notion of lack as fantasy (*A-O*, 27n). Deleuze and Guattari chose to explore the machinic notion of desire, but isn't this *very oscillation between these two poles that they identify, which Smith points out (642), the way desire is mobilized in post-Oedipal society*? Caught, as it were, between rejecting the transcendence of the phallic signifier as Queer theorizing has shown (especially Grist, 2003), and moving toward a posthuman paradigm (e.g., Rosi Braidotti 2002). I take this to be also the description of the superego of enjoyment in its contradictory demands of permissiveness and abstinence.

In his theory of structuration (1984), Giddens, like Habermas, stressed agency as self-identity in its "capacity *to keep a particular narrative going*" (1991, 54, original emphasis) through lifestyle choices that "concern[s] the very core of self-identity, its making and remaking" (81). The self is parceled out into so many "lifestyle sectors," while the body becomes "reflexively mobilized" (82). This is the apotheosis of the poststructuralist subject. "Institutional reflexivity" has become the norm as each institution is forced to examine its own grounds, just like the self-help industry that focused on individual therapy as reflexive "methodology of life-planning" (180).[2] Both Habermas and Giddens, as sociologists, had affinities with Marxism's questioning of capitalism and its consumerism. However, Giddens has been severely criticized for his overemphasis on rationalism (Mestrovic 1998), while Habermas's theory of "communicative action" (1984)—the core of which was an "ideal speech situation" where an equal playing field among actors was to be maintained through speech acts undistorted by ideology or misrecognition— was equally criticized for its naïve rationalist emphasis (a representative array can be found in Thompson and Held 1982; Johnson 1991).

Reflection, the older term that both Habermas and Giddens attempted to problematize, continues to maintain a subject-object dichotomy, assuming apodictic knowledge and certainty. As Bruno Latour (1993) pointed out, the "modern constitution" was bequeathed to us in the seventeenth century by Robert Boyle, according to whom nature was independent of the speaker, while Thomas Hobbes theorized the social and political order that was independent of material circumstances. Although this naïve self-reflective view has been questioned in posthumanist circles that recognize the extension of "mind" into the environment, what remains missing is, yet again, the endogenous problem of inner conflict that psychoanalysis recognizes as being fundamental to the human condition. Our species is doomed to the metaphysics of desire. We exist between nature and culture. From the side of nature, we seem to be the most advanced encephalized animal, capable of language and technologies that can change our *physiological* nature. From the side of culture, we are overdetermined beings, caught by our own follies, which we (must) believe in.

Be that as it may, Beck and Lash's use of self-reflexion is claimed to be a step beyond the naïvety of self-reflection. Structure and agency are once again rethought in an information age by maintaining their *demise*, which is complementary to a systems theory of complex networks like that of Niklas Luhmann, according to whom agency seems to disappear entirely, his antihumanism being in direct opposition to the humanism of Habermas. Rather than a dualistic reflectivity of agency and structure, reflexivity in the formulations of Beck and Lash now becomes monistic or immanent—the subject is placed "in" the world, recognizing its multiple interconnections. This is not some revelatory tenet, yet—in the sciences at least—it comes as a late arrival. As in Latour's claim (1993), "we have never been modern." The human and nonhuman are intertwined; the more-than-human world of the environment informs humanity. A nonlinear notion of reflexivity takes precedence where a system's disequilibrium and destabilization are produced through open system feedback loops. Complex systems change rather than reproduce as a result of noise or "chaos." The self-reflexive subject is said to be devoid of any stable subject position, but must continually weigh the uncertainty of knowledge in "possibilistic" terms. With a New Age twist to it, self-reflexion can be skewed toward neoliberalist market exploitations as described in *The Secret* (Byrne, 2006), whereby an individual learns to harness the cosmic energy that surrounds it. The illusion of complete agency is restored.

Such a position is contrary to a Deleuzian stance whereby (drawing from Henri Bergson) the ontological couplings of the actual and the virtual are opposed to those of the real and the possible. "The possible has no reality (although it may have an actuality); conversely, the virtual is not actual, but as such possesses a reality. . . . On the other hand, or from another point of view, the possible is that which is 'realized' (or not realized)" (1988, 96–97). For Deleuze, the possible, which lies at the core of Beck and Lash's theory of the subject, is realized through resemblance and limitation. The virtual, in contrast, is actualized through difference and creation. Thus, the possible is that which is "retroactively fabricated in the image of what resembles it" (*DR*, 212), meaning that the possible is always already some kind of representation of the real that appears to preexist it. It appears that the possible is offered as a "real" alternative when it signals an ideal fulfillment of an already given reality. This is basically how *The Secret* is sold to the masses of believers. One need only project what one desires and it will come true. If it doesn't, then the failure rests within oneself for having failed to adequately harness the cosmic energy of the outside.

Beck (Beck and Willms 2004, 63) uses the term *disembedded individuation* to suggest the idea that *individual action* has become the basic unit of social reproduction. The idea of such an autarkic individual fits ideologically with the withdrawal of the welfare state and the emergence of neoliberalism where survival depends on having the skills to play the capitalist game, remaining flexible, and being able to make the "right" decisions and live with contradictions. The ideology that generates *The Secret* is precisely this—the Oprah Winfrey mentality that reaches such a huge population of the North American middle class. This arrangement is best described as a post-Oedipal landscape where phallic power has waned. The family is distantiated, held together at a distance through computer technologies—skype, e-mail, text messaging, and the cell phone. Blended families become more and more common as the birth rate drops while the divorce rate increases. The subject becomes individuated and rule making, more specifically, constitutive rule making, enables a game and its playing field to unfold—from sadomasochistic rituals to video games and computer dating—where a set of parameters determines the array of possible partners so that a "risk" may ensue. With an increase in sociotechnologization in all dimensions of human experience (communication protocols, standards, intellectual property), especially with interactive media, self-reflexivity now occurs at the boundaries of the social and technical (Hansen, 2004). Frag Dolls assure that this self-reflexive gaming world also belongs to girls.

Self-Reflexive Irony

Such a "second-modernity institution" would be identified as being "sociotechnical" (Lash 2003). We have seen the emergence of the "rules girls," where Ellen Fein and Steven Jay Schneider (1995) provide all the rules for online dating, marrying, shopping, exercising, dressing, and so on, but we have also seen such artificial rule making emerge in the arts (e.g., the Dogme films of Lars von Trier). In the task-oriented film *The Five Obstructions* (2003), codirected by Jørgen Leth, specific constraints are given to a filmic problem that must be solved. If postmodernity marks a state of groundlessness, then the ground must be artificially created. This is a way of coming to accept a constructivist universe and a conceptual form of art where the technological constraints determine content, the artist being only a mediator in the process. Conceptual art developed such a posthuman aesthetic to ruin representation. In a film such as *Dogville*, von Trier presents his viewers with a minimalist stage where everything appears to be shown, contributing to the confusion since it creates the illusion of transparency and clarity. In the town of Dogville, authority has been vacated: there is no pastor, no mayor, and people lie to the police. An idealized communitarian community is presented into which Grace, a beautiful young woman and a stranger, is thrown into its bosom while escaping from gangsters. She is adopted by the villagers and told to find her place. This eventually causes the darkest aspects of their being—the X— to emerge from various community members who proceed to exploit, rape, and torture Grace, and relegate her to slavery. All along she remains in the position of a victim caught in the grips of her own masochism. Eventually, to cover up the abuse, the community selects Tom (her professed lover) to call back the gangsters and "rub her out." It is here that the plot twists and that a *disjunctive synthesis* is presented to viewers. It turns out that the mob leader is Grace's father, a loving father at that. She has "used" the inhabitants of the village for her own narcissistic ends to prove that her gangster father was wrong in his assessment of people. Grace as victim now becomes Grace the victimizer. Revenge is sought, and the village is eventually burned. Only a dog is left. As witnesses to the event, viewers remain stymied as to where to place their judgment in such a masochistic-to-sadistic flip-flop, since we have been party to the pleasure of watching her victimization and rallied in the destruction to satisfy our initial sympathies. We face our own "X," our own complicity in the fantasy of the violence we have witnessed, much as we do watching the films of Michael Haneke (especially *Benny's Video* and *Funny Games*).

Dogville illustrates a certain self-reflexive irony, which *is the very way that designer capitalism is schizoid in its inability to find stable ground.* A film such as Shane Black's *Kiss, Kiss, Bang, Bang* (2005) wears this constructed sense of life on its sleeve in every waking moment of the unfolding narrative, even up to the point of addressing the audience at the end of the movie as part of the invisible fourth wall, as the "outside" audience absorbed watching a television movie—*Kiss, Kiss, Bang, Bang*—before being turned off into a black screen by the protagonist, Harry Lockhart, a small-time crook cum actor-detective who has been narrating and commenting on the story all along.

Paranoia within Risk Societies

Latour (2003) has tried to qualify Beck's meaning of self-reflexion and risk, maintaining that these concepts have been largely misunderstood. Reflexivity, he says "means that the unintended consequences of actions reverberate throughout the whole of society in such a way that they have become *intractable*. . . . '[R]flexive' does not signal an increase in mastery and consciousness, but only a heightened awareness that mastery is impossible and that control over actions is now seen as a complete modernist fiction" (36). As for risk, this does not mean more danger than before; rather, "that we are now *entangled*, whereas the modernist dream was to disentangle us from the morass of the past" (ibid).

Latour qualifies risk with the word *network*, which refers to "whatever deviates from the straight path of reason and control to trace a labyrinth, a maze of unexpected associations between heterogeneous elements, each of which acts as a mediator and no longer as a mere compliant intermediary" (ibid.). The reflexes, characterized as "I am I," are indeterminate and immediate—quick decisions. Latour's own response to agency, his ANT (Actor-network theory), takes into account human interaction with material-semiotic nonhuman networks, decentering the arrogance of anthropomorphic agency and intentionality and casting a wide scope of heterogeneous associations between humans and nonhumans that ends with stochastic probabilities of control, thereby curbing the relativism of constructivist thought. However, ANT's poststructualist leanings suffer from an inadequate grasp of power in the way humans dominate networks and in the way researchers identify which actors in such networks are given prominence. In contrast to ANT, the psychoanalytic understanding of "inhuman" desire challenges the intentionality of knowledge (coming from Edmund Husserl and phenomenology as adopted by Beck) and hidden interests (coming from critical theory) by forwarding unconscious desire and the *jouissance* of the drives as informed by the memories of the virtual past. Agency is repositioned as a singularity of the unconscious, an acephalic "actor" not entirely in conscious control. Self-refleXivity is the recognition of this inhuman self that stalks the paranoiac and schizophrenic narratives of the television series examined.

In an important book, *Latent Destinies,* that bears directly on the thesis of this book, Patrick O'Donnell (2000, 9) presents five summative theses as to why paranoia is embodied in the fantasy formations of designer risk societies. These are symptomatic of the "temporal contradiction in postmodernity" that reveals anxieties concerning identity, power, nationhood, technology, knowledge, and history. To paraphrase his well-articulated insights:

1. We are paranoid because paranoia remains the last refuge of identity where we are made aware of ourselves as constructed beings, assembled through desires to the point of parody.
2. We are paranoid because postmodern societies are approaching the commodification and virtualization of temporality itself. As a result a nostalgic past is remade "to provide a virtual depth to a future that has been brought entirely into the present."
3. We are paranoid because paranoia is fun and pleasurable. It allows for the possibility to perceive "self-referential depth in the fantasy of the totalized world of available objects." This then provides for an enfoldment of "personal history, destiny, and temporality that fantasy itself attempts to erase or revise as immediacy."
4. We are paranoid because we seek to escape the totality of capitalism by seeking to control the "interface (our bodies) between libidinal economy and that of our own vestigial selves."
5. We are paranoid because paranoia is "the last epistemology, the final form of human knowledge before it passes away into information." At root, paranoia is a form of knowing ourselves in relation to others "as having the capacity to be known, to be seen, to be objects of desire and attention."[3]

The anxieties associated with "risk" have been answered in a number of ways, all of which have a direct bearing on the television series that are analyzed. First has been what Alain Badiou (2002) has called a "passion for the real"—that is, for what is immediately practical, here and now. To ease the anxiety of uncertainty, it all comes down to what heuristically works in the context itself; hence, the obvious shift from moral principles to situational ethics. Second is the continual development of the cynical subject as first developed by Peter Sloterdijk (1987), where the new conformity manifests itself as the narcissistic aggrandizement of the ego through designer consumption. Third, in one sense at least, designer capitalism has absorbed the schizophrenic self that Deleuze and Guattari thought would lead to capitalist dissolution. The schizophrenic is supposed to represent the "limit" of (designer) capitalism. "[S]chizophrenia is the exterior limit of capitalism itself or the conclusion of its deepest tendency, but that capitalism only functions on condition that it inhibit this tendency, or that it push back or displace this limit. . . . Hence schizophrenia is not the identity of capitalism, but on the contrary its difference, its divergence, and its death" (*A-O*, 246). The schizophrenic is supposed to "escape coding, scramble the codes, and flee in all directions . . . [schizophrenics are therefore] *orphans* (no daddy-mommy-me), *atheists* (no beliefs), and *nomads* (no habits, no territories)" (Seem, *1983*, xxi). In the *Smallville* narrative, I try to show that the relationship between Lex and Lionel Luther embodies this schizophrenic contradiction of global capitalism.

Deleuze and Guattari wrote their *Anti-Oedipus* in 1972. It was translated into English in 1983, the same year and the one following Fredric Jameson wrote his two influential essays and later a book (1991) on the "logic of late capitalism." Jameson (1983) makes it quite clear that schizophrenia is defined by "the failure of the infant to accede fully into the realm of speech and language" (118), and further that such an experience is one of isolation and disconnect where the sense of self fails to attach to a coherent sequence. How should one interpret this—as an alarm or as hailing a new posthuman subject? It is worrying, however, to note that autism is the fastest growing "pathology" in the United States (Kantrowitz and Scelfo 2006), suggesting that many more children are unable to break out of the Imaginary into the Symbolic Order, as if refusing to engage in the "real" material world. Such a stance is reminiscent of Günter Grass's (1962) brilliant book *Die Blechtrommel (The Tin Drum)* and Volker Schlöndorff's 1979 film of the same title, in which Oskar Matzerath opts out of the Nazi order on his third birthday by disrupting and repressing its sense-making apparatus by aggressively drumming at its symbolic structures, especially during Nazi rallies. One could say that Oskar snapped into autism. While such an autistic epidemic may be disputed, or at least put into doubt (Grinker 2007), the very idea that it has become alarmingly visible in a contemporary, aestheticized society continues to raise interesting and disturbing speculations as to the affects of media consumption.

In designer capitalism, phallocentrism has been slowly deterritorializing—with authority seemingly evacuated, prohibitions lifted, and permissiveness encouraged, with perversity on the rise. The superego commands us to "Enjoy!" At the same time, a reterritorialization continues through media screens to retain the relations of production and private property and to reinstate humanism in more clever ways through the "back door" of New Age spiritualism, so to speak. Like the Argonauts' boats that are dismantled and rebuilt at the same time so that the journey across the oceans becomes possible, humanist capitalism survives. We see this everywhere as the recoding at the level of the Imaginary where the potential of a schizophrenic self has been continued by the multiple mirrors of ego production: the steady stream of makeovers—beginning with the early rise of Madonna in the 1980s, the "true" material girl morphing from one persona into another, to online dating sites where people redesign themselves to articulate their pseudo-individualities, to Internet chat rooms where they shed their "real" roles and adopt new ones. The Imaginary schizophrenic mirror is constantly *reflexing* back a "new" look, or attempting to confirm the reflective look that stares back—even obesity is fine given the right set of designer clothes. Big girls can be sexy. We can drink our liquor, smoke our cigarettes, and be happy. There is no need to change lifestyle for reasons of health. A technological or pharmaceutical fix will be found. As Žižek so often maintains, just take the poison out of the poisoned fruit, the fat out of fatty food, the nicotine out of cigarettes, and so on, and all will be fine, for there is no "One" telling you what to do anymore. No need for performative demands. And, if you have *The Secret*, and have learned to radiate positive waves to harness the cosmic flows, how could anything go wrong? And, if it does— there's only *you* to blame.

Has not desire been freed from the neurotic, familial Oedipal insistence that neo-Freudians clamor for? Designer capitalism "is constantly arresting the schiz-ophrenic process . . . as though it saw in this process the image of its own death coming from within" (*A-O*, 34; 245). The new authority has been evacuated from the old despotic figures—the patriarch, the priest, and the politician, and has migrated over to celebrity status—pop-icons who take the Law into their own hands through lawyers (the Michael Jacksons, Naomi Campbells, Paris Hiltons, and what's left of Anna Nicole Smith's estate) and high-profile adoptions of Other children (Madonna, Angelina Jolie). Authority in the Symbolic register has shifted to its perverse side—the Imaginary register. In this sense the schizophrenic revo-lution has been "betrayed" (*A-O*, 379). Lacan's desire, theorized as lack, continues to triumph in designer capitalism, while the schizo desiring-production as a sub-ject group (opposed to a subjugated group) can only be found in mongrel identi-ties and artistic cells like the Critical Art Ensemble (CAE).

Self-RefleXion: In between Nature and Culture

Our species "lives" or exists in the *gap* between nature and culture. This is the abyss of freedom but also the source of our pathology. I name this gap the "X" in self-refleXion as a way to distinguish such thinking from self-reflection and self-reflexion where knowledge as a negative function, as an ignorance of our self, is not accounted for. From a Deleuzian perspective, the X is the gap of becoming. He maintains there is an internal self-differing within difference itself; the differ-ent differs from itself in each case and hence everything that exists paradoxically only becomes and never *is*, informed by time and movement. While *all* of Nature is not known, nor can it ever be known, it has been in the interests of science to grasp its physical manifestations within given heuristic parameters. And while culture is an equally troubling term, we know that technology is our ability to influence Nature through material and instrumental means that then shape and modify culture. This is what makes our species unfinished. Radically stated: the Magdalenian culture of the late Upper Paleolithic was developed by Homo sapiens who differed from us contemporary humans physiologically and psychologically, as well as psychically. They were "wired" differently. Although the Magdalenians belonged to the same species, their paleontology would suggest remarkable differences.

The Nature-culture dynamic over this unexplainable gap—X—generates our species being that is prone to fantasy and desire. I take this realm to be where psychoanalysis as a form of anthropological philosophy straddles both the biological individual and society, both Nature and Culture, and attempts to confront the impossible contradictions of a species being that is "out of joint" compared to the rest of the animal kingdom. This is either an arrogant anthropocentrism or a profound recognition that we are defined by an "original" ability for "modifying" our environment which refleXively comes back to shape our very physical, psychological, and psychic well-being, whose responsibility cannot be escaped. As a species we do not merely adapt but alter the species Being at the molecular level. Inexplicably, within this gap our species psyche changes as our physiology changes as does the culture we generate. Again, the "cave" painters of 20,000 years ago may be the same species (Homo sapiens), but their brain circuitry differed from that of contemporary humans living in an information age. While I am not advocating some sort of technological determinism, there is an obvious difference between the Egyptian *Book of the Dead* in which there is no future tense and our own phenomenological experience of future time that is now being questioned as an ever recurring present—the time of perpetual "now" due to "live" media broadcasting.

If our species is saddled with this gap, a gap that will never be filled out with a recovered "missing link," but perhaps remains an accident of Nature, it is this gap that we must "work" with and theorize. If the human infant is born as a helpless being in distress (*Hilflosigkeit*), who needs caregivers to survive and hence learn, then s/he must grapple with the enigma of the Other's *jouissance*: "What does this caregiver want of me?" Almost immediately the infant faces the enigma and choice of identity. But this fundamental gap between the infant and its environment, which includes its caregivers, remains as a Real psychic order—as the level of the virtual in Deleuze that is "actualized" through difference and creation. The status of this *inhuman remainder* is always at issue. What happens when the ego does not form, which is possible only through the recognition of the Other? Or what if this ego remains autistic without recognition of the Other, and the infant lives only in the Imaginary register? Is this not a passionate attachment to an unconscious Self as a struggling ego refuses the Symbolic? Isn't this precisely what consumer society wants? That ultimately we gratify not only the ego, but also our deepest repressed wishes?

By maintaining this X to be the seat of subjectivity of becoming—the acephalic singularity of an "I" at the *bodily level*, as the BwO—before it becomes a body image—as a body without an image—immediately brings us over to Deleuze's side so that we recognize that this is difference itself, since identity requires the Other that follows with the formation of the ego. We might conclude that to *truly* live with "difference" is to live with those who remain asocial and autistic. Shouldn't such a conclusion worry us when both "ends" of existence are deemed valueless and unproductive: the "special needs" kids on one end and those who suffer from Alzheimer's disease on the other; not to mention Giorgio Agamben's (1998) claim of the "nowhere" places where "bare life" has been abandoned, without protection by any state or Law? X then is the place of the Real and of materialism—the place of difference and of the posthuman—a gap where the pathological stain of our species remains, an enfolded space, a source of our strength and our weakness. One might ask now whether the "authentic [political] act"—what Lacan calls the "passage à l'acte"—which Žižek (1999) constantly returns to in his writings and which Badiou (2005) calls a "truth event" that directly addresses this X, cannot be equated with the schizo self. After all, if such an act places one *outside* the symbolic order, or if it is supposed to change the symbolic order, or at the very least suspend it with the actor suffering "subjective destitution," doesn't the schizophrenic experience offer a similar "event"? If schizophrenia is only to be metaphorically understood in Deleuze and Guattari's sense, isn't the authentic Lacanian act "schizophrenic" in its metaphorical traversing of the fundamental fantasy? Could it be said that "traversing the fantasy" is precisely the process of breaking down the imaginary body's topological matrix, setting loose its intensities and affects, and in effect reaching the BwO? If the BwO is the degree zero of any possible assemblage—that is, the baseline from which all intensities are immanently differentiated—then "subjective destitution" becomes a self-refleXive act of horrific proportions. If such an act is without agency, not subject to conscious will, there is no author-agent involved, but an acephalous subject through whom the act takes place—something takes "over" me. This is not unlike the schizophrenic. Not the subject of enunciation—rather the subject of the enunciated has become paranoid, psychotic, schizoid—which? To "*posit your self as your own cause*" (Žižek 1999a, 14, original emphasis) means that you are no longer determined by the symbolic order.

So, is this not the heroic artist-scientist absolutely gone "mad," the one who creates the new *ex nihilio*? Like the iconic figure of Dr. Frankenstein, who is paradoxically responsible for such a creation but did not *intentionally* wish to release a monster that acted out his own unconscious desires. What of all those "failed" artists whose acts ended in the clinic, failing to change the Symbolic, leaving them subjectively destitute? One is reminded immediately of the forgotten but important book by Rudolf Wittkower and Margot Wittkower, *Born under Saturn* (1963). Some artists could not comprehend the Copernican revolution; they fell into states of perpetual melancholia and were unable to resuscitate their art. Thus, the paradoxical wager: is the schizophrenic a divine human being or just another "nut case"? He or she is both, of course. These unforeseeable and unpredictable acts, as somewhat miraculous, events happen and shatter lives. If this is indeed the way the "divine" enters our lives, the "madness" of the shaman as the chosen one to lead takes us toward various ways of betrayal, an interesting proposition when examining such a narrative as *Smallville*, where Kent is led to believe that his destiny is to save and/or destroy the earth! The line between madness and genius is just that—a line.

In the Deleuzian sense, the "X" in self-refleXivity can be understood as a resistive potential, as *a* life. The way Deleuze describes this life approximates the notion of authentic act in Žižekian terms, "the life of the individual gives way to an impersonal and yet singular life that releases a pure event freed from the accidents of internal and external life, that is, from the subjectivity and objectivity of what happens" (Deleuze 2001, 28). The "X" as the inhuman is "an inhumation of the intelligible body" (Schefer 1995; 1976). It may well be said that the Real is nothing but the BwO, which is the body subject to affects and intensities of the figural body. Thus for Lacan, the unconscious is the inhuman. The Real is the inhuman—where the taken-for-granted human meets the vitality of uncertain Nature as explored by Deleuze and Guattari through their vitalism.

X as the Meeting Place between Lacan and Deleuze

In this remaining section I want to argue that a lacandeleuze assemblage can be envisioned in the gap of the X as the *virtual Real*. In chapter 6, there are sections where I try to advance this discussion more deeply. The question is how to dispel lack as it is usually (mis)understood in either/or terms: as an incompleteness of any structure of differences or excess that escapes structuration.[4] To establish this possibility, I turn to an emphasis on play—the space of creation. The paedomorphic development of youth manifests itself in a postmetaphysical climate where the binding and unifying ontological ground has become suspended (in the Greek sense of *epochè*) in a number of ways. *Play*, in particular, has become central in order to grasp the changing ontology where *becoming*, as the site of the in-between of presence and absence, requires a new understanding of *time* as movement that is *separate* from action (Küchler 1994). Such origin*ary* movement of time identifies an *emergence*—a bringing-forth of a "pre-sense", which can no longer be attributed to an original presence (*archè*) that will be completed by, as yet, an absent *telos*. A final cause takes us outside and beyond the sense-making signifier formed by this metaphysical dichotomy of presence and absence, best illustrated by representational language. Telos is therefore invested with *possibility*—the possibility of *utopia*, which is yet another form of representation.

Transposed into Lacanian terms, to avoid representation requires the (nowhere) *site* of the Real, while the Imaginary (sight) and Symbolic registers (cite) provide the closed circuit of absence and presence as famously established by Freud's *fort/da* game and reinterpreted by Lacan (1979 SXI, *Four Fundamentals*, 62) as sense-making activity provided by the phonemic opposition of vowels o-a (the "o" in *fort*, gone, absence—the "a" in *da*, here, presence). As he argues, through this process of signification, the drives (*Triebe*) are pacified. The "unary" signifier ("o") to which the frustration and anger of losing the toy (reel) is attached becomes soothed over as soon as the toy (reel) is found ("a")—the signifying circuit of meaning becomes complete, plummeting the child into the symbolic order of language and inaugurating imaginary desire. Here lack applies. In such an understanding, "fort" is an origin*ary* signifier. It is nonsensical; there is no signifier into which it can be translated. It enters as a trace into the synapses of the unconscious mind as the affective bodily drives impinge on it. It is "doubly" inscribed, as Freud claims, in the Imaginary as well as in the unconscious Real.

The first point to note in this frustrating, temper-tantrum-ridden game is that this nonsense signifier "fort" is repeated over and over again, symptomatically, until the Imaginary self (ego) becomes satisfied through the completion of its meaning, staving off the drives. The "sense" of the self is temporarily restored.

The second point is to recognize that this unary or origin*ary* signifier belongs to the *site* of the unconscious, the in-between postmetaphysical *site* of becoming. It is situated between Being (presence as such, the infant as seemingly One with its environment—in this case Freud's grandson thinks the toy is part of him) and absence (as meaning that is "seemingly" available through language of the symbolic order—the field known as the Other in Lacan's terminology). Lacan names this nonsense unary signifier *objet a*. The unconscious is therefore the *site* of *becoming* while *objet a* is the mark of *difference* achieved through *repetition*.

This opening discussion on *play*, and its significance for theorizing youth *undercover*, now takes another turn where Lacan and Deleuze come together. Two forms of play can be culled from the Freudian-Lacanian take on the fort/da game, as supplemented by a second game that Freud recorded his grandson playing later. He would hide beneath a mirror for a time, jump up and see his reflection appearing in it, and then laugh wildly in delight. In this second playful game, he became the toy (reel), quite unlike in the first game where the lost toy (reel), as a part object that belonged to his being, made him a subject of *lack*; that is, a subject of desire. The two games offer two forms of play that will "figure" in the *becoming* of youth on television by their oscillation between one another. In the first game, Freud's grandson chose sense making as part of the frustration of Being. This sense making continually fails to secure pure Being. In other words, language, in and of itself, never provides a conclusive end to desire as lack (*manque*). Repetition in this first sense of play is structured by renewed representation (presence/absence). The game is repeated endlessly with the "false" hope of finally capturing "that" which escapes Being (the gap of becoming, the X) to achieve a complete and unified identity once and for all. This direction is toward absence (lack) in the field of the Other. Every sense-making episode that ends the repetition sublimates the drives, but only for a time. The circuit of completion weds time to the action. In the Derridean (1978b, 259) sense, this game presents a "strict economy" where play becomes a closed system yielding knowledge and meaning.

The second game is Deleuzian. The choice is not one of sense making; rather, it is in the direction of *becoming present*. The repetition is driven not by desire as lack, but by satisfaction, a positive sense of desire in Deleuzian terms, satisfaction that goes specifically under the name of *jouissance*, which in my opinion has close affinities with affection, the *zöe* of intensity—of life itself. When the drives predominate over desire, Lacan claims that the intimate core of our being is no longer framed and sheltered by sense. It becomes exposed. What is involved in the drive is "*making oneself be heard*" or "*making oneself seen*" (S XI, *Four Fundamentals*, 195). Rather than a *negative* sense of desire, caught by the "defiles" of the signifier, there is another operative desire that has a *positive* spin to it, which is productive (as well as destructive) of Being. This is a "general economy" in the Derridean sense (1978b, 271), an open system where there is an indefinite destruction of value and meaning. It is, once more, the place of the death drive.

The well-established, but false, option between Lacan and Deleuze emerges in this differentiation between desire and the drives.[5] Deleuze (and Guattari) are praised as presenting a *positive* and productive notion of desire [what I take to be the drives], while Lacan is accused of dwelling only on lack—*negative* desire.

From my reading, which will be supported throughout this book, as I look at youth "undercover" in television, this false opposition will always be problematized by showing the transpositions that occur between *late* Lacan and Deleuze and Guattari. Difference, becoming, and repetition as the three key themes of Deleuzian corpus that are said to challenge Lacanian psychoanalysis have their transpositional equivalences. It is often forgotten, for example, that Baruch Spinoza was a primary source of inspiration for Lacan from 1932 until 1946, as he was for Deleuze, and he also influenced the way Lacan thought about ethics in 1960 (S VII, *Ethics*). According to Elisabeth Roudinesco (1997), as early as 1932 Lacan had already "rehabilitated paranoia as a 'discordant' equivalent of a so-called personality" (55), the term discordant coming from Spinozian writings on ethics. Lacan made a distinction between *Wiederholung* and *Wiederkehr* (both mean repetition), which bears the same distinction concerning repetition made by Deleuze four years *later*. Writing in 1968, drawing on Friedrich Nietzsche's Eternal Return, Deleuze (*DR* 1994, 40–42) stresses the becoming and transformation that takes place when difference is introduced to identity; identity now becomes a "second principle" (a becoming), turning around the different—as "one of the multiple" (of possibilities) rather than identity being a "first principle" of sameness.

Lacan had already developed the same conceptualization with different language. *Wiederholung* is simply the repetition of the Same, what he refers to as *automaton*. Left here, Freudian psychoanalysis can be charged for limiting repetition to representation where the idea is to stop the symptom from repeating itself, thereby "curing" the disorder that gave rise to it. However, Lacan realized that even when the cause of the symptom was found, behavior did not necessarily stop. He shifted the discourse from symptom to *sinthome* in S XXIII, *Le Sinthome*, which he delivered in 1975 and 1976, indicating that there is now a fundamental fantasy that holds one's world-reality together. Change it, and life becomes unraveled. This is a marked departure from identifying the "Name-of-the-Father" as the *only* solitary and predominant change agent, a position he began to question since S XVII, *Envers* (1969–70) when he *rejected the Oedipus complex* as being psycho-analytically "scientific" and reduced it to a form of myth along the lines of Claude Lévi-Strauss's structuralism (see Grigg 2006).

To arrive at such a position, Lacan (1977) had rethought the nature of repetition in his S XI, *Four Fundamentals*. In contrast to repetition as *Wiederholung*, he introduced repetition as *Wiederkehr*—an "encounter with the [R]eal" (53), or transpositionally put, an encounter with difference. He utilizes the Aristotelian term—*tuché* (as if by chance) to identify the moment of this happening with difference. It marks the same place of becoming as in Deleuze where the coimbrications of the virtual real and the actual real are continually splitting. The Lacanian Real can be interpreted as difference itself—the X, as difference differentiating itself in these chance moments of *touché*. *Wiederkehr* is a repetition that turns (*kehr*) in on itself affecting the unconscious structure, and thereby enabling a change, a becoming of the Subject when this difference is encountered. In this sense it, too, is a "positive" power (*puissance*) of transformation. Both forms of repetition, as in Deleuze, are informed by memory.

It should also be noted that Lacan is referring to the *intensities* of the *bodily* drives (*Triebe*) in terms of pulsations with different speeds, which the Deleuzian paradigm elaborates on. Too much intensity leads to trauma, the heart of the conflict between the pleasure principle and the reality principle. This is then a missed encounter with the Real. From this, it should be obvious that the psychic order of the Real refers to the body's affective dimensions *prior to its imaging*, which is where the Deleuzian paradigm excels and becomes most useful for this study.

The Subject for Lacan is located in the unconscious Real. Hence, Lacan's tripartite psychic divisions—Real (*je*, I), Imaginary (*moi*, me, ego), Symbolic (subject of the social Law)—that intertwine in all their complexity, are transpositional to Deleuze's own tripartite divisions developed in *Difference and Repetition* (1994, especially 246–47), where he elaborates the distinctions between individuation, Self, and I. Like Lacan's Real unconscious Subject, which (may surprise some?) is machinic in its functioning,[6] individuation is that process of "pure" difference, or "disparateness" of intensities as a continuum of heterogeneously organized multiplicities that characterize the BwO, which then become discrete through extension. This pre-individual is comparable to Lacan's "body in pieces," a state prior to the mirror stage.[7] Deleuze uses the term "differentiation" to characterize the pre-individual field characterized by flows and singularities. The "pre-individual field is a virtual-field made up of differential relations" (*DR*, 246) He reserves the term "differenciation" (257) when addressing the Self and I, both of which are extensions (representations), stratified from this chaos. From this emerges the differenciator, or that which differenciates differences—known as the "dark precursor," which might well be transposed as Lacan's *objet a* since it is that which "sticks" out causing a change of direction, another line of flight. In Žižek's (2004b, 82) interpretation, the dark precursor is none other than Lacan's phallus, which then is phased out in Deleuze's later writings.

There are further parallels between Lacan's Real, Deleuze's virtual BwO, and Daniel Stern (1985). Working between the fields of psychoanalysis and psychology, Stern coins the term "Representations of Interactions that have been Generalized (RIGs)" to identify experiences (intensities and flows, interactions) that are coded as identical in terms of their activation contours that form the core of the "emotional schemas." In Wilma Bucci's (1997) terms, these RIGs are "built up through repetitions of episodes with shared affective states . . . [which] consist of clusters of sensory, visceral, and motoric elements, which are largely subsymbolic" (195). This is the process of individuation consonant with the way Deleuze would understand it. It is the unique singularity of thinking itself. The Self, on the other hand, "forms the psychic organization" (*DR*, 257). Like the Lacanian Imaginary, it partitions and organizes thinking that belongs to the quality of human being as a species—designated as I. The "I" is the thinking subject belonging to our species being.

It seems fair to say that the Lacanian Real is equivalent to Deleuze's reality of the virtual. So, to conclude: The three terms, self-reflection, self-reflexion, and self-refleXion, constitute the triadic subject as shaped by three registers. Self-reflection can be attributed to a naïve understanding of the symbolic order constructed by language of representation—even including its obscene supplementary side; self-reflexion can be construed as the Imaginary caught by the constructed deceptions of self-reflexive irony that are so predominant in neoliberalist designer capitalism; and finally, self-refleXivity can be seen as the site of the inhuman unconscious—the place of monsters and aliens. Self-refleXivity is crucial because the X must deal with the excessive moment of "madness" that is inherent to *cogito* and that is identified as "diabolical Evil" in Kant and as the "night of the world" in Hegel (Žižek 1999b, 62). The cogito is pathologized, and at the same time part of that pathology identifies the paranoia of subjectivity. One might also say that a "savage" part of the cogito remains open, impossible to civilize. While singularity as "life" defines the way the becoming of this pathological stain is ethically met.

Part II

Self-RefleXive Narcissism and Alienation

3

Dawson's Creek's Reflexivity: Savvy Poststructuralism

Prelude: Horrific Screams of Teen's Hidden Angst

I watched all six seasons of *Dawson's Creek*, right up to and including the final episode(s) (622–23), where the triangle between Dawson, Joey, and Pace, which had been circulating in an open-ended teenage version of *Jules & Jim*, finally resolves itself and the series comes to an end. That's 128 episodes later. After that, I felt I could rest. In preparation for this chapter, I had borrowed the entire series on DVD from my friend Brad Smilanich, and had started watching them, right from the opening pilot, all mercilessly free of the dreaded commercial breaks. The characters grew on me. I began to care, to suffer with them in their love affairs. I watched as other characters moved into their lives, left, and came back again, and I watched them grow up, leave high school, and enter college. I was hopelessly hooked. How could I fall for such shallow pap?

Prime-time serial melodramas (soaps) have this way about them, don't they? And, if I am to understand Will Booker's (2001) analysis of *convergence* regarding the *Dawson's Creek* and *Capeside* Internet site and various other fan sites on the Net, I could conceivably continue to reside interactively in the fictional town and keep the characters alive for as long as I please. I may never have to leave. I could dress like them, wear the Capeside high school T-shirt, complete with the fictional logo, send e-postcards to friends, listen to the songs, go to various bulletin boards to continue plot developments for the future, or register hate mail if need be, and also have an extended grasp of what the characters lives are about off screen. I could even peer into Pacey's computer's "hard drive" posted online.

Unlike the deranged fan Annie Wilkies in Steven King's horror story *Misery*, there was no need to torture and kill off the author to ensure that the fantasy would sustain itself. Kevin Williamson, the series' creator and the high-profile screenwriter of the *Scream* series, left long ago. The series may be over (1998–2003), but it's not over . . . for some. I viewed it as one long flow, in its compressed form, without commercials and without weekly anticipated delays and possibly missed episodes that would involve a six-year commitment. Driven by an academic desire to see it to its completion so that I might gain some distance from it, to overcome the personal empowerment it had over me, almost a full year later I am able to write a response.

In the context of the opening theoretical chapters, I am going to argue that *Dawson's Creek* (*DC*) is an exemplary television series in the way it masks and manages teenage anxiety in a time of post-Oedipalization where the contradictions around feminism (second vs. third wave), romantic love versus partnership (so-called confluent or pure love in Anthony Giddens's [1992] terms), queer closeting versus queer outing, psychotherapy versus "normal" teenage angst, missing versus present fathers, and missing versus present mothers, have coalesced and are now all on display through the realist façade of the self-reflexive expressions of its characters living in the sleepy, picturesque, hidden tourist town of Capeside, a small fishing village, supposedly somewhere in New England, 40 miles southeast of Boston (Mangles 2000, 164). This underlying anxiety of American youth has been made palatable and processable into the twenty-first century.

Basically, my primary argument is that the *auteurship* of Kevin Williamson, upon whose fantasy of high school *DC's* narrative is based and who publicly outs himself as gay during its second season, is the very *inverse* of his *Scream* series trilogy. *Dawson's Creek* is Williamson's "silent" scream, the one painted by Edvard Munch, which was simply dramatized by him in the movie series. In *Dawson's Creek* the anxious scream that cannot be *heard* is brought out only by completely suppressing the unconscious through the seemingly rational, self-reflexive, and nonalienated spontaneous self-therapeutic discourses of his characters. Self-refleXivity as formulated in the previous chapter is nowhere to be seen. The "X" is never exposed. Rather, *DC* is Williamson's "talking cure" with the audience whose members become his listening and patient analysts, countertransferring their angst onto the characters as another variation of pop psychology. Individual agency, self-mastery, and self-expression that are so evidently on display in the *DC* series are the very qualities that are prized by the self-reflexive risk society of neoliberalism. While the *Scream* series provides viewers with Williamson's unconscious, repressed grasp of post-Oedipal angst, *DC* exposes us to it in the open, as it were. His outing came at a time when he had worked through his own trauma in those first two years of the series. There was no need to stay on—so he left.

Scream and Scream Again: The Pleasures of Self-Referentiality

As Deborah Lupen (1999, 170–71) explores in her examination of "risk" in its various dimensions, the gothic genre of literature and the horror film are generally perceived as sites where the transgressions of cultural boundaries occur, where excess over order, sadomasochistic eroticism, and strong affective feelings over everyday banal realities triumph. This in itself is nothing new. The gothic novel was a genre that combined romance and eroticism, where young female victims were tortured in the claustrophobic spaces of deserted and decayed castles. But what happens to the horror and gothic genre when we posit the appearance of the Father of Enjoyment? When the very limits of safety, sanity, and normality *demand* to be broken so as to increase consumptive pleasure? How does one then set up a boundary that can *still* be played with once the Father of Prohibition has been removed and the security of authority has gone? Answer: by adding self-referentiality and self-reflexivity within the horror genre itself to provide a minimum psychic space between fact and fiction so as not to be completely swallowed up by the Real. Self-referentiality, based on popular media references, provides an Imaginary construction as the necessary scaffold to hold on to. Authority is transferred away from authority figures that have become ineffectual in the narrative, and onto the viewer through cognition—namely, knowledge of popular culture by fans (see also Hill 2003). The "quoted" signifiers contain the bloc of pleasure and affect.

Such a ruse has been, mistakenly I believe, identified as a longing for *nostalgia* (Birchall 2004), but Deleuze's (1990) notion of the simulacrum makes more sense. It could be argued that this is an example of Nietzschean "powers of the false" in the way that these references "counteractualize" the horror genre as it was previously narrated. It becomes a simulacrum—as an appearance of the corridor of films that make up this genre. Drawing from that genre, it repeats and falsifies a potential for metamorphosis (becoming) that is already immanent within it. "[The powers of the false] is *art* which invents the lies that raise falsehood to this highest affirmative power, that turns the will to deceive into something which is affirmed in the powers of the false. For the artist, *appearance* no longer means negation of the real in this world but this kind of selection, correction, redoubling, and affirmation. The truth perhaps takes on a new sense. Truth is appearance. Truth means bringing of power into effect, raising to the highest power" (Deleuze 1983, 103, original emphasis). This might be a way to grasp such trickery.

Williamson's *Scream* series can be understood in this sense of art affirming the lie as truth. Its success cannot be grasped without the sociocultural development of designer capitalism with its superego formation of productive enjoyment. This was Williamson's genius, enabled perhaps by his own angst of being Othered, remaining closeted as a youth, caught in the role of an impostor (or double agent) by heterosexual hegemony where theatricality was his way out. Growing up Southern Baptist in the Bible Belt meant that it was safer to stay undercover, dating his best friend Fannie through college. As a student of drama and theater, his attempts at being an actor, and his love for television and film, especially the horror genre and the Americanized fantasies of Spielberg, provided a way for him to cope with his artistic sensitivity and fears as a queer youth, a way to push back everyday reality. In the Deleuzian sense, it is not necessarily (after Freud) that something is repeated because it is being repressed (William's gayness), but the other way around: his gayness is repressed so that it can be repeated in another register—the register of art. His acting out wasn't because Williamson had somehow forgotten his gayness; rather, it is forgotten so that its role *could* be acted out. Desires or events, which cannot be represented as objects of remembering or reflecting in consciousness, can be dramatized through modes of repetition. What is being performatively repeated *is* desire itself along the plane of immanence at the molecular levels. There is nothing beneath the mask, only its repetition. The horror genre freed Williamson through his appropriations of its repetitions, and through his vast imaginative memory archive of popular culture. It especially enabled him to imaginatively address the superegoic law that remains heterosexualized but that is post-Oedipally in decline.

While this is neither the place nor my intent to continue to psychoanalyze Williamson, it is the place to explore the underlying unconscious of the *Scream* series to grasp *DC* better as a form of its inverse repetition—*as the silent scream of youth anxiety and paranoia.* Williamson is no "schizo." If anything, the *Scream* series once again illustrates how capitalism capitalizes on schizocreativity. One of the disappointments of Anna Powell's (2005) attempt to provide a Deleuzian, as opposed to a psychoanalytic (Lacan), reading of the horror film[1] is her neglect to mention and deal with the *Scream* series, which introduced a reorientation to viewing film—what I am calling the *savvy poststructuralist subject of designer capitalism.* Here I would follow Matt Hills (2003) and maintain that such "reflexive cultural capital" "of pop cultural knowingness [. . .] fantasizes away issues of cultural power by making popular culture all that protagonists need to know in their life and death struggles." Trivial pursuit perhaps, but it reverberates the satisfaction of being "in the know." "What counts as knowledge and expertise by the time of *Scream 3* [which was *not* written by Williamson], unsurprisingly, is as much intratextual across the franchise as it is filmically intertextual. Reflexive cultural capital therefore becomes 'proprietary'; it is knowledge about the film series" (Schneider 2000a, 83). Savvy ironic self-reflexivity, however, does place youth "undercover," reinforcing subcultural bonds through shared knowledge that separates them from their parents' generation. The *Scream* series made that possible for "girlculture." Its figurality resonated with a youthful generation that saw a new bodily potential emerging as to what a "gurl" could do.

Andrew Tudor (1995) makes a strong dichotomous distinction between what he terms *secure* and *paranoid* horror films, maintaining that secure horror narratives assume a secure world where authority is prevalent to protect its citizens against all manner of external threats that can be defeated. The constituted authorities "remain credible protectors of social order although, as always in popular culture, they are not immune from mockery" (35). Paranoid horror Tudor reserves for the society of risk (Beck), which is just the opposite. The world is unreliable. Authority and institutional protection are ineffective as normative social relations collapse. The home becomes an uncanny place. If expertise is ineffective, protection rests with the self. People cannot be trusted even though outwardly they appear reputable, because there is something inextricably *inhuman* about them. This inhuman—what I referred to in chapter 2 as an "X"—is in this case a disordered psyche, inexplicably psychopathic for which there is no explanation. "Unruly bodies and unquiet minds [. . .] are the tangible articulations of the distinctive risks and fears of late twentieth century social life" (40). The ultimate horror film in this regard might be Mikael Håfström's 2007 film *1408*. The title refers to the number of the room in a New York hotel, The Dolphin, where 56 guests have died by either suicide or "natural" causes. Based on a Stephen King story, Mike Enslin, a writer who debunks paranormal phenomena, must face all his inner psychic demons, a metaphor for the unconscious Real that the room throws at him for an hour of entrapment. Redemption can be found only through a self-cleansing, symbolized by Enslin setting the room (and himself) on fire. The *Scream* series (the first in the series that appeared a year after Tudor's article was published) is also a paradigmatic example of a paranoid horror movie. As Williamson said, he "made the killer so self-aware of his psychosis that it was all played up" (Mangels 2000, 58). The other killer, when asked by Sidney the power-girl protagonist what his particular motive was, replies, "peer pressure." The self-reflexive joke cannot be missed.

It is the home, especially the hegemonic middle- to upper-class white bourgeois America that is being threatened in the *Scream* series, with *girlpower* and *girlculture* forwarded as its best defenses against the potentials of date rape and male aggressivity in general (see Karlyn 2003). The boyish "Final Girl" (Clover 1987, 1992) in the slasher movies is finally allowed to stand up for herself at the end of the millennium in a fantasy of control. The "chick flick" is born. There is a love-hate relationship between femininity and feminism set up by the relationship between Gale Weathers and Sidney. Weathers, a cheesy tabloid reporter, is presented as a phallic woman, toying with Deputy Dewey, in control of the camera(man), always seductively dressed and enjoying the attention. Sidney, as the name indicates, is the resignified "Final Girl."

Williamson's gay sensibility has both psychotic killers pre-Oedipally fixated. Billy overidentifies with his mother, while his accomplice, Stewart, overidentifies with Billy in a homoerotic bond. (Randy says to Steward in *Scream*, "You are such a little lapdog [for Billy]." While in *Scream 2*, he says, "He was a homo-repressed mama's boy.") The killers are Williamson's joke on psychosis, where it is the over-bearing mother who is to blame for Norman Bates's pathology in Alfred Hitchcock's classic *Psycho*. Psychoanalysts have often stereotyped the mothers of gay men as being phallic, smothering their sons, but the psychoanalytic truth is not far removed, given that the gay son is conflicted in his desire for the father as the primary love object, with his mother becoming the chief rival for the father's affection. This causes aggressive and competitive feelings toward the mother. Quite often these are repressed and masked within a heterosexual family, given that the boy's physical anatomy creates a set of expectations of desire on the part of his parents that are incongruent with his psychic life. As a child, the young boy cannot make significant changes in his environment so, as a "double agent," he must sequester his homoerotic longings, including those toward his father, as well as his aggressive feelings toward his mother. He intuits that he must present himself as a boy with the very opposite set of impulses as he attempts to identify with *either* gender. The conflict often remains unsolved until adulthood (Goldsmith 2001).

Dysfunctionality, as a descriptor for the neoconservative middle-class white American family only emerges when the core values of what holds the fantasy of what a family "is" or should "be" becomes decentralized and threatened—that is, *All in the Family* (1971–79) to *Married With Children* (1987–97), to *The Simpsons*, which began in 1989 and continues to chronicle the American middle-class family, going into its nineteenth season in 2007–08. As a cartoon, this family never ages. Its becoming is handled through the same strategy of self-reflexivity. Its characters act as a palimpsest of the imperceptible changes that are constantly taking place. Williamson's screenplay(s) has the mother blamed for the breakup of the family.

The father remains exonerated or weak—at least in the first two screenplays that he wrote. She is identified as a slut (Sidney's mother) or is accused of committing maternal abandonment (Billy's mother) and then seeking revenge in *Scream 2* for Sidney having killed her son, perhaps out of guilt. Either way, the mother is not permitted her own desire outside the family and/or relationship, as brilliantly developed in Stanley Kubrick's surrealist masterpiece in 1999, *Eyes Wide Shut,* where he shows cinema's incapacity as a patriarchal institution to understand and represent female desire. Williamson's treatment of the mother throughout the series would be a creative way to deal subliminally with his own aggression.

Carol Clover (1987, 1992) provided a psychoanalytic explanation as to how the slasher films of the 1970s and '80s were a response to the "trouble" going on in the Oedipal household. As she wrote, "the typical patrons of these films [were] the sons of marriages contracted in the sixties or even early seventies," a time characterized by "the women's movement, the entry of women into the workplace, and the rise of divorce and women-headed families" that "would yield *massive gender confusion* in the next generation" (1992, 62, my emphasis). To recall her argument in brief: the Final Girl is a girl in boy's drag, a "congenial double for the adolescent male," while the killer is really a woman in man's drag—and on rare occasions, as in *Friday the 13th*, the killer *is* the phallic mother. To extend Clover's thesis: the breakup of the household that was emerging—with Wes Craven's fantasy horrors seen as the chronicles of the dysfunctional family through this time—enabled young men to psychically work through their trauma by disavowing the fantasy that they were being "beaten" by their fathers; that is, by abandoning them. Their love for the father, although tenuous, is not abandoned. In effect, the blame is passed onto the mother. The Final Girl in drag with whom they identify with acts as the agent of revenge on the evil Father/and on the phallic Mother, thus satisfying their repressed feelings. This cross-gendered fantasy now becomes: "I am being beaten by my mother." But, what about the girls' anxieties in this *gender confusion*?

Enter the *Scream* series in the late 1990s, which sets up the discourse surrounding the maternal superego in a consumer climate where the demand to "enjoy" is hard at work. Williamson's gay sensibilities put to work in the *Scream* series explore how the "slut" and maternal "abandonment," both perverse feminine transgressions of the mother, are to be psychically confronted by daughters in the new permissive climate. The question of Billy's mother's abandonment is answered in *Scream 2* in an ironic way. We might say the Oedipal myth is replaced by Williamson's gay aversions to Orestes and Aeschylus' series of plays called *Orestia*, which would be consistent with the resolution to his own intrapsychic conflicts. Orestes murders his mother to avenge the death of his father in this "negative" Oedipal stage (see also Goldsmith 2001). Against the mise en abîme of the college play *Agamemnon*, Clytemnestra, as its tragic queen, becomes Mrs. Loomis, Billy's mother, while Sidney is given the role of Cassandra. Compared to the Greek play, the very inverse occurs. The abandonment of the father (Agamemnon) is answered by an extramarital affair by the mother (Clytemnestra/Mrs. Loomis), but she fails in her attempt at revenge for the loss of her son. Nevertheless, in the closing scene of the film, Mrs. Loomis comes across as a strong demonic figure who is not to be pitied; rather, her madness is a self-refleXive act of self-destruction that is meant to put an end to the family as we know it. The maternal superego, although dispatched by Sidney, is still given legitimacy as a defender of the family. Casssandra/Sidney, who in Aeschylus' play is a powerful and "mad" prophetess who is beheaded by Clytemnestra, ends up being a "fighter" who "faces her fate," as her drama teacher reminds her. The Final Girl becomes the postfeminist exemplar of someone completely in control of her self-being—make that sexual being. To referentially acknowledge that it is white middle-class America that is continually on display in Wes Craven horrors, *Scream 2* goes out of its way to intentionally "pepper" the script with African-American actors from the beginning of the film, where a young black couple argues over Hollywood's racial politics, through to a wise-cracking Eddie Murphy-like cameraman for Gale Weathers, and then completed with a female black bodyguard for Sidney.

The "absolvement" of Sidney's mother as slut is reserved until the final sequence, *Scream 3*, but its narrative cannot be completely attributed to Williamson. Mangels (2000, 269–70) reports that he wrote 30 pages of the script and had already outlined the entire trilogy earlier, but a mental breakdown prevented him from being fully involved in the final screenplay. Ehren Kruger was given credit for that accomplishment. The haunt of Sidney's ghostly mother, classically as a "return of the repressed" in Freudian terms, presents a monstrosity that must be laid to rest, lest Sidney become like her. The bottom line is that Sidney's mother, Maureen Prescott, is exonerated for her "slutty" behavior in a rather lame plot when Sidney discovers that she, too, was a "rebel," who as a young starlet in a horror film refused to sleep with the Hollywood director (John Milton) and was subsequently raped and left pregnant. She then began a new life by leaving Hollywood. The Orestian plot thickens when Sidney's half-brother, Roman Bridges, the child of Maureen Prescott and John Milton, ends up killing his mother because she rejected him, and then goes after Sidney. Of course, Sidney kills him, bringing to a close the unresolved mother-daughter relationship by having Sidney *traverse* her fantasy by the end of the trilogy. Knowing that her mother had also been brutalized by an unjust system that she had fought against enables Sidney to confirm her strength of spirit and will.

The Final Girl's Scream

The safety of sex has disappeared. Its paradox as a commodity and a gift is not only threatened by HIV/AIDS, but, generally, having sex has become "risky" business. The tropes of freedom and choice of self-reflexive neoliberalism harbor paranoid anxieties. The argument will be put forward that the self-objectification of women as figures of autonomous, active, and desiring selves has become a defense mechanism, a *neomasquerade* in the psychoanalytic sense as first developed by Joan Riviere (1929), whereby, in order to cope with the threat that bright, clever, and powerful women pose to male hegemony, they must play *in and with* the new femininities that are being constructed by designer capitalism, but do so as forms of *simulacra*. This is *not entirely* a question of hypernarcissism (see Tyler

2005 for a contrary view), as much as it is being backed into a corner to survive the "game" given—namely, that the designer gaze is all-persuasive and the only game in town. Men, as well, have to display a "six pack" to show that their bodies don't leak, while women have "makeovers" to stop the fluids from leaking. In a neoliberal climate where the youthful look reigns and one can only sell oneself to the market, what is left, so to speak, is precisely to play the "feminine card" as the performativity of conscious display; that is, as *simulacra* based on reflexive knowledge of femininity itself. As a performative gesture, the norms are variously played with depending on the cultural context, which I have tried to develop elsewhere (jagodzinski 2003a, 2005), identifying how, for instance, even the "virginity card" can be played for both perverse and normative ends of chastity to claim autonomy of self. Good, old-fashioned second-wave feminism no longer works. Which primary signifiers of identity are reconfigured (or "articulated" as Stuart Hall used the term) varies according to cultural contexts: ethnicity, gender, class, sexuality, religion, and so on. Designer capitalism's gaze of sexual performativity affects the entire globe. There is no escape. Islamic Occidentalism, for example, is shaped by it simply as a reaction to the unholy, unclad women who have no shame in the eyes of Allah.

In this regard, I am reminded of that fateful shot Kaja Silverman (1993, 39) refers to from Harum Faroki's amazing 1988/89 film, *Bilder der Welt und Inschrift des Krieges* (*Images of the World and Inscription of War*) (see Alter 1996), where a pretty Jewish girl tries her best to stave off death by displaying her feminine charms, posing for the camera of an SS (*Schutzstaffel*) officer as if she were simply strolling down a street—not in Auschwitz! The constitutive distinctions between vision, visuality, and visibility that Jacques Lacan makes in S XI (*Four Fundamentals*) indicate that the overdetermined relations that position a woman as a spectacular object, even in the worst of conditions, cannot be escaped. A heterosexual gaze that remains ephemeral nevertheless confirms the superego's demand for feminine display. The "backlash" is one of punishment, as if the superego of enjoyment is saying, "So you [feminists-women] want autonomy and equality, eh? Well, we [the amorphous structuring gaze] will give it to you but on *our* terms!" Playing performatively with this spectacularity, as exemplified by Madonna in the mid-1980s, ends up simply furthering designer capitalism's exploitation by having only a thin layer of heterosexual women given the privilege of "returning" the gaze, so to speak. The ability of designer capitalism to market an array of sexual desires, both queer and straight, leads us into a renewed discussion of perversity. The French Connection clothing company may have reached an ironic end point of such exploitative appropriation in 2002 with the "fcuk campaign," but the capitalist schizomachine is likely to find its way out of this endgame as well (Botting 2004; Scott Wilson 2000; Godfrey, Gavin, and Jones 2004).

Such a development has left feminists puzzled over its (dis)identification by young(er) women (Scharff 2007). There seems to be a general consensus between second- and third-wave feminists in the way each perceives the other. The politicized second-wave feminists see third-wave women (their "daughters"), many of whom "still" perceive themselves as feminists but do not center their identity on this primary signifier but on sexual emancipation, as being caught by an exploitive neoliberalist capitalism that promotes narcissism and self-love, "women *pleasing themselves* and freely choosing" to do so (Gill 2003, 103, original emphasis). In their minds, this play with sexuality is self-defeating, for once again it simply reproduces and reconfirms the popular stereotypes the second-wave feminists fought over (McRobbie 2004).

The anxieties surrounding postfeminism's self-objectification come in many forms. There is the fear of not having one's "looks" validated or of "loosing" those looks through aging. Of course, the most obvious is loosing control over body weight and appearance. There is also the fear of finding Mr. Right since, as an object of desire, date rape and violence are always possible. Third-wave feminists, by embracing sexual desire, perceive second-wave feminists as simply being unfeminine, man-hating lesbians, and antimale, caught by "normative" sexuality wherein their own pleasures are denied (Sharpe 2001; Storr 2003; Holland 2004). The complication between third-wave feminism and postfeminism is furthered by a distinction that places a wedge between the two terms. Leslie Heywood and Jennifer Drake (1997) maintain that "postfeminism characterizes a group of young, conservative feminists who explicitly define themselves against and criticize feminists of the second wave" (1). For Heywood and Drake, the third wave should be preserved as a continuation of the second wave in terms of sociopolitical action. It seems that there is self-indulgent, personal, apolitical experience attributed to a narrow definition of postfeminism, and then there is personal experience that is political. As I am forwarding it, the *simulacrum* of femininity is the play of a "feminine card" in a heterosexual context, which is perceived as a conservative backlash.

Post-Oedipal Screams

We enter post-Oedipalization most fully in the last two decades, from the mid-1990s to contemporary times. Desire in its queer and feminine forms begins to open up as *liberal* feminism begins to decenter not only with women of color complaining, but also with lesbians emerging out of the shadow of heterosexual feminism once an academic base had been established, as most prominently theorized by Judith Bulter's influential theory of performativity in 1990. The so-called third-wave feminism, often disparagingly identified as postfeminism, makes its appearance as *neoliberalized* girlpower (jagodzinski 2005) where femininity and feminism form a new hybridity. The heterosexual claims of psychoanalysis centered around mothers' desire (Jessica Benjamin, Julia Kristeva, Kaja Silverman) has also been challenged by Hortense Spillers (1996), who attempts to open up the heterosexist, nuclear familial structures by introducing race through the psychic dramas of the marginalized in their everyday life (see Driver 2005).

The question of feminine *jouissance*, its absence in the patriarchal symbolic order, had already been signaled and written about in the 1970s and 1980s by Luce Irigaray; Michele Montrelay; and Parveen Adams (1991), who provided the missing girl's fantasy in Freud's classic beating fantasy. Lesbian *jouissance* was forwarded by Monique Witttig, Judith Butler, and Elizabeth Grosz, who fever-ishly searched for its theoretical grounding, first in Lacan, then in Derrida, then in Foucault, and lastly in Deleuze as championed just as feverishly by Rosi Braidotti against the Lacanians. Gay *jouissance* has not been overlooked either with the theoretical writing on desire by Guy Hocquenghem, Jonathan Dollimore, and Lee Edelman. As Jean Baudrillard put it in *The Transparency of Evil* (1993), "the sexual body has now been assigned an artificial fate. This fate is transsexuality—transsexual not in any anatomical sense but rather in the more general sense of transvestism, of playing with the commutability of the signs of sex . . . we are all transsexuals" (20–21). Post-Oedipalization points to a "trans-genderism" where the circulation of desire decenters the biological male/female polarity through the *simulacrum* (Deleuzian not Baudrillardian) and where the play with sartorial, gestural, and morphological signs of sex remains performa-tive. That said, the politics that surround the plurality of desiring bodies are hard at work for hegemony, especially in their neoliberal forms exemplified by *Dawson's Creek,* as will be discussed in the postlude of the next chapter.

While Baudrillard's provocation has been dismissed by some (Felski 1996), this idea of transsexuality or transgenderism speaks to a shift in the psyche as conditioned by the superego's command to enjoy. While neurosis was the general and ambiguous term used by Freud to indicate the anxiety of the age, dropped now from the *Diagnostic and Statistical Manual of Mental Disorders* (DSM), per-version seems to have emerged as the new term that captures this turn to decen-tered heterosexual desire. It has been mobilized to put to doubt the usual binaries of sexual difference: male/female, straight/queer, black/white, to rethink the sub-ject from a reflective to what I take to be a self-refleXive subject, the *creative* core of the Real so as to escape or place into doubt the established ontological cate-gories and patterns. The instability of the subject and its identifications emerge precisely here.

As a general and ambiguous term for the contemporary society of enjoyment, perversion frees up that part of the libido that brackets the procreative act. Foremost, it is sexual promiscuity applied to an assortment of acts not tradition-ally defined as heterosexual, whereby a normative economy of procreation is pro-moted based on the reproductive capabilities of opposed sex/genders. In short, the pleasures of the body, regardless of sex/gender, not only drift toward the contro-versies that surround the philosophy of the bedroom à la Marquis de Sade, but introduce the uncontrollable body of the drives. Desire is found there alone, regardless of sex/gender, hetero/homo. For Deleuze and Guattari, desire is the amorphic creative term that opens up the possibilities of "n-sexualities," that is, multiplying the possibilities that the binary male/female enclose. As Tim Dean (2000) has persuasively argued, this position and that of Lacan's notion of *objet a* are similar and complementary formulations with the transcendental Phallus decentering and dropping away in particular contexts where authority can no longer function easily. The geopolitics of its force remains uneven—hence, "*pos*tal" in its effective delivery.

The subject may well be in permanent flux, but one is hard-pressed to find evi-dence that this "flux" is highly unstable and chaotic, not subject to repression, ego defenses, and so on. Derailment from "normalized subjectivity" is not a *conscious* choice, but an act that is self-refleXively contingent. One cannot predict love, for instance. It just "happens." Nietzsche's aphorism *amour fati*, that we embrace and celebrate our fate, equally applies. Even one's "coming out" is not entirely a conscious decision, but one that is shaped by social circumstances that always involve risk. The "volitional tactic of positive perversion" (MacCormack 2004, 29) is suspect, since one cannot control drives *entirely*. An ethics of the Real comes into the picture. "To pervert one's static self" (30), that is, "to use perversion tactically without acknowledging issues of power, control and oppression in relation to sexuality," is, as MacCormack maintains, "unethical" (30). Perversion does not necessarily lead directly to the pervert, but this slippage is impossible to maintain. If "[p]erversion describes the open circuit of the flow of desire (existence *as* desire not with desire)" (30, original emphasis), this is none other than a strong affirmation of the Freudian drives. To say that desire is defined through lack (the usual retort against Lacan), which demands an object *choice*, is to move desire onto a conscious level.

This slippage happens easily, as in Rosi Braidotti's discussion of monstrosity, which ends up in object choice. "[T]o become monster we must desire monsters" (quoted in MacCormack, 34). It is not possible to maintain monstrosity as a becoming in a resistant and ambiguous form without slipping into signage. *But*, Braidotti maintains, there is a difference of this monstrous desire from a Lacanian frame: "in order to desire a monster one cannot be monster. One is fulfilling the monstrous lack in the hitherto normal subject" (quoted in MacCormack, 34). "That is why," she concludes, "woman is the primary monster because man is the primary nonmonster and desires only what he lacks" (ibid.). Lacan is saddled again with the specificity of heterosexual desire when he makes a specific claim that desire holds no specific sex/gender distinction. Unlike Braidotti and Bulter, sex for Lacan cannot be historicized (unlike gender). It remains in the Real. *But*, desire read as "abundance" (productive and positive), according to Patricia MacCormack, somehow escapes any such accusations, for "the desire for a monster changes both the subject desiring and the monster of desire" (34). As if in the Lacanian sense, this did *not* happen, as if unconscious desire as lack continues to maintain an enforcement of otherness.

These conclusions are egregiously wrong. The *objet a* as the cause of unconscious desire confuses any system of self/other, inside/outside. By forwarding the discourse of woman being the *first* monster of man reinforces yet another binary. It becomes the antithetical discourse to postfeminism. The monstrous woman (Braidotti 2000) presents another opposing hybridity—monstrosity and feminism versus femininity and feminism. In this context it becomes impossible not to think of Charlize Theron portrayal in Patty Jenkins's *Monster* (2003), the fictionalized story of Aileen Wuornos, a Daytona Beach prostitute who became a serial killer. The monster-woman can only remain a screen fiction who can just as easily transform herself back into the glamour of Hollywood—as Theron did to receive her various nominations and awards, *seven* in total as best actress, including her Oscar (2004)—and become a feminine-feminist, yet another screen fiction. This very interchangeability seems to indicate that they are two sides of the same coin.

My prelude to *Dawson's Creek* was intended to highlight the way self-reflexivity has become a way for youth to go "undercover" by being in the know and deriving pleasure from this. The *Scream* series is a landmark in this regard for these films also subvert the Oedipal relationships pushing them in the direction of the "post." The development of postfeminism, I have suggested, is a form of simulacrum, a neomasquerade in defense of the impossible escape from spectacularity. While it brings its own "post-Oedipal" screams, I have also suggested that such a development within the heterosexual discourse is matched by the resignification of perversity in the queer discourse. Both developments decentering the Phallus as the paradoxes of the superego manifest themselves in consumer societies.

4

Dawson's Creek: The Postlude

Kevin Williamson's *Scream* series must be understood as a prime example of the postmodern culture of the *simulacrum*, where the relationship of its narrative shifts to the spectators themselves in its perpetual "wink-wink," "nod-nod," through its referentiality (or intertexuality). *Dawson's Creek (DC)* pays homage to a whole host of other teen series: *90210* is often evoked. Episode 201 ("The Kiss") addresses Luke Perry, while episode 220 ("Reunited") mentions the Peach Pit diner, and episode 305 ("Indian Summer") references *Sweet Valley High*. Most often references are made to the teen "brat pack" movies of the 1980s of John Hughes, who Williamson claims had a big influence on him. Episode 202 ("Crossroads") refers to *Pretty in Pink*; episode 508 ("Text, Lies and Videotape") refers to *Sixteen Candles,* while episode 100 ("Emotion in Motion") refers to *The Breakfast Club*. However, as in the *Scream* series, his references are meant to be repetitions that evoke the "powers of the false." Not only is the naïveté of *90210* exposed, but also in episode 106 ("Detention"), a clear reference to *The Breakfast Club*, the Hughes movie is purposely evoked and discussed among Dawson, Jen, and Joey so as to question its worth as a narrative. While Claire Birchall (2004) has called this *nostalgia* that extends the viewing pleasure to the "young adult viewer" and the baby boomer, an alternative reading is that *DC* places stress on *nostos*—as an idea of "return"—rather than on *algos*—the pain or emotion of the regret or longing for the conditions of a past age. A return brings with it the possibility of difference, and a rewriting and exposure of the flux of a situation (e.g., *The Breakfast Club*), given that "moving on" and change are so much a part of the dialogue on *DC*.

DC's ironic mode of address distances viewers from barbed linguistic violence and, at the same time, speaks to the audience by inviting them to participate as knowledgeable and savvy viewers. The attempt to increase interactive audience participation has become a standard device since the mid-1980s through the so-called open text, already theorized by Umberto Eco (1979) in 1959 and updated by Roland Barthes (1974) as "writerly" as opposed to "readerly" texts where the reader/viewer is said to become an active producer rather than a passive consumer of texts. The hypertext, of course, has become the paradigmatic example for this claim. But film and television in their postmodern textual forms are unable to push this interactive dimension as far, so the narratives invite audience interactivity in other ways. Ironic self-referentiality has become the standard fare. The author function (often a team) becomes machinic and decentered, while the director tugs at the strings of the audience à la Hitchcock. The writer/director becomes a knowing participant who indulges in jokes and asides with the audience. This produces a *suspension* of the taken-for-granted past that the genre has established, or that has become hegemonic (often claimed as a return of nostalgia, in this case, to the horror genre).

Writer/directors highlight this past, bringing it into relief as a memory by juxtaposing a similar narrative that introduces difference through a series of repetitions. Thus, there is a suspension of the "identity" of the original, as well as a suspension of the object of desire and knowledge of this taken-for-granted original. A good example is Gus van Sant's 1998 remake of *Psycho*, where, as a gay man, he attempts, like Williamson, to dispel the easy read that Bates's mother bears the weight of his psychotic break by queering certain scenes and thereby drawing out the queer subtext in the "original" (Schneider, 2000b). Authority's ability to show or control this original thus wanes. It shows exactly how repetition through simulacra is able to put the original in doubt and drain it of its power and influence. Also, the fundamental separation of the visible from the articulable can no longer be maintained; rather, image and word come together, crisscrossing in their hybridity territory explored by Jean-Luc Godard for some time now.

In many respects *DC*'s first two seasons, which were written and directed by Williamson, provide a *simulacrum* of teen romance as a "silent" scream in relation to his slasher movies. While *Scream* was a trilogy, *DC* as a televised prime-time serial (PTS) included up to 24 episodes a year, which obviously required an entirely different narrative structure to capture its audience. Michael Z. Newman (2006) has usefully examined and described the way PTS narratives are able to capture and maintain their audiences through a fairly standard structure where repetitiveness, redundancy, and recapping of the story are mandatory but are done in such a way as not to irritate the audience. Newman explains the overall PTS structure in the following comprehensive way: the micro level is composed of "beats" (these are scenes composed of short segments, often less than two minutes long), a middle level of the episode (which is usually divided into four acts of equal length—to accommodate commercial breaks—requiring a resolution to the conflicts with various thematic parallelisms running through them), and the macro level or multiepisode arc. The PTS is a character-driven form. Each character has an arc that plots his or her story.

An arc, as the character's journey, Newman (23–25) explains, is shaped by two salient commercial constraints. The first are the questions that dangle week after week throughout the season to maintain suspense. Obviously, on *DC* it's the questions surrounding love and friendship among the four main characters. The second is organizing the season into segments, of which there are five based on sweep periods that set advertising rates according to Nielsen ratings. A season normally premiers in the fall (September–October), with the fall sweeps occurring in November. There is a holiday rerun period (December–January), followed by winter sweeps in February. Another rerun period follows (March–April), with the spring sweeps and the season finales broadcast in May. Lastly, there is the summer rerun season. The three sweep periods enable acts to be constructed in units of six to eight episodes. With 24 episodes to a season, there are three acts (not arcs) that come to strong closures at the end of each sweep period. At this macro level, character arcs share a shape with the season acts, since characters' lives and their arc trajectories are intertwined; often the arcs and acts come to a resolution at the end of the season or they are left in a dramatic nonresolution.

Beats, episodes, and the arcs that shape the season make up the formal PTS structure. *DC* is no exception to this winning formula. One of the most extraordinary aspects of *DC* is its so-called *realism*. It does away with anything that is appears ambiguous—conflicts of whatever magnitude become framed through full, transparent speech acts. Nothing remains "unsaid" for very long. Whenever advise is given by one teen to another, or by an adult to a teen, or even visa versa, that advice is already internalized by the enunciator in the hope that he or she is already a living example of the advise that is being given—which is not necessarily the case, but presents openly the flaw of being "human." The success of this moralizing discourse has provided some researchers with an opportunity to explore teenage moral reasoning as measured against the Kohlberg-Gilligan developmental scales (Aimée Dorr and Sandra Irlen, 2002). *DC* is, on all accounts a Norman Rockwell aesthetic composed of a pastiche of traditional families whose conflicts are made visible in such a way that, through Dawson's desire, the audience wants that 1950's image restored with Mitch cutting up the turkey on Thanksgiving Day, his marriage restored. And, indeed that is precisely the arc that happens after the illicit love affair Gail Leery has with her news coanchorman, Bob, complete with a new member added to the family, baby Lily, at the beginning of season four. Its affective diagram is rigidly territorialized, tight with little given to chance.

Throughout the six seasons, I can only recall one episode, early in the fourth season, in which narrative time was played with in a circular fashion. It was episode 403 ("The Two Gentlemen of Capeside"), where Dawson is told that Joey and Pacey are now together, and he experiences the trauma of that realization. Otherwise, each episode is shot as a "movement image" in the Deleuzian sense, with such feeling for romantic illusion that each scene is perfectly framed with optimum radiant light. However, that said, like David Cronenberg's *Blue Velvet*, which presents the illusion of Lumberville as a small town with a picket-fence aesthetic, there is equally a dark side to the post-Oedipal dysfunctional families that the cast of characters attempts to sort out.

Not all is well in Capeside despite appearances. From Jen's Bible-thumping fundamentalist Grandmother to her alcoholic mother and rejecting father, all of whom have abandoned her; to Dawson's parents who become embroiled in divorce as a result of extramarital betrayal; from Pacey's parents—an overbearing father, an absent mother, and an older, perhaps queer, brother who has a "steady," law-abiding job as a deputy and is used as a foil by his father to degrade Pacey's efforts; to Joey, whose dad is in jail on narcotics trafficking, while her mother is absent—dying early of cancer. If that's not enough dysfunctionality, there is her sister who is marginalized and barely surviving, unmarried with a child with an

African-American, and looked down upon in white, middle-class Capeside. Jack and Andie, who are brother and sister, introduce us to a father who hates his queer son and must come to terms with this; their mother seems absent once again. Then, late in the fifth season (501, "Bostonians"), we are introduced to Audrey Liddel, who is caught up in drugs; she is also from a dysfunctional family. So, it's not that there aren't all kinds of problems circulating throughout the idyllic white middle-class of Capeside; it's the way that they are worked through that provides the greatest concern—cognitive self-help therapy among friends: *The Secret* teenage style.

There Ain't No Rap but Capeside Pap

As in all teen melodramas, music is used to affectively underscore the emerging romantic relationships. Kay Dickinson (2004), who specifically addresses the music heard on *Dawson's Creek* in some detail, maintains that the large amount of music (at least six tracks per show) is "tied in with a specific and highly appealing lifestyle, aesthetic and hegemony" (103). The official soundtrack website enables extended consumer activity to take place. Clicking on links takes potential buyers to the featured artists' home pages. As part of the Sony group, Columbia TriStar Television, which is responsible for *DC*, is able to extend sales for Sony Music, and it also distributes a number of films directed by Dawson's idol, Steven Spielberg. Through her careful analysis, Dickinson comes to some rather startling conclusions: African-American performers are underrepresented and, if heard at all, are presented delivering "quirky, mainly lyrical commentary" (105), and performances are by "classic" artists like Louis Armstrong, Ella Fitzgerald, the Weathergirls, and the Temptations. Rap is out, as are performers such as Marilyn Manson. Goth, hip-hop, and nü-metal are also conspicuously missing, leaving what? Dickinson claims that what is left is a Christian agenda with such artists as Jessica Simpson, the Newsboys, the Elms, Sixpence None the Richer, Tait, Switchfoot, Beanbag, Sarah Masen, and Say-So, perhaps "trying to soothe a concerned Christian demographic into thinking that the challenging themes of the TV show are, in fact, 'safe'" (105). To drive the conservativism of the music home, she points out that most of the soundtrack is music from the boomers' teenage years: Bruce Springsteen, Bryan Adams, Chris Isaak, Curtis Stigers, and the Corrs. This leads her to conclude that tapping into the older markets "is an adult culture interfering in an opportunity for youth to develop in a manner distinct from its parents; a grown-up voice droning on about how things were better in its day" (107).

Dickinson makes a further valuable point as to why *DC*'s baby boomer soundtrack is hegemonically conservative, promoting, in the final analysis, what could be considered a neoliberal agenda that promotes enterprise, achievement, and self-determination. So many of the songs have a self-help narrative about them. Following Lawrence Grossberg's (1992) lead, she maintains that youth are caught in a contradiction of being either powerless adolescents or college students. In contrast, the baby boom generation has economic clout and refuse to grow up, taking the category "youth" as their life trajectory. They continue to maintain their "cultural supremacy . . . through the regimentation of the music which gets the most circulation" (109). A subtle revisionism takes place where the folk-style song and lyrics are "strangely devoid of the leftist politics marked out by the work of, for example, Bob Dylan" (ibid.). Paula Cole's theme song for *DC*, "I don't wanna wait for our lives to be over/I wanna know right now," ends up in the ambivalent space of a liberal sense of freedom, in the sense of having "missed" out on something, as well as a call to the immediacy of getting one's life in order.

Young Love, Pure "Confluent" Love?

The idea that "youth" is an intergenerational category that defies an easy classification is what I have argued in the seminal book of this tripartite series, *Youth Fantasies* (2004). Simon Frith (2004) in his "afterword" to a book that examines the problems encountered in maintaining Birmingham's Centre for Contemporary Cultural Studies' (CCCS) approach to youth—that is, in viewing them as definable subcultures—confirms such a stance. He writes, "And here lies the most significant shift in youth studies before and after subculture. Then youth was an age category; now, it seems, it isn't, or isn't necessarily. . . . On the one hand, . . . 'youth' as constructed in subcultural and postsubcultural discourse describes lifestyles and means of identity that are no longer age specific. . . . The implication is that 'youth' has become a different sort of category altogether. On the other hand . . . youth must be approached 'through actual practices of individual groups in real social settings.' . . . as a process of transition rather than a stable social role [that] freezes youth into a particular moment of consumption and display" (177). This contradiction is especially evident in *DC*. The characters act with a maturity that is well beyond their "teen" years. Pacey says, "What's with all the psychobabble insight? How many teenagers do you know that talk like that? (210, "The Kiss"). Dawson's idol, Steven Spielberg, also exemplifies the crossroad between the "late modernity" as outlined by Anthony Giddens and the reflexive modernity of Ulrich Beck. He is an adult who never quite grew up, but made it selling the fantasy of *E.T.* (1982) at about the time that American families were experiencing change because both parents had to work to make ends meet, and feared abandoning their children. *E.T.* happens to be Dawson's favorite movie.[1]

Matt Hills (2004) has argued that *DC* exemplifies the transformed love relationships of "late modernity," the shift from "romantic love" to "confluent love" or the "pure relationship." Giddens (1992) believes that globalization and the rise of expert systems have wrought changes in every type of relationship, especially in intimate sexual relationships. Giddens traces love from its being a form of disruptive divine passion—as "cosmic fate" in premodernity—to the late eighteenth and nineteenth century when alongside it arose the idea of romantic love where a "flawed individual is made whole" (45). The romantic novel for women narrated quests "in which self-identity awaits its validation from the discovery of the other" (ibid.). The one true love would be found sometime in the future leading to a lifelong (heterosexual) marriage assuring some form of psychological security. Such romantic relationships revolved around ideal visions of manly strength and womanly virtue.

Things changed in the second half of the twentieth century. "Pure" or "confluent" love is a relationship in which "a social relation is entered into for its own sake, for what can be derived by each person from a sustained association with another; and which is continued only insofar as it is thought by both parties to deliver enough satisfactions for each individual to stay within it" (58). So while an attempt is made to know the other intimately through constant communication, this is not necessarily a permanent commitment, but a contingent one. If the implicit agreement in terms of the values, interests, and identities of the partners begins to diverge, then there is no reason to sustain it. Doing so (for the sake of the children) plunges the partnership into misery.

DC tests the waters of such confluent love by setting up a triangle between Pacey and Dawson with Joey as the girl in the middle drawn both ways: the direction toward Dawson would confirm "true" romantic love culminating the friendship they've had since elementary school; the direction toward Pacey would lead in the opposite direction. Dawson's best friend has another set of values that is more suitable for Joey—namely, actual experiential adventure as opposed to just the fantasy life on the screen (Dawson) and a bad-boy heroism that attracts Joey as opposed to Dawson's good-boy conservativism. One might say that it took six seasons to resolve this conflict of Joey's moving from the constraints of the traditional romantic love of "soul mates" toward a "pure love" relationship eventually with Pacey. The conflict itself as played out through the various arcs of Joey with Dawson and then with Pacey and then back to Dawson and then back to Pacey is simply the same shift from liberalism to neoliberalism; from rationalism to a hypercognitive rationalism in the myth of control when facing the uncontrollable. If powerlessness and the threat of victimization and exploitation tend to produce paranoia, *DC*'s characters are so assured of themselves that the thesis of this book appears to be in jeopardy. However, like the white picket-fence aesthetic, there is profound insecurity in their bravado.

Giddens's account of the rise of these pure relationships is related to globalization and the growth of expert systems. The authority of tradition is undermined by the decontextualization of knowledge, while globalization offers an array of lifestyle choices, which, for Giddens, form the core of self-identity. In good neoliberal, rational fashion, an individual must weave together a coherent narrative of self-development from the threads of the past and present and anticipation of future lifestyle choices. Giddens calls this the "reflexive project of the self" (9), where one gravitates "towards relationships that center on authenticity and self-disclosure, on the pursuit of similar lifestyles, that are sufficiently contingent in that they do not threaten to block unanticipated lines of personal development" (Gross and Simmons 2002, 536).

DC certainly provides prime examples of individuals who pursue self-actualization and become reliant on self-generated therapeutic discourses among themselves. They are individuals who continually "conduct a self-interrogation in terms of what is happening" (Giddens 1992, 76) in the relationship so that the status of the relationship and its dynamics can be assessed. Emotional communication and reflexive questions play central roles. Above all, perhaps, is how the moral/ethical obligation is maintained since there is no longer a Bible to believe in.

Jen's adamant fight with her aunt about God and religion highlights this. To ensure trust, intimate partners have to be sure that the other will not take advantage of them. This trust depends on "the opening out of the individual to the other, because knowledge that the other is committed, and harbors no basic antagonisms towards oneself, is the only framework for trust when external supports are largely absent" (Giddens, 96). Such "opening out" among the characters on *DC* is a defining characteristic of *pure* love characterized most often as *soul mates*.

Pop psychologists like John Gray (1993) posit men and women as *aliens* to one another: "men are from Mars, women are from Venus." Barbara DeAngelis's (1990) self-help books for women put the male on another planet defined by a host of biological differences. How to love an alien (as explored by the *Roswell* series) becomes turgid and dangerous and an arduous expedition. Romantic love can be obsessive, addictive (e.g., Norwood 1985), placing the woman at risk and making her vulnerable, open to the predatory exploits of the male. Having an orgasm and sex is but a small part of intimacy and friendship between partners. It's the "rest" that counts, enabling the "X" of *desire* to be kept in check. Good rapport, for instance, is considered far more important to women than good sex. Trust and friendship are, therefore, at a premium and help explain why straight-gay relationships have become popularized on television (*Will & Grace*) and in the movies (*My Best Friend's Wedding* (1997), *As Good as it Gets* (1997), and *The Object of My Affection* (1998). *DC* is no exception in terms of the relationship between Jen and Jack where their friendship is eroticized. Male-female friendship is privileged over romantic love (Dreisinger 2000; Battles and Hilton-Morrow 2002). This takes me to the next section.

Confluent Fag-Hag Love

The way the gay character of Jack McPhee interacts with troubled straight-girl Jen Lindley illustrates perfectly well a neoliberal confluent or pure relationship as theorized by Giddens. A trusting friendship is exchanged for sex of any sort. The sexual act is taken out of heterosexual romance, leaving a safe eroticism. At the end of season six, a dying Jen gives up her one-year-old baby, Amy, to be raised by Jack, confirming her unconsummated love for him. Their relationship is the melodramatic counterpoint to the comic relationship between NBC's Will Truman and Grace Adler (*Will & Grace,* 1998–2006). Michaela D. E. Meyer (2003) has applied "relational dialectic theory" to claim the worth of such interpersonal dialogue when understanding Jack's gayness via his friendship with Jen. The pejorative "fag-hag couple" is put to work by the scriptwriters to explore gay sexuality, but I would argue (contra Meyer) in a very safe way as if we have entered a "post-gay" period where the struggle for gay rights has already been won; where the responsibility for coming out of the closet is placed squarely on the individual, as is the rejection of a homophobic attitude. What follows is taken largely from Meyer's convictions.

I begin with Giddens making the further point that, besides globalization and expert systems of knowledge, it is the decline of fertility and the growing acceptance of contraceptive technologies that have made confluent love possible. Such interrelated developments have enabled "a progressive differentiation of sex from the exigencies of reproduction" and ushered in an era of "plastic sexuality" where, especially for women, "sexuality became malleable ... and a potential 'property' of the individual" (1992, 27). Plastic sexuality as the severing of sexuality from reproduction made sexual fulfillment as *ars erotica* a condition for remaining in a relationship. "[H]eterosexuality is no longer a standard by which everything else is judged" (34). Such a logic of plastic sexuality gave cultural support to "interest groups and movements ... claiming social acceptance and legal intimacy for homosexuality"(ibid.) that, in principle, does not rely on assumptions about "natural" gender complementarities.

Both Jack and Jen, individually (in their independence) *and* as a "couple," beginning with the third season (in their interdependence), exemplify this development. Jen, struggling with heterosexuality—her inability to "handle" her erotic attraction toward men and men toward her—sees Jack as a "safe" bet. Jack, struggling with his gayness, sees Jen equally as a confidant. Such self-refleXive, unconscious attraction is not dialogically discussed; instead, when Jack breaks his arm halfway through the football season, Jen "self-sacrifices" her cheerleading since it is no longer associated with him. She now shuns being treated as a "sex-object." The reason for the repetition of continually failed relationships with men who cheat or reject her, the root of her unconscious desire, is never directly tackled. Neither are her drinking and drug taking resolved through counseling, which begins when Jack finds Tobey. Neither a psychologist nor a psychiatrist (yet alone a psychoanalyst!) can help (416, "Mind Games"); *only Jack can.* This is explained as her need for him to affirm her identity. The resolution to her "man problem" is perfectly engineered in Hollywood. In season six she is dying of a heart condition and has a child! Out of wedlock, of course. And who will be the baby's father when she passes on? A no brainier— Jack! Her unconscious desire for the impossible male partner in her life is finally fulfilled at the cost of her life.

Television series such as *Will & Grace* have made the gay and straight couple a trope to explore different relational sensibilities as their names indicate. Jack's coming "out of the closet" in February 1999 made no impact on the news media (Dow 2001). *DC*'s episodic arcs dealt with all aspects of Jack's coming-out process: high school students' reactions to queer students (301, "Homecoming"); his explorations of Boston's gay bar scene (310, "First Encounters of the Close Kind"); his visit to an organized meeting of queer people in Boston (410, "Self-Reliance"); Jack's firing from his peewee coaching job because of parental fears of pedophilia (216, "Be Careful What You Wish For"); the violent beating of his boyfriend Tobey because of his sexuality (419, "Late"); his acceptance into a fraternity (512, "Sleeping Arrangements"); and his dismissal by a closeted fraternity brother who accuses Jack of making a move on him (514, "Guerilla Filmmaking"). All along, this is presented as foregrounding his personal struggle, with Jen acting as his conscience, continually pushing him to be true to himself, reminding him that he has to face his gayness. *DC* draws on the cultural convention of treating homosexuality as a personal, rather than a political, issue; or rather it shows how Jack is trapped in this contradiction. It takes into account the social consequences of Jack outing himself on a personal level. As B. J. Dow (2001) argues about Ellen DeGeneres's personal media-saturated coming-out narrative, as it is practiced in popular culture; it often degenerates into a politics that "can serve a masking function as representation [of visibility that] is mistaken for social and political change" (137). The discourses that surround the positioning of the gay subject are avoided. Most often in the episodes mentioned above, gay sex between Jack and a potential partner is contained through the conventions of male bonding. At the most, the audience is exposed to kissing.

In a marked contrast, Meyer (2003) argues that it is Jack's "desire to use sexuality to inform identity rather than constitute his entire self" (269). She takes this as being an "adolescent perspective that wishes to avoid falling into some preconceived stereotype" that is confronted by an "adult-oriented position that sexuality must constitute identity" (270), a position taken by Tobey (Jack's boyfriend) and Jen, who maintain that politics and queer activism cannot be avoided. Jack's attempts to pass for straight and be accepted as just another one of the guys on the football team or in the frat house continually fail. This blending of adolescent and adulthood perspectives provides not only an extended viewing audience, but also a safe way for queer identification to take place, thus making it tolerable. The straight and gay alliance between Dawson and Jack that begins at the end of season three and the beginning of season four (the arc of 323, "True Love"; 401, "Coming Home"; 402, "Falling Down") is not well developed. Queer identity as filtered through heterosexual hegemony is possible up to the point where sexuality is removed from representation—an acceptance of intimacy but without any exposure to same-sex escapades. Bisexuality is, for the most part, a missing discourse for explorative representation. There are the proverbial moments as in most gay/straight narratives of a possible sexual encounter between incongruous partners to reassure the audience that it "could" still happen, thereby further normalizing heterosexuality. One such moment takes place when both Jen and Jack are drunk on a school ski trip after Jen's breakup with Henry Parker (402, "Falling Down"). But Jen breaks it off. On another occasion Jack "proposes" to Emma so that she doesn't need to marry Gus just because she does not wish to move back home (614, "Clean and Sober").

DC leans heavily on Jack's naïveté as he explores his gayness. His anxieties, as mediated by Jen, present a "tolerable" context for a hetero-audience that can now handle handholding, hugging, and kissing as long as it is not so passionate that *DC*'s sponsors will complain. In episode 623 ("All Good Things . . ."), Jack's kissing his partner, Sheriff Doug Witter (Pacey's brother), is done as a comedy sketch as he is pulled over for speeding. The mention of handcuffs for a possible lovemaking session in the evening is meant as a joke to relieve audience anxiety. The sheriff remains, in Jack's terms, a "paranoid closeted freak." As a teacher, however, Jack comes across as a gay activist, but he condemns Doug's inability to come out of the closet, recapitulating the insensitivity to his institutional plight. They are unable to reconcile their differences, and they split apart only to come together again in a Hollywood ending where Doug is willing to support Jack's sudden fatherhood.

Ironic Self-Reflexivity—The Final Episode's Joke on Us

So, to what extent is the constant "self-therapy" among the characters a form of "talking cure" in the neo-Freudian ego psychological sense? Is Dawson Leery the Dr. Phil of neoliberal youth? Principal Green says to Dawson, "You think like people twice your age . . . Reclaim your youth" (301, "Like a Virgin"). Or, as Pacey says, "What's with all the psychobabble insight? How many teenagers do you know that talk like that?" (210, "The Kiss"). There is now even a research paradigm that has developed from such dialogical interactions. Baxter and Montgomery (1996; Montgomery and Baxter 1998) call this "relational dialectic theory," which is "a belief that social life is a dynamic flow of contradictions, a ceaseless interplay between contrary or opposing tendencies" (3). Applying dialectical tensions to the context of interpersonal relationships exposes the way such tensions define and redefine relationships toward intimacy. Relational dialectics theory is said to expose these tensions within interpersonal relationships, and at the same time the assumption is that a continual maintenance and repair of those tensions will take place. In other words, there is a marked absence of any recognition of an unconscious at work. Each character acts as the other's therapist, which is the promise of self-reflexive cognition. There is no repression in relational dialectical theory, and in *DC the unconscious does not exist.*

So, although youth may not *talk* that way, the claim is that they *feel* that way; the signifiers carry all affect. The dialogical exchanges are meant to engender an affective state between friends and the audience, to expose how they *feel.* The exposed teenage angst is subjected to reflexive, rational examination to promote the healthy teenager who is, by and large, searching for conservative family values (Dawson wants mom and dad to get back together, which they do), safe sex and only when ready (did Joey sleep with Pacey while they were adrift for months on a boat together between the end of season three and the beginning of season four? The answer turns out to be, no!). Joey "saves" herself for Dawson and staves off Pacey through several developmental arcs while striving to attain the American dream by establishing a name for herself through her writing by becoming a junior editor. Dawson wants to be a film director/producer, while Pacey is the daring adventurer-entrepreneur, "sailing" through life, successful at any job simply by applying himself.

DC as a romantic melodrama defers (following the classical formula) the desired consummation of the couples until the endgame of the sixth season, in the complementary episodes 623 and 624 in which the producers finally "show their hand" through a mise en abîme effect of a story within a story, a frame within a frame, a fiction within a fiction. The *ménage à trois* turns out to be a variant of Freud's joking triangles (Flieger 1991, 176). It is never "truly" resolved, for desire always escapes resolution, becomes deferred or deflected. The joke falls on us as the Other, the witnessing public, seeing rather than hearing the joke being told. As the fourth term, we now become exposed.

As *DC* addicts caught within its circuits of desire, we have been watching a story that *frames;* that is, that gives context to or *mirrors* an autobiographical television series that Dawson Leery is writing and producing called *The Creek,* starring Sam (as Joey), Colbey (as Dawson) and Petey (as Pacey). Episode 623 ("All Good Things") opens with Joey lying in a luxurious New York apartment, wine glass in hand, faithfully watching *The Creek,* a television program that comes on every Wednesday. Here is the opening dialogue between Sam and Colbey that rehearses and conflates the many episodes that were shot in Dawson's bedroom where the tomboy Joey would visit him through the window and spend the night as young kids.

COLBEY (about 12 years old?): Feelings and emotions have a subconscious way of manifesting themselves not always in self-aware behavior.
SAM (same age): Your verbal deconstruction of teen angst is really outdated. There is nothing going on between Petey and me. He's just a friend . . . your best friend I might add. I have no unconscious subliminal intentions towards him.
COLBEY: Just a friend, huh? .
SAM: Yes, that's all. Period. End of sentence . . . dissertation and postmodern diatribe. Now can we go to sleep?
COLBEY: So is Petey a friend like you and I are just friends?
SAM: Yes, of course.
COLBEY: That's what I was afraid of.

Joey's boyfriend, Christopher, a writer, hates the series. Here is some of what he says while gleefully turning off the television and coming to sit on the couch with Joey:

CHRISTOPHER: Thank god that's over. You know that show . . . it's like bad airplane food. You know, the teen hyperbole . . . it's bad in your stomach. The writers must sit around with a thesaurus just seeking out four-syllable ways to abuse the English language. Who talks like that Colbey guy? He's like some mutant English professor psychotherapist freak.

After the usual trailer that introduces the series, we cut to the writing room where the team of writers of *The Creek* are discussing how to end the series. A large white-board with all the color-coded arcs of the characters (Petey, Sam, Colbey) are shown. Prominently displayed is the saying, "If it's not in the Frame, It Doesn't Exist." This opening is an extraordinary "tongue in cheek" play to make two obvious points: that *DC* is a simulacrum (in the Deleuzian sense) and that psychoanalysis as a discourse is to be rendered laughable or negligible, yet all along providing the ambiguity that it is still in effect as the dialogue between Colbey and Sam indicates.

After a memorable rehash of the different relationships made possible by Jen's death, we come to the concluding scene (624, ". . . Must Come To an End"). Joey is back in her New York apartment watching the final scene of *The Creek,* where Sam, falling through Colbey's window and into his room, asks, "I can't take it anymore Colbey . . . *I can't wait for my life to be over. I want to know right now* [the title song of the series] what will it be?" Colbey gently kisses her, pulls back, and says, "You and me . . . always." Sitting on the couch by Joey's side is Pacey—crying. She has made her choice. With the flurry of a two-minute montage that recaps the multifarious relationships between friends through six seasons with the voice-over of Chantal Kreviazuk singing "Say Goodnight not Goodbye," the series ends.

What is to be drawn from this? As Dawson says, "life has no opposite. The opposite of death after all is birth" (624, ". . . Must Come to An End"). The idea of *soul mates* is reinstated: Jack and Jen/Dawson and Joey, as couples only having sex falls off the radar; sex is given a displaced, overrated value. This is not sexual ecstasy or physical passion, but "friendship, tenderness, caring, understanding, passion, loyalty, and the ability to rise above petty exasperations," what the pop psychologist Dr. Joyce Brothers calls "second stage love" (1981, 247). Pacey is with Joey, but Dawson will always remain her soul mate, implying no sex. To be generous we could say that a new BwO emerges, one that has reorganized and reeroticized the body parts away from the genitals to the fantasy of a holistic embodiment formed through the memories when coping with *life*. Compared to such heights of togetherness, the "X" of such unconscious desire doesn't seem worth bothering with. Jen's sexual trouble with men, her constant repetition of her symptom that leads to a child out of wedlock, and her atheistic beliefs are never examined, nor do they need to be. She and Jack, the fag-hag couple as they call themselves in the final episode, are soul mates because they never belonged to Capeside; they remained perpetual outsiders—undercover. Jen grounds Jack while Jack displaces her impossible relationships with hetero men.

Dawson constructs a fantasy world (e.g., *The Creek*) that has been challenged by Joey since grade school. Reality "bites" when he is around her, grounding him. She will always be his soul mate for that very purpose and reason. But Dawson's root obsession with the media and his escapes into its fantasy space are never examined either. Why Spielberg of all directors? An answer appears obvious enough. Joey is always running away from relationships and has anxiety whenever a long-standing commitment must be made. With Pacey of course, she can live an adventurous life. But this deep-seated anxiety—her X—is never unearthed, and there is no certainty that their relationship will last. Can the haunt of her mother have something to do with that, and the instability of her family life? Pacey, on the other hand, is a womanizer in need of grounding. Will Joey's relationship be enough to sustain him? All these major and minor characters on *DC* (Audrey with her depressions and alcoholism; Andie with her cheating ways and pill swallowing, with her striving to be the ideal student and then a medical doctor) have symptoms that would have required a different dialogical script, one that acknowledges the place of unconscious desire that unleashes their singular anxieties shaped by the neoliberalist discourses that are at work.

It seems to me that Jen, Joey, and Audrey suffer from symptoms that emerge with postfeminism (see also Gill and Herdieckerhoff 2006; Feasey 2006). Joey is highly independent and thus unable to settle down with any one man. She fears entrapment. Jen, also independent, is unable to find a man she can love and so she falls into promiscuity through her searches to find the "right" man, while rich spoiled-girl Audrey is overwhelmed by *jouissance*, addicted to alcohol and an excessive lifestyle. She simply has too much freedom, like a Paris Hilton, a Britney Spears, or a Lindsay Lohan. Indeed, she is billed as having lived in L.A. next door to the famed Osbournes. Jack Osbourne is her friend.

The young men do not fare any better. Dawson's fictive dreaming and family values are pitted against Pacey's womanizing and his *gritty realism*. Dawson strives to achieve the American Dream of independence through the Hollywood model of success, while Pacey does so through entrepreneurship (he eventually owns and manages the Ice House Restaurant, before becoming a successful stockbroker). Jack is caught in the contradictions of his gayness—his politics of outing are confused.

The neoliberal ideals that these young people espouse and seem to seek suggest that surviving *life* in a post-Oedipal age requires the solidarity of friends as exemplified by such postfeminist series as *Sex and the City* (1998–2006), the sisterhood of *Charmed* (1998–2006), and the bonding that takes place among the six young people on *Friends* (1994–2004) or in such singing groups as the *Spice Girls*, who reunited in 2007. These have become the new ersatz family, the "undercover" of confluent love. On one level, pop psychology has reworked *soul mates* to match New Age thinking in a world where control and agency seem limited and relationships seem tenuous and temporary. If there is a paranoia at work here, the language of self-reflexivity is meant to "shoo" it away. Their symptoms, as I have tried to show, are far from being acknowledged. Their self-reflexion is a failed self-refleXion. But that is perhaps only part of the story.

In Beck's risk society of AIDS, divorce, separation, and sexual abuse, a "beyond" to romantic love has been found in the realm of the *pure*—the transcendent *soul* that dwells in the "virtual Real" shared by a couple that protects each other in the games of capitalist survival, a crystal fortress that is able to sustain the crisis of life as these young people search to find a place to ground themselves as they emerge from school. This is the real surprise of the final episode. Among all the psychobabble and the deferral as to whom Joey will choose lies the deconstruction of the series by way of the positing of a soul mate, a relationship that injects a transcendent place where "difference"—the "X"—can dwell without each consuming the other—at least that is the fantasy I leave with.

Freaks and Geeks: "I Don't Give a Damn 'Bout a Bad Reputation"[1]

I don't know if I could have entertained writing on the long-standing *Degrassi* series, which began broadcasting in 1983 and continued to follow the kids through junior high school (1987–89) and on into high school (1990–91), complicating things even further with *Degrassi, The New Generation,* which aired in 2001. It is now in its eighth season, making it the longest running teen drama set in a school environment, and it has won many awards. Quintessentially a Canadian production—Degrassi is the name of a street in Toronto, Ontario—its varied narratives dramatically follow the lives of teenagers through interweaving plots and arcs, always with some touch of comedy to lighten things up. In contrast, *Freaks and Geeks* is quintessentially white, middle-class American and stakes its ground as a comedy-drama. It takes place during the 1980–81 school year at the mythical McKinley High School in the town of Chippewa, Michigan, a fictional suburb of Detroit. While geographically near Toronto, relatively speaking, about the only thing the two series share is perhaps Joe Flaherty, who plays the character of Harold Weir. Flaherty, an American, earned his comic reputation in Toronto as part of the Second City Theatre troupe starring on the television hit SCTV.

Freaks and Geeks, unfortunately (but fortunately for me), aired only a sum total of 18 episodes (from 1999 to 2000), on NBC rather than on WB, the dominant teen network. This was about a 14-hour investment of time if one watched the episodes straight through.[2] I watched the complete series twice thanks to a remarkably well-crafted DVD set produced with care and containing a hilarious commentary by the executive producers and cast members, pretty much a comedy track. I first watched the series in 2006 and then again in 2008 when I realized that I had no choice but to refresh my memory in order to write this chapter. It was not difficult. Watching the pilot all over again with a more discerning eye, I was hooked once more.

For those who have not seen this series, a quick introduction to the characters will help facilitate my exploration of the series below.[3] The four sophomore Freaks are represented by their semi-tough-looking leader, Daniel Desario (18); his wild-at-heart girlfriend, Kim Kelly (17), who has a tough reputation and "does it"; Ken Miler (17), with the sarcastic one-liners; the pothead drummer Nick Andopolis (17), with Sean (16) as a floating extra Freak. The threesome of freshman Geeks are represented by 14-year-old Sam Weir, a star character in the series, and his close friends: the "comedian" Neal Schweiber, whose Jewish background reverberates with his character, and the allergy-ridden Bill Haverchuck, who prominently wears "tear-drop" glasses that dominate his face. Bill is tall and lanky, but uncoordinated, while Sam and Neal are about the same height but have yet to experience the characteristic teen "growth spurt." A fourth Geek is added about midseason, Gordon Crisp (8, "Girlfriends and Boyfriends"), a heavyset kid whose abject status is even more pronounced—he "stinks" because of a medical condition and is more of a mama's boy than Bill is.

Representing the Brains is "smart-girl"[4] Lindsay Weir, Sam's sister, who is the key star of the series, and their middle-class parents, Harold and Jean Weir. Harold runs the A-l Sports center on 16 Mile, while Jean is a stay-at-home mom. Mom is solicitous and protective of her two children, while dad is overbearing, hard-edged and paranoid about their future and the lifestyles his children lead. Completing the core group of main characters is Millie Kentner, Lindsay's evangelical childhood friend and mathlete who has been kicked off to the side.[5]

In the "background" are the Jocks and Cheerleaders represented by head cheerleader, Vicki Appleby; Cindy Sanders, Sam's love interest; jock Todd Schellinger (Cindy's love interest); and a small host of minor characters: the bully Alan White, who is always picking on Sam; Harris Trinsky, a sophomore geek who mentors the threesome in the ways of romantic desire; Maureen Sampson, a new girl at school who befriends both the Geeks and the cheerleaders. The Geeks had hoped to raise their status by being publicly intimate with Maureen in the cafeteria and down the hallways before, as Neal says, "she is overtaken by the 'pod people' (referring to the film, *Invasion of the Body Snatchers*) like the head cheerleader, Vicky Appleby" (7, "Carded and Discarded"). Finally, there is Eli, a "special learning needs" student who appears only in several early episodes.

The array of adult school authority figures is represented predominately by three characters: Coach Ben Fredricks, the out-of-shape physical education/health teacher, a man's man, who ends up having a relationship with Bill's mom; Mr. Kowchevski (no first name in order to assert his authority), the school's hard-ass rule enforcer, the math teacher, and coach of the mathletes; and long-haired counselor Mr. Jeff Rosso, who has a soft spot for delinquents having undergone his own "rocky" transformations as an ex-hippy social activist who still plays in a band. He is a counselor who can't counsel (or at least, not in the traditional way), a point I shall revisit. Problems funnel through his office before they move on up to the principal's office. While always trying to be hip to reach the Freaks (and sometimes the Geeks), he never quite succeeds. Guitar playing in his office, becoming a friend who cares (call me "Jeff"), sharing "horror" stories from his own youth as a deterrent strategy, cajoling Lindsay to take on the "responsibilities" of her intellectual prowess (to ask George Bush Sr. a vital question when he visits the school for a photo op in episode 17 ("The Little Things") and to live up to her destiny as a summit debater at Michigan State University during the summer after she graduates (18, "Discos and Dragons"). When he pushes the Freaks to determine what "truly" is eating them, he gets no answers, because there aren't any. Ken tells him about his concerns with Amy the transsexual; Neal blurts out that he is unable to get over his father's illicit affairs; Lindsay is not really allowed to be heard at all regarding her existential angst. High school counseling, while well intentioned and full of hope, is in the end a way to reterritorialize student desire so that they will stay in the institution. Jeff is good at giving psychological and vocational tests to determine one's "destiny" in life!

Remarkably, almost all the central characters are introduced in the pilot. The series splits the time relatively evenly between Lindsay Weir and the Freaks and Sam Weir and the Geeks. The plot line follows Lindsay, a good, smart girl who joins the Freaks, while Sam's exploits trying to date Cindy and discarding his Geek status are equally followed. I will argue in the following chapter, utilizing both Lacan and Deleuze on desire, that Sam and Lindsay have opposite trajectories: by moving toward the Freaks, good-girl Lindsay breaks with the Oedipal Law but does so not along the path of Joan Jett's Grrrl culture as the theme song suggests, but by finding her own surprising "line of flight." Sam, on the other hand, moving toward the Jocks and the Cheerleaders caught by Oedipal Law, ends up facing his own fantasies, having gotten "the object" of his demand.

Freaks and Geeks (now *F&G*) is based on a memory. Its writer and creator, Paul Feig, graduated from Chippewa Valley High School in Clinton Charter Township, Michigan, in 1980, and its coexecutive producer, Judd Apatow, also attended high school in the early 1980s. The series takes places during the school year from September 1980 to the summer of 1981, the beginning of the Reagan/Bush Republican presidency. With its historical specificity and geographical location, it makes no pretense of representing the diversity that exits in contemporary schools of the new millennium. The demographics, as can be gleaned from the characters' names, are largely a mixture of descendants of western and eastern European immigrants. Its one obvious ethnic character, Neal Schweiber, is a German Jew whose name is typically anglicized by his teachers (they confuse the "i" and the "e"). He is also mistakenly referred to as "Ned." As a Geek, with his runt-like stature, he remains an invisible and misperceived entity, a "no name" who must inflate his image and worth as a comedian and lady-killer to garner self-respect. McKinley High is a "white" school. On the DVD commentary voice-over, Feig and Apatow laughingly discuss how the single African-American male extra is perceived as a cool guy in school. NBC blocked an episode Feig wanted to do that was based on a nasty racial incident that had taken place in his own school, but they insisted that at least one black appear in the script (2, "Beer and Weirs").[6]

Murray Milner Jr.'s (2004) sociological study *Freaks, Geeks, and Cool Kids: American Teenagers, Schools, and the Culture of Consumption* attempts to update these high school categories for the contemporary scene. It is useful to develop some of his conclusions here, since it plunges youth studies into contemporary debates as to how one should go about conducting the research (more below). Milner's study is basically the inverse of *F&G*, since he concentrates on the hierarchy of status as power—the cultural capital that structures high school youth, who, by-and-large, have little economic and political power to influence outside events; power is imploded within the institution itself. For Milner, status is therefore "inexpansible" (95). He sees high school students organized into sets of crowds and cliques with distinguishable identities that, once established, remain "relatively stable" for the most part "after the first year" (1983–85).[7] Such identities are shaped by the usual norms: beauty, athletic ability, clothes, style, athletic uniforms and letter jackets, speech, body language, popular music, humor, collective memories, and the ability to dance and sing as played out within the territorialized spaces and specific times.

In his book *Cool*, Marcel Danesi (1999) articulates how "small cruelties" (put-downs and harassing the weak) in the form of speech acts police bodies and maintain territory. This is well illustrated by both Kim and her tougher girlfriend, Karen Safoli, who belittles Sam, writing "geek" on his locker with lipstick (4, "Kim Kelly is My Friend"). Such status linked to power, Milner (96) notes, begins to break down as students become older and are able to participate in other forms of power by having more money to spend because of part-time jobs. *F&G* brings us to the cusp of this later development in the figure of Neal's older brother, Barry Schweiber (15, "Noshing and Moshing"), who graduated from the same high school two years ago and sees college as a whole different life of liberation.

In such a hierarchical system, anxiety and paranoia are manifested primarily in the minority groups who are the least secure about their identities and who are concerned about their bodies and fashion. The cheerleaders are the closest to the "source" of the "school spirit" that is generated by school sports and rivalries—for example, McKinley versus Lincoln. Hence, cheerleaders are the perceived "goddesses" of the school and are closely associated with the performance of the transcendentally sacred games on the football field and basketball court. They perform school rituals and master the ceremonial techniques of the community. The school mascot, a Norseman (or Viking) in McKinley's case, embodies this spirit. The grinning giant head of the Norseman is ironically "invaded" by the Geeks when Colin has an accident and is unable get ready for the final showdown with Lincoln. First, Sam wins the audition to wear the Viking head and to practice with the cheerleaders. When he realizes it's impossible to do the routines while actually wearing the big head, Sam takes over with disastrous results (9, "We've Got Spirit"). He turns the mascot's role into a farce.

This spiritual body is but a supplement to the spiritual mind of the school. In *F&G* this is represented by the mathletes under Mr. Kowchevski, who competes for the glory of the school's reputation, mathematics being the king of subjects. Such a structure, of course, reflects Cartesian humanism with its mind/body split and its hierarchy of distinct subject areas. Here this split is along gender lines—boys occupy the discourses of the body (sports) while girls covet the mind (mathletes). Good grades, however, especially for boys, do not guarantee them status within a school.[8] Moreover, empirical research indicates that nerds more so than geeks are constantly harassed by the controlling popular students (preps and jocks). Nerds are expected to lower their grades, not study "too hard," and not get too chummy with the teachers, but they are expected to spend their time socializing and valuing classmates for their prowess and attractiveness (Bishop et al. 2003,

2004, 249). A point is reached by some nerds, geeks, or freaks where such harassment and the inability to fit in results in suicide; worse yet, as Jesse Klein (2006) argues, a psychotic break happens that leads to school shootings to seek revenge against the jocks who harassed them, ex-girlfriends who rejected them, girls who scorned them, teachers who belittled them, and preps who put them down.[9]

In the 1980s, the Geeks occupy the Audiovisual Room as their sanctuary, the "lowly" machinery of 16 mm film and film loop projectors that enable supplementary entertainment to complement the serious subjects being taught. Ironically, it is the cigarette-smoking Geek, the school's audiovisual (AV) technician, Mr. Fleck (18, "Discos and Dragons"), who describes for them an imaginary trajectory of a jock's life after high school that ends with him serving hamburgers and fries while, in contrast, the geeks inherit the earth via acceptance into Ivy League schools. In the mid-1980s, the AV room slowly began to decenter and to infiltrate every classroom as AV instruction and computerization took command, somewhat confirming Mr. Fleck's scornful boast. John H. Bishop et al., (2004, 235) also confirm that students of both genders who achieve high grades earn higher wages after graduating from high school than do those with lower grades. Geeks only improve in status during the dot.com boom during the prosperous Clinton years when the iconic geek of all time comes into prominence, Bill Gates (see Witse 2004).

According to Milner (63), the taboo against associating with other cliques does not apply when it comes to schoolwork. Friendliness is allowed with people in other strata when required by the school (e.g., science labs, where partnership is teacher-assigned. Bill gets to "experiment" with Cindy while Sam is stuck with Gordon Crisp) or when a distinct advantage can be had. Lindsay attempts to tutor Daniel in math to little avail. Eventually, he charms her into cheating for him (5, "Tests and Breasts"). Daniel regularly relies on "brainier" students to do his homework for him (18, "Discos and Dragons"). Clubs and associations are also spaces where links are formed across groups. So Sam joins the Yearbook Club (the classic space occupied by the popular crowd, since this is where the school's media are controlled and disseminated) in order to be close to Cindy when she does a "Sylvia Plath-like" reading of her poem for the yearbook (which is voted down, except by Sam of course) (8, "Girlfriends and Boyfriends"). Oddly, neither music nor drama as pockets of counterculture where "drama freaks" and "drama queens" adopt distinctive styles of dress and behavior were explored in this first season of *F&G*.

For a "brain" like Lindsay to break into a Freak clique is an easier transition than the other way around—a Freak is more unlikely to join the Geek crowd. Downward mobility is easier to negotiate than upward mobility. As Bishop et al. (2004) indicate, some cliques are absolutely impossible to break into because of obstacles relating to money, prestige, and status. All such expressive relationships are socially regulated, with sex and eating being the most primary forms. Lindsay must successfully negotiate and be let in on the secrets, rumors, and gossip as forms of intimacy that continually circulate to either strengthen solidarity or set up hostilities. The high school party, where couples kiss and flirt, drink, and deviate from adult standards, where status is determined according to who is and is not invited, becomes the fertile ground for status negotiation (2, "Beer and

Weirs"—Lindsay's Party; 16, "Smooching and Mooching"—Mona's party). In the 1980s dating was still on the radar, with Sam attempting to have an actual date with Cindy, which he plans and executes. Contemporary forms of "hooking up," however, can mean anything from kissing to oral sex to sexual intercourse, with no strings attached. In this regard, *F&G* is pre-girl power. Lindsay's performativity as a girl is quite different. While curious about sex, she will not go to "second base" and has difficulty knowing how to break up with Nick, who ends up somewhat inadvertently being her Freak boyfriend.

In part 3 of his research, Milner (2004) attempts to contrast the modern from the postmodern school,[10] which troubles his hierarchical schema to some degree, as does the question of power. His research shifts to what has been deemed post-subcultural studies (Muggleton and Weinzierl 2003; Hodkinson and Deicke 2007), more of which will be developed in the next chapter. Racial and ethnic pluralism (lacking in *F&G*) changes the school dynamics significantly. Milner's research becomes framed by lifestyle relativism. "Pluralism . . . means that subcultures are relatively equal in status, that claims of superiority are contested, and that tolerance of other ethnic and racial groups is the social norm" (101). "Lifestyle pluralism" (128) (as first developed by Anthony Giddens) decenters the "popular crowd" into many pluralistic groups based on extracurricular activities, generating status systems built on lifestyles. The Yearbook Club, for instance, would continue to be a high-status club to belong to.

Milner speaks of voluntary segregation between white and black groups in classrooms, hallways, parking lots, football bleachers, and so on (103). Yet, interpersonal relationships between white and black groups do take place in the cafeteria. However, race and ethnicity as markers of identity remain inalienable (124). Status remains inexpansible; hence, an "increase in school size increases the likelihood of pluralism" (128). While broad categorizations of status can be maintained—the preps as stereotypically middle-class, with suburban backgrounds on one end and the rednecks, usually from working- and lower-class, rural backgrounds on the other, with the middle filled in by an alternative category (hippies, freaks, weirdos, skaters, punks, Goths, and straight-edgers)—Milner admits that this no longer captures the complexity (115). Gradations and ambiguities militate against easy categorizations. "Students are often reluctant to label themselves or even their clique—though they seem to have little trouble categorizing others" (116). In short, the pluralism of status groups confound easy hierarchization, but two ideal types of pluralism emerge, the first based on racial and ethnic pluralism; the second, on lifestyle pluralism.

Hegemonic Masculinity

F&G presents an obvious heteronormative image of hegemonic masculinity wherein both the Freaks and (especially) the Geeks fail miserably. This ideal of masculinity has been well researched in schools (see Klein 2006 for a review). Competitive athletic prowess is perhaps the most important. In *F&G*, Todd Schellinger, in typical Hollywood fashion, scores the final basket in the last seconds to give McKinley the championship over their long-standing rivals, Lincoln. Yet, the difficulty of keeping this hypermasculine image up is briefly exposed as Neal sees Todd throwing up in the washroom before the big game (9, "We've Got Spirit"). Maintaining a strong, powerful body and continuing to perform heroics on the sports field are a source of pride but also a source of an underlying anxiety leading to various forms of psychic damage (Frosh, Phoenix, and Patman 2002; Frost, 2003). Other characteristics of such masculinity involve a dominant relationship with girls, a sexual objectification of women, a certain savoir-faire concerning relationships, a distance from femininity and homosexuality, fighting prowess when necessary, and a higher socioeconomic class.

Daniel as a Freak obviously scores on most of these points; his only failure is that his territory is outside the school, not in it.[11] While savoir-faire and interpersonal skills are used by boys to become more popular by appearing more socially sophisticated, while at the same time manipulating, domineering, and controlling, Daniel uses his charm to have others cheat for him or to play the system by feigning being a victim of its meritocracy. The Geeks, on the other hand, struggle to attain this masculine "norm." Sam is afraid to take a shower because his hairless body—devoid of chest and armpit hair (and perhaps pubic hair as well)—and small penis would be laughed at (6, "I'm With the Band"). "Weir is queer" rolls easily off the tongue, and Bill is certainly identifiable as a "sissy" or a "fag" and suffers from allergies. The bully, Alan White, takes advantage of this and puts a peanut in his sandwich, making him catatonic; Bill almost dies (13, "Chokin' and Tokin'"). In this episode we learn that Alan was rejected by the Geeks in the third grade and that he has hated them ever since. Neal's runt size also makes him an easy target to push around. As for Ken, one of the Freaks, when his girlfriend Amy tells him about her transsexual operation as a baby (17, "The Little Things"), he is at first repulsed and wonders whether he is queer. Anxieties abound. Hilariously, he performs a self-examination by comparing hetero and homo porn magazines for a reaction. The trajectory for the two Geeks—Sam and Neal—is to participate somehow in "normative" masculinity through dating and to eventually be seen as "normal."[12] Sam tries to impress Cindy by dressing up in what is considered to be the latest in men's fashion, a blue one-piece jumpsuit, which, as it turns out, he doesn't have the confidence to wear to school for fear of being stared or laughed at. However, when his under-shorts are stolen in the shower locker by the bully, Alan, Sam is forced to "streak" naked through the school hallways; that scores him points with Cindy! Just the opposite of what he had thought would impress her.

Resistance, Rebellion, or Deviance?

Resistance, rebellion, or deviance, which is it to be? *F&G* takes place in 1980 and 1981 when the link between the specificity of rock bands, consumerism, and youth subcultures seemed particularly strong. Dick Hebdige's seminal work on subcultures in the Birmingham Centre for Contemporary Studies tradition came out in 1979. This makes the series suitable to such an analysis, although, the heterogeneity of a youth subculture back in the 1970s and '80s has been seriously criticized for its estimation of coherence and fixity (Hodkinson and Deicke 2007) and its comprehension and negotiation of power as simply a top-to-bottom affair, a tendency of Milner's (1999) work as cited above. Within such research, power seems to be a closed system concept—inexpansible. The subtleties of micropower, which presents resistance through biopower—the ability to reinvent the body by creating new modes of desire and pleasure—as theorized by Michel Foucault appears absent.

Just how Foucault's (1988) later work on the "technologies of the self"—where individuals create their identities through ethics and forms of self-constitution—differs significantly from the regimes of neoliberal governance that seem to promote similar discourses of self-scrutiny, self-formation, and self-governance is at times difficult, if not impossible to ascertain. Can a distinction be easily made between localized individual practices and individualism, especially since aesthetic self-stylization plays such a big part? Humanist and antihumanist discourses seem indistinguishable in this formulation. Pirkko Markula (2003) maintains that a resistant, progressive, and feminist "technology of the self" is possible in high performance sports, but she ends her comprehensive discussion by wondering just where the "critical self-awareness" among female athletes is to be found. "A physically active woman, then, must become aware of the limitations of discursive femininity and the athletic self in order to reinvent herself" (104). An ethics is obviously missing. In other contexts, transformative and resistant strategies by girls calling themselves Geeks to assert difference turn out to be nothing more than a reiteration of the neoliberalist discourse forwarding girl-power to differentiate themselves from other forms of popular femininity (e.g., cheerleaders and sexy-dressing girls) still caught by "inequality." They enact a form of essential feminism that identifies them as "naturally" sensitive and emotional (Currie, Kelly, and Pomerantz 2006, 433). This appears to be a form of "counter-identification." In *F&G*, I will argue below that only Bill Haverchuck performs a "technology of the self" that has ethical import, but in a very Deleuzian way.

Subcultural theory approaches resistance as deviance and appropriation. Framed in this way Daniel and his girlfriend Kim would be marked as delinquent and working-class from "broken" homes. Kim constantly quarrels with her working-class mother; she has no respect for her mother's boyfriend, while her brother is ill. She has no father, and there is a history of drug use—her West Coast aunt had a cocaine addiction. Authority has been evacuated from the home. Hence, subcultural theory would "read" Kim as being out of control. Daniel on the other hand has a sick father and a brother who is addicted to painkillers. His working-class mom appears tired and worn down by shouldering the full burden. Daniel's rebellion would be "read" as fleeing from authority, as not wanting to take the place of his father to "look" after the family. He only reluctantly fetches a drug prescription at his mother's pleading.

Freaks also practice a form of appropriation. In an ironical gesture, Daniel wears his Molly Hatchet T-shirt to church, a sign of irreverence, while Nick's pothead phase—a sign of unengaged participation, truancy, and a disengagement from school itself—is an imaginary escape either through a "lifeless" BwO on dope or its polar opposite; he plays the live track of Rush while wearing headphones, and drums along, imagining himself to be Neil Pert, their drummer. Here we have two multiples of Nick's body formed by two different machinic assemblages. When he connects with "dope," specifically when school and his father are too much to bare in their intensity, he needs to become a dope to cope—literally to disconnect and become lifeless. The opposite effect takes place when he sits surrounded by his 28-piece drum set. The intensity of the drums gives him life. Nick's body is fundamentally trapped within these two opposing assemblages—student/drummer, unable to escape their contradiction of being either dead (on dope) or alive (on drums), mixing day with night in good vampire-like fashion. Psychoanalytically, such a contradiction would characterize Nick's obsessive symptom, "Am I dead or alive?" Nick is only alive when he is hooked into his drum assemblage and dead in the school's regime. He would prefer to live in his imaginary world.

On September 24, 1980, when Led Zeppelin's drummer, John Bonham dies from choking on his own vomit while intoxicated, Nick symbolically "dies" as well, and uses his depression to excuse himself from trying to go to "second base" with Lindsay (removing her bra). Neil Pert (Rush) and Keith Moon (The Who), Ginger Baker (Cream), and Bill Ward (Sabbath) are possible reincarnations in Nick's Imaginary. When his father sells his drums, the *objet a* of his Imaginary idealization, the magic object that frames his dream, he is devastated and goes into self-exile, sleeping at friends' homes and then moving into the Weir household. He is, in effect, a walking zombie, catatonic, caught in a death drive as he searches for a new assemblage to occupy, thinking that the Weir's might be it. And, indeed, he does find it, becoming appreciative of the big band great Gene Krupa, thanks to Mr. Weir.

Ken is another story. While he does have a specific rock 'n' roll mind-set ("Led Zeppelin rules" often issues from his mouth), it is his mouth assemblage that wields him power—the linguistic skills of sarcasm that take the dominant cultural symbols and values and turn them around, or simply suspend them as a question, introducing a hesitancy in speech performatives. He is a cynic, waiting for his dad to pass on so that he can take over the company. Always in the background, Ken is the "second" in command who continually puts Nick down, policing his moves: breaking his guitar so that he will not sing the song he wrote for Lindsay ("Lady L"); he heard Nick sing it before, off-key. Eventually he ridicules Nick about his disco "fever." Ken is an enforcer whose *jouissance* (vampire's blood) is satisfied only by sarcastically putting others down so that he can prop himself up. Nick is the weakest member of the Freaks—not fully street smart and not a "mouth" like Ken, more willing to escape from the world by tokin'. As a drummer for the band, he is characteristically the "dummy" of the group; only when he sets a beat for a song is he ever listened to, and that's questionable as well. Both Ken and Daniel perceive Nick as a looser, headed for the army as his dad (who is in the air force) has threatened to make him do.

For traditional subcultural theory, Ken is an anomaly. In episode 17 ("The Little Things"), he tells Amy, his tuba-playing girlfriend, that he comes from rather well-off parents who let a nanny raise him. His resistance in the form of sarcasm may well be aimed at the "missing" parents in his life, a phenomenon that only became more pervasive as Reaganomics ended up forcing both parents to work and spawning the feminist movement. Hypocrisy in the expectations of people with power over his life could generate such an attitude in the way the world "truly" works, forcing him undercover. Ken's self-doubts of being a "man" emerge when his girlfriend, Amy, shares a secret with him: when she was a baby, she had a transsexual operation to make her a girl. This secret changes the perception of her Being and Ken begins to see her as some sort of mutant or monster; an irreparable damage has stained his idealized image of her. Conflicted, it takes a considerable amount of self-conviction to change things around—happening only after listening to Sam explain why he wants to break up with Cindy (they have nothing in common and it's boring being together)—and for him to overcome this difference and restore his idealized image of her. It is an example of self-refleXion at work, for Ken did overcome the "strangeness" within himself by reevaluating his affective relationship with her.

Among the Geeks, it is only Bill whose resistance is ethical in the sense that Foucault may have meant it. Bill recognizes the weaknesses of his body (his allergies and clumsiness) and his looks (he "looks" like a dork) in the larger picture of having a reputation in relation to key identity markers—sports and girls. He lives with his working-class mother, a waitress in a restaurant. It is uncertain where his father is. To sustain his ego, Bill undertakes to lead a vivid imaginary life in his head, culled from movies and games like Dungeons and Dragons and his favorite television show, *Dallas*. He also looks specifically to television comedy (*The Larry Sanders Show*) to help cheer him up. To work on the girl side of things, he learns the latest dances ("funky dance," a quote from the film *Napoleon Dynamite*). He "wins" a date with Maureen (by cleverly wetting the lottery ticket), and while studying with his lab partner, Sam's heartbeat, Cindy, he concludes that she is flawed. She eats gingerly and doesn't admit to farting! In other words, she's not "real," too pure. Bill can also charm women in his own special way. He manages to "make out" with head cheerleader, Vicky Appleby, in their "Seven Minutes in Heaven," the reward for spinning the bottle that lands on the same person three times, only because he is able to create the imaginary space of fantasy; his looks are no longer at issue in a darkened closet where the two spend their "heavenly" minutes.

However, it is in sports that he is able to make structural changes. Bill recognizes that as a clumsy Geek he will never be the first pick on a team, that he will be punished in dodgeball, and remain out in "left field" waiting for the baseball to come his way—forever. He recognizes that these injustices occur because of the way sports are defined in high school, and he does something about it. After stealing the telephone list with all the teacher's names on it, he calls up Coach Fredricks. Feigning the deep voice of a parent, he tells him of the injustice and demands that the Geeks be given a chance to play as well. At first the coach resists, but as fortune would have it, Coach Ben falls in love with Bill's mother, Gloria, giving Bill more leverage. Eventually, the coach's machismo is whittled away by Bill's refusal to take part in games until something gives. The day comes when the two Geeks, Bill and Gordon Crisp, are the designated captains; they can choose their own baseball teams (14, "Dead Dogs and Gym Teachers"). During the game, Bill, playing shortstop, catches a pop-up fly. While an insignificant incident to most, this "catch" signifies his acceptance into sports. He is no longer a "looser." This confirms what a body can do when placed in a different assemblage, rerouting the circuits of desire.

Bill exhibits what Deleuze (1988b) maintained was the key to grasping Foucault's technologies of the self: he operated on the "inside" and "outside" terrain at once through a doubling or "folding" of the outside force. Such an "inside" dimension "derives power and knowledge without being dependent on them" (101)—it is a "will to power" in this sense, the singularity of Bill's life. In Foucault's conceptualization, this is a "double" move, a type of interiorization of the outside. Such a relationship is never "a projection of [just] the interior; on the contrary, it is an interiorization of the outside" (98); the outside being the discursive forces at work on Bill's body; namely, the unjust hierarchal practices of high school sports. These require a "folding" back in on the self. Bill must "double" his relationship with Coach Ben. Through such a subjectivization, power-relations (Coach Ben becomes helpless, his authority drained as he comes to recognize just what he is doing) and Bill's relation to knowledge (his grasp on sports inequality) enable a transformation to take place. He becomes reborn (he makes the "catch"). Bill is therefore practicing a Spinozian ethics that informs Foucault/Deleuze, where to be "free" is not a negative gesture. Bill is not caught by lack; he knows where he stands in the structure of things. Rather, to be free is to arrive at a greater power by producing effects that come from one's own singularity: Bill recognizing that he is not "free" and "equal" to participate in sports; this is only useful as positive knowledge. But, it is the first step (as the "outside"), to see that his effects are not wholly his, leading to the second step ("interiorization") that produces effects that are his own.

In contrast to Bill, both Sam and Neal are afraid of authority. They do seem to lack. Sam worries about what his parents would say if they found out that while they were away, his sister Lindsay was having a keg party. So he dreams up a scheme to substitute the "real" beer keg with a nonalcoholic one so that no one will become drunk (2, "Beers and Weirs"). He is a good boy, still protected by his mommy. Neal by and large follows suit. He does not step out of line and, like Sam, calls on teacher authority to stop the bullying. It takes a "dummy" or rather, as Neal insists, his ventriloquist's "figure" to transgress and resist, and only after he learns that his father is having an illicit affair. This divides his loyalties between his parents and tarnishes the image he has of his father. It is his father, after all, who forms his Imaginary as a ladies' man. "Schweiber men are irresistible to the ladies" is often repeated to Neal. "Morty" was to be Neal's way of "controlling life" and becoming rich and famous like Billy Crystal on the sitcom *Soap* (1977–81). But, just the opposite happens, as his figural alter ego, Morty, eventually possesses him, as in the final scene in the classic film *Dead of Night* (1945). When Neal is asked to perform his ventriloquist act by his dad at his parent's cocktail party, "Morty" begins to tell obscene dentist jokes (his father is a dentist). Soon everyone stops laughing as these jokes begin to penetrate to the heart of his father's infidelity.

The impact of Neal's dummy/figure presents a moment to clear up a misunderstanding concerning voice that many Deleuzians attribute to Lacanians. The usual reading has been to follow Louis Althusser's (1971) appropriation of Lacan to develop his celebrated "interpellation thesis." But, this is not Lacan, rather not all of Lacan. Lacan places the voice in the Real, which is closer to Deleuze and Guattari's (1987) discussions of music and the voice in *A Thousand Plateaus*. Mladen Dolar[13] develops the full implications of this in his *A Voice and Nothing More* (2006). It is the voice as an uncanny object, a force of sound and intensity that can deterritorialize beyond the signifier, belonging to a "subject before subjectivation" (Žižek 1989, 43–47). Within that subject lies the "object voice." The question is whether this inhuman subject or X is being theorized only as negation (lack). It can, as Dolar develops it, be a transgression that occurs by an explicit productive immanence.[14] The relation between Neal and his puppet is mediated by the voice as signifier, back and forth in dialogue. But then something uncanny begins to happen: the puppet begins to pull the strings of his master (Neal), rather than the other way around. (This is signaled humorously by Bill, who, sitting by Sam's side on a couch, says, "Hey, I told you that thing would take him over.") Dolar explains this as a breach in causality, "an excess of the voice-effect over its cause" (10). The voice comes to occupy the space of this breach as the missing link. Invoking Lacan: "There is a cause only in something that doesn't work" (Lacan 1979 *Four Fundamentals* 22), meaning that at "the point of hitch in causality" appears the *objet a*—as the object cause. And it is here where Dolar meets Deleuze and Guattari as he goes on to say that this is what should be called "thought"—"the search for what exceeds language and meaning" (11). For a fleeting moment, Neal's uncanny voice was heard but immediately silenced because it would have opened a crack in the sanctity of the Norman Rockwell-like household. Neal must now learn to live with his dad's indiscretions, since his mother has accepted them as a sacrifice to "protect" her two sons. The economic exchange has been exchanged for the price of repressing this secret, maintaining dental clients, and providing both sons with a college education.

F&G's Music Scene

The sociology of music as seminally developed by Simon Frith's *The Sociology of Rock* in 1978, where there is a fairly neat fit between youth subcultures and the music played and heard, has undergone significant scrutiny. *F&G*'s taking place in 1980 and 1981 remains susceptible to such subcultural rendering. However, Paul Hodkinson and Wolfgang Deicke (2007) in their edited book *Youth Cultures: Scenes, Subcultures and Tribes* provide an updated overview of the changing debates. The notion of neotribes and musical "scenes" (see Barry Shank [1994] and Will Straw [1991, 2001] for two different interpretative approaches to musical scenes) has emerged to replace the more static term—subculture. There is an ongoing debate and dialogue among sociologists as to whether any of these terms (subcultures, scenes, tribes) are satisfactory. David Hesmondhalgh (2005) wishes to replace them with the more "flexible" approach that combines genre with Stuart Hall's celebrated notion of "articulation." Others, like Andy Bennett (1999, 2005), who were early in fully incorporating Michel Maffesoli's (1996) concept of neotribalism ("tribus") into their studies of youth music, maintain that the concept still remains productive; whereas Stewart McCulloch et al. (2006) still wish to reinstate the distinctive subcultures as they relate to social classes that they identified in Edinburgh and Newcastle as Chavs/Neds, Goths, Skater, and Charva.

On the whole, postsubcultural studies (see Blackman 2005 for a critique; Bucholtz, 2002; Muggleton and Weinzier 2004 for a review) have arisen to find a way to cope with the postmodern shift that was imperceptibly occurring in the early 1980s where *Freaks and Geeks* is positioned: prefeminism, pre- and post-Oedipal, the downturn from organized religion, and the shift away from distinctive well-defined classes. All of these are cracks that are beginning to show in the various episodes: Lindsay sees her father as patriarchal and her mother as his slave (10, "The Diary"); the grip of parental authority is lessening, being transferred over to peers; Sam is already shopping to dress up; Mille's religious piety is marginalized, but respected; Mr. Schweiber is involved in an affair—yet his wife stays in the marriage for the sake of the kids and her own economic well-being; the self-sacrificing mother is the norm, and some of the Freaks come from single-parent households, which was yet to become an established trend.

Again, following the sociological theory of Giddens, members of a status group share commonalities of lifestyle, patterns of consumption, and use of symbols and rituals, but they are not defined by simply sharing a common economic or political location. Maffesoli's tribalism takes into account how identity based on class, occupation, locality, and gender ends up being a "performative orientation" whereby the homogeneous identities of a mass decenter into temporary groups and circles—communities or tribes held together by affect (Shields 1992). To be part of a tribe is a state of mind, a moving shape where there are no definitive practices of inclusion and exclusion to maintain strict boundaries; they are held together part-time rather than fixed. The specificity of site and the temporality of its formation in terms of the ebbs and flows that take place form a neotribal grouping of a heterogeneous range of individuals—to extend the claim—pulled together by a particular desire or cause (peace activists, legalize cannabis groups, antinuke groups, reclaim the streets movements, and so on). While the community is not given first billing, its network possibilities are what meets each member's satisfaction or needs. It remains a moot point as to whether the desire of a network neotribal community such as peace activists places such an ideal above their own individual satisfactions of belonging.

Musically, *F&G* rolls out a long list of well-known '80s music that never seems to stop: among the most prominently mentioned within the series are Led Zeppelin, The Who, and The Grateful Dead. In the background we hear Rush, Van Halen, Styx, Kenny Loggins, Deep Purple, Santana, Kiss, Cheap Trick, Steve Martin, Bachman-Turner Overdrive, Rush, Billy Joel, Bob Seger, Super Tramp, and so on and so on. What is rather amazing is that no Led Zeppelin is ever heard as background music, despite the prominence given to them by the Freaks. Why is that? Music in *F&G* is obviously crucial. Paul Feig himself is a musician (a former drummer), guest spotting as the guitarist for the band Dimension when Nick auditions to be their drummer (6, "I'm With the Band"). He delivers the bad news. Like the music of *Dawson's Creek*, which was argued to be baby-boomer-driven and religiously squeaky-clean, the question emerges whether the nostalgia of the '80s music is not that of a generation behind—like actor Paul Feig and Judd Apatow, an executive producer of some note (beginning with *The Larry Sanders Show*)—who are making an impact in Hollywood.

The Power of Refrain

To come to terms with questions such as this, rather than following the subcultural or postsubcultural path, I turn to Deleuze and Guattari's way of analyzing music, applying some of its basic insights to *F&G*.[15] For them, "It has been said that sound has no frame" (1994, 189). In *A Thousand Plateaus*, they take as their starting point their analysis of music beginning with the concept of the "refrain" or *ritournelle* ("little return"). The opening page (311) of their eleventh chapter, "1837: Of the Refrain," presents a tripartite structure of refrain as a rhythmic pattern that serves to mark a stable point in a field of chaos. The refrain is a framing effect, which they further elaborate in *What is Philosophy* (1994, 189ff). It is a simple but powerful schema that addresses the refrain's ability to territorialize and reterritorialize; music, on the other hand, has the ability to deterritorialize. One captures, the other opens up, with difference already lying within the same—the potentiality of sounding different while sounding the same. The three functions of the refrain are developed in their specificity. First, refrain has the ability to create a calm and stable center in the heart of chaos, like a child who sings to him/herself in the dark to relieve fear and anxiety and find his/her way home. Second, the refrain is able to create a "home," a sheltering frame, "a wall of sound, or at least some sonic bricks in it" (311) so that it becomes a place to return to when the forays into the world become too much. Such a "refrained home" is a particular gesture that fortifies and envelops an uncertain and fragile center or interiority that helps create a reserve of inner strength. Third, once such a secure refrain has been established, a risk can be taken to venture out into the world, bringing that secure interiority of the home within oneself. The song becomes a future of one's own dreaming. As a "block of content proper to music," the refrain serves these three functions at once: a block of sound—more specifically "*a bloc of sensations, that is to say, a compound of percepts and affects*" (1994, 164, original italics)—is a way home, the creation of a home, and a home that lies in our hearts. *Music*, in contrast, deterritorializes the refrain.

Popular music as refrain, argues Ian Buchanan (1997), plays with the second function of refrain—territorializing a home by creating a unique block of sensations, thereby creating a niche in the public sphere for its listeners (e.g., Goth, Beatles, Punk, Disco, Rap), which can open up the previously closed system of the meaning of popular music. A "new" home is created that can be inhabited leading to the third function of refrain as an "enfranchisement of its faithful listeners." Buchanan then makes the move by maintaining that popular music at this stage can be considered to serve the first function of refrain: teenagers as listeners of popular music "use the voice it gives them to enunciate themselves differently and in so doing make habitable the objective condition of their existence (paragraph 18)." This then is a "becoming-minor"; that is, "a becoming-public of the otherwise private individual (paragraph 19)."[16]

It seems that the function of popular musical refrain is quite evident in *F&G*. Nick's constant return to Rush's "The Spirit of the Radio" with earphones on, believing he is like Neil Peart (complete with cowbells so that he can follow Peart's electronic bells in the song). This is "home" for Nick, the 28-drum set is his wall that protects him. It does enable him to have the courage (with Lindsay's persuasion) to audition with Dimension, to venture out and meet the world. When that fantasy dies (he is rejected by Dimension, and his father sells his drums), Nick goes into a self-exile after a row with this father and moves into the Weir household. Mr. Weir introduces him to his generation of music, the drumming of jazz and big band great Gene Krupa and the music of Buddy Rich. Nick is hooked on the idea of taking formal drumming lessons, rekindling his dream. Yet, Nick flips 180 degrees, a willful display of a "technology of the self" within a new assemblage: a new girlfriend (Sara), no more pot. His lethargy is replaced with a new affective body of disco dancing as his new "home," and, just perhaps, since this was the last episode of the series written by Judd Apatow, his turning away from his freak friends who deride his "disco fever."

And of course, it is Lindsay who listens to Grateful Dead's song "Box of Rain" on their *American Beauty* album, which was given to her by counselor Rosso, who said that it consoled him in times of trouble (18, "Discos and Dragons"). She listens to it over and over, finding her home in it as time passes and the day seems to become brighter and brighter. This would have been the initial step; it became her inner song. Then, after talking to Deadhead fans (Laurie and Victor) in the cafeteria and hearing how carefree and joyful it is at their concerts, where there is no judgment, she proceeds to become affectively embodied by the Dead and finally escapes Chippewa, skipping her big chance to attend the academic summit at the University of Michigan. At the end of the episode, we see her get on—what else, a VW (Volkswagen) Microbus driven by the Deadheads so she can follow their tour from Texas to Colorado for a week and a half.

In another episode (14, "Dead Dogs and Gym Teachers"), The Who concert presents an escape from home, with Lindsay trying to convince her parents that this is good, "clean" music. After all, The Who wrote an opera (*Tommy*) and even Mille is going. Harold Weir threatens that he will be listening to their music backwards to pick up on any satanic verses. Daniel enacts a particularly poignant moment to show how the refrain is able to set up that solid, protective wall of music (15, "Noshing and Moshing"). He comes home and enters his room, exhausted after his mom had been on his case earlier that day and he had gotten into trouble at school. He puts on a vinyl record of Black Flag's *Damaged* album and plays "Rise Above." The refrain of "rise above, rise above" indicates how this song speaks to his interior being.

So, where's the music if the refrain is always territorializing? Where is the reterritorializing? We see how in one sense both are happening. For Lindsay the Grateful Dead are deterritorializing, as The Who are for Mille; she is "drawn" to them, but her mother puts a stop to that by making her feel guilty. But two other moments might be mentioned as being "music" in a counterintuitive sense.

According to Deleuze and Guattari, music deterritorializes when it no longer gives primacy to the formal relations and structures, but focuses on the sonorous material itself. The musician is no longer caught by the note function as it relates to the harmonic or melodic axis. Rather, it is the sound in its singularity, as a pure force that is sought after. Such an act of deframing opens up the sonorous forces of the "Cosmos"; that is, a certain limitless plane of composition becomes evident, setting up a deterritorializing "line of flight." Unquestionably, when the Freak's band (Creation) plays Cream's "Sunshine of Your Love," it is not recognizable, yet the intensity of their enjoyment when they finish is indescribable. They produce music, not simply consume it. While Kim wallows in this "noise," Lindsay squirms and, with much more reserve, joins in the appreciation. As the episode develops (6, "I'm With the Band"), when Lindsay suggests that the band should practice more to get the cover song "right," she ends up being accused of breaking up the band, taking the joy away from the music, and draining their *jouissance*. Why?

Daniel, Sean, and Seth have no interest in the "Battle of the Bands," but Nick does. He is the only one who is "serious." As Daniel says, "Rock 'n' roll is in your crotch." For him, it has nothing to do with practice. Their skewed punk-sounding DIY songs are "music" to their ears in the deterritorializing sense of Deleuze and Guattari. Rock music, even when played badly, enhances their feeling for life. It invigorates them. They are not interested in comparatives, criticism, or judgment. The act itself is cool enough—for them and their girlfriends. Daniel, on hearing that Iggy Pop uses three chords, even promises to learn a third one! Their garage band is not looking so much for their "own sound," as they are in enjoying the fantasy of being rockers swept up by the physicality of sound. They are intoxicated by the inhuman, the X that creates an excitement at the level of their BwO's, which becomes drained when the molar authority (Lindsay) begins to "correct" it.

The same can be said of Nick's composition of the song "Lady L," first tested on Ken to see what he thinks. Composed of rather silly lyrics and sung with a falsetto voice that ends with a dramatic sounding moan, Nick's love song is meant to woo Lindsay in a "folkish" kind of way with his acoustic guitar. Of course, Ken spits at it. When Nick tries to play it to Lindsay as they wait around for The Who concert, Ken even smashes his guitar "to save him" from himself. This is Nick's attempt at a personal expression (refrains do not express). He is reaching out to corral Lindsay into his sonorous voice, not really knowing how it "sounds" to other ears. It is him "singing a song" in the dark because he is uncertain of Lindsay's "true" feelings—a way of calling her home.

6

And the ~~Geeks~~ Freaks Will Inherit the Earth

The Limits of Post-Subcultural Studies

All of the categorical descriptions discussed in the previous chapter, with exception of the closing music section, rely on the dichotomy of identity and difference as such—difference being in the first instance *negation*. Freaks are separated from Geeks, and both are separated from Jocks/Cheerleaders. Friend and enemy are spaced apart. In post-subcultural studies (Muggleton and Weinzierl 2003; Hodkinson and Deicke 2007), there is recognition of the increased complexity and pluralism that has emerged among youth subgroups, but identity politics continues to assert itself; boundaries are redrawn in clever ways through new media technologies, the Internet being the most prominent, to secure cybercommunities like Goth sites (Hodkinson, 2003) and sprout various forms of subcultures of cyberactivists, as well as of right-wing militia groups (Kahn and Kellner 2003). A structural plurality is presented with demarcated territories, which establish identities as precariously bounded collectivities.

While identities are seen as unstable, or performative for those sociologists[1] who follow Judith Butler (1990, 1993), there is a *hegemonic* heteronormativity or *hegemonic* masculinity that is posited, which as argued below, continues to theorize difference within the dichotomy of sameness. For those sociologists who follow Pierre Bourdieu, *mimesis* becomes a key concept in the form of mediating impressions between the inner and outer world; this then reinstates another dichotomy—inside/outside. If Michel Maffesoli's tribal theory is adopted,[2] the shift is certainly to flows and temporary formations of youth networks, yet the dichotomy of identity and difference is still maintained. We have space conceptualized as a homogenous medium in the broadest sense, within which the complexity of pluralism exists; the terrain of school is constituted by the identities and differences of groups who struggle to take up discrete geographies (cartographies) within it. The mapped space that is presented in most subcultural and post-subcultural studies, such as Murray Milner Jr.'s (2004) study that was cited in the previous chapter, is already a removed abstraction, a flattened image of a more profound order of movement and relational activity of productive desires—the virtual as a fully Real excess inhering in Being. In post-subcultural studies the metaphysical categories of essence and accident, inside and outside, universal and particular, form and matter, self and other, and finally universal and particular continue to assert themselves, but they do so with greater complexity, and with finesse.

The relationship between micropolitics and macropolitics of youthful activism, the celebrated rebelliousness and resistance first introduced famously by Manchester's Centre for Contemporary Cultural Studies (CCCS), suggests yet another dichotomy that is continually strained. Youthful "tactics" as opposed to "strategies," as Michel de Certeau (1984) influentially theorized it, can be apolitical (downright hedonistic) or not political enough. On the other side of the ledger, radical democracy that retains its Gramscian roots—for followers of Erensto Laclau and Chantal Mouffe (1985), such as Oliver Marchant (2003)—present an articulation between the universal and the particular. At the level of the particular, each single-issue neotribe comes together in an alliance or network regardless of background to form a universal front in opposition to neoliberal global capitalism or to its more neoconservative leanings that latch onto populist appeals of religion, ethnocentrism, and security. The universal is theorized as a temporalized totality with a "constitutive outside," characterized as a fundamental antagonism that makes this plurality of differences possible. This continues to be the most sophisticated direction that posits hegemony as a key concept. Hegemony sets up an already individuated *idealized* mythical position that is considered normative within a changing historical formation, ascendancy to which assures power and status. Such idealized normativity is shaped by the circulation of models of admired social, gendered, and economic conduct exalted by religious organizations, the media, and the state so as to express widespread ideals, fantasies, and desires. One learns how and what to desire within a particular social order to ensure being seen favorably. This is a powerful theoretical model for critical sociology.

Questioning Hegemony

To challenge the hegemonic model appears to be necessary if categorizations of youth are to be overcome. The idea of hegemony—taken as *heteronormative* in many queer studies, or predominately as *hegemonically masculine* in gender studies—affirms a pluralism that rests on a politics of horizons and frontiers as fluid territorializations between subgroups, genders, the abjected, and the like.[3] But, where there is particularism, there is also totality. What "holds" this totality requires the positing of something beyond its limits (an irrecoverable excess) so that the particularities within can establish a *unity in difference*. For Ernesto Laclau and Chantal Mouffe (1985), this beyond or "constitutive outside" is characterized by a "fundamental antagonism" generated by a form of radical Otherness (as negated, nonrecognized identities) that is different from the already recognized identities in their differences as such. There is an irresolvable antagonism between genders, for instance, in the case of hegemonic masculinity, or an irresolvable antagonism of class distinctions when it comes to establishing an egalitarian democracy. Positing this "beyond" is what differentiates his theoretical proposal from a synthetic Hegelian dialectic. He does Hegel one better, so to speak, by escaping closed-system totality as a teleological endgame.

As for the universal, drawing from Lacan, Laclau maintains that this is best theorized as *empty master signifiers* in the Real, conditioned by the logic of both/and—inside and outside the system at once, thereby overcoming any easy dichotomization. It is the empty place of power that needs to be filled in order to act as a "quilting point" (*point de capiton*, as a knot of meaning) that temporarily stabilizes the system (master signifiers such as progress, ideal masculinity, freedom, human liberation, emancipation, and so on). Empty signifiers act as hingegates that both open and close the social symbolic system. They also enable the possibility of any one element within the system to become hegemonically universal thereby initiating a new rebinding because of the uneven antagonistic system of power that exists in such a decentered structure. An *equivalency of demands* is posited between the pluralities so as to fill out and hegemonize its content (Laclau 1988). However, there will always be exclusions as determined by the master signifiers. Hence, this nontotalized decentered field becomes a place of *play* (Derrida) in a struggle for hegemony as the political game. It is an agonistic democratic system. Further, this empty signifier (as a potential hegemonic universal that paradigmatically temporizes the system) is marked by an unconditional ethics suggestive of the gap that exits between the "is" and the "ought," requiring radical subjective investment (Laclau 2002).

How far Laclau escapes from G. W. Friedrich Hegel and modernity through his poststructuralist agenda has raised a great deal of debate.[4] The main concern seems to be the way totality is cleverly slipped in through the back door as an implicit appeal as a particular becomes hegemonically universal, propped up by a master signifier on the grounds that this is an instance of radical democracy, when all along such a moment proves to be impossible. It requires a totality to achieve this hegemony when the theory presupposes that such a gesture is not possible to begin with. For such a master signifier to work, it presupposes that a discourse is in place that totalizes all the particularities. Yet, there is no a priori reason to maintain that it will be the Left that will perform such a totalization, nor that the competitors vying to assert their "particular universal" are indeed democratic antagonists and not enemies. Worse, the master signifier as the political symbol par excellence that claims the "full" possible community, tying together as many particularities as possible in the name of democracy, *always already presupposes an excluded absence.* Universal cultural agreement cannot be secured democratically as Laclau would have it. If no particular group can assure universality, but only temporarily occupy the empty place of power so as to claim that this is the best that is possible, then this takes us back to an ideological illusion that the universal (however temporary) truly represents the absent fullness of all the particulars concerned; in other words, this is a fall back to essentialism that was being escaped from (see Boucher 2000). The Left or the Right can claim a particular universal with ethics unable to resolve the dilemma.

Laclau's revision of hegemony as a radical egalitarian particularism ("radical democracy") has also been taken to task by Nathan Widder's (2000) Deleuzian account. One way to characterize Widder's complex argumentation is to say that it hinges on Laclau's dismissal of the possibility of particularity (difference) that does not depend on evoking a totality (universalism) even if it remains empty. Laclau's dismissal of Foucault for his "pure particularism" is a failure to recognize the possibility of *multiple negation* that is characterized by a logic of neither/nor, an unlocalizable, excessive difference that is always untimely, a difference that is *neither* particular *nor* universal but *singular*. This reorientation to Deleuzian difference presents a constitutively and virtually hidden realm that underlies the actual organization of differences via identity politics. Widder rolls out the "disjunctive synthesis" card of neither/nor logic that relates forces according to their differences. Folds and warps become the new figures with which to grasp the complexities of spaces that are no longer separated by distance, as in representational subject-object relationships. As a synthesis through difference, an "excess of the in-between" is opened up.

Another way (perhaps?) of seeing the dispute is to observe the distinction that can be made between power (still theorized in terms of sameness and difference) and force. The former requires agency that exercises a right or a prerogative, something that is apart from the self, while the latter, in contrast, exerts itself. It does not imply any wielding or willed coercion of one thing by another. While power has an exteriority that imprints itself as form, force has an interiority that is creative. "Forces [. . .] are disjointed singularities. They form a virtual field of relations which in turn generate meaning and sense in accordance with the way they are articulated" (Widder, 127). The fundamental contention is to theorize immanent forces against the overarching hegemonic power of politics. Why this becomes important is because it leads to ethical and critical practices of the self as Foucault developed them, as the "technologies of the self," which present a different political agenda by the minority.

The constitutive outside is not Nothing, as in Hegel, which then generates the Something; nor is there a "fundamental antagonism," as posited by Laclau and Mouffe, but what if it is simply chaos itself, the virtual Real waiting to be actualized? The "Real of antagonism" that Žižek rolls out could be interpreted in this way. The "in-between" as the marker of difference is already antagonistic.[5] Shifting to this possibility has the advantage of linking the nonhuman with the human— an (a)theistic (perhaps intolerable) radical position.

There is a way to skew this argument and to radically suggest that hegemony as an empty signifier is but another version of God.[6] The anti-Hegelian anthropologist Ludwig Feuerbach, a materialist from whom Marx drew his inspiration, maintained that God was simply the personification of man—human, all too human. God's omnipresent gaze becomes a guarantor of identity as literalized by the sacred books of world religions (the Bible, the Qur'an, the Book of Mormon, the Torah). Can one ever do away with God? In Lacan's terms the existence of the big Other is still preferable to an ensuing psychosis, although the big Other "does not exist," nor does "society" exist. It is one complex process with no definable boundary. The chaos floods in, since some form of frame of fantasy needs to exist to keep the Real at arm's length. The symbolic order becomes the said and unsaid (obscene) rules that give the illusion of relative stability without some secret code waiting to be discovered that would clear it all up. The response to this is either tragic or comic, laughing or crying according to Helmuth Plessner's (1970) account, and the vast variety that is the "in-between" of these uncontrollable bodily breakdowns. I will return to *Freaks and Geeks*, this time trying to read it as other than a simple representation. But, before doing so, I would like once more to find transpositional ground between Lacan and Deleuze, this time concerning the multiple.

Lacan–Deleuze on Multiplicity

Is a shift toward a D+G position possible within cultural studies?[7] Could perhaps a hybrid assemblage emerge by reconciling Lacan with D+G? The dominant theories of representation in post-subcultural research are characterized by One and its multiples,[8] where difference is subsumed under sameness. The notion of hegemony can still be useful if it doesn't fall into a universalism, but is thought of as a "singular universal," a necessary construct to mark the terrain of constant struggle, a never-ended becoming, funded by the antagonisms of difference; difference, that is, that escapes sameness. Lacan's "formulae of sexuation" already presupposes "difference" as articulated by Deleuze. Masculine/feminine is marked by a difference that can never be symbolized as forms of opposition, inclusion, exclusion, and so on. These terms resist any attempt at reconciliation; hence, they name a "deadlock" or trauma, as Žižek would say. Masculine and feminine are two "different" solutions to an impossible reconciliation. Difference, whether it be Lacanian or Deleuzian, becomes the place of impossibility that remains *nonrepresentational*. Žižek extends such antagonism to politics as well. Left and Right function in the same way as Lacan's masculine and feminine. For the Left, it will always be class struggle, a question of social injustice; for the Right, it is always a question of moderation and social stability. To reconcile their differences in some sort of complete harmony would be the end of politics. I am tempted to include yet another fundamental antagonism, the a-signifying pair—lack/excess—which are irreconcilable as well if applied to closed and open systems respectively, between-1 (incompleteness) and +1 (excess).

This meeting place of Lacan and Deleuze concerning the "purity" of difference is the *virtual Real*, a place of ontological groundlessness of *life* itself, Nietzsche's will to power. We are also closer, I believe, to seeing some transpositional room concerning the concept of multiplicity. Lacan's *objet* is an *immanent cause of desire* that is *constitutive* of desire itself. Desire is *not* preexistent, nor is it transcendent or an emanative cause. *Objet a*, after all, is a virtual object. There are three points that come to mind concerning Other, gaze, and the formula for fantasy, which establish Lacan's own multiplicity. First, "the desire of the Other" is a constant and reoccurring claim in Lacan, yet Other here cannot be pinned down to representation. It is a chameleon of many colors, about which no one can say, "this is it." This indicates the complexity of "Other" in Lacan's lexicon.

Mark Bracher (1993) attempts to explain its ambiguities within the field of desire. First, desire can take either the passive form (to be) or an active form (to have). Second, Lacan's formulation of the word "of" further complicates things concerning desire. "Of" functions as both subjective and objective genitive, "indicating that the Other can be either the subject or the object of desire" (20). Third, "the Other" can be "either the image of another person in the Imaginary register, or the code constituting the Symbolic order, or the Other Sex and/or the *objet a* of the Real" (ibid.). This schema generates a plethora of possibilities: It can mean that we desire to be desired or to be recognized by the Other. It can mean we desire the Other. It can mean that the Other structures our desire; or that desire can be the Other's desire or the desires of the Others with whom we identify; the Other can also refer to the discourse of the unconscious.

Second, the gaze (as a reconceptualization of the superego) fares no better in being less complex. No "One" possesses the gaze, although the "look" tries to capture it but can never fully control its power. This already suggests the circulatiuon of micropower equally complex and complicated as Deleuze's or Foucault's explications. The gaze in S XI, *Four Fundamentals*, is ephemeral, radically deanthropomorphized, identified simply as "light" and hence nonrepresentational. In effect, what Lacan does by introducing the gaze is to deconstruct the perspectival *space* of the look, thus subverting the spatialization of time and, like Deleuze, he introduces movement *in* time of the Real. In his example in S XI, *Four Fundamentals*, of light reflecting back at him from a floating sardine can, when this "object looked back" at him is an instance of a movement in time. He is no longer "in the narrativized picture," his being is "out of joint" as a gap in his Imaginary is im(pressed). The gaze, in effect introduces the Real of time, its interiority and intensity as a *force*, thereby its relation to *power* is further complicated.

To complicate things even further, Joan Copjec (2006), who has steadily theorized the gaze throughout her theoretical career, adds another twist by arguing how Lacan's nonsensible gaze is activated by the subject's own surplus-*jouissance* as "the libidinal knock or beat of the signifier on some part of the body" (102). This is an interior, not an exterior, affect. Such a contingent moment of time (not *accidental* time) is, once more, time that is "out of joint." It is *jouissance* (or affect in Deleuze's language game), the inhuman "X" that "not only singularizes us, but also doubles and suffocates us" (ibid.).

Finally, Lacan's formula for the *frame* of fantasy is $\$<>a$. This is most often read as "the barred subject related to the object that it *lacks*." But why is there an insistence on lack? The lozenge between complicates things and further introduces the multiplicity that the Other and the Gaze already indicate.[9] In his S X, *Anxiety* (1962–63) (Seminar 14: Wednesday 13, March 1963), the fantasy frame that emerges in the relation between a barred subject and its virtual object is "a relationship whose polyvalence and multiplicity are sufficiently defined by the composite character of this diamond shape $<>$, which is just as much disjunction, [or], as conjunction [&], which is just as much greater, $>$, and lesser, $<$, $\$$ *qua* term of this operation." In this formulation, lack would be only *one* formation of the fantasy frame and only *one* of many possibilities as a regime of signs most often associated with the sacrificed remainder in Oedipalization.[10]

However, in post-Oedipal scenarios that are perverted, it is precisely the inverse formula that is at play: a $<>$ \$. The relationship is not defined primarily by neurotic lack, but as a denial of sacrifice and castration and as excessive satisfaction. In other words, the forces of *objet a* productively prevail in relation to the subject. It is obvious that the matheme for fantasy as perversion makes evident an exclusive disjunction (either/or) and a conjunctive synthesis (&). An exclusive disjunction (as a negative affirmation) takes place in the case of suicide when the *objet a* as Thing overwhelms the subject. But, this already presupposes an existent imaginary frame (on the side of the Subject of *actualization*). The subject has *already* been produced by the cause of desire, namely *objet a;* in the above case of suicide, the imagined frame of identity cannot be sustained, while the "in-between" of the Imaginary and the Symbolic can no longer be mediated. This directly addresses the ontology of desire.

It seems to me, on the other side of the ledger, the *objet a* as "cause" of desire confirms the ontogenesis of desire D+G put forward in *Anti-Oedipus*, as three *affirmative* disjunctions formed by paradoxical logics. The virtual, like Lacan's *objet a*, operates as an immanent causality. It cannot be abstracted from its actualizations. We move from actualization to virtualization given that *objet a* is virtual *partial* object, existing in the Real. It is capable of performing the various connections and effects of affirmative desire, since the unconscious Real has no capacity for negation; it is incapable of absence—there is no "no." The *connective synthesis* of production (the paradoxes of and then . . . and then . . . and then), the *disjunctive synthesis* of recording (the paradoxes of either . . . or . . . or . . . or, which can also take the paradox of neither/nor) and the *conjunctive synthesis* of consumption/consummation (the paradoxes of attraction and repulsion of being born and reborn in a series of states) form the ontogenesis of affirmative desire.[11] Taken together, they are sometimes referred to as *inclusive disjunction,* since they all deal with the paradox of affirming disjoined heteronymous terms. It is easy to see why this is a creative, "agentless" (so-called machinic) endeavor that goes on in the virtual Real. Now, it's time to get back to *F&G*.

Laughing with Daniel in the Lion's Den

F&G's 18 episodes can be grasped as a self-contained complex assemblage, a haecceity of complex becomings[12]—the affective "this-ness" of its narrative process that is uniquely singular. It is a *crystal* moment of time and space in the sense that *F&G* is a series of constructed and connected memories that briefly captures a year of high school life from a particular angle of repose. As a simulacrum it provides a particular "lie" as to what high school was like in the imagination of its writers, especially Paul Feig, who had already written many of its stories in *Kick Me: Adventures in Adolescence* (2002). *F&G* is not a question of how "true" the representation of high school that is being presented is. Rather, it presents us with characters who have lives animated by its actors and writers. Their fictitious lives are stalked by excess as much as any empirically led life. The writers and actors cannot totally control their characters.[13] As an art form, *F&G* is nothing but the creation of falsehood—as "powers of the false." Deleuze (1983) repeats Nietzsche's insight in this regard:

> The world is neither true nor real but *living*. And the living world is will to power, *will to falsehood*, which is actualized in many different powers. To actualize the will to falsehood under any quality whatever [. . .] is always to evaluate. *To live is to evaluate*. There is no truth of the world as it is thought, no reality of the sensible world, all is evaluation, even and above all the sensible and the real (184, emphasis added).

Truth, values, and affects emerge or emanate from the way we live; the way we evaluate, and the perspectives we *create* within the restrictions given. Subjective identity means little if a judge has pronounced that you are a criminal, and you "know" that you are not. In the molar (symbolic) order of things, you remain a criminal. If we were to think of the differential categories of freaks, geeks, jocks, and cheerleaders being caught by a *dialectic of negation*—what Nietzsche calls a "slave ethic"—we can then say that they are characterized by an "ideology of *ressentiment*" (Deleuze 1983, 121). School shootings have been linked to such ressentiment (Klein 2006). Such subject/object dichotomies continue to keep categories apart—the "outside," or the unknowable Other as nonself, remains unbridgeable and raises ethical questions as to how to live with difference.[14] The dialectic understands the differential forces of the will to power—difference itself—as a power of the negative. Herein lies the difference: Nietzsche's empiricism is an affirmation of a force's constitutive difference—it is creative action that produces becoming, whereas the (Hegelian) dialectic succumbs to identity only through negating differences. The will to power ends up being a "no" to the Other. Difference is not negation in the Deleuzian system; rather, it is the "the object of affirmation and enjoyment [*jouissance*]" (Deleuze 1983, 9). The force of difference is affirmative. "What a will wants is to affirm its difference" (ibid.). It is *not* a search for a motive or an object. That enjoyment of difference, I would add, is the object-cause of desire—*objet a*. This immediately raises again an ethics of the Real. How does one deal with *ressentiment*, in Lacan's terms—the way the Other enjoys at my expense?

In this respect, "heteronormativity" and/or "hypermasculinity" are forces of the dialectic that react to forces that challenge it or try to dominate it, and guard against its collapse. In *Freaks and Geeks*, the principal's office is hidden from site/sight/cite, strangely missing as part of the narrative. Only Mr. Kowchesvski, as its representative, fully reveals his hatred (*ressentiment*) for Daniel as a loser who pulls others down, as when Lindsay asks him for an exam extension on Daniel's behalf (5, "Tests and Breasts"). Given the missing center of authority in the school, the orthodox Lacanian reading of Daniel's "rebellion" would suggest that he, like Jim in Nicholas Ray's *Rebel Without a Cause*, is struggling with the missing father of a dysfunctional family.[15] Daniel's father is (tantalizingly) presented as being sick at home while Daniel's mother wants Daniel to take on his father's shirked responsibilities. But another reading is plausible. It could be said that Daniel is no slave and no "pleb." He is aggressive in maintaining his difference. Nietzsche presents the dialectic as a thinking of the slave. The relationship between master and slave is *not* in itself dialectical, but becomes so when the slave thinks of *power as being representational,* as a transference of superiority to a Master as a recognition of the Master's Will. It then becomes a competition and a fight for the establishment of values. Daniel avoids the fight. His aggression is not that of a leftist Fool (as discussed in Lacan's S VII, *Ethics*) who tries to "steal" *back* some of the Master's *jouissance,* as presented by the heroic subcultures such as punks and anarcho-punks or Goths. He is certainly not the cynical Knave either, who plays into the system to *outdo* the Master. Daniel knows he cannot "win." What then is his stance toward authority? He is either feigning being a victim of school abuse (claiming he was categorized as "stupid") so as to use the system's weakness for his *own* satisfaction, pulling the fire bell to declare *his* state of emergency, or he is dodging tests by "cheating" (smart kids do his homework) and escaping from the confines of the institutional boundary when possible, skipping classes—all stretched to the point of still being *in* school for he knows it is a no-win situation. As he sarcastically tells his mother, as a dropout he would be earning $2.50 an hour (15, "Noshing and Moshing"). He is not a slave, and he is not a hero. He is, however, surviving through his own *will to power,* as creative as the rest of them, trying to "perform" punk, for example, to get close to Jenna Zank, the McKinley dropout (15, "Noshing and Moshing"), realizing in the end that he does not belong to that scene when Zank reveals she is a lesbian. If he exhibits a form of nihilism, then it is a negation as an affirmation that has been denied him. Even Eli, the special needs boy, is presented with more sympathy because his difference is so pronounced relative to what is considered the "norm," so he is given extra help.

F&G, as a singular memory of high school, can be grasped productively as the crossroad meeting of superegoic power and creative force, a force that "laughs" at power through the form of comedy, as suggested by the two possible readings of Daniel's self-refleXivity. The superego as the myth of the Father that underwrites its reign can be understood as "nothing other than that very narcissistic *jouissance—jouissance* as the core of being—which we encounter in anxiety, *in an altered form.* The transformation that produces it could be described as the conversion of a *force* (that of *jouissance* as core of being and object-cause of desire) into a *power* (that of the superego)" (Copjec 2006, 108, original emphasis). In Daniel's case, the superego is suspended; the anxiety is continually pushed away so that his will to power triumphs. I think this force/power differential is best shown through comedy, but not in the cynical, humorous way of *Dawson's Creek,* which ends with a joke on us. Comedy speaks to the question of finitude that all the main characters acutely face in high school, as they must repeatedly "die" symbolically in order to continue to work through the difficulties life presents.

Simon Critchley (1999) has persuasively argued that tragedy seems to be the overriding aesthetic of the post-Kantian settlement in philosophy as to how the regions of pure and practical reason (ethics) that Kant had divorced could be bridged. As he puts it, "the question of the meaning and value of human life becomes a matter of what *sense* can be *made* from the fact of finitude. . . . It is a question of what forms of aesthetic production and creation might begin to fill the void left by the historical self-consciousness of the death of God" (220, original emphasis). In the tragic-heroic paradigm, it is death conceived as a possibility that enables freedom and hence "authenticity." In contrast, the comic-paradigm presents death as impossibility. Finitude is ungraspable. For the former, death is certainly "on the table" when it comes to heroic action. Critchley wonders to what extent the heroic paradigm casts away materiality; to what extent the striving for the transcendental posits evil within matter itself. In *F&G* the mathletes and athletes operate within this tragic paradigm. To be a mathlete is already a transcendental affair—mathematics being a form of application rather than a creative, as yet unfolding, abstraction, while the athlete speaks to an always already accomplished body. There is no room for the "Bills" in the world, an uncontrolled, as yet unorganized body capable of doing something else.

In the tragic paradigm, a "redemption card" is played, since there is nothing to fear in death; death is a liberation from evil. The hero will come back to score again if he has failed. Heroes can redeem themselves and be restored by a confirming gaze. Comedy, on the contrary, is "an eruption of materiality into the spiritual purity of tragic action and desire. . . . The body, in all its dreadful fallibility, is the site of the comic" (230). The heroic "Rocky" moment is played for laughs as Bill, playing shortstop, catches a pop-up fly (10, "The Diary"). The comic recalls the weakness and vulnerability of the body. "[T]he super-ego observes the ego from an inflated position, which makes the ego itself look tiny and trivial" (224), and for this reason laughter becomes an acknowledgment of finitude that cannot be fathomed, as a confrontation with the Real. "Laughter returns us to the limited condition of finitude," and so Critchley concludes, "only comedy is truly tragic," for it shows the frailty of the body. It is, risks Critchley, a "site of resistance to the alleged total administration of society" (235). François Roustang's (1987) "How Do you Make a Paranoiac Laugh?" brilliantly adds to Critchley's insight. Drama certainly reveals "man's" attachment to his suffering, the pleasure that he enjoys wallowing and repeating it. "Tragedy reveals the extent to which suffering can disfigure and alter, in short, show that man (*sic*) is without contest the most *inhuman* of all animals (712, added emphasis). But laughter, says Roustang, reveals suffering quite differently. Its explosive bursts confirm our incertitude, giving us a fleeting moment and distance "from the suffering which comes with the weight of destiny" (710). If "one happens to die bursting with laughter [. . .] such a death is likely to keep us [going] for quite a while" (ibid.) The confrontation with the Real is staved off if one "dies laughing."

F&G is such a haecceity of explosive, repetitive laughter. When Lindsay laughs hysterically at the end of episode 5 ("Tests and Breasts") as Daniel repeats his "sob story" of being a victim of the meritocratic school system in Counselor Rosso's office, having been caught cheating on his math test, it is a confirmation that the forces of Daniel's will are playing with the power of the superego. Although he may look tiny, he is "looking back."

Sam: Be Careful What You Desire

Both Sam and Neal wish to shun their Geek status; both desire to overcome their "mommy's boy status," to be "men" by standing up to bullies, being good at sports, and having girlfriends as the accepted norm. One would think that the gaze here is in the eyes of their fathers who form their identity in the Symbolic order. Both Harold Weir and Dr. Schweiber are exemplars of patriarchy. But perhaps this identification is not entirely the case. In Neal's case his Oedipal identification seems more evident. Mr. Schweiber is always telling Neal that the Schweibers are lady-killers. With Sam, the gaze of his mother predominates, as there is little to indicate that Harold pushed sports on Sam, although he owns a sports store. In one episode, she embarrasses Lindsay by telling her to tell her brother that he has a "lovely body." The heirloom that Sam's mother gives him (her mother's pendant), which Sam in turn gives to Cindy, also confirms her gaze. As *objet a*, this gift of a pendant is to bring Cindy symbolically into the family fold, but she rejects it. It is a hideous object for her. Sam must reckon with the superego of his mother and not his father.

Cindy as Sam's object of desire—as a *concrete* object—embodies his demand to be accepted as normal. Possess her, and he possesses manhood. Feeling that there is something between them at the bodily level, Sam does not "fear" her, but from the start she is an object of anxiety. As Lacan puts it in S X, *Anxiety,* via a liotes or understatement, "anxiety is not without object." In other words, it is an encounter with an object that is more than an actual object, a sure indicator of its signification. Cindy as his fantasy-girl-come-true would be a transformation of his entire geek-dome that he cannot escape from—namely, his mother gazing upon him as "her boy."

Anxiety is a response to *objet a*, in this case to Cindy's enigmatic desire: "What does she want from me?" "How does she see me?" "Why is she talking to me?" Her "beauty" is somewhat overwhelming, and the fantasy frame he has of her at the start makes it difficult for him to approach her. It is only after a number of contacts occur and Bill "levels" her somewhat (a girl who doesn't admit to farting, who is rather rigid in her eating habits) that Sam is able to engage and ask her out, trying all sorts of ways to fit into her fantasy frame—new clothes, a more "with-it" hairstyle, joining the yearbook club, and so on—eventually only to find out that she really likes the basketball jock, Todd Schellinger, and that Sam is only a *friend* to whom she can talk to.

When Todd dumps Cindy, Sam is able to live out his desire, and here I mean his conscious desire to have Cindy as his girlfriend—as an object. When Lacan claims that the ethics of desire consists in "not ceding one's desire," one interpretation is precisely what Sam has done—attained the "object" that he thought he desired; he begins to act out his fantasy, but living it out only to find that the frame that holds Cindy as an object in the first place begins to disappear or fade. She is drained of desire as *objet a* vanishes. Cindy begins to become a monster—controlling, deciding on all the "pseudodates" where they should go, boring, not liking the same films as Sam, and so on. Fantasy, which is a defense against the enigmatic desire of the Other that gives a response to "What am I to you?" becomes revealed. Cindy dates him because he is "nice"—because he is a Geek, not a jock who treats her badly.

While Sam *suffers* through this dating spell, trying to figure it out, he does come to terms with his unconscious desire, *jouissance* or X—but in a surprising way. He discovers that Cindy *also* does not know what she desires. Disappointed, he does *not* suffer subjective destitution. As a self-refleXive moment, *there is a collapse in his identification back on itself*, a confirmation of who he is. Separating himself from Cindy as "object" had paralyzed him in his demand to be less of a Geek—to achieve his fantasy of being gazed at by Others (his dad; his fellow Geeks, especially Harris Trinsky; jocks in the school) as someone who has a cheerleader as a girlfriend and is hence a "stud." Instead, she confirms his "geekiness," a gesture adumbrated by her refusal to wear the pendant.

His frame of reference has now once again changed, reassuring his identity among his friends who thought that they had "lost" him, that he was no longer their friend (sitting at the "other" table in the cafeteria, taking time away from them, and so on). As in Charlie Chaplin's *City Lights*, where the little tramp, who wants to blend into the modern city life, is constantly thwarted by having swallowed a whistle that emits a sound, which prevents his inconspicousness. It constantly signals his presence to himself. Sam finds himself equally "riveted to being"—his "X." As Joan Copjec (2006) explains, this phrase from Levinas:

> The sentiment of being riveted to being is one of being in the forced company of our own being, whose 'brutality' consists in the fact that it is impossible either to assume it or to disown it. It is what we are in our most intimate core, that which singularizes us, that which cannot be vulgarized and yet also that which we cannot recognize. We do not comprehend or choose it, but neither can we get rid of it; since it is not of the order of objects—but, rather, of the 'not-without-object'—it cannot be objectified, placed before us and confronted (100).

Sam must live with himself—live with his X after this self-refleXive moment.

As Copjec further explains and explores, the anxious moment when the very core of our being is encountered (as X in self-refleXivity) is a moment when "we are uncannily doubled by an alien and yet intimate other, this is because the confrontation with *jouissance* as the 'origin of [our] own person' confronts a doubled or forked time where who I am in the present converges with who I am in the past" (104). Lacan and Deleuze meet again, for this *past* as reminiscences presents "time out of joint." Such a *past* is not a modality of the present but belongs to the virtual Real, not as actual or realized events but in the Bergsonian-Deleuzian theorization: as that part of the biographical self "not actualized," as the virtual potential "stored" as it were in the brain of an unrealized past—a "pure" past. Sam confronts his own *jouissance*—he is not having any "fun" with Cindy and must accept this, willing to go up to her and break off the relationship, to let go of what he thought would change his life—a gesture of affirmation rather than of negation.

Deleuzian Ethics: Good Girl Becoming-Freak

I now turn at last to Lindsay—she is, after all *a* key figure in the series who starts her trajectory from good-girl mathlete to Freak, attracted initially to Daniel as a potential love interest and his band of Freaks who seem to be having *fun*—but why this sudden fork in her life? What is the possible cause of her desire? We learn in the series' pilot that when her grandmother died with Lindsay alone by her side, she conveyed to her the emptiness of life. Much later in the series, Lindsay describes to Sam this moment of subjective destitution that simply remains beyond his comprehension. "Can you see God, heaven or light—anything?" she asked. But, her grandmother said there was "nothing." Lindsay concludes that she was a good person all her life and that's all she got—Nothing. There was no afterlife to look forward to—we live in a godless world. The essential finitude of the human being hit Lindsay hard. How should this be interpreted?

Psychoanalytic theory has it that when an abyss appears, chaos emerges, and an *event* in her life happens that changes her entire perspective on living—turns her around. Is such an event to be read as a lack? Does she now turn toward hedonism? An event does not come into being *from* the world, but *by* not being attached to it, as Alaine Badiou (2005, 327) might have said. Lindsay's event does blow a "hole in her knowledge"; it's just not a seismic event like the Copernican Revolution. Instead of a world defined by creative continuity, there is a founding break. Time is "out of joint," for such a moment remains "subjectless," uncertain, and incomprehensible. Its relationships have yet to be realized. As a potential multiplicity it "speaks," "thinks" or "acts" in the form of an "undetermined infinitive" in Deleuze sense.

If Lindsay remains faithful to this singular "event," she produces the "truth" of her subjecthood in Badiou's (2005) terms. Since there is no transcendental subject that discovers truth, it unfolds. The truth here is suspended and could be thought of, as Lacan did, in the future anterior tense as to what Lindsay will become given what she was before.[16] The future anterior was Lacan's way of articulating becoming, and one might ask whether this is not the same concept for the Deleuzian virtual as Brian Massumi (1993) distinctly puts it, "the future past of the present: a thing's destiny and condition of existence" (37). The object-cause of desire is what "prefigured" Lindsay's momentum.[17] Lindsay's body begins to move at a different speed, her BwO's flows change, as does her desire. Is this how Lindsay's subjective destitution should be interpreted? There are many possibilities: as a "symbolic death" (Lacan), as a cut/break (*coupure*) (Foucault), or as a schism, a discontinuity or deterritorialization (Deleuze and Guattari). These can all be theorized as an encounter with the virtual Real—as a temporality that confronts a pure difference or disjunction in Deleuzian terms. Either way, this is still an ethics of the Real. It initiates a new individuation—at first a passage from knowledge to "thought in thought" and then a search for a founding signifier, since this is a "groundless" state. We might say that Lindsay becomes a schizo self. "Why are you throwing your life away?" asks Sam, the concern conveyed through her best friend, Mille.

We might also take this "event" as a collision with death—in Deleuze's terms, as the advent of a "dark precursor" that takes over. It is from the point of view of Lindsay's life that death is affirmed, rather than the inverse. Her grandmother gives her an, as yet, unknowable gift of life, but it certainly does not appear this way at first. From a Lacanian perspective, it is not *what* she desires, but it is the *objet a* as the *cause* of desire—which is not an *object* of course; there is no object that desire's desire—that sets Lindsay's desire in motion. *Objet a* makes it possible for a frame or stage to define itself as the psychic emergence of an *excluded middle*. This frame mediates the inside and outside. In this case it is the performative haunt of Lindsay's grandmother's words (of Jean's mom) that are the object-cause of her desire. Her dying words unhinge the identity Lindsay once had of herself in the symbolic order. It is the haunting gaze of her grandmother that sets her off in the direction of the Freaks, attracted by the *jouissance* of Daniel, the way he "enjoys" in school. Her grandmother was always a "good" person, always looked at favorably by the familial gaze as she fulfilled her expected role. But now that ideal that Lindsay once had as to how to lead a life that once defined her, becomes shaken. She becomes unhinged—an uncertainty appears. As her identification fades away, what remains is the excess of her subjectivity. The "X" in Lindsay's self-refleXivity begins to "think" on its own; it is an acephalous, unconscious subjectivity now in a search of affirmation.

In S XIV, *Logic of Fantasy*, Lacan begins his seminar working through Descartes' *cogito ergo sum* and its multiple transformations around either "I think or I am," from which he generates multiple possibilities: either "I don't think or I am not," "I am where I don't think," or "I think where I am not." He eventually maintains that the *cogito*, the "I think," belongs in the unconscious, which is heterogeneous to consciousness itself. As he famously put it, "I think where I am not, therefore I am where I do not think" (see also Žižek 1993). This is the place of the *process of individuation proper*—of becoming itself.[18] Lindsay (one must think of her here as that "strange" creature that is an assemblage of the writer's narratological imagination—Linda Cardellini's take on her character—and the excess that escapes both when acted out) is poised to actualize the potentially problematized state she is in, the now active differential field of the virtual Real. Her movement is drawn toward a new intensity for resolution that has now become "possible." We could say she is in a schizostate, as are all the Freaks and Geeks, undergoing different individuated singularities at different speeds and movements. All their desires are "prefigured" by an unconscious that "thinks" on its own through the BwO. Self-refleXivity is the process of coming to terms with the virtual X of that process, as an ethics of the Real.

Lindsay's Ethical Turn

Such self-refleXivity has much to do with Nietzschean eternal return. I take several points from Deleuze's discussion of this important idea (1984, 68–72). First, "As an ethical thought the eternal return is the new formulation of the practical synthesis: *whatever you will, will it in such a way that you will also will its return*" (68, original emphasis). Second, "The eternal return is the *being of becoming*. But becoming is double: becoming-active and becoming-reactive, becoming-active of reactive forces and becoming reactive of active forces" (71, emphasis added). It is the becoming-active that requires refleXion, for becoming-reactive leads to nihilism. In Lacan's terms the same distinction is made in S XI, *Four Fundamentals*—repetition as *wiederkehr* (the active affirmation of becoming) rather than *wiederholen* (the repetition of reactive negation of the same).

I would take this as an ethics of the Real of self-refleXivity within a socius as conduct amid relationships. Like Deleuze, it is the self always already becoming-other at the unconscious level of both body and mind.

Later in Deleuze's (1997) thought, this eternal return can also be marked as a form of "stuttering" and "stammering" of language—as the "poetic comprehension of language" (109), language becoming material, reaching its own negation. I can't stop thinking of the Freaks' band (again) playing "Sunshine of Your Love" (6, "I'm With the Band") as "poetic" noise (in the Jacques Attali [1985] sense). Of their noise (rather than language) as a form of "stuttering," since its affectivity is all that matters for them becoming-other. It, too, reaches the limit of silence—certainly to the ears of Nick's father, as well as to Lindsay. Such "stuttering" marks a threshold of in-betweeness of heterogeneous coexistent forces: Hence the "X" of self-refleXivity is the immanent virtual differential marked by stutters as they become actualized. So, to what extent is Lindsay self-refleXive after this encounter with the Real? Does she fall into the nihilism of so-called Freak life? Like the "death" that her dad is always warning her about through his moralistic "fascist-like" raves. Or, is her line of flight an ethical one? [19]

This impingement of self-refleXivity—her schizo initiative—is only revisited once during the 18 episodes. When Lindsay is stoned, her first experience with marijuana, she drops her defenses and lets the world of sensations impinge upon her (13, "Chokin' and Tokin'"). Talking to Mille, who has come with her to the neighbor's house to help babysit Ronnie, since she was in no condition to do so alone, the following conversation ensues:

LINDSAY: (to Mille) . . . God . . . I don't believe in God . . . faith . . . faith based on what? . . . What if all this is a *dream* and it's not even our dream . . . it's that dog's dream (motions to the dog on the couch). Maybe we are just existing in his mind and all of a sudden he will wake up to go to drink out of the toilet and we will be gone. What would happen to us if that dog wakes up? It will be over!
MILLE: Life is not that dog's dream. We live in God's world.
LINDSAY: (looking at Mille) What are you doing?
MILLE: I am going to wake up this dog!
LINDSAY: Don't do it! I don't want you to (pleading).
MILLE: Have faith . . . rise doggy . . . have faith.
(Lindsay is wide-eyed wondering whether she will now disappear.)

While this scene is played for laughs, it is "deadly" serious. Many may recall the irrational things seen, said, and laughed at during their first experience with "grass"; marijuana effects and affects each person differently. For Lindsay it is not an escape from the world (as is often thought); rather, it becomes another plunge into the abyss—the X. The exchange is revealing psychoanalytically, taking us back to Lacan's commentary on Choang-tsu's dream of the butterfly in S XI, *Four Fundamentals*.[20] Lacan's point is that Choang-tsu recognizes something about his innermost being when he dreams that he is a butterfly. And so it is with Lindsay. The dog is telling her something about herself. It gazes back at her, puts her in the picture of a precarious existence. Here the anagram between god and dog reverses the question of transcendence and materiality.[21] As when Diogenes pisses on the street in Plato's *Republic*, it is somehow disturbing to think that our life is an illusionary dream with so much that is out of our control that even a dog could control who we are, a paranoid moment of realization that the "Other does not exist." When Lindsay is "off" marijuana, this "illusion" disappears—but not "really," for it continues to structure her unconscious.

Unlike Mille who has God,[22] Lindsay carries this question of the missing signifier into Freak territory covered by a new skin, her green army jacket, ready for combat with her unknowable Self. This is her self-refleXive move. Lindsay's becoming-Freak, her singularity, is a response to this event, and the 18 episodes should read as a haecceity, as a long arc that leads her "gratefully" into *Dead* territory. This is her line of flight out from blocked desire. Is this an escape from responsibility, which is Counselor Rosso's continual concern, or an escape from *judgment*, the judgment that is always made based on predetermined rules as to who is the best—in athletics, in solving math problems through application in a given time (this is not creative math), or in being the best debater at the upcoming summit at the University of Michigan?[23]

Let me shift ground from the moral judgment of the Oedipal world as humorously represented by the Weirs—the self-sacrificing mother and apoplectic Harold, whose warning about drugs, having children out of wedlock, prostitution, hitchhiking, premarital sex, devil music that the kids listen to, in short all the paranoia surrounding the rules and the morality of being a "good girl"—to ethics.[24] Again Deleuze is useful here. "Ethics, which is to say a typology of immanent modes of existence, replaces Morality, which always refers existence to transcendent values" (1992a, 269).[25] Life is a question of selection and affirmation, not of judgment which presupposes an otherworldly truth represented by metaphysical idols and moral symbols. The signifier "good" got stuck in Lindsay's throat during that fateful day. One presupposes that her grandmother must have been religious, since her haunt is often evoked by Jean as a ghost who still judges "What would your grandmother have said?"

Deleuzian-inspired ethics involves a typology of our modal affects in terms of joy and sadness (Goodchild 1997). Joy and sadness are not predetermined states, and such a typology is always conditioned by each new encounter, and appears only according to local and singular conditions. Lindsay tests this in one of the episodes (11, "Looks and Books"), where she decides to join the mathletes again, mostly out of guilt: she smashes up her mom's car when the Freaks want her to transport some amps to a gig. She dresses down and tries to win her spot back as a first tier mathlete to challenge Shelly Weaver, who is currently perceived as being on top. But this experience does not give her more joy; rather, it saddens her even more as she realizes that she must bump Mille (not Shelly) to get her "first bloc" spot back. Worse, Shelly's arrogance and mean-mouthing her Freak friends ends up stoking Lindsay's competitive fires. The mathletes beat Lincoln in the competition, but Shelly freezes under fire and has a breakdown. All of this gives Lindsay no joy as she leaves the company of the mathletes once again, reconfirming that the school's system of judgment ruins lives.

Lindsay is willing to risk different relationships with the Freaks. The ethical dilemmas are met continually throughout the series as her actions seem based purely on affect within the circumstances she finds herself in. It is never a question of the "right" thing to do. Rather, she is often as much surprised at her "self" as those around her are, suggesting that she is continually actualizing her being, weighing things out as they unfold. It is a practice of being curious in the sense that Foucault meant it, to "get free of oneself" (1985, 8). It is a form of "erring" where one makes errors and one also wanders about, " becoming altered and having one's expectations disrupted" (Zalloua 2004, 239). First, it is Lindsay's relationship with Nick. To make him happy when he was down, she became his girlfriend, but then realized this was not making her happy; she had to find an ethical way to disengage bodies. (The messenger of doom, however, turned out to be her mother.) Then with Kim, who proved to be a bitch, protective of her territorialization of Daniel as Lindsay moved in. But Kim eventually befriends her as this threat is lessened. Here again the ethical question arises when borders break down; Lindsay is willing to lie to Kim's mom, Cookie, and tolerate her threats when Cookie comes over to the Weirs' home to straighten out her daughter's relationship. Judgment in each case is suspended. "It not a question of judging other existing beings, but of sensing whether they agree or disagree with us, whether they bring forces to us, or whether they return us to the miseries of war, to the poverty of the dream, to the rigors of organization. As Spinoza had said, it is a problem of love and hate and not judgment" (Deleuze 1997, 136).

A Diagram of the Good Girl's Escape

The scene is Harold and Jean sitting on the bed in Lindsay's bedroom (10, "The Diary"). They have discovered her diary (brought about through the coaxing of Cookie, Kim's mother) and contemplate whether they should read it, to uncover Lindsay's "secret" life. Jean begins to read as Harold listens:

> DIARY: I'm sick of living in this claustrophobic suburban world.
> HAROLD: (commenting) Oh, yeah! Get used to it!
> DIARY: Everyone is trying to fit in. I feel like I'm living in a world of scared robots. Honestly, this is terrible but the two worst ones are mom and dad.
> HAROLD: What! What does that mean?
> DIARY: They are the most boring, repressed people on the face of the entire earth.
> HAROLD: (commenting) Repressed? I'll repress her!
> DIARY: They say that they love each other, but who knows? Probably just part of their routine; anyway, can robots be in love? . . . Their whole life is this monotonous routine. She cooks dinner, practically the same meal every night. He comes home barking like a fascist dictator . . . who's scared his penis will fall off if he ever cleared the table, and she lets him walk all over her. I love them, but it's not the life for me. No thank you.

This diary entry exposes the two "incompossible" worlds that Deleuze defines as the virtual and the actual. The actual world that affects Lindsay is the representational world, such as Lacan's Imaginary and Symbolic registers, where signifiers shape the representational beliefs. However, there is also a virtual perspective at work here. It is a felt bodily perspective. But there is also a virtual world of a body and its affects, which coexist heterogeneously to one another. What I am referring to is the virtual Real, the "X" of her self-releXivity that is governed by a different set of relations: the unconscious body and mind. This is a world of multiple phantasms that is formed by her past memories, a place of unconscious evaluation and desire. As Deleuze puts it, "Evaluations, in essence, are not values but ways of being, modes of existence of those who judge and evaluate, serving as principles for the values on the basis of which they judge. This is why we always have the beliefs, feelings, and thoughts that we deserve given our way of being or style of life" (1984, 1). What the Weirs are reading "between the lines" then is the tenor of her existence, the various intensifications of her life, her virtual world, which is an indictment of the Oedipalized life as being boring and limiting, blocking desires.

Lindsay (unlike other good girl's in so many youth series, see Conaway 2007) does not follow the usual makeover to become a popular girl so that she can score a guy. Both Lindsay and Kim have a mind of their own, adumbrating third-wave feminism (Rich 2005). As the series draws to a close, in episode 17 ("The Little Things"), Lindsay displays a profound act of disruption. Given a chance to ask Vice President George H. W. Bush a question, the one she submits is refused and replaced by the Bush staff with a banal, harmless question as to what her favorite place to eat in Michigan is. When her moment comes, she turns it around and asks why her question was rejected, and why the vice president was afraid to have an open discourse with students![26] It is an outrageous act in front of her parents, the administration, the media, and her friends. It is her statement that institutionally she has had enough. It is precisely because Lindsay is "bright," an ideal student in the gaze of the school administration, who has gone somewhat astray, that such a moment is conceivable. One "could" follow Lacan (and Žižek 1998) here and maintain that this is an ethically authentic act. For a moment there is a "suspension of the Other." The sociosymbolic system, which guarantees Lindsay's identity, is no longer "covered up" by the big Other. Everything is exposed during that one awkward moment. Is Lindsay indeed "suspended between two deaths"? This standing up to authority, however, does not result in a subjective destitution, but one of affirmation. It seems the shock has to be absorbed, the embarrassment played down, for it was the school's administrators who made the call to have Lindsay address the vice president. This penultimate scene sets up her escape.

For Deleuze in his study of Francis Bacon (2003), it is the diagram[27] that enables the deterritorialization of the figure (as subject) by the figural (what lies "under" the subject's organization/organism) to take place. The diagram is an a-signifying bundle of energy flows, producing the BwO that underlies representation. For Lindsay to jump on the VW bus to go on the Grateful Dead's concert tour in the last scene of the very last episode would have meant that she had produced a different BwO of flow—a different diagram. It is perhaps the case that *F&G* could *only* have lasted 18 episodes, the last episode written by Paul Feig, because the writers knew the series was to be canceled. We might think of the diagram of all those signifying and a-signifying occurrences as Lindsay's experiences with the Freaks and mathletes, finally arriving at her destiny/destination. What is called destiny, for Deleuze, "never consists of step-by-step deterministic relations . . . [D]estiny accords so badly with determination but so well with free-dom: freedom lies in choosing the levels" (1994, 83). Certainly the series was "fig-urative" rather than "figural," with many episodes seeming like clichés, with the narrative constructed around youth themes (first love, competition, gym classes, and so on), but that is not all. There was the figural of the inhuman at work as well: the self-refleXivity that stretched, twisted, stammered, and eventually rup-tured Lindsay in her liberatory flight. This was her productive encounter with chaos, which led to a new rhythm and a new order once she was on that VW bus. The new map of sensation, as an action of forces impinging on the body, led to The Grateful Dead. This turned out to be the call of her dead grandmother. Her haunt was affirmatively put to rest in the belief that a nonjudgmental space could be found with the Dead Heads and the counterculture hippie movement. Is it any wonder that Bob Weir, one of the key Grateful Dead musicians, was perhaps a different father figure? After all, her friend Kim joins her as well to escape Cookie.

So we end with the question of whether Lindsay's flight out as a Dead Head is a revolutionary-becoming in D+G's terms, practicing a micropolitics that creates a difference. Unquestionably, many viewers would say that this is simply an opting out of society, another turn to nihilism or to hedonism with the next episode of Lindsay caught as a dope head, no better off that Nick once was. But, to follow Deleuze, who argues that in a society of control like ours, where we are inundated by capitalist competition (what Lindsay is escaping from) and especially by the con-tinuous communication and flow of information, might not creative-becoming be found precisely in "no longer getting people to express themselves, but providing little gaps of solitude and silence in which they might eventually find something to say[?] Repressive forces don't stop people from expressing themselves, but rather force them to express themselves. What a relief to have nothing to say, the right to say nothing, because only then is there a chance of framing the rare, or even rarer, the thing that might be worth saying" (Deleuze 1992b, 288–89). Deleuze wrote that in 1985 in the middle of what he took to be a literary crisis where the market was promoting only best sellers and books by journalists had become the standard. To break or interrupt the flow of communication so that a transformative potential might take place requires an "escape." "[T]he revolution-ary potential to transform the current system involves a becoming revolutionary of our desire. It requires taking time out, an interruption, a self-imposed leave of absence from the continuous process of control and communication" (Jeffrey Bell 2003, 29). In this sense, Lindsay performs a creative revolutionary-becoming. "DEAD FREAKS UNITE" was the legendary notice placed by Hank Harrison inside the *Skull and Roses* album. And, didn't "flower power" change, at least for a brief moment in history, a perspective on the world before capitalism reinstated its command?

Lindsay went undercover.

Part III

Real Paranoia

The Death Drive's at Stake:
Buffy: The Vampire Slayer

Although most of the good titles have already been taken—*Fighting the Forces: What's at Stake in Buffy the Vampire Slayer* (Wilcox and Lavery 2002), "What Makes Buffy Slay?" (Udovitch 2000), "'You Slay Me!' Buffy as Jurisprudence of Desire" (MacNeil 2007), "Fans with a Lot at Stake" (Bloustein 2002), and even from the series itself, "Being A Vampire Sucks" (4003, "The Harsh Light of Day,"[1] I have come up with a title that captures what will be a predominately Lacanian reading of the series. This chapter and the next were first written in 2003 when the series ended, and they were meant to be included in the *Youth Fantasies* (2004) book, but never made the "light of day." At that time I had watched all seven seasons and had the Buffyverse quite well in hand (somewhat "backwards" I must add, beginning with the first season after I had found a way into the series for myself, as shall be revealed). It seems apropos to revive them now, some five years later, recognizing that the scholarship on *Buffy: The Vampire Slayer* has not waned. Footnotes will update some of the discussion. In these two chapters, I have retained my idiosyncratic approach to youth by retaining the signifiers gurl/girl/grrl that I developed in *Music in Youth Culture* to address the question concerning the specificity of postfeminism. The exploration of *Buffy: The Vampire Slayer* is placed in the middle of *Television and Youth Culture* as an enfolded space that reaches out to the other two books, making the trilogy complete. Theoretically, chapter 1—"Madness and Paranoia"—addresses the postgothic of *Buffy*, as it does that of *Roswell* and *Smallville* that follow.

Buffy: The Vampire Slayer (cited as *Buffy*) began in 1997, a historic moment when the disgruntled concerns of the third-wave feminist daughters that had been percolating since the early 1990s began to see the light of day as a confrontation with their second-wave feminist mothers (de La Rosa 2000). Buffy took a page from Kevin Williamson's *Scream* series and hyperbolized girl-power through its fighting sequences. Buffy's mother, Joyce, is totally oblivious to her daughter's struggles until the end of the second season—the start of the new millennium. Parental authority, as I show, is suspended throughout the series. In 1997, Sarah Michelle Gellar, who was 20 at the time, took on the role of Buffy, a 16-year-old who is destined to fulfill her Call: "As long as there have been demons, there has been the Slayer. One girl in the world, a Chosen One, born with the strength and skill to hunt vampires and other deadly creatures . . . to stop the spread of evil. When one Slayer dies, the next is called and trained by the Watcher." Over the next seven years Buffy grew up. Besides Joss Whedon, the series' creator, other writers—most notably Marti Nixon since season five—began writing episodes; the narrative obviously underwent a number of changes.

In the first three seasons, Buffy and the Scooby Gang were students at Sunnydale High School. At the beginning of season four, Buffy and the Scooby Gang became freshmen at Sunnydale University. She was now 19. Season five marked a shift in the series as Buffy turned 20 and was "reborn," not quite herself. By season seven, Buffy, now in her early twenties, returned to Sunnydale High School as a counselor, completing the cycle. Joss Whedon, who is openly gay, established a campy, self-referential, witty pun(k) style to capture Buffy and the Scooby Gang's struggle with their psyches—first in high school, then in college, and finally in the case of Buffy as a counselor mentoring a younger generation. Whedon managed to find a narrative structure that cleverly explored in a humorous way the fears and anxieties that impact youth today.

The Usual (Objectionable) Suspects

Buffy has become a huge enterprise. It is easy to become a fan(addict) of the series.[2] Theologians and academics[3] alike have bitten into Buffy's apple as both a poison and a cure. Not only did it last seven seasons—spin-offs include *Angel*, an animated *Buffy*, and a BBC spin-off featuring Giles, the librarian—but the series has also generated an elaborate cyberspace following: Websites (two in particular deserve to be noted: Buffy.com and PlanetX.com), chat rooms, and the usual slash fanfics where erotic relationships between the characters are developed, played with, and pushed even further (Stengel 2000; Graham 2001). There are also sophisticated discussions by academics (hopefully, including this one) on the moral and ethical dilemmas of the series, its plot structures, its marketing schemes, and so on. *Slayer: On-Line International Journal of Buffy Studies* boasts a sophistication that now makes even the *X-Files* series pale by comparison. "Everything Philosophical About Buffy the Vampire Slayer," a former website, also treated the series with equal sophistication. Let me first dispense with some obvious interpretations and objections before proceeding to my own, hopefully, unique thesis.

Buffy, first of all, can be read as a perpetual "final girl" of the horror genre as developed by Carol Clover (1992; see also Barbaccia 2000). Her gurl performativity of kicking, fistfighting, and stabbing—that is, "slaying"—is an obvious link with "girl-power," while her grrrl roots will be discussed later.[4] Kevin Williamson's *Scream* series of teen horror flicks in the late 1990s revitalized the slasher genre in one parodic swoop, and disarmed Clover's "Chainsaw thesis" into the "Final gurl" laughing. There is the usual complaint that *Buffy* is just too Anglo-American centric, but as Geraldine Bloustein (2002) shows, it is a series that has an amazing appeal in numerous countries, indicating the profound psychic resonances that it has managed to strike. *Buffy* websites can be found in the United Kingdom (UK), the Netherlands, Portugal, Spain, Italy, Sweden, Israel, Germany, Brazil, France, and Singapore. "It is screened in Argentina, Australia, Brazil, China, [Canada], Denmark, Finland, Hungary, Israel, Japan, the Netherlands, Norway, Poland, Portugal, Spain, Sweden" (Topping 2001, 54), and Austria, where this chapter was written. No question that there are other countries that belong on this list. Some critics and fans were unhappy with Buffy's heteronormative relationships, but that, too, ended with a lesbian subplot that began in season five between Willow and Tara. That was just a question of time, given that gay romances had become increasingly successful commercially on prime-time shows by the end of the twentieth century. From what had been slash fanfics, characterized by a "best friends" fantasy among girls during the first three seasons when Buffy had a predominately teenage girl audience, began to change, especially in the fifth season when the spin-off *Angel* was launched. Spike/Angel and Xander/Angel slash fanfics began appearing; as did "BadFics," where sexual pairings were between monsters and the Slayerettes (Graham 2001, 25).

There is also the typical complaint of tough-minded critics on the Left that *Buffy* is a shameless display of commodity fetishism. Isn't everything?[5] Filmed in Southern California, both near and in Los Angeles, Buffy is *Sassy* incarnate, wearing Delia's-style slip dresses and spaghetti-strapped tank tops—one might say a Spice Girl in disguise. She is a retail industry, like the crossmarketing of *Buffy* paraphernalia from the Warner Brothers (WB) network and clothing retailer Hot Topic.[6] True. But there is an undeniable integrity displayed behind Gellar's actions that makes one a believer. Sassy gurl Sarah Michelle Gellar had the network executives at United Paramount Network (UPN) by the . . . (you know what) when she (at first) refused to move from the WB network. She made *Teen People* magazine visit the Dominican Republic for an interview (she was on location working for Habitat for Humanity). Gellar also left the *Rolling Stone* magazine photo shoot when things became too "uncomfortable" for her. As for her parodic appearance in the horror film *I Know What You Did Last Summer*, she ironically quipped that she prefers to call it "I Know What Your Breasts Did Last Summer." Gellar is fully aware of the contradictions of the series and uses them effectively for positive ends.

Then there is the complaint about what I have called Buffy's "romanticized transgressivity" (jagodzinski 2003b). This criticism is generally leveled at cultural critics such as John Fiske, who argued in a seminal book, *Television Culture* (1987), that such a stance is the best that is possible within a capitalism system. The *jouissance* of youth's pleasures is able to rupture the stranglehold of ideology. As Rob Latham succinctly put it in his brilliant book *Consuming Youth: Vampires, Cyborgs, and the Culture of Consumption* (2002), "the choice is between Marx's parasitic vampire-rat [capitalism], a verminous beast deserving only of extermination, and Fiske's mischievous mallrats [youth], rebellious creatures avidly indulging their cravings and caprices" (36). *Buffy* does not escape either position, but masterfully negotiates in the space between them by setting up what might be referred to as a *walled narrative* when it comes to its consumption. This concept is not unlike a walled-city (or cyberspace cities like Neocron), but its effects are much different, since its walls are fortified by the very nature of its narrative. *Buffy* is another video game "of sorts," but the stakes (I couldn't avoid that one) are much, much higher—adolescent psyches. *Buffy* was their cult secret that they could whisper among themselves in school. To escape into its fantasy porthole and be enclosed by its protective shell, however, requires work (especially by adults[7]), since its episodes appear like "fluff," just trivial nonsense: a bunch of kids running around putting stakes through demons and the like. What nonsense, and that is precisely its "wall." You have to somehow climb over it, or find a way through it. I admit that I thought at first it was just fluff.

The Heroine with a Call

Before I try to unravel the secret of its fortifications, I must say a word about Buffy herself. Buffy, for the most part, follows a heroic monomyth as classically described by Joseph Campbell (1973).[8] She accepts the challenge to be the ONE; Giles is her guide; she faces her first test—the Hellmouth Master; dies in the whale's belly; is resurrected and comes back to fight him; defeats him and continues on her journey. But this monomyth is completely *inverted*. There is no jumping from one world to the next as is usual in a heroic quest—as an endless puzzle adventure if need be that is the stuff of many video games. Buffy stays *put*. It is an inner psychic journey that she is on, first at Sunnydale high school and then at Sunnydale University, with minor sojourns to Los Angeles. This heroine's guides are all inept. As adults, the Watchers fail miserably in their "guidance." The ONE Buffy also splits into two other slayers (Kendra and Faith), as I shall discuss later. Death and resurrections are common fare in the Buffyverse, as sacrifices are made for the sake of the Cause that have ethical consequences, but raise the question that just maybe the Cause itself is a myth. This heroine turns out to be part demon herself! Does Buffy suffer from a multiple personality disorder? Is this heroine delusional? I shall discuss this as well.

Buffy stages a world that doesn't exist in the classically heroic sense. It is its missing piece, the X that the classic hero avoids, but which structures his journey in the first place. This is the world of his inner demons and "pure" desires, where he journeys either away—from or toward—in his quest. *Buffy* is not a narrative of heroic desire, but of uncontrollable drives: Hieronymus Bosch's *Garden of Earthly Delights* found in the unconscious virtual Real that is structured by an ethics of radical Evil, and the struggle with the will-to-*jouissance*. This is her self-refleXive move, the one I develop in the next chapter. Paradoxically, the Buffyverse is not a fantasy—it's Sunnydale's Hell, a place of perdition where *Being* insists on its suffering. Vampires and sexuality are closely associated in Dracula's Victorian gothic genre (Callander 1999). Vamping (sexual intercourse) turns ordinary women into sexually voracious predators—virgin/slut dichotomies abound. Buffy, however, is able to keep these roles in deconstructive play in such a way that, as I try to show, *the gothic genre itself is inverted*. Is being "vamped" then a fall into the Sadeian world of sadomasaochism (s/m) associated with liberated female sexuality? That is to say, the woman is an equal partner in the pleasures of the flesh. Some have argued this about the Buffyverse, especially in the figure of Spike. Vampires are monsters in human drag, while Buffy defies demonic miscegenation ("excessive exogamy"). She is a slayer coming together with a vampire (Angel), crossing the boundary of their difference. What the teratological imagination of postmodern-gothic explores, however, is much broader than this. I argue in this chapter and the next that the Buffyverse is much more. It addresses the anxiety of youth leading up to what was to become an *event* —9/11.

Opening Up a Porthole: Scratching the Tain of the Mirror

When I first stumbled across the *Buffy* series—the episode (I was to learn later) was entitled "Normal Again" (6017) and aired on March 12, 2002—a scene stayed with me that pried the wall open for my approach to *Buffy*. The episode begins with Buffy walking down a moonlit Sunnydale avenue scouting out a demon hideout.[9] When she gets too close to the hideout, a demon jumps out and attacks Buffy and manages to skewer her with a claw. We cut next to a featureless room where Buffy is being held down by two orderlies, dressed appropriately in white. As she struggles to free herself, one of them jabs her with a hypodermic needle. The camera pulls away to reveal a bed with constraints, a reinforced locked door. Patients are being herded down the hallway outside. We are in a mental hospital. Immediately, Buffy is back in front of the demon's hideout a bit confused. The "cuts" she incurs during the Sunnydale scrap and at the mental hospital cause a rupture of her skin-ego—the force of the skewer and the hypodermic needle. The next flashback to the hospital occurs when Buffy's manager barks at her at the *Doublemeat Palace*, the fast-food place where she is working. This time a nurse is telling her it's time for her drugs, reminiscent of Nurse Ratched in *One Flew Over the Cuckoo's Nest*. Almost immediately, we are back at the *Doublemeat Palace* with Buffy looking at her bemused manager. His threat had caused a brief flashback, a momentary disavowal of his existence.

In the next incident, Buffy collapses when Xander gets into a quarrel with Spike, a vampire who has Buffy as a love interest (it's a long story . . . later). This time, the scene is more dramatic. A kind, soft-spoken doctor is talking to her. He tells her that Sunnydale is not real. The mental institution is where she has been for the last six years (seasons). There is a quick cut to Buffy walking in the cemetery (as if she is now hallucinating this memory *within* the context of the mental institution), and then we are immediately back to the mental institution where the doctor tells Buffy that she has visitors: Joyce and Hank Summers; her parents are here for a visit! (Hank is divorced from Joyce and does not enter into the Buffyverse. He makes a rare guest appearance when Buffy visits him in the second season. Effectively he does not exist.) They are somewhat surprised that she recognizes them, and Joyce strangely says, "stay with us." But Buffy curls up into a fetal position. With the shock of seeing her parents, Buffy is back with Willow, Xander, and Spike who are gathered around looking at her lying on the ground in a fetal position. Buffy tells them that she has been having hallucinations, that Sunnydale is not real. As Willow tries to reason with her, Buffy is again back in the hospital. This time the incident is even *more* dramatic. Joyce and Hank are talking to their other daughter, Dawn, telling her that they hope that Buffy will come back to them. The doctor tells them like it is. Buffy has been living in an imaginary world of her own construction. She has written her own delusions of escape, which include imagining that she has a sister, Dawn, but now these delusions have taken on an opposite effect: Sunnydale has become too ugly a place to stay. Buffy is suddenly back again in Sunnyvale talking to Willow and looking at a picture of the Summers family *that does not include Dawn*, as if the shock of seeing Dawn at the mental hospital has transported her back to Sunnydale.

For regular watchers of the series, Dawn "magically" shows up in season five, as if she came from nowhere. This hallucinatory episode could be interpreted as if there is now something wrong with the hallucination *of the hallucination*. Willow tells Buffy that there is nothing to worry about, that she has never been in an institution. On the contrary, Buffy explains, she was placed in an institution when she first told her parents about vampires. If she stopped talking about vampires, she was not given her daily dose of Thorazine. In a couple of weeks she was discharged. Her parents put the incident behind them, as did she. Buffy tells Willow that she is not sure if she ever left the mental hospital, that maybe she is still there! After a brief scene with Spike and Xander, Dawn (age 15) is miraculously back, bringing her sister tea. Buffy tries to convince Dawn that she's OK now, and that as sisters they have to learn to get along better. That conversation is rudely interrupted as Buffy's mother bluntly says, "You don't have a sister, Buffy." Buffy is on the bed in her cell and repeats her mother's statement. Joyce encourages her to say it again—which she does. Hank insists that her memories of Dawn aren't real, while Joyce then encourages Buffy to "stay with them." They will take care of her. Wanting to believe her mother, Buffy reaches out only to find a hurt look on her sister's face. Buffy is back in Sunnydale. Dawn has heard the rejection (Buffy's repetition of her mother's words) and leaves.

Willow works out a magic potion to make the hallucinations go away. After a lucid incident with Spike, who tells her in no uncertain terms to get off her "hero" trip and to tell her friends about their romance, the shock caused by Spike's directness prompts Buffy to take Willow's cup of potion to her mouth to end the hallucinations. She closes her eyes and then abruptly pours the potion into a bedside wastebasket. She is immediately back at the institution telling her parents that she doesn't want to "go back there." "What must she do?" Joyce and Hank are overjoyed. The doctor explains that she has to destroy the things that are holding her in Sunnydale—her friends. Buffy is suddenly back in Sunnydale and begins to turn on her friends: first Willow and then Xander. Willow is hogtied and gagged with duct tape; Buffy then goes after Dawn, to get her in the basement so that she can become "well" again. Dawn pleads for Buffy to recognize her existence in Sunnydale and wake up from her hallucination. Buffy approaches Dawn reeling off the improbabilities of the existence of vampires and demons, the whole absurd concept of being a Slayer, and the unlikelihood of her ever sleeping with a vampire like Spike. Dawn is gagged and put in the basement.

She stands looking at her friends whom she has been with for six years, and, wavering about what to do next, she is back at the clinic. The doctor is telling her "to make it easy on herself." Back in the basement of her Sunnydale home, Buffy releases a demon, one of several that Willow and the gang had subdued thanks to the investigative work Buffy had done earlier in the episode. She watches impassively as the demon is about to do Xander in. In the meantime Tara comes into the Summers' house looking for the gang. Buffy is suddenly back at the mental institution, where she retreats to a corner of the room. Joyce is there, calmly assuring her that whatever is frightening her is not real. Buffy looks as if she is having a seizure, and sinks to the floor of both *hospital room and the basement as if the two separate worlds have collided.* The moment of "truth" has been reached. An unconscious decision has to be made. A fight ensues between Buffy and Tara, who has now summed up the situation and released Willow. The demon begins to attack Xander. Back to the hospital. Buffy is freaked as her body wrenches and contorts. Joyce crouches next to her, and with all the faith and devotion she can muster, tells her, "I believe in you. You're a survivor. You can do this." The fight continues in the basement. In the institution Buffy, half-hysterical, screams out her best friend Willow's name and pounds on the floor. Joyce continues her encouragement: "You're too good to give in. You can beat this thing. Be strong, baby. I know you're afraid. I know the world feels like a hard place sometimes . . . We have all the faith in the world in you. We will always be with you. You've got a world of strength left in you. You just have to find it again. Believe in yourself." All of a sudden Buffy is very still. She looks up her mother with a smile of gratitude on her face. "You're right," she says quietly. "Thank you." Her facial expression then changes. "Goodbye," she whispers. We are back in the basement with Buffy pounding out the demon that had almost killed Xander. She apologizes to Willow, Dawn, and Xander—fortunately, no harm has been done. Everyone is OK. Buffy demands more of Willow's antidote. Back at the mental hospital, the doctor holds a flashlight and examines Buffy's completely unreactive pupils. "I'm afraid we lost her," he says sadly.

This episode that I have described in detail more than just winked back at its audience, as these episodes usually do through their self-reflexive, ironic fashion. Written by Diego Gutierrez, whose Borgesian influence is clearly visible, it came dangerously close to exposing what I feel is the secret of the Buffyverse narrative. Many fan(addicts), called the "Bronzers" (after "The Bronze," which is the main teen hangout on the show), were "power-freaked" by this episode, since the series came so close to a suicidal self-destruction; it could have gone either way. After six years Buffy might become *normal*—again! It raises the question of an ethics that surrounds fandom. Buffy's resurrection would mean the "death" of the series; the supernarrative of the Buffyverse would end. Fans know what happens then: *Misery!*[10] This is part of the brilliance of the series itself. It doesn't matter whether this is yet another repetition of a death/resurrection episode; rather, I think it exposes the psychic structure of the series itself. In its very mimetic excesses, this episode forwards a "truth" of the Real. Rather than giving fans wry little glimpses of neurotic anxieties, like *Ally McBeal* with its playful imaginary special effects, this episode in particular is a porthole into understanding its structure through which I now escape into.

Paranoid Psychosis: Suspending the Name-of-the-Father

If it were possible to retitle this chapter, it would be something like this: "From the Paranoia of the *X-Files* to the Paranoid Psychosis of Buffy: The Aliens Have Already Invaded." What the *X-Files* does with outer paranoia to the Symbolic Order, Buffy does to the inner paranoia as a psychosis. Buffy presents us with the possibility of turning paranoid psychosis into an ethical examination of Evil, rather than being caught by it as in Hitchcock's *Psycho*. Buffy's world appears psychotic. It allows for narrative structures and changes of and in characters that enable a diagesis to emerge that seems to defy all logic, for it tries to deal with the improbable structures of unconscious memories themselves—the virtual Real.[11] The show's serialization allows for repetitions with a difference, loops and compressions in time/space and a play of clichés by doubling them—truly a hall of mirrors that goes *blank* at the end of each season with a concluding "death," Lacan's anterior future of lived experience—what I will have been is amply demonstrated in *Buffy*, as is the Deleuzian repertoire of time-image signs.[12] Her past inflects and alters her present, "refreshing" it differently each time. This "time out of joint" effect can be simultaneously presented; for instance, we are not sure what role Dawn plays in Buffy's life. Does Dawn "truly" exist? Or is she a delusional manifestation, part of Buffy's virtual Real?[13] In one story line (5005, "No Place Like Home"), she is "The Key," pure energy made human by Glory, a she-demon from another dimension that sucks energy from peoples' brains, leaving them crazy (season five). Or, was Dawn there all along, from the beginning of season one, but a neglected sibling who is finally recognized (5002, "Real Me")? Once created, Dawn's existence changes Buffy's past by revisiting previous memories, and so on; this not unlike the Bergsonian virtual past, which exists as a single dimension where all past events coexist.

Paradoxes and alternative worlds abound, the *Angel* series being one such alternative universe. Buffy is the Persephone of the Underworld, engulfed by the Real, living in her unconscious world. Unlike the bit players of apocalyptic heroic cybernarratives, Buffy is the ONE to save the world—a metonym for the psychic health of the planet. Whether we place Buffy in a permanent coma or make her delusional, the point is that the Symbolic Order as the authority of the Father becomes suspended, and the mOther, Joyce, is never barred. Joyce's death (5015, "The Body") occurs when Buffy has cut her ties with the Council of Watchers and, in effect, takes over the mother role while looking after Dawn. Hank, her father, does not "figure" in the script. Sunnydale's structure remains post-Oedipal. The only time that we have any knowledge of Buffy's father is in the first season. Joyce and Hank are divorced. In episode 1010 ("Nightmares"), Buffy's "nightmare" comes true: her father doesn't want to spend anymore time with her. He is a harsh man who feels that she is not as smart as he had hoped her to be, and complains that she is always getting into trouble. Hank Summers comes across as a negligent father who has vacated the household. While the episode closes with him embracing Buffy as they are about to spend the weekend together, we know Buffy's unconscious fears remain unresolved in their relationship. He typifies the parental incompetence and inept guidance Buffy receives from her two guardian adults, Giles and Joyce.

What authority there is in Sunnydale is ironically represented. The police seldom play a significant role. As in the *X-Files*, they do not believe in demons, monsters, and the like, so why call on them? They remain functionaries like Principal Snyder of Sunnydale High School, who sees Buffy only as a troublemaker. She only pays lip service to his rules. Principal Fludie, his predecessor, was promptly "eaten" in the first season (1006, "The Pack"). The Initiative, on the other hand, has authority, its operations represent the obscene side of the Law. It is a clandestine government operation composed of scientists and commando operatives. Their purpose is to study and harness the power of supernatural beings by capturing vampires and demons. After studying and testing them, they implant these "hostile sub-terrestrials" ("hostiles" or "HSTs") with antiviolence chips to neutralize the threats they pose to humans (4011, "Doomed"). (The joke on adults is obvious, especially the thinly veiled reference to the V-chip that enables parents to censor various television channels because they may be too violent.) The Initiative operates strictly in black and white terms, by the book, which Buffy rejects. Joyce and Giles, Buffy's Watcher and ersatz father, do not have all the answers, although Giles pretends he does. Any other adult who is likely to become Joyce's love interest is equally suspended as an authority figure.[14] Buffy has to rescue them, and not the other way around.

Buffy's world, therefore, is a foreclosure of the Name-of-the Father, the authority of the Symbolic Order. Even when it comes to the Council of Watchers—led by Quentin Travers—they are presented as being inept, quarreling, and bungling things up, like the figure of Wesley, who is a "dork" and sometimes a "jerk." Buffy refuses to listen to him, and refuses the Council's condemnation of Angel (3021, "Graduation Day, Part One"). In episode 3012 ("Helpless"), when Buffy has to pass the "Cruciamentum" test on her eighteenth birthday, she is controlled by the Council of Watchers and learns not to trust their patriarchal powers. This marks a shift in the series where she becomes more autonomous. Their persnickety *theological* "wisdom" becomes highly doubtful and suspect. Giles and Wesley, as their representatives, are most often caught by the "letter of the Law;" that is, they read the rules literally, which Buffy doesn't always accept. In episode 3007 ("Revelations"), the Council lets Faith's new rogue Watcher, Gwendolyn Post, remain at large. In episode 3014 ("Bad Girls"), the inept Wesley is sent to replace Giles. As the term *Watchers* suggests, they are *vigilant*, but their vigilance can also be interpreted as voyeuristic, panoptic, and controlling—as Mob Law. The Council can be ruthless, as demonstrated by their use of commando tactics to kidnap Faith and force her to face a Slayer court martial (3015, "Consequences"). The Council is filled with factionalism and fanaticism, in power struggles and political jockeying; they seem to be bound to omerta, the code of silence of the Cosa Nostra. Tony Soprano (*The Sopranos*) is also "vigilant" and "watchful" over his daughter Meadow, who is a gurl like Buffy in the making. Meadow knows better than to listen to her father, and is often impertinent to him, as Buffy is at times impertinent to Giles. She has her own mind.

As Lacan puts it in S III, *Psychoses*: in psychosis "the repressed . . . reappears in another place . . . in the imaginary, *without a mask*" (104–05, emphasis added). This is what we face in Buffy—the Real is unmasked. What isn't foreclosed is her eternal struggle with the superegoic function of the Father—the Father of Enjoyment in its various guises. Most specifically in the figures of The Master of Hellmouth—an oral evil Father; Major Wilkins's diabolical schema of *Ascension* to enslave and destroy mankind; Adam's *Frankenstein* plot to create a superrace of human demon hybrids; and her battle with Glory, a glamor-girl hellgoddess in season five. Also at stake (how could I resist?) is her will-to-*jouissance* as demonstrated by the conflicting figures of her love life—Angel and Spike—and also by Buffy's own demons and those of the generation that she represents. The demon is the drive personified, always bent on total destruction of the self. In a vampire, the drive forces (*Triebe*) have already overpowered the human will. (Giles: "A vampire appears to be completely normal until the Feed is upon them. Only then do they appear mad" (1001, "Welcome to the Hellmouth"). The drives are always "kicking" and coming at Buffy; she is always fighting and "kicking" back at them when they turn their "vamp" face on. It is a never-ending struggle with the symptoms of postmodernity: addiction, drugs, consumer capitalism, sexual advances, parents in your face, school pressures, joblessness, and so on. We can see that Buffy is the exemplification of self-refleXivity.

In this interpretation, the series does indeed take place *only* in Buffy's unconscious, as her post-gothic Hell. The narrative places us "behind" the mirror. The narrative wall—or *tain of the mirror*[15]—that blocks a noninitiated viewer, especially a parent, from entering into the narrative is the stupidity and self-refleXive humor of the series itself. The tain of the mirror reflects the outside world of Authority and keeps it out. A viewer has to scratch a line into the tain of the mirror and open a porthole to begin to grasp the Buffyverse. The episode (6017, "Normal Again") that I have described is atypical in exposing the scratching that fans of Buffy are constantly doing from the inside out, so to speak, as she battles her own demons and vampires. These vampires reflect and refract her world, giving back to her its demands and desires. Such a psychosis expresses perfectly what it means to be alienated as a youth today: whether one is a closeted queer or an outsider who doesn't fit into a peer group at school.

The Scooby Gang is a pack of rejects. (The name is self-depreciatory in its reference to the gang of teenagers who investigate crimes of supernatural origin in the cartoon *Scooby Doo*. They are "dogs" like the cartoon's Great Dane, Scooby Doo.[16]) Xander plays the teen as Everyman, the teenager who is never cool (enough)—a geek at times, a looser, a freak—an X. Xader is always being jerked around by women: from the "Inca Mummy Girl" (episode 2004) to Cordelia, to Faith, and finally to Anya. Strong women feminize him; Buffy calls him "one of the girls." Xander has no remarkable personal skills. He still lives in his parents' basement, and (in the first few seasons) must drive an ice-cream truck to make money. He's more nerdy, uncoordinated in his fights with vampires. Finally, compared to his friends, who all have some sort of defining talent, he is insecure. Willow is tomboyish, from a strict Jewish household (Rosenberg); brilliant, but fashion-challenged; the typical "smart-girl" in many youth television series. Cordelia is shallow and vain—a Valley gurl; and Oz, the musician, is occasionally a genius, or a rebellious Werewolf (good on the outside and only occasionally bad—once a month during the full moon—on the inside). The vampire, Angel, is a brooding type whom I shall develop later; and his opposite, the Sadeian vampire, Spike (a.k.a. William the Bloody, "Hostile 17"), was introduced in episode 2003 ("School Hard") and remained a regular. The demons can also be read as gang members and drug dealers who transform gullible kids into victims. For Lacan, paranoia manifests itself as a disturbance at the level of the signifier; the subject fails to secure a position in the Symbolic Order. There is a failure to integrate a symbolic identity where the Imaginary predominates. The Buffyverse lends itself to the possibility of such a reading.

The slash/fanfic/perverse genre that might be expected to have been spawned by the series never emerged in the first four seasons. It took off with season five (Graham 2001 paragraph, 25). It remained a straight, heteronormative show for the most part, which is surprising given Whedon's gayness. One has to assume that he played it cautiously, letting out more "alien-monsters" when the ratings were secured and the time was right. As more and more gay and lesbian characters developed on prime time, Whedon began to let the queer folk into Bosch's *Garden* (although he had to back off as fan(addicts) became upset with Willow/ Tara's lesbian relationship). Properly speaking, a perverse sexual range would be possible from the start in such a perverse fantasy frame where "normal" is thrown out the window. With the suspension of the Symbolic Order, sex remains "uncivilized" and polymorphously perverse, not structured by the hierarchy of genital sex. Oral and anal and any other possibility might have been presented. Whedon all along gave hints of queering *Buffy*, starting with episode 2015 ("Phases"), where the jock Larry outs himself to Xander; another hint was the standing joke of Joyce using coming-out clichés to ask why Buffy was a slayer: "Have you tried *not* being a slayer?" and "Why did you *choose* to be this way?" (2022, "Becoming, Part Two). The clincher comes when Joyce even asks her if she is expected to march in a "Slayer pride parade" (3002, "Dead Man's Party"). Besides the lesbian relationship between Willow and Tara in season four, there was the first bisexual vampire (3016, "Doppelgängland"), and a transgendered god (5013, "Blood Ties"). In the seasons where Buffy's demon side is drawn to the love interest with Spike, the rebel vampire ("good" on the outside, but "bad" on the inside), Whedon and his team of writers have not been able to stage outrageously perverse sex scenarios; they remain on the Internet as fanfics.[17]

Psychotic-like Language as Ethical Slayage

Hallucination is a typical form of primary-process "thinking." While present in neurosis, perversion, and psychosis, here it structures the entire narrative. Buffy's dreams are prescient. She has foresight and foreknowledge through them as Night and Day, both metaphorically and actually; they are flipped around in "Sunnydale." *Buffy* positions the viewing audience in the "know" on the edge of psychosis, as in the above example's ambiguous reading of the title, "Normal Again," where the difference between reality (RL) and schizophrenic paranoia is put in jeopardy, as in the *Blair Witch Project*. Fact and fiction coexist in what Lacan (see Miller 1994) called a space of "extimacy," where the binary inside/outside or container/contained does not apply. It was Lacan's way of attempting to show how the unconscious is already part of conscious everyday life; the neurotic is able to socially construct notions of reality through a fantasy frame to keep at bay what is incomprehensible and unknowable. The *Buffy* narrative turns this around, placing the viewer into that very unknown where the normal world (of adults) becomes monstrous. Buffy's fantasies have become so life-like that the frame has dissolved.

This interpretation can be supported by the "psychotic-like" use of language throughout the series. In the first season there is an obvious differentiation made between the Scooby Gang's use of language and that of adults (Wilcox 1998). What happens, however, as the episodes begin to stack up on top of one another, the subtext and supertext continue to develop into a complex hypertext that can be read on multiple levels. The series becomes implosive in its self-referencing through its humor, puns, parodies, and cultural references to countless monsters, television shows, and films. The quoting game becomes hyperexcessive. The fan(addict) develops and internalizes what we would call a special set of "viewing lenses" that enable him or her to *overidentify* with the Buffyverse, stationing a "true" fan(addict) on the threshold between neurosis and psychosis (as if he or she were experiencing the "Normal Again" episode described earlier). It is a schizophrenic kind of looking. As Giles, the Watcher-librarian says, "I believe the subtext is rapidly becoming text." That is precisely the experience I am trying to describe—the overquotation that perhaps Joss Whedon took from Williamson or visa versa.

I can give two examples of what I mean by this. The first has to do with looking at a 3-D "puzzle" image, which doesn't seem to be anything at all but a meaningless blend of chaotic colors. To "solve" such a puzzle you have to stare at its meaningless image long enough to find and occupy the proper point in the imaginary perceptual space from which a 3-D image miraculously begins to form from the nonsense. These shapes emerge "magically" when this happens. It seems as if figures pop out in a 3-D form that had existed there all along. We just couldn't *see* them. This is the experience I am trying to suggest happens when viewing the Buffyverse as a *supertext*. Seemingly "secret" messages emerge, like a psychotic experience—a "call" from the Real—seeing something that others don't see, like a delusional experience. Joss Whedon's gayness has something to do with this approach, since such clandestine communication through overidentification has a "cult-like" trance to it. It is also part of queer culture to be able to reaffirm a communal bond through a counteridentification by communicating "forbidden" meaning that the mainstay audience can't "read." I take this to be a form of textual transgression that works on undecipherable readings, which effectively make many ethnographic studies of *Buffy* somewhat suspect and superficial.

My second example comes from a grade-B movie that is dear to my heart, John Carpenter's *They Live* (1988). The sci-fi plot has the aliens already landed and walking the streets, slowly taking over leading governmental positions in the country. But no one is aware they are aliens, for it is impossible to distinguish them from the ordinary citizens. A white-trash construction worker, John Nada, inadvertently finds a pair of special sunglasses (in the trash, where else!), puts them on, and begins to see hidden messages in advertising that are intended to pacify citizens so that the aliens' smooth replacement operation can continue. With the same glasses, he is able to pick out the aliens from the human beings. John Nada is like Buffy—"is he psychotic or have the aliens (vampires, demons) truly landed?" In a development consistent with my previous argument concerning seemingly indecipherable images, the leader of the liberal forces is able to hack a message intermittently through the television networks. His face flashes on and off with a warning about aliens. The glasses can be read in two ways: not only are they a form of protection, but they also reveal messages that can be understood as a hypertext, the myriad of allusions to a historical past, an implosion of intertextuality so as to be able to see "differently." Maybe I am being a little overdramatic here? But, *Buffy* as a cult series passes on this secret, this indecipherable message that adults are blind to—namely, the ugly, monstrous world adolescents face, which adults do not see, is quite often frightening, and it is the adults who are often the aliens.

The spells that witch Willow casts mean that the words "themselves" somehow possess power. They are *performative speech acts* meant to produce an effect, as if the word as *spell* had contagious power. The word "witch" historically contributes to communal madness; as if what a witch said spread from person to person affecting them like a contagious disease. A psychotic has the sense of being possessed by language that seems to be coming from "outside" him- or herself, and not from the inside. As disembodied speech, it gains its power elsewhere. It is the very "materiality" of language, as if it has a life (*zoë*) of its own, which is what "spells" and "chants" are all about. The dialogue in *Buffy* stretches language to the limit, and it is this special "slayer slang" that speaks to the body's excesses and the isolated affects of alienation that resonate with psychosis.

Michael Adams (1999a,b) has usefully explored the innovations of language that the Scooby Gang plays with, which Rhonda V. Wilcox (1998) at one time began to identify. Adams provides many useful examples of the extraordinary use of cultural and television references; the shifting of proper names into other parts of speech as both verbs and nouns (Xander: "Does anyone feel like we've been *Keyser Sozed*?"—tricked and manipulated by the main figure in *The Usual Suspects*); the reworking of meaningless adult factual information into slayer slang ("oxidation reduction reaction" becomes for Buffy "drastic distraction reduction"), the use of retrosounding words (Slutorama and Disco Dave); the use of "free" as expanding a new lexicon (destiny-free, free-move, fester-free, glib-free); the play with the prefix "un" (unmad, uncool, unbudger, unlife, undead) to refer specifically to the sate of being a vampire; the use of specific teen states of affectivity (overshare, overthinking); the creative exploration of the suffix "age" (sliceage, slayage, foodage, studyage, etc.); the shifting of adjectives to nouns more frequently than usual (the postal, the crazy, a happy, the funny); Cordelia's overemphasis on the word "much," and so on. This self-referential imploded language refers to signifiers that can't find a place in the Symbolic Order. They form an affective BwO of bodily articulation that makes teenagers and twenty-something Scooby Gang members *aliens themselves*, in a form different but related to the demons, vampires, and monsters that already abound. Their *ethical insistence* to be heard using a language that does not belong in an adult vocabulary places their existence in the twilight zone that Lacan called "between two deaths," the forbidden zone of *das Ding*. Like Antigone's brother Polyneices, they have not had a "proper burial." The "adult" Symbolic Order has not answered their ethical demand as yet. Rather, they exist at the entrance to "the Hellmouth."

The Matrix of Players: The ONE=THREE of Buffy's Postfeminism

Buffy is definitely a gurl, like Britney Spears, Shakira, Christina Aguilera, Kylie Minogue, and a host of other teen and twenty-something singers. She is a hysteric (living in a psychotic world) who has displaced the male by possessing the phallus-stake. The racial implications of her whiteness and privilege are not anything that I contest. Yet, gurl sexuality is just as much on display in racially coded Black Hip Hop music with its own strategies of "fly girl" postfeminism to avoid being degraded as a "ho," as it is in other ethnically and racially coded youth locations: Asian American, and Latino-American I read gurl power as a Master signifier which is "empty," located in the Real. It has emerged in post-Oedipalization as a hysterically defined psyche rather than being defined exclusively in (white) racial terms.[18] It is an affective state in relation to the Law that preserves a sexual vitality that is maintained regardless of race, or rather inflected differently in each culture; *jouissance* itself is not racially coded; it is a-signifying. The affectivity of touch belongs to the Real affective body (BwO); color as visible identity belongs to Imaginary body. Although the two cannot be separated, only their relation reworked, gurl power is a particular way of "touching" the patriarchal Other, the Law in which faith has been lost. The problem is determining how to "touch" the demons that are sexually harassing you. What does one do with demon lovers? The Buffyverse raises such questions. Certain forms of "protection" are required. Sarah Michelle Gellar's own sexuality as presented in secondary texts such as *Esquire* and *Rolling Stone* is often in stark contrast to Buffy's (Vint 2000). Yet, Gellar knows full well that the gaze is different in such spaces as opposed to the fantasy space of the series. It is precisely the creation of her alter ego Buffy that enables Gellar to maintain her sexuality outside of *Buffy*; not unlike Britney Spears's strategy (once upon a time) of playing the "virginity card."[19]

Buffy's gurlism struggles with sexual relationships throughout the series, which is its youthful attraction. In the first two seasons, it is a romance with Angel—the name seems to say it all, her first "true" love, who appears much "older," a hybrid vampire cursed with a soul, having to wander around guilt-ridden. Angel's brooding masculinity is not very different from that of the boyz who are struggling with their own familial pasts. When Angel and Buffy first sleep together (2013, "Surprise"), he immediately loses his soul, and the demon inside him takes over. His will-to-*jouissance* supercedes his desire. This seems to confirm Lacan's point (against Kant) that if a man is given a choice between the gallows the next day and having sexual relations with his dream woman that night, he may well choose the latter. He refuses to give up his *jouissance* (as "pure" desire) and feels completely devastated, his life empty of meaning.[20] Angel is denied happiness, raising questions about sexual relations between men and women, which Lacan reads as being fundamentally "impossible" to begin with. Love is the only way to breech the difference. Angel's love for Buffy eventually leads to his downfall. At the end of season two, Buffy has to sacrifice him—kill him so that the demon Acathla will not rise and suck the whole world into Hell!

In the fourth and fifth seasons, Buffy's new love interest is Riley Finn. Approaching twenty during her Sunnydale University stint, Buffy has a love affair with an all-American type, a handsome commando with the Initiative who is eventually betrayed by its leader, Professor Maggie Walsh (a.k.a. Buffy's psychology professor). Buffy breaks with Riley when he decides to pursue his military career. Riley represents a figure of masculinity that truly believes in authority and the system—heroic, patriotic, and idealistic. He is shocked that he has been betrayed by the Initiative, and never quite recovers from it. Dr. Walsh, as the obscene maternal superego, the clandestine underside of the Initiative, gives "birth" to the figure of Adam—Project 314—the fantasy figure of a biocyborg, who kills his creator in good Frankenstein fashion, and then wishes to rule the world.

Seasons six and seven has Buffy drawn to Spike, a punk-rocker type vampire who has been neutralized by the Initiative through a chip implant, another metaphor for a soul.[21] He is unable to kill humans. Spike is eerily reminiscent of the Trench Coat gang in the Columbine shootings. He wears a black-leather trench coat and has spiked peroxide-blond hair. In episode 5007 ("Fool for Love"), he even goes after Buffy with a double-barreled shotgun. But, Spike has already been smitten by Buffy in that episode, and now love begins to bloom. Spike is Angel's opposite. He is a Sadeian type who (to remain with psych-pop here) is "good" on the outside, but "bad" on the inside. His sadism is precisely what Buffy is drawn to and she must come to grips with self-refleXively, for his is a particular masculinity that satisfies her own hysterical refusal of authority. In episode 6012 ("Dead Things"), Buffy beats Spike up after having made love with him just four episodes before (6008, "Smashed"). This incident can be interpreted as a repeated struggle with her "dark"—that is, Sadeian—side (as it was with her dislike of Faith),[22] but it can also be read as a sadomasochistic sexual experience of "rough" sex. A slash fanfic between Buffy/Faith would also be a sadomasochistic relationship. No weaker sex here; both prey on their own desires. Buffy has possibly succumbed to such enjoyment (*jouissance*) and becomes addicted to pain—a rather perverse reading.

Most often, Buffy's relationship with Spike lends itself to a romantic reading. Spah (2000) reads Spike and Buffy's romance in Courtly Love terms. Buffy is a Lady, the unobtainable, virtuous, and Good Thing (*das Ding*). Spike appears as the typical vassal, her slave. Sublime love can flourish because of her unreachable elevation; she is an object that is just too far away to be reached—pure. Reading it from Spah's viewpoint, Buffy is now virginal and unobtainable (see Shalit 2000). Spike in this romantic scenario rids the Evil inside himself, as Buffy's own moral goodness overwhelms him. She extinguishes his cancer, and he is willing to commit his life to her, bound by honor and devotion. It is the Christian story of moving from Evil to Good. A sound theory, but there is that *chip* in the "Big Bad"[23] that goes awry, that leads to "Smashed" (episode 6009) with a very hot, censored sex scene of Buffy coming to orgasm that was made available to fans;[24] the usual conventional reading of the morality play within Buffy's unconscious gets thwarted.

The Boyz/Bois/Boys and Gurls/Girls/Grrrls in *Buffy*[25]

This brief review of Buffy's love affairs identifies a variety of masculinities that are found on the post-Oedipal landscape. The Vampires (Spike vs. Angel) represent pretty well the array of figures that are found in the music scene—the Boyz/Bois. Riley represents the All-American patriot—a "man"; whereas the more nerdy figures such as Xander and Oz, who lasted for two season, we would call "boys" trying to become boyz, who in turn refuse to become "men." They are good on the outside and (sometimes) naughty on the inside, wishing for their first sexual experience, but remaining virgins. Oz is a Werewolf (bad on the inside) who has to be locked up once a month and might be stretched into a skater-type boi? In another context we have termed these boys the "new Castrati."[26] This is especially the case with the inept Xander, who is more representative of the "normative" Oedipalized boy struggling with a "cheerleader fantasy" and the shallow types like Cordelia, and who is always in love with Anya (a former demon whom he almost marries in season six). As a main character, what is surprising is the repression of an outwardly gay character in the Scooby Gang. It is left to the fanfic imagination, unless Buffy is read through Clover's (1992) thesis as Whedon's *alter ego in drag.*

Equally, there is an array of women characters who complement the boys/boyz/bois. The gurl Buffy is complemented by Kendra, a 17-year-old Slayer who appears on the scene to replace Buffy after her temporary "death" and resurrection in the first season at the hands of the Master. Speaking with a Jamaican patois, she is obviously meant to represent non-white identification and to raise questions concerning belief in the occult and spirit world. Her "primitiveness" reaches back to vampire lore (McClelland 1999). Kendra's racial implications have been explored by Edwards (2002), who argues that she presents the tragic myth of the mulatta woman. Belonging to neither black nor white, her fair skin makes her "a symbol of miscegenation by white fathers and hypersexuality for white lovers[;] her existence threatens both ancestral and descendent purity for white women" (88). For Edwards, Kendra's quest for "legitimacy as a slayer is denied because of the threat she poses to Buffy's identity as the slayer and to Buffy's relationships with her lover (Angel) and her father figure (Giles)" (90).

Kendra doesn't last long in the series. She was introduced in the second season and shortly dispatched by Drucilla (Spike's flame) in the second to the last episode (2021, "Becoming, Part One"). Kendra is a representative, in my view, of the Virgin strategy, which perverts patriarchy by wanting to restate the exact "letter of the Law."[27] She has been "chosen." Her parents literally give her up to be raised by her Watcher, Sam Zabuto, in a very strict way. In her case, patriarchy needs no propping up. Kendra has learned to control her emotions, "The Slayer Handbook" providing her with all the necessary rules of engagement. One immediately thinks here of the ritual of becoming a nun to serve God's greater Cause; or of being inducted into some formal organization where the Rules form the Creed; and of the obvious associations with occult belief, and with references to the Chosen Child as the reincarnated Dalai Lama. There is also the Rule Girls' moral handbook that this could allude to. Such intertextualities enable multiple readings.

For Buffy, Kendra is an impossible Ego Ideal—non-white and chaste, an unattainable subject position to occupy. (Buffy calls her "stuck in the '80s.") Her non-white, mulatto coding also helps problematize the imaginary signifier /black/, which is always associated with Evil. Kendra does things "by the book"—that is, she is bound by the letter of the Law as stated in "The Slayer's Handbook." Such rigid training was not good enough for her to have survived. (Edwards (2002) reads her "death" as being a result of her assimilation into Buffy's culture.) Buffy, on the other hand, did not even know that such a book existed. She goes by her feelings and not just by logic. For Kendra "sleeping with the enemy" (as Buffy does with Angel) is strictly forbidden. It is the one warning she has for Buffy—not to sleep with a vampire. She remains a chaste virgin. Kendra presents a strictly formalist moral strategy of Rules. I take "Mr. Pointy," her stake that she left for Buffy when she died at the hands of Drucilla, to be Joss's pun on virginity, and perhaps on race relations as well. It was white (or did I hallucinate this?). Drucilla killed Kendra for good reason. Kendra was Drucilla's inversion—her demon, everything Drucilla hated in herself. Drucilla was a chaste nineteenth-century girl who was to become a nun, the bride of Christ; instead, she became Spike's sadistic sex partner. The playful punning is obvious.

Kendra was then replaced by Faith, yet another slayer who is easily identified as a Sadeian woman, the Slayerslut who just loves the erotics that come with violence. She even makes a "growl" noise when she fights; she is a warrior at heart, equal to any man, and is indeed a grrrl. She goes about seducing Giles and Riley. As to be expected, Buffy's relationship to Faith is as oppositional as it was to Kendra, and Kendra's virginity is at odds with Faith's sluttiness. Faith is the *extimate*[28] inversion of what Buffy is trying to control within herself; namely, her sexual drive personified—to use the pop-psychology of *Star Wars*, her "dark side." Faith is Buffy's death drive personified. It seems as though Whedon went out of his way to make this as obvious as possible. In episode 4016 ("Who Are You"), Faith actually "embodies" Buffy (takes over her soul and possesses her as "pure" drive—as *zoë* or *life* itself). Buffy becomes Faith, and Faith becomes Buffy, with a slugfest at the end for each to get their own body's back. Significantly, Faith is white, the inversion of the signifier /white/ as representative of this "dark force." Such a *femme fatale* appears in video games as "Johanna Dark," and in the short-lived Fox series *Dark Angel*, where her vamp eroticization has been worked out as a hybridic cross between Buffy and Faith in the twenty-something figure of Jessica Alba, who also problematizes the black/white skin distinction by being mulatto.

When Faith and Buffy go at each other (Buffy calls her a "criminally insane woman" while she calls Buffy "Little Miss Goody-Two-Shoes"), they are talking to each other's abject self. These oppositions are replayed over and over in various episodes. While Faith has some affinities to grrrl power,[29] she is placed on the Demon side, more as a Sadeian woman, a dominatrix/porn star, than in the ethical position of the grrrl rebellion. Faith ends up joining forces with the Major of Sunnydale and his mad plot of Ascension (eventually Faith, as the name suggests, is given a redemptive chance on the series *Angel*). The "better" grrrl representative, in my view, is surprisingly Willow, the Wicca witch. Willow embodies grrrl rebellion with her brilliance, nerdy smarts, and computer skills; with her more "boyish" figure; desexualized, androgynous look; preference for pinks, reds, and purples in clothes; and an ambiguous lesbian identity. Grrrl rebellion was also a rich mixture of heterosexual and lesbian youth, so Faith can still be considered here as well. The lesbian Wicca is also a space for exploring lesbian identity as a protection from the Symbolic Order (Winslade 2000). As Buffy's best friend, she is also her inversion: Buffy is erotic, while Willow is not; Buffy is at times mentally challenged at school; Willow is brilliant; Buffy has power and self-esteem, while Willow struggles to gain it through her witchcraft practices, and so on. She could also be a candidate for Joss Whedon's alter ego in drag. As a Slayerette, Willow is also decentered by three subjectivities as is Buffy. Anya is Willow's abject self. She calls her a "thousand-year-old capitalist ex-demon with rabbit phobia." Translation: a reformed bad girl who is off drugs but into consumerism. Tara is her Ego Ideal because of her experience, witch powers, and disposition, and of course, by Buffy as well.

Willow and Tara's relationship can also be interpreted as a straight-lesbian one. Perhaps this is why some lesbian critiques of the Willow/Tara coupling find their relationship improbable. Farah Mendlesohn (2002, 58–60) makes the point that both Willow and Tara are desexualized. The scenes between then are de-eroticized. Eventually Willow and Tara split up (6007, "Tabula Rasa"). But when Tara dies by a bullet meant for Buffy (fired by Super-Villain/Nerd Warren), Willow faces her own death drive in the form of revenge. She can no longer sublimate her drives through her magic; the magic has taken over. Willow was always on the edge of disaster with her attempts at magic, spells, and potions. She decided to give up on magic when she realized she was addicted to it. The death of Tara, however, was too much to bear. Her witchcraft overpowers her, as all her partial drives come together, and her death drive takes over.[30] This is presented in an amazing scene where the knowledge of a hundred magic books is absorbed through Willow's skin-ego, the potent poisoned blackness of the ink seeps through her fingers and flows up to the top of her head, concentrating itself in her eyes, which have now become unfathomable ebony pools, as a death mask appears. Becoming all-powerful and Evil, bent to destroy the world and her friends with it defines the conclusion of season six (6021, "Grave"). Xander is her best friend, and only his love for her is able to stop her rampage. These episodes show that Tara was always Willow's inversion. If it wasn't for Tara's sensibility and gentleness as Willow's Ego ideal, Willow might have spun out of control much earlier. In episode 3016 ("Doppelgängland"), she became temporarily a bisexual vampire seductress in leather pants and bustier, a recognition of her own lesbian desires. In episode 3009 ("The Wish"), as a vampire, Willow performs an act of sadomasochistic sexualized torture on Angel. In these episodes she "acts out" her unconscious desires. In season seven (7003, "Same Time, Same Place"), Willow disappears, making herself invisible to friends. Her magic addiction can be read bulimically, as bingeing (excessive magic in season six) and vomiting (disappearing in season seven). The addiction to witchcraft is too difficult to properly maintain, since it is the one key trait (*enizige Zug*) that she believes defines her more than any other. It is her *sinthome*. Unhinging it unhinges her entire existence, which is precisely what happened.

Finaly, Buffy's 15-year-old sister, who is appropriately named Dawn, "shows up" in season five. Perhaps she is a figment of Buffy's imagination, as is ambiguously demonstrated in episode 6017 ("Normal Again"). Dawn is a character that I would identify as a gurlie (younger gurl) in a gurlie-gurl interval. Dawn is given such names as Little Bit, Bitty Buffy, Tiny Snapdragon, and Bite-sized one. She is literally "The Key" in the fight with a *femme-fatale* demon, Glory, in season five, as if the fate of her soul was in balance, a metaphor for the upcoming Y Generation.

All these webs of inversions among the girls/gurlies/gurls/grrrls, lesbian and androgynous drags, and Sadeian women could be fruitfully explored through the logic and antilogic of a Greimasian semiotic square,[31] as could the positioning of boys/boyz/bois, and Sadeian men, with Buffy as a gay in drag. Slash fanfics explore yet other "missing" impossible relationships, such as Angel/Spike and Anya/Tara. When all three girls/gurls/grrrls come together, they register a complaint on all three fronts of Lacan's psychic registers. The girl addresses the virginity of the patriarchal system in its Lawful state (Kendra). The gurl plays with the Imaginary, established identifications of teens, a hysterical position (Buffy), while the grrrl explores the desires of the Real that have been excluded from the Law itself (Faith and Willow). Yet, only Buffy is forwarded and discussed as an exemplar of postfemininity (Early 2001). While such a structural maze—complex but not rhizomatic—offers an array of identifications, one would think that its Southern California location would not travel well to other countries. But, as mentioned, the success of the series speaks to youth in many other postindustrial countries. As a partial list, we might point out the following themes picked at random (see also Bloustein 2002, 438):

Balancing dating with responsibilities (1005, "Never Kill a Boy on His First Date"); teen insecurities (1010, "Nightmares"); date rape (1006, "The Pack"); domestic violence (2019, "I Only Have Eyes for You"; 2011, "Ted"; 3004, "Beauty and the Beast"); street kids and homelessness (3001, "Anne"); crippling parental/adult pressure and expectations (1003, "Witch"; 2020, "Go Fish"; 1010, "Nightmares"); Internet predator (demon Moloch) (1008, "I Robot, You Jane"); fraternity dangers (2005, "Reptile Boy"); childhood illness, death, and trauma (2018, "Killed by Death"; 5016, "The Body" and 5017,"Forever"); drug addiction (6009, "Wrecked"); family breakup (1010, "Nightmares"); first sexual encounter (with Angel) (2013, "Surprise"; 2014, "Innocence"); irrational parental fears (3011, MOO, Mothers Opposed to the Occult in "Gingerbread").

There is perhaps another reason why the Buffyverse is fascinating for an intergenerational audience, and that has to do with its particular soteriology that disturbs and interrupts the hegemony of the Christian church, offering something different from the quasi-religions of the New Age such as Falun Gong from China, Spiritual Human Yoga from Vietnam, Dahnhal from Korea, Reiki (a *ki*-based Japanese therapeutic system using Buddhist symbols), and Qi-based well-being systems, which are Tao based. These new personal religions, which radicalize the meaning of God, are also sought out on an intergenerational scale as a search for a new ontological myth. The Buffyverse taps into this "longing" (*algia*), and raises aspects of Gnostic knowledge that have found enthusiasts in ecofeminist movements and in philosophy, such as Morris Berman's *Reenchantment of the World* (1981), but it does more than this, as I shall show in the next chapter.

8

The Buffyverse Soteriology: Youth's Garden of Earthly Delights

Hieronymus Bosch's *The Garden of Earthly Delights* (ca. 1504, central panel, Figure 8.1) presents a vision of Hell—a place where the psyche suffers—characterized by excesses of bodily addictions, *jouissance*, and the drives. Metaphorically, it already distances us from the "horrors and delights" of the virtual Real, a place where the division of human beings and nature has yet to be formed, D+G's immanent plane of flows and intensities; nonstratified, unformed intense matter, where both the animate and inanimate, the artificial and the natural come together. This unformed and fluid plane of nature (or BwO) is simply a function of varying its speed and slowness, movement and rest, and intensities within a single physical system. Both the Imaginary and Symbolic psychic orders, as "abstract machines of stratification" (to continue to use D+G's language), protect us from its worst manifestations. As Bosch's paradoxical title suggests, the delights and horrors that emerge from it, seemingly through autopoietic processes, are intimately enfolded within one another: Heaven and Hell are not dichotomies; rather, they are braided together in complicitous and complex ways, like demand and desire, as intertwining toruses (doughnuts). Bosch's painting seems to be a perfect metaphor for the "Hellmouth," the portal through which the demonic forces gain entry to Buffy's Sunnydale.

In 1958, a Harvard art historian, Clive Bell, wrote an important thesis, by now long forgotten, explaining why pagan gargoyles—strategically placed on Gothic cathedrals to remind the faithful that the Church was to protect them from such horrors—began to disappear as the Enlightenment proceeded from its natural theological beginnings to secular forms of rationalism. More recently, Robert Romanyshyn, in his interesting book *Technology as Symptom and Dream* (1989), makes the same claim. Such irrational forces seemed to visually vanish as rationality eventually became an internalized ideology as modernism progressed. Goya's famous etching *The Sleep of Reason Produces Monsters* (1797–98), subtitled *Imagination abandoned by reason produces impossible monsters*, and Foucault's (1965) important study *Madness and Civilization: A History of Insanity in the Age*

Figure 8.1   Hieronymus Bosch, *The Garden of Earthly Delights, central panel*

of Reason are two further historical markers that indicate how our hellish "monsters and demons" have been locked away from sight so that the road to rational secularization could continue. The basement, underground, or cellar—all the metaphorical names Freud and his followers provided for the unconscious struggles with the drives—have yet again come out in the open, working themselves out in music, computer games, television, cinema, and other art forms in various ways. Documenta 11 (8.6–15.9, 2002), the renown postwar art exhibition, held in Kassel, Germany every five years for one hundred days, made this abundantly clear, as many artists presented paranoid states of existence concerning the postcolonial condition and the failures of democracy.

It was Lacan who tried to show that such "monsters" were not repressed in some gothic basement, but could be seen functioning in everyday life through his structural attempts at explaining neurosis (hysteria, obsession, phobia), psychosis, and perversion. These are not states of "madness" as much as they are attempts at living with the contradictions between unconscious and conscious life shaped by the relationship of *jouissance* to the Law of the Symbolic Order. *Buffy*'s narrative is one brilliant form by which to display these contradictions between impossible masculine and feminine relationships that youth grapple with in a post-Oedipalized world. Episode 6017 ("Normal Again") is conscious Heaven rather than the unconscious suffering of Hell. The world of magic, as littered throughout the video game landscape, television, and films, manifests an unconscious search to rethink a new transcendent myth to live by, which would transform the postmodern malaise, where both melancholia and mourning are entwined as *algia* and *nostros*. Rudolf and Margot Wittkowers' study *Born under Saturn* (1963) pointed to the same malaise that prevailed as the Copernican Revolution swept through the intelligentsia. Some artists and writers were unable to make the transition to the new ontology. *Buffy* is definitely on the side of *algia* in its attempts to deal with the Real of postmodern transition.

There have been few filmic narrative structures that have opened a porthole into the unconscious as effectively as *Buffy* does to explore ethical implications of the Real. The most brilliant of these have been time-image films like Taylor Hackford's *Devil's Advocate* (1997) that stage the journey into the unconscious through Lacan's mirror stage as a misrecognition between one's ideal ego [i(o)], how you want to be seen, and the Ego Ideal [I(O)]—how the social order sees you. In *Devil's Advocate*, Lomax, a lawyer who has never lost a case, faces his first possible defeat. During a pause in the trial, he walks into the men's washroom and stares at himself in the mirror. The camera lens voyeuristically penetrates the darkness of one of his pupils through a telescopic zoomed close-up, and we are immediately propelled back to the courtroom as the trial resumes. Cinematically, there has been no cut in the action. It is only much later that we find out that the ethical decision that Lomax must make in the court trial has been suspended as he struggles "within" his unconscious Real with the Devil—John Milton—as to what action he should take. Toward the end of the narrative, the camera zooms back from his pupil, and Lomax is once more facing himself in the mirror, ready to enact his decision (jagodzinski 2001). The port(w)hole to the unconscious is also humorously developed in Spike Jonze's *Being John Malkovich* (1999) as a crawl space that exists on a nonexistent half-floor of a building. There is also Vincent Ward's *What Dreams May Come*, which charts Chris Nielson's journey in an imaginary heaven to find his two children, and then into hell to "awaken" his wife, Sciorra, who has committed suicide, bereaved of her family: her two children killed in a car accident, followed a few years later by Chris who dies in a car accident as well.

Assuming that the Buffyverse is an exploration of the unconscious—its horrors as delights and delights as its horrors—what gives Buffy her power if authority has been suspended? What saves Buffy's schizophrenic, psychotic narrative from simply being the pathology of a narcissistic, grandiose, paranoid ideation? Buffy is egomaniacally positioned at the center of conspiracies and intrigues of a colossal magnitude, like Freud's Judge Daniel Paul Schreber. Her stories of vampires and demons are simply delusions on the grandest of scales. What saves Buffy's psychosis is an "Ethics of the Real" (Zupančič 2000; Jaaus 1997), for within such an ethics lies the heart of self-refleXive thought. As the ONE, in her singularity, undecidability, and urgency, as Jacques Derrida[1] puts it regarding the difficulty of justice, she practices a form of "responsible anarchy," if it can be put this way. Not only do the episodes deal with a host of youth dilemmas, *A Garden of Earthly Delights* with its Sadeian traps, but it is also the way she deals with them that is so powerful.

Buffy is suspended in a space between her call of Nature and the Law, the Sophoclean story where woman defies the law of man (patriarchy) and submits to Divine Justice. She is wedged between the Council of Watchers (Symbolic Order), who have a Scriptural Divine Law as represented by Giles's library, and a realm of Nature that is always "beyond" them, existing in a dimension that is out of reach of rules and the imagination. I would go further and maintain that Nature here is not transcendental in its reach for utopian possibilities. Rather, as Nature, she brings the issues back to Earth. This "fall" is in the direction of Spinoza, Schlegel, and the Stoic tradition, all Deleuzian influences, where divine Nature becomes an immanent god. Pushed further, material Nature becomes a force moving itself, an intelligence in matter, but that does not allow an escape from judgment. We find ourselves on a plane "between Heaven and Earth," a place where *jouissance* flows freely between them, bringing us painful pleasures and pleasurable pains—the joys as well as the sorrows. Buffy has to mediate these two forces through her actions. But, ultimately, the decision rests on her shoulders as a "free," ethical act.

Her entitlement to Nature; that is to say her chthonic powers of the Earth's energy as sacred "natural life" (*zoë*) is inexplicable and out of the reach of the Symbolic Order (institutions, rules, science, Law). She must work out an ethics of the Real, which is always beyond the Law's reach, mediated by the entwinement of Eros and Thanatos. Justice is always beyond rules, and ethics is the negotiation of this "beyond" of the rules. This is precisely why the *Triebe* exist in the enfolded space/time between biological Nature and symbolic Culture. Ethics is always a preontological question. Its questions are always open-ended; its value structures always come after the fact, after the decision has been made. Lacan's discussion of *Antigone* (S VII, *Ethics*) is the exemplar here. Antigone becomes a numinous object by being sublimated and raised to the dignity of *das Ding* for the deed that she does. That is to say, some ordinary object or deed has been elevated to an unconditional position that is valued as life (*zoë*) itself. Her splendor and grace come from an ethical stance against the laws of Creon. Her "madness" (*até*) to obey a higher Law of Nature (*zoë*) meant burying her brother Polyneices despite his offenses against the state. Creon wanted his soul to perpetually suffer in anguish. His burial would raise questions about the weakness of his own rule. But Antigone's sacrifice as an "act" meant her own death. But, through this "act," the very foundation of morals as to what was dichotomously Good and Evil came to be questioned. In the end, Creon is devastated and alone. All his loved ones have committed suicide because of his fixation (Freud's *Fixierarbeit*), his obsession with and on the rules.

To commit an act in Lacan's sense is to change the very orientation of the Symbolic Order, seemingly an impossible task. It is a metaethical act. We have only to think of the founders of (patriarchal) world religions of the "Axial Age"

(*Achsenzeit*) (ca. 800–200 BCE), as Karl Jaspers (1953) called it—Socrates, Confucius, Zoroaster, Lao Tzu, Buddha, Moses, Jesus, and Muhammad, as the founders of Confucianism, Zoroastrianism, Taoism, Hinduism, Buddhism, Judaism, Christianity, and Islam—to see what's at stake (sorry, couldn't be helped!). The Buffyverse revisits the transition of matrilineal to patrilineal family structures. She is the "Numinous Slayer with a Thousand Faces," to echo Joseph Campbell. Buffy goes all the way back to the first slayer—Sineya (4022, "Restless") as the primordial *das Ding*, the Mother, the ONE, in Hegelian terms: the paradox of the genus that contains its opposite—man,[2] where Zero is counted as ONE, the womb as Nothing which already has Something. Creation demands an imbalance of the situation from the start.

The Doubled Road of Ethics

There are two ways in which the seemingly innocuous and frivolous Buffyverse addresses self-refleXivity as an ethics of the virtual Real. The first I would call a Deleuzian solution, where the difference inside us, what is strange within us, is addressed as becoming-animal[3] in D+G's terms, a return to nature where the perspective on life shifts from seeing oneself as an ego (*moi*) to seeing oneself as a flow (*flux*), "a set of flows in relation with other flows, outside oneself and within oneself" (Deleuze 1997, 51). Such flow extends to the life of flux and nonorganic life as orientated to the soul (*l'âme*). Such an ethics means decentering the egoic self, coming to terms with its misrecognitions in Lacan's terms, and extending oneself to the nonhuman and inhuman alike, the "beasts" that dwell throughout the Buffyverse, as animal-machines that every living creature is, subject to DNA reinsciption leading to genetic miscalculations and code errors.[4] "What is individual is the relation; it is the soul and not the ego. The ego has a tendency to identify itself with the world, but it is already dead, whereas the soul extends the thread of its living *sympathies* and *antipathies* (51, added emphasis). The soul is directly tied to the virtual Real. "The soul as the life of flows is the will to live, struggle and combat" (52). I take Deleuze's notion of the soul as a key to an ethics of difference that the Buffyverse demonstrates, as I hope to show. It is a combat with difference that is at stake (I'm letting the pun stand). Deleuze compares combat to war; war being a general annihilation that requires the participation of the ego, whereas combat rejects war. It is the conquest of the soul. "The inalienable part of the soul appears when one has ceased to be an ego; it is this eminently flowing, vibrating, struggling part that has to be conquered" (52).

The second is Lacan's ethical "act" as staged by Buffy, which, as was true in the case of Antigone, has consequences for the Symbolic Order. In Alenka Zupančič's (2000, 249–59) formulation, the ethics of the Real is an "abyssal realization of desire." To break with the premodernist Master/Slave dialectic, where Honor (as Cause) cannot be surrendered, requires rethinking the drive toward Liberty (as Cause). The former is an "ethics of the Master" where the code "better death than dishonor" makes honor the one exception that one is willing to sacrifice one's life for—or anything else for that matter—in order to save face. Heroically, the slave tries to elevate him/herself as a Master. It is an either/or proposition—death or honor. The modernist version, "liberty or death," leads to the paradox where you die, but you have achieved your freedom, with the possibility that the Symbolic Order has changed as well, as during political revolutions. Choice, however, can be dictated by a different logic—neither/nor. "Liberty or death" can be inverted to "neither liberty nor death." The Slave reframes the context of opposition to the Master. This presents the option of sacrificing the Cause itself—be it liberty, honor, or anything else. Death, in this case, may be symbolic in the sense that there is no place in the symbolic order for the Slave. However, freedom is retained and death is avoided! This is an antiheroic position. It seems the act that seals Antigone's fate embodies both possibilities.

In order to explore these two possibilities, we begin with the "mythological," neopagan soteriology presented by Giles:

> This world is older than any of you know, and contrary to popular mythology, it did not begin as a paradise. For untold eons, demons walked the Earth, made it their home, their Hell. In time, they lost their purchase of this reality, and the way was made for mortal animals. For Man. What remains of the Old Ones are vestiges: certain magicks [sic], certain creatures . . . The books tell that the last demon to leave this reality fed off a human, mixed their blood. He was a human form possessed—infected by the demon's soul. He bit another and another . . . and so they walk the Earth, feeding. Killing some, mixing their blood with others to make more of their kind. Waiting for the animals to die and the Old Ones to return (1002, "Harvest"; Golden and Holder 1998, 126).

This mythological tale identifies what Immanuel Kant, a pious Protestant, was unable to adequately explain—namely radical evil, which is repressed so that he may define a universal notion of the Good based on a dutiful vigilance to a "categorical imperative" that rationally universalized good behavior. The question of "diabolical or radical Evil" (the Old Ones) eluded him (Žižek 1993, 83–84). Subjectivity in the Buffyverse myth is already tainted with Evil, but in an ambiguous sense. The usual understanding of Evil as being in opposition to the Good is deconstructed. "Feeding off a human mixed their blood" (the vampire) has several resonances. The first is a matter of survival, while the second is the sense of ushering in the Good in the form of what is distinctly "human." While a third is the coming together of difference itself—as nonhuman with human, a becoming-animal.

From the Deleuzian perspective, death and becoming have a particular relationship to the BwO. It is very close to Lacan's reinterpretation of Freud's death-drive[5] that Slavoj Žižek (2004d) follows—as that which is "beyond" life and death. It is "the terrifying insistence of an undead object." Something is "dead," but it still manages to go on. In other words, we are dealing with a kind of life force that is oddly named, for it has nothing to do with the usual misinterpretation as only being destructive. Willow's magic out of control in season six was her death drive, but this is still an intensity animated by life. This is precisely D+G's formulation as well when they write, "Catatonic schizophrenia [. . .] gives its model to death. Zero intensity" (329). In other words, the catatonic patient will attempt to mobilize and reanimate other parts of the body where possible. As they say, "The body without organs is the model of death" (329). Authors of horror stories know this. We have only to think of all those zombie films as examples of such "living death." They continue to move as best they can, although they are "dead." So it seems absurd to place Thanatos (death) in opposition to Eros (life), the death drive in opposition to the life drive. Their solution, as it is Lacan's as well, is to theorize the death drive as animating life. Deleuze enfolds Thanatos (death drive) within Eros (life drive) to make the "experience of death" that which structures the psyche; as in Lacan, it becomes a "driving" force (hence, the need for a forgetting to allow for change, thought of as the physicality of dying brain cells). As D+G put it, "The experience of death is the most common of occurrences in the unconscious, precisely because it occurs in life and for life, in every passage or becoming, in every intensity as passage or becoming" (330). "Experiencing death" is precisely becoming. It opens up transformative potentialities.

The death drive in this formulation oddly enough becomes a form of Eros, but with significant questions surrounding its occurrence. As the positive orientating principle of repetition, it is also demonic. There is something compelling as well as horrifying about the way it can derail us, take us over, and here we are again in the realm of *jouissance* and the Buffyverse. As Žižek (1993) puts it, "Evil is another name for the 'death-drive,' for the fixation on some Thing which derails our customary life-circuit. By way of Evil, man [sic] wrests himself from animal instinctual rhythm, i.e., Evil introduces the radical reversal of the 'natural' relationship" (96). This is rather a startling reversal of our usual way of thinking of Evil. What is that "natural relationship"? From a Kantian humanist perspective, Evil is a question of conscious subjective (ego) choice. Through "reason" one can subordinate one's own "pathological" nature, or "original sin," and follow one's moral duty. Here, something more radical is being proposed: "Survival" itself becomes ambiguous. An act of radical Evil may result in suicide that may be indistinguishable ethically from the Good. Young Palestinian men and women in their teens and early twenties acting as suicide bombers embody such a deadlock position where Evil suspends the Law of the Good. Evil/Good become reversible terms depending on which side of the Israeli/Palestinian wall you are on. Such activity is "pathological" when taken in the Kantian sense. This is an act that runs counter to egotistical interests, and believes in a Cause that does not yet even exist. Each martyr believes he or she will change the symbolic order through his or her act, and make a qualifiable difference.

It seems an imbalance is required to jump-start things. The primary choice is not between Good and Evil; rather, it is either yielding to one's "pathological" leanings or choosing radical Evil as a mode of becoming. Paradoxically, in this view Evil ushers in the Good. Evil is put in the service of facing "subjective destitution," a metaphorical "death" of one's ego; to allow the fantasy frame that holds it to shatter so as to inwardly face the "pathology" inside when confronted by the "face" of the Other (cf. Emmanuel Levinas[6]). But, how far can this be taken? An ethical act must respond to the alterity in the Other; that is, one has to respond to what is absolutely unknown in the Other as well as to the alterity within one's self. It means to invent a new rule out of the singularity of the situation. Put another way, we are all capable of being vampires. An ethics of the Real analyzes the unconsciously accepted and willed anxiety of a subject who confronts pain, destruction, and even death in the name of desire. When such an ethics of the Real is called into play, the notion of Good versus Evil as opposites begins to be deconstructed to work out justice, which always lies "beyond" the Law—a Derridean position where the face of the Other must now disappear so that a third position (the new law) can mediate the two positions. So there is a limit, a resolution, but we do not know what it is—as yet. This ethico-political decision always has to do with "difference," with what is unknown (*objet a*), the very alterity of a person— what makes a person unique and singular, but also unknowably monstrous. Stretching Deleuze, this means combating the alterity within the soul in order to allow for "becoming" to take place. This is why for Deleuze (1993), Leibnitz's notion of a monad becomes "the entire world enclosed in a soul" (24). The entire world is inflected in the folds of its walls, and it is here that the combat takes place as a form of self-refleXivity.

In contrast to the above position, since the Renaissance, ethics (be it Christian or atheist) has been centered on the "human" side of our potential pathologies, especially "human" coexistence. Such an ethics of the Imaginary, like that of Kant, always has the neighbor in mind, as the commonsense notion of "love thy neighbor as thyself." Nietzsche, in his *On The Genealogy of Morals* (1994), showed that such an ethics ends in mastery and appropriation, since the neighbor ultimately becomes judged in relation to oneself. We treat the Other like we treat ourselves. What appears as an obviously fair and just system hides an injustice. Our neighbor's difference is appropriated in the name of sameness. Forms of postmodern racism arise through well-intentioned ethnographies that stem from the same ethic. We are inquisitive of the Other to the degree that the Other is the same as us. Once difference as *objet a* is confronted, the Other turns ugly and hideous, or its opposite—exotic. The imaginary self, characterized by aggressivity, narcissism, and paranoia when threatened, is unaccounted for in such "conscious" imaginary ethics.[7] In the Buffyverse, the character of Cordelia intentionally exemplifies such an abjection of the neighbor. Cordelia is so insecure that she is unable to gain any distance from her Ideal Ego to even begin to accept difference. We disavow what is "strange" within us so that the neighbor can remain "like" us. The Buffyverse, on the other hand, always attempts to deal with this difference of strangeness through the inversions of characters that are presented throughout the series. This difference is always beyond the human, presented as monstrous alterity. This difference or strangeness within us is what Lacan identified as *das Ding*. It is our deepest "affective law" in the sense of our relation to *jouissance*, the way we enjoy. It structures our deepest relationship to reality as to what we believe or do not believe about the world. It provides us with faith, which is why the slayer Faith as Buffy's Thing is so terrifying for her. She embodies all that Buffy rejects, or struggles to reject. Faith can be thought of as another intensity, another world, and the power of another order.

Beneath the neighbor as my semblant—my mirror image of sameness—lurks the abyss of unfathomable radical Otherness. It is this unnamable alterity that turns him or her into a monstrous Thing—a vampire, a demon, at the same time also a person to love. The unknowable *objet a* is what can make the neighbor a terrifying beast if he or she comes too "close" to me, threatening the Real core that defines me. The Buffyverse always brings these anxieties of difference to the fore, such as the forbidden love between women, between demon and human, between Slayer and vampire. When we address the Other, we always address this alterity—his or her unknowability, but we can never do so directly. It is always mediated by the Symbolic Order. An ethics of the Real asks that we temporarily suspend that Symbolic Order so that the Other as friend/foe might be approached. That is, to extend our "hospitality" as Derrida (1997) has discussed in his book on the politics of friendship. In *Buffy* I have argued that the Symbolic Order has been suspended. In Sunnydale, the friendly neighbor has already become the monstrous Thing. If it weren't for the band of friends (Giles, Xander, Willow, Buffy), the Symbolic Order itself would become monstrous and would eat them up.[8]

In episode 6017 ("Normal Again"), Buffy returns to her friends. Together they are a multiple of ONE. And, the question is to what extent is this multiple, band or "pack" in D+G's (1987, tenth plateau) sense, enabled to becoming-animal by Buffy as their "anomalous individual?" Such an individual is the "animal" in the pack that is situated at its very borders and thus defines its territory. The status of this individual is unknown. D+G say that this individual could be in the pack, on its border, or outside it, and that it could have even left the pack and be traveling alone. Wherever its location, the anomalous individual is to carry "the transformations of becoming or crossing of multiplicities always further down the line of flight" (243–45). Such an individual is always drawing the pack away from stratification toward a zone of new potentials of relating and becoming. A line of flight emerges within this zone as a "block" of becoming, as previous categories dissipate into a hybridic minoritarian position that is politically charged because it challenges the dominant.

To enter that zone is a self-refleXive move. To expand life beyond our limited perspectives is an ethical move of the body. Ethics is tied to its limits and capacities. The Spinozian influence of D+G manifests itself in coming to know what the body can do; what its potential is for interacting with other bodies; whether this interaction is harmful to either body; and whether there is the potential for exchange, a joining together to form a still stronger body. Such are the questions that surround their ethics. "Beyond" humanist ethics lie the death drive, the inhuman (or non-human), and the Real ethics of the unconscious. The Scooby Gang engages in passionate associations with the inhuman element (of abjectness and difference). This inhuman youth culture is the site of drives, illicit desires, and the complexities of sexuality, all of which find their fullest tensions in these seemingly unnatural unions. Buffy does not immediately engage in categorizations of good and evil, and when she does, the episodes always resolve her ethical misjudgment concerning an abject Other. The discrimination against werewolves could be considered a form of bigotry (Oz and Willow), while the elevation of what is defined as "human" can easily fall into a form of fascism.

The human/monster divide that establishes difference is always being problematized in *Buffy*. It is a boundary that is compromised at every turn: from Buffy's love for the vampire Angel to her relationship with the vampire-cyborg

Spike. Buffy's way of knowing is a highly mediated one, dependent on a range of personal motivations, demon motivations, and calls of conscience, exemplifying, in my reading at least, a self-refleXive ethical position. The Buffyverse is able to present a different psychic reality from the dominant social fiction precisely by presenting a psychotic delusion that allows for ethical questions to emerge that deal with difference and not morals (good vs. evil). It is an ethics that necessarily includes the difficult question of radical or diabolical evil.

The *Buffy* narrative places the virtual Real, not as a separate underworld category of unconscious madness, but rather as Lacan did, as effects that are found in everyday life. They exemplify Freud's notion of the uncanny (*unheimlich*), being both strange and at home at once. The Hellmouth is the site/sight/cite[9] of Sunnydale, and visa versa. Grace and spiritual pain are coterminal. Light and dark become a Twilight zone between two deaths. The drives have their own cycles that are not subject to the biological rhythms of day and night. This is the strength of the Buffyverse narrative. The loving relationships of friends in the conscious world are tied to the unconscious world as well. To work out the problems of the unconscious Real does not require a pharmacy of drugs as much as it does the love of close friendships. Buffy, Willow, and Xander live out a Lacaninan ethical maxim that says, "Do not cede to your [pure] desire." Do not be caught by your *jouissance* that blinds your desire. They will not go to any length to avoid being called a "looser"; they endure the mockery that comes with pursuing what they see as right. They take responsibility for their friends. But all this can still be left at the imaginary level. They go further, facing and recognizing differences that sit at the heart of their own anxieties and those of one another. The friendship of the Scooby Gang demonstrates what it means to live with the other's difference, with their impossible Thing or "Monster," or inhuman partner. When Willow is bent on destruction (end of season six), it is Xander's friendship (since elementary school) and his love for her that make her stop her witchcraft frenzy.

An Ethical Act Proper

The first self-refleXive strategy of an ethics of the Real emerges in each episode when a character confronts his or her personal demon—the alien within us as different and monstrous, an Other-as-Self existing in the "extimate" space of inner outer or outer inner. The Demon in each character, as the Real self of the unconscious, means that each is capable of an act of radical Evil. Demon is very close to the Greek diamon, meaning the soul of the person, harking back to the Deleuzian influence of my reading, but also Lacanian in that the *objet a* is the unknowable part of each one of us. We are all capable of radical acts of evil, as well as radical acts of sacrifice for others. As an ethics of the Real, each character is presented with his or her abject difference that he or she must cope with as their demon-lover. I have discussed several of these already: Buffy must face Faith and Spike, Willow must face Anya, and even the Watcher Giles has his demon. He was known as the "Ripper," a member of the dark cult Eyghon (2008, "Dark Age") before he left Oxford to work as the librarian. A "balanced" life when confronting demons (slaying) is of course impossible. As Freud put it, the battle is "interminable." There is only struggle with the love of friendship. The act of "slaying" is itself a traversal of the fantasy; the double meaning of the word—as both attraction and destruction—points to the fundamental defining features of ourselves: love/hate, Eros/Thanatos, human/ non-human, not as opposites of course, but as complicitous enfoldments.

The Real virtual self is ground zero, an abyss where there is an absence of Good—as yet. *Buffy* does not present a moral universe of good versus evil, while pop-psychology is useful only as it provides a recognition of the fact that the opposition of difference is only where ethics begins. The ambiguities of good and evil are tempered by the love and mutual care among friends; love for one another in difference, and confronting this difference. Loving what is "in" the Other "more" than him or her self, without appropriating it; accepting, at times, its monstrosity as well. It is appreciating the very "specialness" of the other person without destroying it, but also intervening as a friend when the Other needs support. To appropriate that specialness—that is, to "attain" it for one's own ends— is to become a vampire, to feed off the blood-*jouissance-objet a* of others. Marx characterized capitalism as being vampiric. Vampires need other people's souls to keep them alive, since they have no identities of their own. They "sire" other vampires, implying that they rape, commit incest, generate intergenerational confusion, and lure others into their clans (2003, "School Hard"). Metaphorically, they represent drug dealers and users, gang members, and abject school kids who fester with hate. Joss Whedon plays with the paradox of vampires and demons as beings far more "alive" than mere mortals because they are not mortified by the symbolic networks, but have been empowered by others.

The difference between a Vampire and a Demon, although never clarified in the Buffyverse, seems to form a scale of worse to worse yet, or "more worse." Everyone is already a nonhuman demon, a "stranger to ourselves," as Julia Kristeva (1991) put it. Everyone is capable of a pathologically selfish act. In *Buffy*, Good as the absence of Evil is not cast as some sort of Universal possibility; rather, it is the possibility of redemption that comes through friendship and love in its many forms that is forwarded. In a sense, the Buffyverse longs for a new religion in its original meaning of *re-legere*, as a new re-binding; what we take to be an ecumenical way of being together, a new "convivence" (Garfinkle 2002, 196). Relationships based on blood ties, marriage, and patrilineal kinship are given a backseat as the Scooby Gang hold on to one another and defend parental interference. For instance, Tara's father and brother want to take her away in episode 5006 ("Family"). She has been fed the lie that she was a demon just so she would remain subordinated to the family and do the housework. The Scooby Gang accepts adoption and the sudden appearance of "family" members (e.g., sister Dawn), which happens in contemporary blended families; they intervene when unhealthy relationship choices take place. Unlike the neoliberalist greed of the individual alone, where teamwork becomes a farce (Sennett 1998, 106–17), transformation remains personal, a unique achievement, but with the help of friends who remain loyal and compassionate and who see the "storm" through. They are band or pack; each Scooby member contributes their unique *objet a* to make the band function: Willow contributes "spiritus" (spirit), Xander contributes "animus" (heart), Giles contributes "sophus" (mind), and Buffy contributes "manus" (hand) (4021, "Primeval"). But, it is the hubris of each of their excessive passions that also gets them into trouble.

I come to the second ethical strategy of the Real, and only Buffy as the ONE slayer can fulfill it. While each character is capable of "traversing his or her own fantasy," a becoming that profoundly changes their lives because they are seeing the world differently, only Buffy can perform the "diabolical Act" as an ethical act. Giles, for example, is able to transverse the fantasy he has of the Council of Watchers. He leaves when their orthodoxy has been exposed. Tara comes to terms with her own demon and realizes she is complete in her humanity (perhaps that is why she is killed in episode 6019 ["Seeing Red"]; she has reached her goal). Faith embarks on her own journey in another parallel universe, the series *Angel*. Oz learns to control the werewolf inside him through yogic meditation; Willow recognizes that her addiction to witchcraft can get out of control and is profoundly changed by Xander; Xander gains self-respect, while Spike grapples with his vampirism, and so on. Yet, it is Buffy alone who shows that the death drive can lead to a radical Act that can change the Symbolic Order, redefining what is possible within the symbolically constructed social space. An "Act proper" is essentially a metaethical Act. It transvalues all previous standards of what is Good and Evil, and defines a new legal norm. In brief, it transforms the Symbolic Order (Žižek 2001, 152–73). It is an uncompromising Act. Buffy insists on "the future of an illusion," in Freud's sense. The splendor of her death drive is Buffy's resolve, her "unconditional insistence of a drive which is more real than reality itself" (167). Buffy exhibits the same "perseverance," responsibility, and commitment (Freud's *Haftbarkeit*) as Antigone (Copjec 1999).

Buffy's traversal through the most fundamental fantasy of the Symbolic Order is done on a seasonal basis as a metaphorical death, a sacrifice and redemption for a Cause—placed always in the grandiose sense of saving the "Earth" (symbolic of *zoë*) with all that such an apocalyptic gesture implies. This Cause is thus illusionary; it is pitted against Evil, but her Act itself is monstrous and Evil. Through her death, the "illusion" of the Cause seems possible. We need only think once again of the young Palestinian men and women whose own bodies become bombs because they believe that they are dying for a Cause and that there is no other way out. They refuse to accept the current ethico-political norm. Is this for honor or for liberty, or for both? Through their deaths, as tragic as they are, the ethics of the conflict are elevated in such an extreme, profound, and painful way. "Diabolical evil, the highest evil, is indistinguishable from the highest good, that they are nothing other than the definitions of an accomplished (ethical) act" (Zupančič 2000, 92).

Buffy, of course, is a fiction, but she stages the ethics of the death drive to its fullest level of accountability. It is her duty as a Slayer. Each time Buffy dies, metaphorically speaking, the Symbolic Order is redefined. The Council of Watchers is shaken up. In season one, according to their Book, she was to die. Yet, she rose again. At the end of season two (2020, "Becoming, Part Two"), Buffy once again faces her own death; this time it is a "choice without a choice" when it comes to her duty. Angel has become Angelus, the vampire that he was. As her first love, Angel has defined her fantasy frame—she loves him, and now she must commit her own Evil Act for a greater Good. She must sacrifice his life—at the very moment Angel gets his soul back—if Acathla is to be stopped from dominating the Earth. The moment she kills him, she has "killed" herself. There is no divided self, as Buffy's killing Angel coincides with killing Acathla as Thing. This is a "free Act" in its highest form. It rests completely on her shoulders.

To whom and to what does she sacrifice her life? Each season, the traversal of the fundamental fantasy is placed on one or more symptoms of postmodernity— the Big Bads. Like James Bond, the world is always at stake (there I go again!), issuing a series of different Masters: Buffy's defeat of the Vampire Master is the central issue of season one—how should we read such a Master? Could it be capitalism itself? The Master creates a plan wherein blood from victims is machine-drained through mass production for increased efficiency. Season two has her dealing with Spike and Angel/Angelus, raising issues of love and abuse. In season three, it's Mayor Richard Wilkins where questions surrounding fascistic power arise concerning his dream to Ascension as Olvikan to achieve immortality. In season four, the Big Bad is Adam the vampire-cyborg, who raises the question of world domination through technology. In season five, it is Glorificus. Buffy must struggle with Dawn and this femme fatale Demon, a transsexual (Ben/Glory) who wants just what the name indicates—glory—and to obtain it by collapsing all the existing dimensions with the "Key" (Dawn); in season six, it is (Dark) Willow, who becomes addicted to magic and is capable of dominating Nature so as to trigger an apocalypse. Season seven concludes with First Evil, an incorporeal entity that can assume the form of any person who has died. This entity cannot affect the world on a physical level; its power lies in its ability to deceive, torment, and manipulate others. First Evil claims to be the source and embodiment of all evil, in my interpretation throughout this chapter, the paradoxical nature of *jouissance* itself. With Willow's help, Buffy heroically leads an army of potential Slayers that defeats First Evil's army of Turok-Han vampires (722, "Chosen"), thus spreading communal female empowerment from Buffy to the symbolic "Slayers." For me *Buffy the Vampire Slayer* has been interpreted as dealing with the Death Drive— slaying the anxieties of postmodern youth by meeting them "dead" on and putting a stake through them, thus preserving the "future of an illusion."

Postscript

A friend discussing the relative scariness of horror movies on a trip to Bali some years ago named *Jaws* the scariest, while his Balinese acquaintance voted for *The Exorcist*. "How could that be," my friend asked, "when you lie surrounded by shark-invested waters?" "Oh, sharks," said the Balinese, flicking his hand dismissively. "Everyone knows sharks hardly ever eat a person. But possession by spirits—that happens all the time!" (Levine 2002, 221)

9/11 Addendum: Has the "Future of an Illusion" Collapsed?

When revising these two chapters that had been written some five years ago, my praise for Buffy's ethical stance crashed when I came across Helen Graham's (2007) article "Representations, Ideologies and Affects of a Newly Post-9/11

'Feminist Icon.'" It was a hard-hitting review of Buffy's "last days." When did our gurl go wrong? Had the "anomalous individual" stupidly led the Scooby pack into America's patriotic war and joined the molar forces of stratification on the War on Terror? Graham begins by pointing out that all the negative press about *Buffy* began after 9/11; more specifically, the criticism was directed at the last two episodes of season seven (7021, "End of Days" and 7022, "Chosen"). The last episode was "aired in the United States on May 20, 2003, two months to the day after the invasion of Iraq had begun" (10). The titles of the criticisms (mostly online) speak for themselves: "Buffy the U.N. Slayer" (Jonah Goldberg); "Buffy the Vampire Slayer Defines Terrorism" (Jonah Goldberg); "The 'Buffy Paradigm' Revisited: A Superhero and the War on Terror" (Phillips 2003); and my favorite, "'It's Bloody Brilliant!' The Undermining of Metanarrative Feminism in the Season Seven Arc Narrative of Buffy" (Spicer 2004).[10] What's going on here?

Graham begins by discussing the pleasure of viewing *Buffy* and refers to Lawrence Grossberg's (1997) gloss on its psychoanalytical use. He confines pleasure to a dualist straightjacket within a closed circuit: zero tension and discharge to maintain balance. This happens to be the fundamental structure of the drive (*Trieb*) mechanism. Fighting, as a signifier of empowerment (leadership, human possibility, and so on) would amount to an expenditure of intensity, starting from zero, which then grows or diminishes according to an infinite number of degrees. To fully satisfy this drive mechanism, to totally exhaust its expenditure of energy, requires the certainty of a utopian effect—namely, some sort of full and complete resolution (the so-called Nirvana effect). As Lacan (S XI, *Four Fundamentals*) maintained, the *jouissance* of the drive is sustained by the very aim of the drive, by its very repetition; even when the goal (utopian in Buffy's case) has not been achieved, satisfaction is still maintained. Fighting, I would say, is a metaphor for the drive itself. This drive mechanism, with its accompanying affect (*jouissance*), is consonant with the primary textual cycle of *Buffy*—as a tension between the plot's construction (narrative suspense) and its cathartic resolution, generally through violence and fighting. This structure, as Fredric Jameson (2003) maintains, characterizes postmodern consumer capitalism as a form of ideological containment. The question becomes, "How do we grasp the relationship between affect and ideology given that televisual practices of excess litter the screens (mostly as computer-generated imagery (CGI) violence)?"

Graham, again drawing from Grossberg, maintains that there is a disconnect or disarticulation between ideology and affect in *Buffy*. According to Grossberg, the ideological/affect relationship is "normally anaclitic, [but] the postwar years have seen it broken" (1997, 142). Now, anaclitic desire (in its Freudian sense, *SE* 14:237–58) refers to the desire to have, as opposed to the narcissistic desire to be. The narcissistic form of desire manifests itself as love and identification; the anaclitic form involves desire for *jouissance* that is fundamentally indifferent, often inimical, to the well-being of both oneself and the other person. If this is the case, then Grossberg has it backwards. It is narcissistic desire that appears "normal" and anaclitic desire that characterizes the post-war period of excess where "our ideological maps and our 'mattering [affect] maps' [are] unable to intersect, unable to articulate one another" (ibid., 4 in Graham 2007). The question is whether this is the case. Is there a disconnect between "mattering maps" and ideology? In this chapter I have argued precisely the opposite. Narcissistic ego desire is more at work. *Buffy* fans are caught up by the ethical dilemmas that emerge and that they can relate to. Buffy's uncertainty (angst) is theirs. But, Graham sees this as a problem—namely, the affect (as a "mattering map") of fighting coded as empowerment supercedes the ideological message; the how supercedes the what. We could say, for instance, the same of Steven Spielberg's films on war and the Holocaust. They are just too aestheticized; the excess of their form overpowers the "what" of their ideological message. Schindler turns out to be more of a prince than he was; World War II was much more horrible than the way Spielberg presents it; *The Matrix's* aestheticized violence prevents us from seeing through its heroic masculine plot, and so on.

Graham takes another gloss from Grossberg's distinction between "non-libidinal affect" and libidinal desire. I take the former to be Deleuzian and the latter to be in Lacanian territory at the level of fantasy. The distinction is between a-signification (what I recognize as *jouissance* in the Real, Lyotard's figural dimension, and what Deleuze often calls a diagram, which is a "mattering map") and fantasy, which is already framed at the level of signification. I argued that "traversing one's fantasy" is essentially disturbing the mapped affect of the BwO, thereby liberating oneself from the stratification of the symbolic order, even if this only means a perceptual change as to how one "sees" the world, even though the world itself has not changed. That is a form of self-refleXion.

We have then three glosses by Graham: pleasure, presented as a dualism (the constancy principle that seeks homeostasis and the Nirvana principle that reduces all tension to zero—as a utopia); anaclitic desire; and non-libidinal affect. When the mutually supportive relationship of affect and representation is culturally disturbed, this causes a disturbance in pleasure, and the viewer becomes discomforted as the ideological fantasy begins to lose its grip. Any perceived change, especially in the Buffyverse metanarrative, would anger fans. And, this is precisely what happens. Is it, however, justified as Graham insists, or is there something else going on?

The simple drive circuit of enjoyment is interpreted by Graham as the pleasure of viewing *Buffy*—namely, as an affective cycle that moves between "certainty" as a utopian a-signifying affect created by Buffy's fighting, and "uncertainty," the doubt expressed through discussion and self-reflection of everyday life (signification). The affect that this "uncertainty" (what is simply angst) brings would envelope or "color" the ethics of the Real that I have discussed. The colors have been somber and dark, accented by the sparks of fighting. I suppose that would be *Buffy's* diagram in the Deleuzian sense. The question is whether the pleasure of watching *Buffy* is indeed structured this way. Is it as utopian as we are led to believe? Graham draws on the affective utopian typology of Richard Dyer's musical dancing bodies—energy, abundance, intensity, transparency, and community—to characterize *Buffy's* "certainty," what might be called its full utopian potential of feeling—Nirvana. Affect changes depending upon which combination of Dyer's emotional components come together. This appears rather intuitively deduced. Community and transparency would support democracy, whereas intensity, transparency, and community become associated with social relationships, and so on. So different representational economies operate with different combinations of affects, the emotional components. It's a bit like mixing aromas to get the right smell for a particular bodily representation.

Buffy's emotional profile, let's say affective diagram, is also characterized by an overall mood. Graham maintains that this affective mood (again glossed from Grossberg as "both quantitative—quality—and qualitative—quality" [6]) is that of feminism. What secures the quality of affective investment in *Buffy* is this "feminism-as-mood" resting on the iconic shoulders of Buffy. Uncertainty (angst) and certainty (fighting), if I can put it that way, is the a-signifying affective mattering map of *Buffy*. Translated within the framework of this chapter: the Real of Anxiety and the Becoming of Fighting. For Graham, this "becoming" through fighting—as an affect—covers over dialogical uncertainty, especially "the uncertainty of the morality of Buffy's actions and their effects on Buffy" (8). The action just happens too quickly for us to process what is "really" going on. Graham maintains that specific clever plot negotiations enable the affect of slaying to take precedence over the broader moral and ideological implications of the series. This could be sustained for six seasons under a thin guise that *Buffy* was a feminist metanarrative that supported community values, cooperation, and hence a democratic ideal, but that came to a crashing end. In the light of 9/11, the pleasure of this cycle in the final series collapsed.

What angered fans was that Buffy fell out of character. Arwen Spicer (2004) wrote a long article on how the Buffyverse metanarrative had been compromised in the seventh season's ending. Rather than being democratic, enlisting the help of her friends, Buffy becomes more certain of her leadership, more arrogant and more autocratic, alienating her friends. Patricia Pender (2004) saw Buffy as a "power feminist" in this last season, foregoing her collaborative community, adopting a "moral absolutism reminiscent of the Bush administration" (169). Her trainee Slayers, who eventually defeat The First Evil have a specific "military flavor" and are assigned an "army-like" role, especially in episode 7019 ("Empty Places") where Buffy is then ejected from the group. Buffy's leadership during the last two episodes is read as offering its viewers the Bush and Blair war rhetoric; she has become a unilateral crusader. The uncertainty and utopianism that made the series so great vanishes. Or, so is the charge.

But what if Whedon risks and sacrifices this character flaw to make precisely the same point about Bush's war? What if Whedon's rewriting the Buffyverse—knowing its end is in sight—presents the strongest critique of Christianity yet—Bush's own heroics? What if this is satire at its best—a form of self-refleXion to make the fan base think? The power that is possessed by the savior of the world (Bush's United States) cannot stand alone and heroic—like *Buffy's* unilateralism, it cannot persist; that power ultimately must be shared. Is not the disturbance in the Buffyverse a precise way to make the fan base hesitate, to lose its pleasure, because it forces a self-releXion over the last six seasons during which an ethical stance was attributed to Buffy, the Scooby Gang, and all those who chose to fight and die beside her? Buffy realizes that as a savior figure she must share "the power" with others; she is incapable of assuming all the responsibility by herself. In an interview, Whedon (2003) went on record in a leading science fiction and fantasy magazine, *SFX*, that he was against the war. Knowing that the series was at its end, his message was almost didactic in its clarity. He redeems Buffy by leaving the fight with The First Evil and its minions to all "Slayers" everywhere through a thinly disguised allusion to the "Women's Movement" represented by an older woman character (7021, "End of Days") who leaves Buffy a scythe, which is used in the last episode to give all the potential Slayers the very same power that Buffy had. She then shares her gift of power with them all—restoring the Future of an Illusion.

Part IV

Televised Paranoiac Spaces

9

Aliens "R" Us: Searching for the Posthuman Teenager

"I am Liz Parker, and five days ago I died; after that things got really weird."

Within the relational geography of the United States, Roswell, New Mexico, continues to function as a key fantasy site as the meeting place between the human and inhuman, so much so that a teen television series was named after it: *Roswell* (1999–2002). For three seasons, most of the series' action took place within its isolated, hot, and desolate embrace—more specifically in three locations: West Roswell High School, the Unidentified Flying Object (UFO) Center (part archive for unexplainable incidents, part entertainment center), and the Crash Down Café, the out-of-school meeting and working place for the cast of characters. All other locations seemed to be within a one- or two-day drive. Only seldom do we find the characters on the "outside" for an entire episode—for example, when they were in New York (209, "Max in the City") and Las Vegas (215, "Viva Las Vegas"). However, despite what appear to be confined and well-defined institutions, one senses that its characters are operating in another space and time, always moving, searching, and driving—nomadic. We seldom see the inside of a classroom, but certainly plenty of hallways, corridors, nooks and crannies, and isolated desert scenery.

Roswell presents the fantasy of another "crash site" that brings the clash of humanist and posthumanist thought together just like its characters. The serious UFO traveler, a true believer, comes to Roswell to confirm the truth of the conspiracy and to verify the military and government cover-up. In the same magical space, the pilgrim meets the postmodern carnival of tourism—the stroller, the vagabond, and the player—each of whom is there strictly to enjoy the entertainment value of playing alien (see Bauman 1996). None other than Jonathan Frankes of *Star Trek* fame hosts the UFO Convention (112, "The Convention"), a wink to the audience that this is all good fun and make-believe. So, believe while you are there, but don't really believe all this nonsense.

This very contradiction between hoax and truth is played out throughout the series: the serious pilgrim, like UFO Center owner and scientist Brody Davis, meets the playful tourists who inhabit the Crash Down Café in an inverted paranoid narrative that comes off tongue-in-cheek at times in season one. But late into season two, the wink to the audience is given up front. Starting with episode 215 ("Viva Las Vega"), Maria DeLuca, one of the alien-human alliance members, acts as a schoolteacher in front of a blackboard and begins each episode by directly addressing the audience and recapping what has happened previously. This stops with season three, as if the producers were unsure to what lengths they wished to continue to frame such a self-reflexive ironic tone.

Raising Sleeping Beauty from the Dead

The story line is about three high school undercover aliens—Max Evans, his sister Isabel, and their friend Michael Guerin—who are joined by a fourth alien, Tess Harding, late in the first season (117, "Tess, Lies, and Videotape"), who will act as a foil for Max's love interest—the earthling Liz Parker—in the manner of other teenage melodramas such as *Smallville, Dawson's Creek,* and *Buffy.* Their crash on Earth leaves them orphaned and without knowledge of their parents or their destiny. Max and Isabel are found wandering in the desert and are adopted by kind loving parents, Philip and Diane Evans, while Michael suffers the fate of being in the custody of a drunken foster parent who lives in a trailer park. Tess, on the other hand, is protected by a planetary shape-shifting guardian named Nasedo (who later turns out to be a double agent). All they have been left to go on are a few alien artifacts, the Granilith (a transportation machine to take them back to their home, the planet Antar) and an indecipherable book written in their native language, which they are unable to read but which could provide them with answers. The narrative is therefore an unfolding detective story as to what their destinies are and what role each of them will play in it. They must remain undercover and pass as humans. Culture must become indistinguishable from "nature" if they are to be treated as authentic human beings. They are, in this respect, an uncanny, undetected element—queer folk living among "normal" human beings.

By the end of the first season, the destiny of the foursome is revealed: The four turn out to be clones of royalty from the planet Antar: Max is king, and Tess is his wife. Michael turns out to be second in command, and we learn later (207, "Wipeout!") that Isabel, his sister, may well be a clone of Vilandra, who betrayed Max's family by falling in love on Antar with his enemy Kivar. The foursome survived the spaceship's crash, landing near Roswell, because they were still in their incubation pods, hatching from them as six-year-old alien-human hybrids. Their "royal" essences had been duplicated and mixed with human DNA so that they could assume human form and be adopted. Their mission is to return to Antar and retake the throne from Kivar. As products of miscegenation (mixing alien and human blood), they are racial bastards.

In this postmodern Sleeping Beauty story, 16-year-old Liz Parker, while waitressing at her parents' restaurant—the Crash Down Café—is accidentally shot while witnessing an argument between two customers. Max awakens her from death (sleep), not by a kiss but by placing his hand over her wound, thereby healing it. The experience bonds them irreparably together in love—a bud-light form of Vulcan mind-meld—as each is able to feel and imagine the other's memories during moments of heightened awareness; this becomes useful during the unfold-ing saga. Eventually, Liz finds out that Max, his sister, and his best friend Michael are aliens, and she eventually shares the secret with her best friend Maria DeLuca, and much later with Alex Whitman (107, "Blood Brother"). The cell of six forms friendship bonds and uneasy love relations with one another: Michael with Maria and Alex with Isabel, the latter of which is less than successful. Thrown into the mix are the town's sheriff, Jim Valenti, and his son, the football star Kyle, Liz's early love interest. As the series progresses, both Kyle and his dad come to protect the aliens. Jim Valenti acts as their surrogate father.

Paranoiac Split

Roswell began broadcasting on the Warner Brothers (WB) network in October 1999, just before the new millennium, and it ended in May 2002, a few months before 9/11, a time frame that rode the end wave of alien paranoia in the 1990s, best exemplified at the time by *The X-Files*, which began broadcasting in 1993 (Burns 2001). Jason Katims, its creator, executive producer, and writer, should be credited for its success, in line with Kevin Williamson for *Dawson's Creek*, Joss Whedon for *Buffy*, and Paul Feig for *Freaks and Geeks*. Unlike the paranoiac ter-ror of *The X-Files*, however, *Roswell's* ironic meditation on paranoia itself exposes its structure as a projection of the divide within us. In Lacan's terms, the very struggle surrounding identity is one engaged with a problematic split-in-belief.

> At the basis of paranoia itself, which nevertheless seems to us to be animated by belief, there reigns the phenomenon of the Unglauben. This is not the not believing in it, but the absence of one of the terms of belief, of the term in which is designated the division of the subject. If, indeed, there is no belief that is full and entire, it is because there is no belief that does not presuppose in its basis that the ultimate dimension that it has to reveal is strictly correlative with the moment when its meaning is about to fade away (Lacan S XI, *Fundamentals*, 238).

This split within the subject is most clearly illustrated by Max, who specifically states, "My whole life I've been thinking that this alien side of me was this bad thing. This thing that made me a freak. This monster" (218, "It's Too Late and It's Too Bad"). As a hybrid human-alien, he is placed on the border of Lacan's division of the subject. He has no "home," or rather he has only a vague recollection of his alien planet, and is torn between wanting to return to it or remaining human and staying on Earth. Memory flashes trouble all the aliens as haunts of the past, of hav-ing led another life that they can't quite fathom. Their enemies are certainly human beings. "In paranoia, the primary function of the enemy is to provide a definition of the real that makes paranoia necessary. We must therefore begin to suspect the paranoiac structure itself as a device by which consciousness maintains the plural-ity of the self and nonself, thus preserving the concept of identity" (Bersani 1989, 109). So while paranoia may appear to be an epistemological angst, addressing the reliability of knowledge, evidence, and history, it is more deeply an ontological problem in which the subject endeavors to determine the nature and security of his or her own existence. Too great an insistence on the static security of identity can plunge the subject into an aggressive form of paranoia.

Max's paranoia is played out through his romantic involvements, between his earthling romance with Liz Parker and his alien romance with Tess Harding. Unfortunately, this bifurcation of love partners repeats the virgin/whore dichotomy made visually famous by the "two Marias" in Fritz Lang's 1927 classic *Metropolis*. Liz Parker is pure, saving her virginity for Max. Tess, on the other hand, is always scheming and succeeds in becoming impregnated. She is presented as a femme-fatale; not only can she mind-manipulate, and hence seduce men, but she also knows exactly what she wants—to return home as queen with Max as her king. Further, she kills (her intentionality is deliberately obscured) Alex Whitman, a member of the alien-human alliance. In the final episode (318, "Graduation"), she is required to sacrifice herself by becoming a suicide bomber in order to destroy a military base so that the cell can escape pursuit. Only then is she "symbolically" forgiven.

What is further troubling is that Tess (like the Skins, who are branded as evil aliens) represents the abject alien part, that part which crosses the line of human acceptance. Betraying Max, Tess is allowed to return home (pregnant) to Antar via the Granilith transporter, but only by the narrowest of margins, when the alien-human alliance is asked to vote on her fate (221, "The Departure"). She is ejected from the symbolic order like those young women in the past who had their out-of-wedlock babies some distance from school and home to avoid familial shame. Max is left behind, enabling his romance with Liz to continue.

Ultimately, the aliens are more drawn to "human" culture than to their own alien planet, not unlike second-generation children who were very young when their parents left their home country to stake out another life. Such children are caught between two words: the traditional world of their immigrant parents and the new culture they find themselves in. Roswell's aliens are no different when searching for their identity. Isabel in particular ends up feverishly desiring the married life with Jesse Ramierz, a lawyer in her dad's firm (306, "To Have and to Hold"). Her feelings of guilt at being unable to tell Jesse that she is an alien finally make her snap, and she imagines what their marriage would be like if her secret was finally outed. This is ironically staged through a dream sequence with a 1960's feel. Isabel becomes the figure of the witch Samantha Stephens, reenacting the television series *Bewitched* (1964–72), with shades of *I Dream of Jeannie* (1965–70). Jesse plays Darrin Stephens complete with brown suit, briefcase, and pipe, and like Toni on the *I Dream of Jeannie* series, Isabel (unlike Jeannie) is not his Master trying magically to make his every whim come true. Rather, Jesse is constantly annoyed and confused by her magical antics (311, "I Married an Alien"). Her independence as the decorator and ruler of the household is firmly maintained both in this dream sequence and in their lived life, which only leads to more problems. Michael, on the other hand, must learn from coworkers what friendship and responsibility are all about (302, "Michael, the Guys, and the Great Snapple Caper").

The famous July 9, 1947, military "cover up" of the UFO crash is revisited early in the second season (204, "Summer of '47"), when the characters are able to reenact, again with tongue-in-cheek, what might have happened through a flashback recounted during an interview that Michael conducts (for a school project) with a veteran World War II survivor, Captain Hal Carver, one of the original members of the 509th Bomb Group that had investigated the crash site. Besides retaining the mystery of the crash (it was only a radar-tracking weather balloon, not a "flying disc"[1]), the episode sets up the plot arc of season two by introducing their doppelgänger doubles—Captain Carver tells Michael that there were eight pods in the crash, not four! Known as the Dupes (208, "Meet the Dupes"), Zan (Max's clone), Rath (Michael's clone), Lonnie (Isabel's clone), and Ava (Tess's clone) are presented as their vilified doubles (the allusion to "dopes" is obvious)—punk rockers whose alien guardian, unlike Nasedo, left their pods in the sewers of New York.

One way of reading this doppelgänger alien foursome is that it differentiates one alien from another, reinstating the boundary that is continually slipping between humans and the aliens throughout the life of the series. Presenting their home planet as being engaged in a war of rival monarchs also distances them from the "democracy" of the United States, but it also bestows on the teens a curious kind of status. As good, hybrid aliens of royal decent, they carry a certain dignity and command a respect that is to be welcomed. It is here that *Roswell* marks a distinct departure from Chris Carter's critical revisionism of the hard-boiled, film noir detective fiction in *The X-Files* to explore the cultural paranoia of ethnic and racial instabilities and racial "othering" through alien motives (Jagodzinki and Hipfl 2001; Burns 2001).

Facing the Alien to the Side

Roswell again provides us with the post-Oedipal landscape. Its narrative symbolizes the common fears and anxieties experienced when facing the alien Other: the not knowing who we are, the experiences of being a foster child, and of keeping secrets from parents and other authority figures. There are also the risks and trust required for making close personal connections with others, keeping friends, and experiencing being in or from a strange world. Facing the alien Other also presents an ethics of the Real. Liz Parker and her friend Maria DeLuca must face Max's and Michael's strangeness as aliens. When Max saves her from a fatal gunshot wound in the series opener, she must let his "strangeness" in, so to speak, and face her own fears. In her diary, as a record of her experiences, she tries to distance herself from, and thus alleviate, these fears; to record and contain them as any teenager does. The *Roswell* series can be read as one long diary of a girl's fantasy life.

The aliens in *Roswell* are presented as a tourist attraction, in typical cartoon fashion. The Greys appear on billboards, postcards, children's toys, and are represented by Roswell's annual Crash Festival and sci-fi themed food served at Crash Down Café. Throughout the series, the gap between humans and inhumans is just barely maintained, for they have come to earth in the form of hybrid creatures, hatched from pod-like cocoons, a clear reference to the infamous *Invasion of the Body Snatchers* (1956) as masterfully explored by Neil Badmington (2001; 2004a,

135–51; 2004b). The film became infamous when the director, Don Siegel, was prevented from releasing the director's cut by Walter Wanger (the producer) and Allied Artists, which backed the project. They refused to accept the bleak ending he had engineered in which there was no hope in stopping the alien invasion. *Roswell* presents a simulacrum of this narrative. There is a similar plot to invade the Earth by the Skins, rebel aliens led by Kivar from Antar, who are pitted against the small band of heroes. They, too, have plans to replace earthlings with clones grown in pod-like structures (206, "Harvest"). Most are represented as members of a Zombie horde. Their leader is Nicholas, a teen who is controlled by his over-bearing mother. This ironical accent is furthered by the cunning intelligence and mind-manipulating powers of Nicholas, who is hot for Vilandra. Nicholas's kissing Isabel on a bus plays out the fantasy of every schoolboy who has fallen in love with his older teacher (207, "Wipe Out"). A renegade Skin, Courtney (206, "Harvest"), provides insight into their mission and the clue to how the Skins might be destroyed—based on their need to inhabit human "husks." The molting of their skin not only provides a trace of their presence, but it also further abjec-tifies their "animal" nature, distinguishing them from the royal three.

Unlike Don Siegel's *Body Snatchers,* where the sudden contagion of paranoia in the small town of San Miro, California, erupts as the citizens are replaced by the unrecognizable, perfect pod-people doubles, who lack the emotion and passion that constitutes humanness, we have the inverse happening here. All three aliens show remarkable passion, indistinguishable from that of humans. Even Michael eventually becomes protective of Maria. Only he is able to reach the psychotically paranoid Laurie DuPree, who has been locked up in a psychiatric ward by her aunt and uncle to prevent her from getting her grandfather's billions (212, "We Are Family"). Fear of the visual double creates a particularly intense anxiety for the paranoid. Aliens can perfectly mimic a human's outer form, as could the trio's guardian, Nasedo. But, in this episodic arc, it turns out the alien as double (Michael who looks like Laurie DuPree's grandfather) passes as her savior-hero once she gets over the family resemblance. The dividing line between alien and human once more collapses.

Alien Love

Roswell, according to Badmington (2004a, 85), provides an example of alien love, which under most circumstances is better grasped as Alien Chic. Following Tom Wolfe's logic in his sense of Radical Chic, the movement from hating the alien to embracing the alien Other is rather superficial, and might also be thought through as an example of postmodern racism or "neo-racism" following Etienne Balibar (1991), which is to say that the celebration of the other as Other, as being entirely distinct from the self, simply reinstates the divide or gulf between "Them" and "Us." In this way, difference collapses into sameness, with the tenets of humanism being reinstated again in a very clever way. It appears that there is a true interest in the Other, to the point of showing love and affection, which can just as quickly turn to hate if the alien Other does not cooperate with the generosity given or does not live up to the rules imposed. Up to that point, there is tolerance and respect, but the line is not to be crossed.[2]

It is to Badmington's (2004a) credit to have read *Roswell* "otherwise," arguing that its narrative avoids the trap of falling yet again into a humanist discourse; it's not just more Alien Chic. He suggests that the familiar theme of teenage alienation should be taken literally in the series. "[H]uman teenagers are almost as alien(ated) as the aliens they befriend and desire. . . . Teenagers . . . would not be teenagers if they did not act a little inhuman, a little alien-ated from time to time. The inhuman (alien) passes for human (teenager) by appearing inhuman (alien-ated truant). And the traditional opposition between the real and the simulated suddenly finds itself in crisis" (127). Once again, this is the power of the simu-lacrum in Deleuzian terms. A mimetic copy always already puts the original to doubt and strips away its authority. Aliens keep collapsing into humans, while humans at times are "wannabe" aliens. Kyle hopes that he might inherit some of the same powers that Liz does, for he, too, had been "raised from the dead" by Max when he was shot. In episode 312 ("Ch-Ch-Changes"), Liz becomes physically ill from being around Max. Her body is remapped as a new BwO. This is "an affec-tive, intensive, anarchist body that consists solely of poles, zones, thresholds and gradients. It is traversed by a powerful, nonorganic vitality" (Deleuze 1998, 131). When Max comes near, her body's electrical circuits become rewired, illustrated visually by her glowing red and green while electrical currents appear to jump from place to place all over her body. She remains ill and weak, unless he draws away. There are no psychoanalytic ego defenses at work here. This is entirely at the level of the bodily unconscious, an affective state of repulsion, as if she is just unable to "feel" Max's difference any longer. At the molecular level, her intercon-nection with Max has been lost. Max is not open, and their desire is blocked.

Badmington (2004a) willingly admits that "*Roswell* unearths resources for rethinking of the relationship between the human and inhuman, between 'Us' and 'Them.' Within its stories, the signifiers 'human' and 'alien' are rearticulated until the relationship between them is no longer one of absolute difference. Neither the human nor the alien is ever entirely revealed in the plentitude of opposition; there is a repeated deferral, an endless retreat from humanism" (134). This slippage not only collapses into the alien of teen alien(ation), but also into transgressions against the law, which enable a "body" to do what it could not do before. For instance, Max and Liz hold up a convenience store where an alien spaceship is concealed, acting out a Bonnie and Clyde number of transgressive behavior (301, "Busted"). This sequence is shot as film noir—once more with tongue-in-cheek—bringing back shades of the hardboiled detective and alluding somewhat to *The X-Files*. Their desire has no boundaries even if it means jail time. In contrast to a series like *Dawson's Creek*, here inhuman desire is released by way of an impossi-ble love that couples Max and Liz, Maria and Michael, and even Isabel and Alex, for a short time. It is not profoundly rationalized and deferred as in *Dawson's Creek*; rather, it raises the ethics of the stain of strangeness that lies at the heart of the purity of being soul mates. There is an implied inhuman "X" that is con-stantly there as Liz, Maria, Kyle, and Sheriff Valenti must grapple with the dis-ruptions in their lives on a daily basis.

What appears straightforward heterosexual love between these couples asks its audience to imagine that a queering is taking place, a coupling between the human and inhuman to find a line of flight outside the Oedipal fix. It is the woman in each case who presents the opening to the posthuman. In the Lacanian logic of "not all," the feminine is infinitely exposed Otherness, while the pretense of the masculine remains a transcendental Other, claiming to speak for a totality, and thereby negating the possibility of real Otherness. To risk an insight developed by Irigaray's ethics, Liz inserts an interval between herself and Max to live with his difference ("X"). This interval is like a "firewall" that prevents the collapse of difference into the same. It is marked by the word "to" in Irigaray's phrase, "I love to you," as explored in her book by the same name (1996). The "to" indicates a refusal to encapsulate the Other in an image or expectation. "I love to you means I maintain a relation of indirection to you. I do not subjugate you or consume you. I respect you (as irreducible). . . . The 'to' is the site of nonreduction of the person to the object" (109). This interval—the "to"—"safeguards a place of transcendence between us, a place of respect which is both obligated and desired as a place of possible alliance" (Irigaray 2001, 19). Such a space is possible only in a sphere of immanence, a space that must retain its sensuous embodiment and environment and not through the workings of an illusionary autonomy. Liz Parker is good at finding this space between them, going about this quietly and patiently, even if Max struggles to find what human love is. What comes across in the series is his charged sensitivity to this space that matches hers. At no time does the monster in Max show itself. It appears only as a split figure, an identical Max called Zan, who has affiliations with the Skins (208, "Meet the Dupes"). Even when Max tries to persuade an alien shape-shifter, Kal Langley (305, "Control"), to help him steal a spaceship hidden in a military base, he is unable to bully him. Kal ends up obeying him only because he "must," as a guardian, if a direct order is given by the king of Antar. His ambivalent leadership finds some resolution for the first time.

Often throughout the series, Liz intentionally distances herself from Max before coming near him again, as if that very "difference," the alien "X," cannot be respected or lived with. But, that distance is put to the test near the start of season two when a *Nachträglichkeit* (afterwardsness) experience is introduced to suspend Liz and Max's love affair (205, "The End of the World"). Max returns via the Granilith from the future (the year 2014 to be precise), and tells Liz that she must terminate their love affair or else the lives of everyone they know will be lost. The request plunges Liz into a masochistic state for the rest of season two as she makes the ultimate psychic sacrifice by staging a lovemaking scene with her former boyfriend and confidant, Kyle—sheriff Valenti's son. The "future" Max witnesses this, draining his desire. Liz must now silently suffer her intended betrayal to save "mankind." This is the acid test of her respect for that place between them. Such a betrayal is just the opposite of Tess's, of course, a gesture of love rather than a devilish plot. At the end of the episode, when Liz dances with the "future Max" after she has "broken his heart," making the "present-day Max" think that she has betrayed him, he simply vanishes. At that moment she and the audience realize what she's done: changed the course of history. That version of Max 14 years hence will never exist, making the sacrifice bearable.

It is the secret of knowing that Max is alien and living with that secret that makes Irigaray's "to" possible. It brackets something out of existence, a *remainder* that enables desire to sustain itself. And, this holds true to a greater or lesser extent for all the alien-human alliances, to the point of collapsing that interval of the "to," as when Ramirez finally discovers the "truth" about Isabel. He is unable to live with her difference. All of a sudden the world has changed for him. Isabel is a liar, not the person he married. It is another Isabel who is stained with a difference that he is unable to cope with. Alien love has turned into alien hate. Alien difference, the "X," may never have its place of existence. Unlike *Dawson's Creek*, for example, such a transcendent place that Irigaray calls for is filled with enunciations and smart, clever, totalizing statements about transcendent reality. The teens talk like cognitive analysts of the neo-Freudian kind. A soul mate in the truest sense would open up the space of the "to." It is perhaps the deconstructive space that *Dawson's Creek* also offers in the last episode.

Post-Oedipal Flips

While Liz most often has a love struck, "doe-eyed" look, remaining the princess whenever Max is around, Max always speaks in a soft-spoken voice of desperation as a sensitive and feminized King who only seldom puts down Michael when he acts as his foil. In teen melodramas, the matching up of sensitive and insensitive male roles, played by handsome, self-sacrificing men (Banks 2000), has become a standard way to explore different sides of accepted "manhood," such as Seth and Ryan on *The O.C.* (Orange County), Dawson and Pacey on *Dawson's Creek*, Spike and Angel on *Buffy*, and Clark and Lex on *Smallville*. Perhaps this is also to welcome a gay viewing audience? By forwarding the sensitive, self-sacrificing heroic male who is able to articulate his emotions, who is thoughtful and obedient and only occasionally rebellious, seems to represent a call for a new masculinity that will replace the former emotionless, stoic, and more rigid one. Max's destiny (like Clark Kent's) is open; after all, Michael is "second" in his army and often loses his cool. But toward the end of season three, we find him changing, remaining impetuous, but being more thoughtful and more protective of Maria. A flip has taken place.

The same masculine encounter is replayed between Sheriff Valenti and his son, Kyle. After being "touched" by Max and healed from a fatal gunshot wound, like Liz, Kyle transforms into a gentler, more ecologically minded, and more meditative person, at times disappointing his dad because of his lack of aggression. But, then another flip occurs. His father is fired as sheriff and ends up trying to make it playing cowboy songs as a member of a "saloon band." Kyle has to find steady work so that they are not evicted from their home. Liz and Maria are similarly cast, not so much in opposition to each other as gradients of good and bad depending on the context, with Maria being much more adventurous and daring, not only with her choice of clothes, but with her mobility (she drives a Jetta) and willingness to put herself out on a limb—for Michael. Liz, on the other hand, "listens" to her parents. Maria's mother, Amy DeLuca, who is rather "loose" herself, recognizes teenage promiscuity and worries about her daughter's possible (mis)adventures. These partnerships are well matched, leaving Isabel, who is elegant, mature, sexy, and more reserved (an "Ice Princess"), open to relationships with other types of male characters, such as the geologist Grant Sorenson; and then in season three, she has a hot romance with the Mexican-American attorney, Jesse Ramirez (301, "Busted"), as the series attempts to include minorities on its roster of characters. Isabel gets a new "look" (more mature and more elegant), while Alex remains nerdy, at times awkward, still searching for the "right" girl. He is written out of the script by the end of season two when he is killed by Tess, having been driven to mental exhaustion deciphering the only document the trio has with which to try to grasp what their purpose was before the crash.

Alien-Angels

The powers of these aliens are truly "low-grade" in comparison to, say, the mutants of the X-men or any number of other superheroes. Isabel is able to reheat food or turn on appliances with the wave of her hand; she has psychic premonitions and is able to travel into the dreamworld of others. Michael can open locks and bend metal with a wave of his hand, but he is also capable of killing another human being by radiating energy from his hand. By contrast, Max is a healer, but his curative powers work only within limits. Liz, Kyle, and Sheriff Valenti have all been saved from dying by him. His own "death" to revive the dying and aging body of Clayton Wheeler (314, "Chant Down Babylon") presents another example of human and inhuman exchange and (forced) sacrifice. Tess, on the other hand, is a creator of illusions, which goes along with her (be)witching character. All are, however, very vulnerable and mortal. Isabel is dramatically shot fleeing from the Meta-Chem Corporation (313, "Panacea") and must fight for her life, since no regular doctor could be called on to operate.

All these powers come at a price, and the ethics that surround them are often explored throughout the series. When Michael kills, he is shocked and disturbed that he is capable of such an act—again addressing this inhuman self. Isabel worries about invasion of privacy, as she can enter into the dreamworld of others; moreover, when premonitions warn her of danger (in 318, "Graduation," she sees all of her friends being shot down by FBI agents), or when she has flashes warning her that someone needs help (211, "To Serve and Protect"), she feels obligated to exercise that gift. Max, however, remains the most complicated gift bearer of all. In episode 210 ("A Roswell Christmas Carol"), Max is riddled with guilt, haunted by the ghost of a father who sacrifices himself to save his daughter from being run over by a car. Max felt that he should have saved him. To "balance" things off, Max ends up curing the children in a cancer ward in Phoenix. "Are you an angel?" asks one of the children as heavenly music plays in the background. Tess, who is living with Sheriff Valenti and Kyle, ends up having "more Christmas spirit than Christmas spirit," in terms of Baudrillard's (1983) hyperreality, by cooking a magnificent meal and inviting Amy DeLuca, Valenti's former love interest, over for Christmas supper. In the meanwhile, Isabel organizes carol singers and Christmas pageants. Dubbed the "Christmas Nazi" by Michael, she also finds the perfect present for him to give to Maria. While not quite positioned as gods, they are just one rung below them.

In contrast, monstrosity clearly rests on Antar, that faraway seat of the inhuman "X," where the struggles for power are lived. Kivar, its leader, attempts to lure Isabel to return with him to be his queen (as Vilandra in her former life), turning her into a monster and betrayer of her own Antar family (307, "Interrupts"). When Max "dies," having been forced to revive a dying old millionaire by his sexy young wife (played by Morgan Fairchild in a tongue-in-cheek allusion to Anna Nicole Smith) (313, "Panacea"), a tattoo mysteriously appears on Michael's chest, and begins to glow, indicating that he is the king of Antar now that the former leader is dead. But his leadership becomes monstrous, alienating everyone (315, "Who Died and Made You King?"). The four pod duplicates of the Royal Four (Zan, Rath, Vilandra, and Eva) that were also "hatched" at the crash site are presented as punk rockers and belligerent New York scum, and are clearly binaries (208, "Meet the Dupes"). In all these episodes, the inhuman is banished to Antar and its culture, differentiating just "which" alien difference it is possible to live with. The Freaks are kept at bay while the three aliens are presented as good-hearted kids, doing everything to survive so that they might come to terms with each of their destinies.

Abductions

Abductions, as Badmington (2004a, 70) informs us, are encounters of the fourth kind, the other three being observation only, a UFO that leaves a record of some kind, and the presence of an alien as reported. As a phenomenon of belief, abductions are usually sexual and erotic. Badmington cites the work of Joe E. Mack, a professor of psychiatry and the director of the Center for Psychology and Social Change at Harvard Medical School, who, after studying the phenomenon and publishing his book *Abduction: Human Encounters with Aliens* in 1994, concluded that abductees experience the aliens in another reality or time dimension with obvious sexual overtones—operations, probes, better sexual orgasms with aliens, and so on. Badmington maintains that a close reading of Mack's abduction narratives leads him to argue that these narratives are an exercise in self-reflexivity, once again as developed by Anthony Giddens. He quips, "I am abducted, therefore I am" (83). The humanist discourse comes flooding in. In these abductions, the alien is the repressed unconscious that is being addressed, verging sometimes on the point of psychosis. Aliens are the ones that "know." And, as Jodi Dean (1998) has persuasively argued, abductions are part of the larger paranoia of postmodernity and the crisis of humanism. Conspiracy theories abound—endlessly fueled by false tracks made possible by the Internet where one clue leads to another.

In *Roswell*, abductions are treated as a form of communication. Max's friend and ally, the alien Larek, regularly abducts the millionaire Brody Davis, who owns the UFO Center, in order to act as an interplanetary communication link between them. Larek/Davis, for instance, warns the alliance about the magic power of the molecular organism/mineral gandarium that can synthesize life to "bridge the gap between DNA and RNA in third stage amino acid sequencing" producing the human-alien hybrid (214, "How the Other Half Lives").

Conspiracy theories also abound in *Roswell*. The clandestine activities of the FBI, and the paranoid distrust of centralized government power, represented by Agent Ms. Topolsky as a substitute teacher (101, "The Morning After"), are introduced at the beginning of the series. The clash between local law enforcement and the FBI is further strengthened and again feminized in season two when Sheriff Valenti is interrogated by FBI Agent Susan Duff, another woman character, for holding back information (211, "To Serve and Protect"). While Sheriff Valenti is a "man's man" (he's not afraid to kill people, loves football, does carpentry, and is Oedipally haunted by the dismissal of his father, who was also a sheriff caught up in UFO intrigue), as his family name suggests in the Italian feminine plural ("being worthy or relevant"), he has a soft spot for the alien four, and in effect becomes their surrogate father and protector.

Liz, too is driven by the intrigue of conspiracy as she problematizes the death of her friend Alex, displacing her mourning as a form of investigation to come to grips with her grief. When Max kisses Tessa on prom night, the ground is cleared for her to undertake her own paranoid detective pursuit, insisting that Alex's death was alien-related. Perhaps Leana, the girl Alex met in Sweden, was one? A photograph of the two of them leaning against a building that had been torn down in 1994 raises her suspicions. Liz dons the mantle of Detective Parker, an act that, while far from being hard-boiled, causes a riff between her and Max and the rest of the group.

Queering Kinship

With aliens being products of miscegenation, one would expect (as in *The X-Files*) the usual paranoid narrative pegging aliens as Other, with the fear of their birth echoing the fear of sexual exchanges across racial and cultural boundaries. However, we learn in a developmental four-part arc—beginning with episode 211 ("To Serve and Protect") and ending with episode 214 ("How the Other Half Live")—that Michael's human donor was the uncle of a young girl, Laurie DuPree, who has a psychic link with Isabel. Her uncle had been abducted and looks just like Michael, which at first frightens her. As an experimental host, her uncle has queered the kinship relationship between them. "Is Laurie then my granddaughter?" Michael asks. It turns out only those with a rare blood defect can be cloned. "Bad" blood is given a positive genetic twist. Laurie may be carrying the same defect. She is being pursued by a "Queen crystal" who controls her crystal drones, called the Gandarium, which have lain scattered around the crash site for the past 50 years awaiting activation. These are the very crystal parasites that enable a bridge to be made between human and inhuman blood to produce the hybrid clones. If the "Queen crystal"—who has infiltrated the body of the geologist Grant Sorenson—is fully able to take over Laurie DuPree's body, then an unstoppable global epidemic will be unleashed.

The scene where the Queen crystal is killed is an ironic wink to *Aliens* and *Star Trek's* Borg Queen. As Michael creates a vacuum with his powers in a bomb shelter that looks like a lab, the Queen crystal bursts from Sorenson's chest, looking more like an organic sperm balloon than the phallic head of the monster in *Aliens*. The Queen crystal starts to "sizzle" around the room like a balloon losing air, smashing herself on the glass window of the door, dropping to the ground—dead. Michael not only saves the day, but because of his family looks, he is also able to restore Laurie DuPree's rightful inheritance that her grandfather had left her. The episodic arc has many affinities with the gothic genre—for example, plot lines similar to those in Mathieu Kassovitz's film *Gothika* (2003). There is always someone unjustly trapped in a mental asylum, just waiting for retribution. The plot line where Bobby and Meredith, Laurie's aunt and uncle, keep her locked up in a state mental hospital in order to grab her grandfather's estate is typical in this respect.

The agent who is blamed for the global pestilence scourge exists in the very gap between the human and inhuman, between the organic and inorganic. Neither humans nor aliens are blamed, but the substance that brought them together as a vanishing mediator providing an interesting twist. Once the Queen crystal has been eliminated, Kyle and Alex are able to emerge from a cave where drone crystals had trapped them. Laughing hysterically, Kyle says, "We have saved the world," meaning that it took the cooperation between aliens and humans and the local sheriff and the soft side of the FBI to do it. Agent Duff is not about to reveal the secret either. Each and every time, the alien Other is safely enfolded and protected through friendship.

The *Roswell* Beat

Melodrama, as is well-known, is a genre that draws from its base root—*melos*, the Greek term meaning "music." Music as the aural background characteristic of this genre is meant to underscore the unfolding drama, to provide an emotional base for the audience and tie them to the various thematic tropes of human existence. It has been argued that the music in these teen melodramas is usually very distinctive, earnest and regulated to underscore the dramatically changing moods of characters; to promote the "teenage cool" of mostly white, middle-class kids, the music selected no less by a baby boom generation that wishes to preserve its "forever young" status by replaying the musical landscape of the time when they came of age (Dickinson 2004). Careful attention to the soundtrack makes it obvious just how it reinforces the moods of the scenes. While dreaming of Alex, who has been killed in a car accident (217, "Cry Your Name"), Isabel is relieved of any guilt feelings for having caused his death. As he leaves her dream, one hears the words "so long, so long" softly sung by Jane Silberry ("Calling All Angels"). Such reinforcement of the emotion with music is typical throughout the series. In episode 208 ("Meet the Dupes), the soundtrack allows *Roswell's* producers to play the cynical and barbed tunes of goth, nü-metal, and rap (sound mixed by W. G. Snuffy Walden), which are sidelined throughout the three seasons, as are African-American rappers from most teen melodramas (Dickinson 2004). The soundtracks

are played most often during scenes in the Crash Down Café, and are meant to further the romances between various characters, but especially Liz and Max. The
theme song, "Here with Me" (as well as "Honestly" and "OK") by Dido, pretty
much sums up the never-ending love affair between Max and Liz: "I won't go, I
won't sleep, I can't breath, until you're resting here with me. / I won't leave, I can't
hide, I cannot be, until you're resting here with me."

The Alliance as War Machine

In *Dawson's Creek* we have already come across the importance of a "closed-knotted"
group of friends. *Roswell* strengthens that friendship even more. This mix of alien
and human forms a cell, which is held together by a secret, a contractual social set
of relationships that engenders a feeling of togetherness. Following Michel
Maffesoli (1996), one could maintain that this is a neo-tribe, forming an affectual
community generated around the notion of "alien," thereby exposing what is the
projected alien/ation of contemporary teen anxieties. Maffesoli's claim is to suggest that late modernity's stress on "the logic of identity" has given way to "the
logic of identification," which he refers to as a process of disindividuation. This
process of neo-tribalism, maintains Hetherington (1998), "act[s] to promote individuality as well as provide intense experience of communion into which that
individuality is subsumed" (85; also Sweetman 2004). The lifestyle choice is made
between aliens and friends who keep their cover no matter what in a conspiracy
of actions would invite exposure. Given the self-refleXivity claim, it is the secret
that bonds their affectual, aesthetic, and communicative lives together. There was
no rational decision for the group to come together; rather, it begins with an
extraordinary "encounter" between aliens and humans that generates this cell.

We have then a good example of Deleuze and Guattari's "war machine," an
organization that opposes the dominant state; it does not dissipate but attempts
to deterritorialize boundaries. The alliance of humans and aliens operates with
different speeds, spatial and temporal coordinates producing a smooth space from
within the institutional, striated space they struggle against (parents, school, the
military, and the FBI). They meet in isolated places. Maria is always driving off on
some adventure with Michael and Max, worrying her mother. Their trajectories
are erratic and unpredictable as they search for clues to their destiny—ending up
in caves, on Native-American reservations, on military (keep out) installations,
and so on. It is a nomadic existence, verified in the closing scene of the last season
when the cell leaves, narrowly escaping the clutches of the FBI after they have been
discovered. In this respect, they have indeed "graduated" from high school!

Posthumanist Line of Flight

Roswell does not present us with the terror of a hybrid figure like Ripley in *Alien
Resurrection*, where the ethics of the Real are intensely played out. Given birth to
by the Queen, Ripley must terminate the alien Other. More drastically, in *Alien 3*

Ripley's womb hosts the alien Other that must be terminated once again through an act of suicide. In contrast, the baby Zan, born to Tess and Max when Tess returns to earth (317, "Four Aliens and a Baby"), is presented as "human" (with albeit unknown alien powers, of course). Like Max and Isabel, whose difference the Evanses have now accepted, the hybrid-alien baby is fondled with loving care. Yet, Max must give up the boy for adoption, signaling that a "species difference" will be released into the world, indicating posthuman hope for change as well—a living with difference. A further hybridization would be possible if and when Max and Liz have offspring.

Lasting only three seasons, the very last scenes (318, "Graduation") lead up to the proverbial happy Hollywood ending, with Liz marrying Max, suggesting the potential for a new becoming. Liz risks becoming-alien by leaving behind home and its security, but she is still caught by the frame of institutional legitimacy. Isabel however, with her secret out, does not risk life with Ramierz. She leaves him dangling. The nomadic element of the new cell, the human-alien alliance, suggests that while the monster threatens us with subjective dissolution, infecting us through contact (which is in tandem with the way we are nevertheless drawn to strangeness, to meld with it out of curiosity and experimentation), the abrupt ending to the series provides a potential line of flight out of the Oedipal bind. One would like to think that they are all schizoid in the way they tried to free up desire. However, it is difficult, if perhaps impossible, to envision Max, Isabel, and Michael as anything but human aliens rather than alien humans. But, is this is not perhaps precisely the transformation they were seeking? It still makes for a hopeful, posthumanist scenario.

"I am Liz Parker, and I am happy."

Smallville, Somebody Save Me! Bringing Superman Down to Earth

The usual spoiler warnings apply!

Marvel-ing Superman

Smallville, compared to the other teen series that I have viewed, deals with an epic co(s)mic theme—saving the earth! It is the quintessential American myth, and as a British-born Canadian, I may never quite fully comprehend the place Superman has in the American psychic Imaginary. It is "almost" impossible, however, to have escaped confronting its myth. One easy and somewhat facile reading is that when Superman first appears in 1938, a year before the start of World War II in Europe, his granite features and muscled body are then ideologically put to work as an idealized soldier-machine, part of the war propaganda battling Nazis, forwarding nationalism and patriotism.[1] Such an armored body, as Klaus Theweleit (1977–78) has disturbingly shown, would suggest the need to symbolically present him as a delibidalized body turned machine.[2] The postwar televised series *The Adventures of Superman* (1952–57), starring George Reeves, has him foiling post–World War II Nazi activities and consolidating U.S. social and economic status.

Another view, almost its direct opposite, presents this orphaned alien figure as a unifier of the immigrant experience, exhibiting pride, self-confidence, and integrity. In this scenario, American culture between World War II and the 1980s was characterized by unassimilable stereotypes: the Ox-like Swedish farmer, the German brewer, the Jewish merchant, the fighting Irish drunk, and the Italian gangster (Engle 1987, 20). As an alien, Clark must assimilate into the culture in order to "pass." His creators, Jerry Siegel and Joe Shuster, had purposely downplayed his origins, reducing his background in *Action Comics* #1 to a single page with seven panels.[3] The nation's desire to unify, which the heroic Second World War was eventually able to do, was waiting for just such an iconic fictionalized character to pull together and "quilt" the floating signifiers. The ideological space just needed to be materialized—and the time was right for doing so. In the 1940s and '50s, often referred to as the Golden Age of comic books,[4] Superman represents the Eurocentric American Dream. What needs to be added to this general account is the role the "Man of Tomorrow" played in mediating the paranoia that surrounded modernization—the scientific discoveries and technologies that, if blocked, threatened progress. Superman's villain became the mad scientist (iconically represented by Lex Luthor) who uses chemistry and the power of the atom for selfish and destructive purposes. The hero could overpower any runaway technology and defeat any evil brainiac who was up to no good. Superman stood as a symbol of technology under control. In this Golden Age (1938–55), Superman was also the champion of the oppressed, outwitting generic, no-name evildoers—the factory owners, mine foremen, corrupt mayors, and so on. Corporate America was to be kept in line so that social reforms could take place. The Man of Steel, oddly, adumbrates the cyborg as a fail-safe mechanism. Not quite man and not quite machine, the "something more" of Superman was a fantasy that mediated the frail body and the powers of science and technology as Thing, which could easily take lives through work-related accidents, just as the atom bomb could destroy the earth. As a fantasy frame during a time of precarious scientific progress, Superman provided a veil, a screen or a shelter, with which adolescent boys could identify and feel protected.

Umberto Eco (1972), in a fascinating account of the Superman myth (of the 1960s), articulates what was required to keep his character emblematic, fixed, and easily recognizable. He makes the point that "*the only visible form evil assumes* [in the 1960s] *is an attempt on private property* . . . [whereas] *good is represented only as charity*" (22, original emphasis). Superman fights an endemic underworld of organized crime that preoccupies all his efforts. In contrast, evil from outer space at this historical time is casual and transitory, simply added spice. Civic consciousness, confined to the sphere of a small, enclosed community, is completely split from political consciousness. This was to drastically change. During the 1960s and '70s the Superman ideology turned to the Cold War (Eagan 1987, 94). Writers had him saving the earth from supervillains who came from other stars or parallel dimensions and multiuniverses (Earth-Prime, Earth-1, and Earth-2), making the narratives confusing. For many young readers, Superman had become campy. The major change came in 1986 with John Bryne, who pared down the narrative.[5] Significantly, Lex Luthor was no longer a mad scientist, but a wealthy, scheming businessman, xenophobic and lusting for power, whose plans to better Metropolis by any means available are foiled by this meddlesome alien. Krypton is rendered as a cold, dead ice world, as in the 1978 film *Superman: The Movie* (Pevey 2007, 25). However, sales continued to plummet. In 1995, DC Comics even "killed" and "resurrected" Superman in the multi-issue story arc given the title, *Death and Return of Superman*; the result was a momentary halo effect that increased its sales for a brief time. Since the early 1960s, DC's pantheon of superheroes—Superman, Green Lantern, the Flash, Batman, and Wonder Woman (so-called Silver Age characters)—were engaged in a long, loosing battle for sales with Marvel Comics, whose superheroes were more youthful and more angst-ridden: the Fantastic Four, Spiderman, the X-men, and the Avengers.

This pantheon was more socially conscious and antiestablishment in their fight for justice. Both Superman and Batman continued to uphold the Law and the status quo, a black and white world where good must prevail and the social order must be maintained (see Vollum and Adkinson 2003).

In the post–9/11 era, the hero required a complete makeover. The Yellow-Brick Road that led to the pot of gold called *Smallville* began to be paved by Mark Waid. In 2003 he was asked by DC to "re-imagine Superman for the twenty-first century." Waid's (2005) investigative work for the task uncovered that youth could no longer relate to Superman. His invincibility and lack of history (no traces of scars on his body) didn't jive with their view of lived life. As Waid put it, they perceived the world around them to be "far more dangerous. Far more unfair, and far more screwed up than my generation ever did. . . . [T]heir world is one where unrestrained capitalism always wins, where politicians always lie, where sport idols take drugs and beat their wives, and where white picket fences are suspect because they hide dark things" (5). In an age of terrorism, there is no safety for anyone. "Post-industrial subjectivity is about consumerism, the constant management of 'crisis' and the exploitation of its contradictions" (Braidotti 2002, 188). The shift by youth was toward antiheroes (social outsiders) like Wolverine (a homicidal, feral, brutish half-beast and libertarian), Batman (a paranoid schizophrenic, a brooding loner, tormented mentally), and Spiderman (a guilt-ridden, wisecracking teenager, always pushing the edge like the Torch of the Fantastic Four). The direction of the superheroes lay in humanizing them for example, Spiderman became a symbol of the uncertainties of youth in the 1990s and beyond. As Anton Karl Kozlovic (2006) put it, he was Superman-lite. Waid wrote *Superman: Birthright*, a twelve-issue comic book limited series published by DC Comics in 2003–2004, as a way to invert Clark's superpowers, to make them a burden rather than a gift. But, as Aaron Pevey (2007) points out, this never worked out despite later attempts, such as the seven-issue series, *Infinite Crisis* in 2005 and Grant Morrison's rewrite of Superman in the ongoing series, *All-Star Superman*, to restore his 1950s' persona.

Waid obviously had it right in one sense.[6] The disciplined masculine body had been decentering; masculinity was under siege (jagodzinski 2001). Postmodern neoliberal capitalism needs a morphing, flexible, fluid body that can adjust to different tasks, raising new anxieties for youth to cope with. The turn to body piercing and tattooing was just one way of "grounding" the body's history (jagodzinski 2002b). But it was the overall anxiety of being unable to control the body that became predominant, addressing the adolescent directly. The schizos were let loose by the teratological imagination: freaks, replicants, androgynes, hermaphrodites, zombies, vampires—the new postmodern gothic, Buffy being another obvious example, as has already been discussed. With biopower operating in a centerless way, the "society of control," as formulated by Deleuze and others, provides the illusions of freedom and mobility.[7] This cast of characters desires to deterritorialize borders. Their excesses point to an unstoppable passion made possible by the ceaseless pulse of their drives (*Triebe*), Zoë as opposed to Bios.[8] Pain becomes the "authentic" marker of feeling. In the comic tradition, the superpowers of the Mutants came to replace the Man of Steel.

The "X-Men" and the "Ultimate X-Men" speak to self-refleXivity in the most startling way. Either through a scientific experiment gone wrong or through a genetic defect (the "X" gene), the Mutant powers, manifested during puberty, point precisely to the inhuman within. They struggle with their volatile gifts that are equally their burden; their bodies are all surface, directly exhibiting their character—either visibly or invisibly—as if their bodies' drives have been exteriorized when they "freak." "The mutant body is explicitly traumatic, armored against the world outside, yet racked and torn apart by complex forces within. The mutant body is oxymoronic: rigidly protected but dangerously unstable. In its infinite malleability and overdetermined adolescent iconography, the mutant superhero is a locus of bodily ritual" (Bukatman 2003, 51). Some Mutants go undercover to hide their "true" nature, not surprising as the series deals with minorities, racism, and "coming out." "[T]hey are, first and foremost, subjected and subjugated and colonized figures" (73).

In the series, *Ultimate X-Men*, they have no secret identities, wear no uniforms; the Mutants are a visible minority. As thinly disguised adolescents, they remain genetic mistakes that cannot be trusted, and hence their slogan: "sworn to protect a world who hates and fears them" (*New X-Men* #134: January 2003, in Trushell 2004, 162). The statement is meant ironically, of course, poking fun at adults who cannot tolerate teenagers.[9] Despite their difference and obvious freak status, they, nevertheless, attempt to defend the world from peril. There is this inhuman "X" that they try as they might to control, but never fully succeed. This marks the status of the body in contemporary technoculture: "*X-Bodies* as in taboo; *X* as in impure and polluted and under erasure: but also *X* as in X rays, with their power to reveal; *X* as in extreme; *X* as in *ex*—the *ex-men*" (Bukatman 2003, 73–74, original emphasis).

Self-refleXivity is the mediation of the internal forces with eternal ones, as a battle waged within themselves and as a team. It is not a question of being accepted; rather, it is a question of accepting oneself—pushing this further, accepting the singularity of one's *sinthome*, experiencing the joy and suffering unique to oneself—against an inescapable groundwork of interwoven connections. This is beginning to sound like D+G's "transcendental empiricism." The Mutants find themselves on an unlimited field where the dualistic distinctions are not yet in operation as a division between the physical and psychic world; it is a world of neither subject nor object. There is no stable matter/form relationship formed as yet, only molecularizations of flow. It seems to me the Mutants are indeed molecularized bodies. Mutant freaks are *always experiencing*—which "freak" as a verb indicates: to become or make frightened, nervous, or wildly excited. Then there is "freak out;" to enter into a period of irrational behavior and emotional instability. The particular part of the BwO that has mutated continually reorganizes experience at the level of the plane of immanence. By virtue of being a freak, they escape stratification. The Spinozian ontology applies here as well. The Mutant is just the network of his or her relations with the world, totally externalized in it. The happiness of survival, their conatus or "will to live," is the mutant's recognition of being part of the word despite being rejected by it. But, am I perhaps pushing the analogy too far?

If the original X-Men (Angel, Beast, Cyclops, Iceman, and Marvel Girl)[10] were "children of the atom"(Newman 1999, in Trushell 2004, 153), then today's X-Men are the paranoiac children of genetic experimentation—the *homo superior* of viral or parasitic subjectivity, caught in the postnuclear predicament of a permanent anxiety over the present and the future. As freaks, they are born with their trauma already materialized—inheriting a very uncertain and polluted world. "Mutant superheroes bear overdetermined inscriptions of marginality revealed in every body trauma and transgression" (Bukatman 2003, 72). This becomes a way to queer the body, since what is "normal" disappears; if all members are Mutants, then no members are outcasts. They are *never* normal. What the mutant Freaks reveal is the ambivalence of the body's status relative to contemporary culture. So, will they be the ones to inherit the earth as argued in chapter six? Not if "Smallville" (as Lois Lane calls him) is around!

It was a televised serial and *not* a comic book narrative that "saved" Superman and projected him into the twenty-first century. *Smallville* addressed the two pitfalls of earlier attempts that failed to reach youth—invincibility and history. By staging Clark's adolescence, it enabled the writer/producers (Alfred Gough and Miles Millar) to position Clark, in his disguise, somewhere between a high school freak and geek (freaky geek?), making him vulnerable to all the human emotional traits that have to be "controlled"—lust, love, hate, temper, anger, and so on. Like the *Roswell* series, *Smallville* does not present Clark as an alien. He is a vulnerable teenager whose eyes often tear up. His effeminate, sensitive ego is forwarded (Lois Lane ironically calls him "Smallville"), while his phallic side remains repressed—there is no need as yet to don the famous glasses to indicate meekness, bookishness, and so on. He is that already. Furthermore, Clark regularly undergoes near-death experiences, sometimes dying, when caught in the grips of kryptonite. In one case a "scar" from a knife wound appears on his body, but later disappears, of course (320, "Talisman"). But, a history of the body has been recorded.

This history is further developed as he grows to discover his superpowers and how to use them properly (no pornographic peeping with his x-ray vision for instance!). As an audience we already "know" Superman the adult well enough. This allows *Smallville* (here designated *SV*) to explore his "virtual past" in the Bergsonian sense. It suspends time as movement and enables the youthful viewers to experience Superman's adolescence as a long duration (*durée*). A universe opens up; the writers can explore his pure past as a time-image (Deleuze 1989), opening up the full potential that is available to them. His virtual past becomes a dense crisscrossing of memories, characters, incidents, temporal distortions, and so on, that are rhizomatic in their complexity, perfectly suited to the serial repetition that televised media allow. Common sense as an unfolding spatial narrative no longer becomes a necessity as past, present, and future collapse into one another. As a haecceity, each season is forwarded to bring the "presence" of Superman back to youth so he can continue to *endure* in the American psyche.

In brief, *SV* succeeded in enabling the myth of Superman to "live" once again, paradoxically by recovering the memory of what Superman eventually came to *be* (his future that was already known) by exploring what he was not yet. That enfoldment of time in *SV* turned out to be an enormous hit for the "family- and youth- orientated" WB Network as it was going into its seventh season—no small feat—complete with the usual fan base, Internet sites, blogs, slash fanzine narratives, and so on.[11] I watched six seasons that were available on DVDs and read the descriptions of seventh-season episodes before the dreaded Writers Guild of America (WGA) strike began on November 5, 2007. During the first four seasons, Kent is still a high school student and remains in Smallville before shuttling back and forth to the big city in seasons five, six, and seven—but he is not yet "Clark Kent the reporter." In episode 513 ("Vengeance"), he drops out of Metropolis University to help Martha on the farm after Jonathan dies of a heart attack, and then he decides to go to Central Kansas A&M, which is nearby.

Near the beginning of season six, the nonmutant Oliver Queen (Green Arrow) is introduced (604, "Arrow"). Midway through the season Oliver rounds up a band of Mutants to further the cause of justice (611, "Justice"): There is Bart Allan (Impulse), a wise-cracking young(er) speedball, who is faster than Clark (405, "Run"); Arthur Curry (Aquaman), who is as handsome as Oliver and equally as "loose" and who first shows up in episode 504 ("Aqua"); and Victor Stone (Cyborg), Clark's football team mate in high school, now turned machine in one of Lex's experiments, who first appears in episode 515 ("Cyborg"). Together, they form the Justice League, an obvious marketing clone of Marvel's successful *X-Men* series. Season six also introduces the Martian Manhunter, an intergalactic law enforcer sent by Jor-El to protect Clark/Kal-El. In episodes 608 ("Static") and 612 ("Labyrinth"), he saves Clark from two Zoners, escaped convicts from the Phantom Zone whom Clark is tracking down and killing that season (thus preventing him from joining the new Justice League). In season seven, Kara (formerly Supergirl), Kal-El's cousin's arc, is developed to add some dysfunctional family dynamics, as is Lois Lane, who becomes a full-fledged reporter. Her promotion is complicated by her dating the new editor-in-chief of the *Daily Planet*, Grant Gabriel, who turns out to be a clone of Lex's brother Julian. Lana seeks revenge on Lex and reunites with Clark as his doppelgänger Bizarro! The Black Canary, a vixen siren, is introduced in episode 711 ("Siren") as a possible member of Oliver's Justice League. All these arcs obviously appeal to various dimensions of postfeminism.

So now, given the profound role Superman plays in the American psyche, what kind of ideological duty is the young Superman performing in the post–9/11 era of anxiety? What's the narrative telling the youth, and why does *SV* captivate them? My thesis will be that *SV is managing the anxiety of difference—* that it is taming the threat of difference that is invading America's borders and invading boundaries across ethnic, racial, and sex/gender lines—to ensure that the inhuman X is contained where it should be, and *that the posthuman becoming-animal of Freaks is stopped.* Ultimately, *SV* is fundamentally a Judeo-Christian narrative that promotes the utopian vision of idealized community, as well as answering to the fears of technological and biological manipulation generated by corporate America in a globalized world that is rapidly changing the urban/rural relationship.

Into the Vortex of the Tornado

The setting of *SV* in Kansas, in America's Midwest, is perhaps beyond my full comprehension in terms of its place in the American psyche and in its history as well. Smallville lies in the American Heartland, and I naïvely ask, Is this the place of rural communities and farmers' fields that are threatened by the currently expanding global marketplace and by increasing urbanization? Is this the place of down-to-earth Christian family values, lying between the la-la land of the West Coast (California, Oregon, Washington) and the intellectual realism of the East Coast (Washington, DC, New York, the New England States), a mythical meeting point that collapses into an abyss that shapes the myth of America's expansion of the Wild West? and Does the infant from Krypton crash into the heart of the American psyche? Perhaps Metropolis (the city of "sin and crime") is Chicago— not quite Rupert Murdoch territory, but it has a rich history of gangster activity and is home to *The Daily Herald*, *The Sun-Times*, and the *Daily Tribune*, where the haunt of Conrad Black still floats about. In the *Superman* movies, it is always blatantly New York—but that's not a "mere" three hours by car from Smallville as the myth goes!

To help me ponder such questions, the *Wizard of Oz* readily comes to mind. With the start of season two (201, "Vortex"), Lana is saved by Kent as she is swept up by a tornado, an obvious allusion to the famous narrative. Dorothy lives with her older aunt and uncle on a farm during the Depression, just like Clark does with his younger adopted parents, Martha and Jonathan. The Kent farm is the stage for the conflict between the "small" farmer and the "big" corporation—the rural/urban split that may have political parallels in the Midwestern states in various forms of heroic democracy.[12] All this is speculation, of course, but as Peebles (2003) articulates in his remarkably incisive essay, some of which is purposefully ironic and tongue-in-cheek, the heartland of America—the Midwestern plains— served as a Utopian dream for nineteenth-century Europeans fleeing from European industrialization and establishing utopian rural communities built on a mixture of communist and Christian ideals. Among others, he mentions the Zoarities of Ohio; the Swedes of Bishop Hill, Illinois; the Amana colony in Iowa; the Bethel colony in Missouri; and "the Rappites" in Butler County, Pennsylvania (a cult around George Rapp). What emerged in the Midwest were many attempts to bring Christianity and Marxism together as a way to combat the worst consequences of industrialization.[13]

Perhaps, what clinches *SV* as the seat of ideological struggle in America is Thomas Frank's (2004) political analysis in his book *What's the Matter with Kansas: How Conservatives Won the Heart of America.*[14] Frank maintains that Kansas represents the measure of American normality both in terms of the psychic Imaginary of its citizens and as a place for market research companies to test their products. He further argues that the Republican Party and the George W. Bush administration have harnessed turn-of-the-century agrarian populism by calling on the Midwestern cultural capital of honesty, innocence, and "traditional" values to fuel the cultural war concerning moral issues. For Frank, this diverted the public's attention away from the Bush economic agenda that favored deregulation, privatization, and lower taxes for wealthier people. In hindsight, it seems that Frank was right.

So, starkly put, the "failure" of a resolution between Christian morals and communist idealism can be characterized as one between idealism and materialism, between spiritualism and crass capitalist gain, between a tight-knit system of self-sacrificing neighbors and a general system of selfish commercial trade. This has been *one of the fundamental antagonisms that have shaped the American psyche*. It's two-party system, the Republicans and Democrats exchange roles as to which side of this divide the country is leaning toward during election years. The Evangelicals (the Christian Right), who support strong Christian morals and "family values," have historically not (necessarily) had a problem with capitalism, as was made evident by their support for G. W. Bush's second term.[15] So, two interesting questions arise: To what extent is the myth of Superman's *Smallville* an allegory of American Judeo-Christian values in their relation to the progressive advances of capitalism? and How is the American psyche structured by the Real of the anxieties of the age with the 'help' of this imaginary myth?

Wholesome Goodness

Keith Murphy and Jonathan David Tankel (1998, 60, in Taylor 2007, 349–50) make the claim that 91.5 percent of the superhero comic-book audience consists of white, middle-class, adolescent males. If one is to accept the quantcast.com demographics of *SV* (the caveat being that they have "sparse" data on *SV*), it clearly shows that it appeals to 18–24 year-olds, with 25–35 year-olds a close second. The surprise demographic is the so-called "ethnic" audience, which shows that both African Americans and Hispanic Americans far outweigh the Caucasian audience, with Hispanic Americans being the clear leader in terms of ethnic demographics. This is rather amazing (and more than likely inaccurate) considering that *SV* makes no appeal to being "politically correct" (PC); although it does reflect the demographic fact that fewer African Americans live in "America's Heartland." The one African American who is introduced in the first season—Pete Ross, as Clark best friend, who shares his secret—is never fully developed. There are no racially charged episodes, and at the end of season three, Pete quietly disappears after telling Chloe that his parents are divorcing. In the last episode (321, "Forsaken"), he moves to Wichita to live with his mother, Abigail Ross, who had been given the status of judge in a previous episode (310, "Whisper"). Pete makes a surprise return four years later in season seven (713, "Hero") with his own superpowers! It seems that *SV* makes no attempt to be PC. The paradox of being PC is that the admission of guilt nevertheless centrally locates the dominant white position. While denying white to be a particular identity, PC renders it neutral, thereby marking the place where the truth concerning the others' oppression becomes knowable. *SV* announces that it is white, episode after episode.

In terms of cinematography, the lighting used in *SV*—with its rich sunrises (the stock shot of the Kent farm in particular is bathed in sunlight), sunsets, and clear nights; with its candle light shots and it soft focus on its key stars—presents a pastoral realism not unlike a Norman Rockwell picture. Yellows and reds predominate throughout the series, with, of course, blue used as an accent. Using side lighting for the principal characters to make their best features stand out is simply a given.[16] Day shots of Smallville are confined to establishing shots of the Talon (an ex-movie theater), which is the local coffeehouse and hangout located on the Main Street, and of the Smallville Medical Center and the Kent Farm (it's actually shot just outside of Vancouver, in Cloverdale, British Columbia, to add an ironical twist). Ground shots of the LuthorCorp Plaza and the Daily Planet building (shot in Vancouver) by day and bird's-eye view shots of them by night establish Metropolis as "the city." All the rest of the interior scenes are shot on sets, with liberal use made of computer-generated imagery (CGI).

The Kent family is under the strong moral guidance of Jonathan, who in season five runs for the U.S. Senate (506, "Exposed"). Later in that same season, he dies of a heart attack (512, "Reckoning"). Jonathan's death is in keeping with the Biblical narrative that I will come to later. Jonathan and Martha may just as well be Mary and Joseph, having received Jor-El's (God's) "only son" (Jesus) through a virgin birth (orphaned). Joseph probably died in Jesus's youth. He disappears from the scriptures, and Jesus is referred to as Mary's son; she is a widow.[17] Jonathan's senatorial work continues to be carried out by Senator Martha Kent. As is well-known, melodramas are typically female-orientated. The primary audience is women whose *jouissance* is satisfied through an act of identification with the protagonist that produces the usual tears and weeping. Classically, they stage the Oedipal drama within a bourgeois, patriarchal social order where the father structures moral authority and guidance, while the mother is a self-sacrificing family caregiver, attempting to live up to impossible ideals of femininity and motherhood.

Within *SV* the self-sacrificing mother is somewhat modified when Jonathan dies. At first, a motherly superego tries to intervene (410, "Crusade"); Martha enables Clark to kill his split self, Kal-El, taking her son "back" from Jor-El (his biological father). But this does not hold consistently throughout the rest of the seasons. Martha moves steadily toward the influence of Lionel Luthor, not entirely seduced by power, but drawn back to her own social background; her father is a prominent corporate lawyer. Martha mostly reassures Clark that it's human to suffer, love, and show emotions. Generally speaking, the costume/mask/logo of the superhero marks the symbolic birth or "rebirth" into the symbolic order (logos). At that point maternal power is lost and patriarchy steps in. Here, Martha plays a "dual role" as a female senator, updating the dynamics to post-Oedipal proportions, even making it to Washington, DC, in season seven. Martha is most often presented in a desexualized way—not Puritan in dress, but close to it, occasionally dressing up modestly to perform her senatorial duties. An unconsummated love relationship develops between Martha and Lionel Luthor, the founder of LuthorCorp—their entangled relationship is an allusion to "sleeping with the enemy," of senators selling out to big business since it seems almost unavoidable.

SV, like most teen dramas, agonizingly tries to suspend sex between teens, so much so that Lana Lang has (literally) a virgin pregnancy with Lex Luthor in season six (607, "Rage"). We find out that the pregnancy had indeed been "cooked" up by Lex (618, "Progeny"). The characters on the show are all extremely attractive, even "baldy" himself, Lex Luthor, the refined, piano playing, accomplished Renaissance man who is juxtaposed to "farmer" Clark Kent, who dresses in a lot of plaid shirts and blue jeans. But this is necessarily so, as I develop this below. Clark never aggressively goes after sex; he shies away from it. Sex is always coming at him, mostly steamy, heavy make-out sessions with Lana, as her football-hero boyfriend, Witney Fordman, fades at the end of season three and then her sordid love affair with Jason Teague through season four ends in his death at the start of season five. Sexual aggressivity for Clark is permitted when he is "not" himself—when he is under the influence of red kryptonite (204, "Red"; 613, "Crimson") (more below) or in a "wet" dream in which he is floating off his bed (304, "Slumber"), or even in a dream-like memory (306, "Relic").

Clark is also placed in a triangle (like Dawson and Pacey in *Dawson's Creek*) with Lana Lang (the hazel-eyed, dark brunette cheerleader who comes across as pure, chaste, and sensitive, but then borders on being a femme fatale in seasons four and seven[18]) and Chloe (the blonde, green-eyed "smart-girl," who is a new character specifically penned to play a Scully-like *[X-Files]* detective). All this harks back to the long tradition in the *Archie* comics where Archie is torn between Betty and Veronica—but with a huge difference: all the women characters are clearly third-wave "emancipated" postfeminists, especially Lois Lane.[19] An army brat who is the daughter of General Sam Lane, she enters the narrative in season four (401, "Crusade") and is quite apt at playing with the phallus.

In high school it's still a ménage-a-trios conflict, but at the end of season five some love decisions "appear" to be resolved. Lana slowly moves over to the "dark" side to be by Lex's side, although she and Clark are still much in love (612, "Labyrinth"; 616, "Promise"). Their love continues to smolder through season seven via Bizarro (Clark's doppelgänger). Finally, Clark and Lana "do it" in episode 707 ("Wrath"), causing (no less) an earthquake! Chloe learns Clark's secret in an arc developed during season four, and becomes a "true friend" and confidante as the characters transition from high school to Metropolis. This division of love relationships repeats a transcendental/materialistic heterogeneity within the series, which I develop below. Lana grounds Clark to Earth. "You're still the same Clark Kent to me," she says, even when he reveals to her that he is an alien, Kal-EL (622, "Phantom"). His secret has lost its power of *being* a secret; the condition of *trust* is no longer a factor. Chloe remains wedded to his transcendentalism via her investigative powers. Adumbrating Kent's future attraction for Lois Lane as Chloe's cousin, the occasional incident is thrown in to indicate this arc: she sees Kal-El (Clark) naked with amnesia in the middle of a cornfield when Jor-El sends him back from the Fortress of Solitude after a scolding/lesson (401, "Crusade"); then there is a magic kiss that lingers when Clark plays the Green Arrow to give Oliver an alibi to ward off Lois's suspicions of him (610, "Hydro"); but the "kicker" comes in episode 613 ("Crimson"), when Lois's red "meteorite" lipstick has the episode bordering on "adult entertainment" if left unchecked.

The Alien Messiah: No Flying Allowed!

Given where I left off with Lois and Clark, one of the more surprising discoveries I made while doing research[20] for this chapter is the number of Christian youth blog sites that embraced *SV*'s moral dilemmas, and what they took to be the right choices against a background of clear-cut divides between good/evil, right/wrong. *SV* also offered a pedagogical road map for Christian youth ministries (Dean 2004). The name "Jesus" is equated with "salvation" ("YHWH," the Hebrew tetragrammaton representing the name of God means "will save"), which is further equated with passion. The route to salvation is therefore passion. Tap the passion of youth; link it to Jesus, who shows unconditional love for humanity; and you will be "saved"—just as in Remy Zero's theme song for *SV*, "Somebody Save Me." Superman unconditionally saves people like Jesus.

To further map out the obvious Judeo-Christian allusions of the story, Gary Engle (1987, 25) mentions that Superman's alien name, Kal-El, a neologism penned by George Lowther in his 1942 comic strip, directly refers to the Hebrew "el" that can act as a root and an affix. As a root, it is the masculine singular word for God, while angels in Hebrew mythology are called *benei Elohim*—literally the sons of God—or *Elynim*, meaning higher beings. Used as an affix, "el" is translated as being "of God" and is included in names scattered throughout the Old Testament (Ishma-el, Dani-el, Ezeki-el, Samu-el). In Semitic mythologies, angels are equally so named (Israf-el, Aza-el, Uri-el, Yo-el, Rapha-el and Gabri-el). Michael, the warrior angel who is Satan's principal adversary, would fit Superman's role perfectly. Moreover, Engle adds that the morpheme "Kal" bears a linguistic relation to two Hebrew roots: kal means "lightness" or "swiftness"; it also bears a connection to the root hal; the "h" is a guttural "ch" as having *ch*utzpah. Hal translates into "everything" and "all," so Engle concludes Kal-El can be read as "all that God is." Kent is also a form of the Hebrew kala, where its k-n-t form in the Bible means "I have found a son." An interesting bit of hermeneutic speculation.

The www.hollywoodjesus.com/superman site adds to Engel's claims, specifically cueing in on the classic *Superman: The Movie* (1978), directed by Richard Donner and starring Christopher Reeve. Specifically, they mention that Kal-El means "Star Child" in the Kryptonite language, tying Jesus's birth to the announcement of a special star (Matthew 2:2). Krypton sounds like "Tikkum olam," a Hebrew concept of restoring the world's wrongs. Clark Kent's journey to the Fortress of Solitude in the North[21] to get his education is like Jesus's wandering out in the desert to gain solitude before he starts his ministry. This list can easily be extended, and indeed Anton Karl Kozlovic (2002), comparing *Superman: The Movie* (1978) and *Superman II* (1981), came up with 20 Superman-Jesus parallels to the Bible! Plus, he further identified eight Christian character traits that pretty much speak to followers of Christ's ministry: humbleness, gentleness, friendliness, and goodness; being a caring and upright man and an outsider; and having divine testiness and even a dual identity. Apparently, Christ, too, had a double identity: "As Clark was the mask of the Man of Steel, Jesus was the mask of God" (9).[22]

The writers/producers are quite aware that they are playing with and to the myth of the "alien messiah." And, they do it brilliantly. The question is to what degree the *allegorical imagination* is being played with. The not so subtle references already start with the pilot episode. The obviously crucified Clark is left in the middle of the cornfield by the high school football team with an "S" painted on his chest (for Smallville), unable to move because of the kryptonite around him. Then there is the scene with him fortuitously standing in front of a statue of an angel in a graveyard at night, during a meeting with Lana by her parents' gravesite. His silhoutte fills out the statue's form so that it appears as if he has sprouted angel wings (in the series' pilot). The more subtle references deal with the relationship between Lex and Lionel Luthor, which I will say more about below. Lionel, the CEO of LuthorCorp, comes across as a Pontius Pilate-like figure, not quite certain as to where he stands with Clark/Kal-El and torn between exploiting and/or caring for him. Is this capitalism in the guise of a caring human face? He has named both his sons after famous Roman leaders: Lex (Alexander the Great) and Julius (Julius Caesar). He runs LuthorCorp (Roman Empire) through shrewd business deals and secrecy and by being one step ahead of Lex. He is continually concerned about its welfare, at times referring to Roman history as a source of business knowledge.

Lex has a paranoid relationship with his father; he is always unsure whether his father is plotting for or against him. Lionel's only interest is to make sure Lex can run the corporation in the future—but not yet. Lex is short for Alexander, and one immediately thinks of Alexander the Great as a figure who conquered territory for the Roman Empire but also stretched it too far. In episode 103 ("Hothead"), Lionel tells Lex that the Caesars sent their sons to the farthest reaches of the Empire to see how the world works, and compares this to his sending Lex to Smallville to run his fertilizer plant. Unlike Lionel, Lex appears to be the perfect embodied figure of the schizophrenia of capitalism and the impossibility of its demise. His clandestine activities are all involved in the paradox of *both* saving the world *and* conquering it through the scientific experiments with the freaks of the kryptonite meteorite storm, or by harnessing alien power. One never knows for sure. Totalitarian schemes of grandeur abound. In episode 603 ("Wither), for his costume party, Lex even dresses up as Julius Caesar to Lana's Cleopatra. This episode consummates their love relationship, and in episode 610 ("Hydro"), she accepts his marriage proposal—given that she is now "pregnant" with Lex's child and has been rejected by Clark.

Fate/Destiny/Choice: Earning His Angel Wings

In *SV* Clark has not yet earned his angel wings—his cape. He does not yet know what his destiny is. He is *grounded*, unable to fly—as yet. But, boy, can he run—around! All this is in keeping with the need to thin out his steel skin for today's youth. Clark must suffer and feel pain, and the best way is to place him in a masochistic position, as a St. Sebastian-like figure. His is a mortified body, haunted and "kicked around" by the meteoric debris of his planet Krypton that he needs to sweep up, battered by the freaks the green kryptonite produces, threatened by the crimal ghosts that have escaped from the Phantom Zone, tortured by his inability to share his secret with the woman he truly loves (Lana), torn between the haunts of two fathers (Jor-El/Jonathan), as well as of a third (Lionel), who knows his secret and acts as a distant father. He is an ersatz father who Clark can never be sure he can trust, despite Lionel's care and concern for Martha. Clark has friends, but solitude is his primary friend. Can it get any more painfully masochistic than that? Clark is crucified on Earth.

There is the *jouissance* of his suffering and the desire of his lack. To recall the distinction in Lacan: Lack founds the subject as a member of the social-symbolic order. It is desire that propels the subject toward the social world in a never-ending search for a person or object to fill that foundational gap in being. It is shaped by a fantasy that is always already structured by the Law. Clark, the "alien," has to be tamed, so to speak, for that is the social contract of "civilization." Desire must find both its origins and limits in the social order. *Jouissance*, on the other hand, belongs to the virtual Real. It is the excess, an expression of drive energy (*Trieb*)— of *zoë*—that is erotic and/or aggressive, which exceeds the limits of social rule and restraint. It is "beyond" any rational calculation of the subject's interest, beyond pleasure principle, and beyond preservation. It is pure pleasure as "enjoyment," the inhuman "X" that we must contend with. Clark/Kal-El obviously has the same human problem.

The paranoia that surrounds his possible destiny—to "rule" the earth as Jor-El says (217, "Rosetta")—and his paranoia of being discovered are worked out in the first four seasons through a series of arcs as an Oedipal conflict between two Fathers: these can be taken both transcendentally—Jor-El (God) and Jonathan[23] (Joseph)—or materially: Jor-El (biological father) and Jonathan (adopted father). In the Deleuzian logic of a disjunctive synthesis, where two heterogeneous parallel elements coexist without interference, such logic deals nicely with the post-Oedipal era that young men find themselves facing. Christian youth may identify with the transcendental side, while the other choice remains for any young man who does not come from the place of a traditional family. Queer youth can identify with Clark remaining closeted. The haunt of Jor-El never leaves Clark (just as the haunt of who one's biological father or mother were never leaves an orphan). This is made obvious in the classic *Superman: The Movie* (1978). Before placing the infant in the rocket ship, Jor-El II (to be specific) and not his mother, Lara, blesses his son with Biblical sounding words: "We will never leave you. . . . All that I have, I bequeath you, my son. . . . *You'll carry me inside you all the days of your life . . . the son becomes the father, and the father the . . . the son*" ("Thus *spake* Marlon Brando!").

Interpreted from a Christian theological position, Clark has to figure out his "calling"—the desire of God his Father. "What does my Father want of me?" At the end of season two (223, "Exodus"), Jor-El speaks to Clark via his spaceship, telling him that he must leave Smallville, his parents, and his friends to fulfill his destiny, at which point Clark attempts to destroy the spacecraft and Jor-El's spirit along with it. When he does so, he injures both earthly parents, and Martha, who was pregnant, miscarries, doubling his guilt in relation to these two symbolic "Fathers." By disobeying Jor-El, Clark ends up in Metropolis under the influence of his drives (*Triebe*), addicted to his power when he is under the influence of red kryptonite (his "drug" of choice). He is branded with an S on his chest by the power of Jor-El as a "reminder" of his destiny (301, "Exile"). This again "historicizes" the body-in-pain to show that he is capable of becoming mortal. Jor-El comes across as a stern father, taking Clark's powers away from him for failing to return to the Fortress of Solitude by sunset the next day as had been agreed on, thereby siding with the humans by placing Chloe's health ahead of his promise (501, "Arrival" and 502, "Mortal").

For the Church, destiny translates as a vocation, or "calling"; for today's youth this destiny amounts to existential angst in an uncertain world of neoliberal showmanship. This is what secularism provides. Jonathan as Joseph can only give Clark moral guidance, the foundation of Christian values, so that he can consciously and *freely choose* to make a responsible decision. This is yet another fantasy of existentialism, freed from the burden of the unconscious—nevertheless a fundamental pillar of liberal democracy. Having two names (Kal-El/Clark Kent) is of significant psychoanalytic importance, and is something that many immigrants, especially East Asian people, experience. Their so-called "good name," which is traditionally given to them by their fathers (as Kal-El), bathes them in the gaze of their fathers' traditions, languages, and values, which they find to be at odds within the new culture that they must embrace (as Clark Kent). There is a split between the Ideal-Ego [I(O)] and the ego-ideal [i(o)],[24] which is the psychic turmoil Kent is undergoing—a clash of values. "What do these two fathers want from me, since I am a hybrid of both and do not entirely belong to one or the other?" We have an updating of the immigrant's psychic experience that is no longer one of assimilation as it was in the 1940s, but clearly conflicted and hybridic. Clark's anxiety over his difference is what is at issue.

There is a limit to what an "earthly" father can do in terms of destiny for a "god made flesh." Joseph/Jonathan comes to face this limit. Thus, the authorial position of these two symbolic Fathers is made even more ambiguous when Jonathan has to "cut a deal" with Jor-El to save Clark, whose *jouissance* has overwhelmed him via the red kryptonite. The arc goes something like this: In the very beginning of season three (301, "Exile"), Clark, under the influence of a red kryptonite class ring, has become a criminal in Metropolis. The only way to stop him is for Jonathan to be imbued with Kryptonian powers so he can "put him in his place." The exchange with Jor-El to attain such power takes place in the secret and sacred Kawatche Native Caves[25] that are in Smallville, near Miller's Bend, a "temporary" site for Clark to work out his destiny by collecting a number of "keys" that will lead him to the Fortress of Solitude at the end of season four, where more of his destiny will be revealed. It becomes obvious as season three unfolds that (in keeping with the chronological Biblical narrative) Jonathan isn't going to hang around. He has betrayed his covenant with Jor-El, which was to give Clark back to his biological father. Jonathan has sacrificed his life for his son by tapping into Jor-El's power whenever needed, yet not delivering Clark to him. In episode 310 ("Whisper"), during his heart attack he speaks off camera ("Not now! Not yet!") as if he were addressing Jor-El, telling him not to terminate their agreement, as Clark leans over him. In episode 317 ("Legacy"), Jonathan is summoned by Jor-El's octagonal spaceship key, and Clark saves him as he falls off the roof of the barn. Jonathan then slips up and calls Clark, Kal-El. In episode 320 ("Talisman"), Jonathan, via Jor-El, is able to heal a wound Clark sustained when he was cut with a sacred knife. It all ends in the last episode of season three (322, "Covenant"), when the wrath of Jor-El comes through: he will kill Jonathan if Clark doesn't obey and join him in The Fortress of Solitude to be "reborn" (the three-month break between televised seasons provides a time for Kal-El's scolding and/or education by Jor-El).

Why A Third Father? Reforming the Criminal CEO

A further complication to Clark/Kal-El's conflicted desire and his struggle with his enjoyment (*jouissance*) presents itself. There is yet another "father" Clark has to contend with—none other than Lionel Luthor. This impossibility is set up early in season four (406, "Transference") when Lionel and Clark exchange bodies using one of the Kryptonite stones (Stone of Water). This exchange cures Lionel of his fatal liver disease, and so one presumes it has also affected him in other ways. He is reborn, initially at least, as a more caring person and father, although somewhat too late to change his relationship with Lex.[26] This reformative arc is further developed in the fifth season, beginning with episode 503 ("Hidden"), where Lionel becomes a conduit for Jor-El so that Clark (who has been mortally wounded, no thanks to Jor-El, who has stripped him of his powers for having disobeyed) can be saved. But the price for Clark's rebirth is high: someone close to Clark will die. This is a fate from which there is no escape. Jor-El continually sets himself up as a stern, unforgiving father.

Lionel's increased involvement and presence in the Kent family can only emerge once Jonathan is off the scene, so to speak. Hence, season five presents such a transition where he tries to befriend Clark and develop a love interest in Martha. Episode 512 ("Reckoning") is a pivotal episode for the development of such a possibility. Jonathan dies of a heart attack "caused" by Lionel's exposing a photograph of Clark as Superman (one presumes). In this particular time-image narrative Clark tells Lana his secret, only to have her die; such a fate has already been forecast by Jor-El. Time is then replayed by Clark, calling on Jor-El in the Fortress of Solitude to give him a crystal that will produce another potential actualization and save Lana. Lana's death is replaced by Jonathan's death, sealing Clark's fate and leaving him guilty of causing his father's death, ultimately because of his disobedience to the Law (Jor-El/God).

In episode 519 ("Mercy"), Lionel informs Clark that he knows his secret. He then becomes an oracle through which Jor-El "speaks." In the same episode, Jor-El's spirit works through his body, and he scribbles something unknowingly in Kryptonian scrpt. Episode 521 ("Oracle") follows with an interesting haunt of Jonathan appearing to tell Clark to kill Lionel, as if his unconscious repressions have been materialized. Jonathan's ghost turns out to be Milton Fine, who is a form of Kryptonian artificial intelligence (Brain InterActive Construct, a.k.a. Brainiac). In this episode, Lionel reveals to Martha that he knows Clark's secret, and he comes clean as to how Jonathan died. Lionel once more becomes a conduit for Jor-El via a Kryptonian script warning Clark that Zod from the Phantom Zone is coming, and saving him from Brainiac. In the last episode of the fifth season (522, "Vessel"), he tells Clark how to deal with Zod.

In other incidents Lionel always appears helpful and supportive, providing an alibi for Clark to draw Lex's suspicion away from him (611, "Justice"). In episode 619, "Nemesis"), he tells Lana that he forced her into marrying Lex so that Clark could remain protected; in episode 621 ("Prototype"), he translates a Kryptonian symbol as "mirror," and in the season's closer (622, "Phantom"), we learn that he is a collaborator with the Martian Manhunter in the plan to capture all the phantoms in the Phantom Zone. Lionel had been an emissary of Jor-El's all along! It turns out that Lana married Lex so that she could spy on him and keep Lionel informed!! Speaking in her role as a senator, Martha tells Clark in episode 619 ("Nemesis") that Lionel has changed but that she is not willing to entirely trust him. In season seven there is no change in this general direction. In episode 706 ("Lara"), it reaches a point where Lionel says to Lex: "Can't I take an interest in my son's well-being?" To which Lex replies: "Oh, and which son is that? You spend as much time protecting Clark as you do pushing me away. Exactly whose father are you?"

So what's going on here? The writers, while retaining his ambiguity, present a potential redemption scenario whereby even (perhaps) a ruthless CEO and criminal can continue to reform. Given the corruption in American big business that unfolded during the span of its seasons (the 2001 Enron scandal, being simply the tip of the iceberg[27]), prompts all sorts of questions. We are no longer in the realm of the "underground" crime of yesteryear, but the "overground" of business corruption—among the Martha Stewarts of the world who are, relatively speaking, still only lightly dismissed for just stepping over the ethical business line. Like the Luthors who own and control the media, controlling one's public representation is crucial. The reforming CEO, in this case Lionel as a protector of Clark as mediated by Jor-El, is the signal that big capitalism can still save the "farm," if I can put it in those terms. Capitalism can still "save" America. Its corporations can defend the country from other companies: metaphorically when Zor-El (Kal-El's uncle) attacks Lionel in season seven when Lionel refuses his demand that he make Clark trust him (708, "Blue").

Lionel himself is conflicted in his relationships with Clark (whom he has often called "son" since finding out his identity) and Lex. To cut through continuous paranoid exchanges between Lex and Lionel is to expose the schizophrenia of capitalism itself—Lex being the excess of what is supposed to be the "more" legitimate ways to run a corporation as exemplified by Lionel. The stark contrast between Lex's baldness to Lionel's long hair metaphorically mark the extreme and pradoxical limits of capitalist growth—bankruptcy and unlimited spending. As two sides of the same capitalist coin—one interior, the other exterior—they can only annihilate each other at a point that is 'beyond' capitalism itself. The logic of baldness is not a question of *not* having hair. Rather, the relation between baldness and long hair in *Smallville* is presented as an enfolded space. Baldness is the internal limit of capitalist growth. Paradoxically, Lex has *too much testosterone* (DHT—dihydro testosterone). He is always ready to risk it "all" to achieve power and control. The boldness of the Phallus is completely exposed in its tumescent state. Lionel, as the exterior limit of capitalism paradoxically has *too little testosterone*. He has to pull back on his schemes otherwise he might lose it "all." In prison, Lionel cuts off his hair to match his son's baldness as a sign that he is willing to exceed his limit. He is ready to "up the stakes"—this change occurs when he is convicted and sent to prison because of the actions of his son Lex (322, "Covenant"). Both sides go to the extreme edges, with Lionel condemning Lex to the Belle Reve asylum (309, "Asylum") and with Lex not helping his father get out of prison. In the cutthroat world of corporate stakes, Lionel constantly tries to stay one step ahead of his son to prevent, allegorically speaking, capitalism from becoming a totalitarian paranoid schizophrenic system that engulfs the world through its excesses of *jouissance*.

Disjunctively Speaking

The struggle between the two superegoic authorities is worked out self-refleXively in the Fortress of Solitude, not surprisingly via "crystals," which has a Deleuzian ring to it.[28] They are, indeed, "crystals of time" that are the trapped memories of Krypton, and hence we can call them the virtual past that Clark is dealing with; the potential of actualization is yet to take place. When he activates a crystal, he is simultaneously split between past and present. They mark a cut or a disjunction. (Crystals also trap Kryptonian criminals as images and memories). The Fortress of Solitude, when movement is frozen, becomes the place of the virtual Real where Clark faces the omnipotent, god-like "voice" of Jor-El. His message is necessarily confusing. "Does he want me to 'rule' the world with my superpowers?" "Am I to hate humans because they are imperfect and weak?" and "Do I obey or disobey him?" Such are the questions of the superego that every teenager asks himself or herself, Christian and atheist alike, as guilt feelings emerge, and as transgressions against the Law arise. Here, of course, we are talking about transcendental, not secular, laws when caught up in their theological implications, but we can shift to the ground level as well.

The disjuntive syntheis of *SV* operates on the material secular level when we replace Jor-El as God with Jor-El II as the briliant scientist on Krypton. In the former scenario, Jor-El (God) sacrifices his son to humanity; Superman as a God on Earth is always trying to redeem humanity, making them "better." As Superman, Clark sacrifices himself as a representative of humanity, thus giving up the possibility of being God on Earth. In this scenario the unanswered question is: "What's in it for Jor-El as God?" Or, rather: "What is the haunt of his biological father?" "What does he want from this exchange between him and humanity?" "What is his ranson?" We are stuck following this narrative as an entirely religious allegory. Biblically, this becomes a stickler. The Christian believer has to repress the stern God of punishment and forward the God of unconditional Love. Or, more heretically: Christ's sacrifice that delivers humanity from the Devil (Satan) was the price God had to pay the Devil (our "owner" when we live in sin) in order to set us free. They become partners in an exchange![29]

In the latter scenario, Jor-El II is no longer omnipotent. According to the *Kryptonian Glossary*, he is a brilliant scientist and the son of Jor-El I, also a famous scientist on Krypton, who also has a younger scientist brother, Zor-EL (a "climatographer" no less!). As such he, too, is subject to his fate and destiny—that things can go wrong with the creations he makes, with dire consequences. The tragic end of Krypton is something he could not prevent. In this reading, his "sacrifice" of Kal-El to "humanity" is to serve as retribution for his own scientific screw-up of not saving the planet; to cover up his own failures, his own lack of omnipotence—to save the honor of the House of El. The El family can turn out to be downright dysfunctional, as the two brother/scientists are at odds with one another, especially over Jor-El's wife, Lara, bringing these gods down to earth as well. This opens up more story line space for the changing post-Oedipal relationships between uncles and cousins. In season seven, Kara (Zor-El's daughter), begins her own rebellion against both her father and Kal-El, who has to deal with his newly discovered cousin. This opens up possibilities for making the obviously Oedipal house look dysfunctional, as Kara (first as an impostor in episode 322 ["Covenant"]) wakes up from her animated slumber in a spacecraft that has been sent to Earth before Kal-El's arrival (702, "Kara") and begins her arc of discovery.

The question in this disjunctive synthesis is whether Kal-El is a vanishing mediator, the figure of the Holy Ghost that reunifies God and humanity. Is he the condition of possibility and impossibility between the two Fathers—the divine Jor-El (God) and the earthly Jonathan (humanity)? Humanity would then be fully united with God in the Holy Spirit. But, the answer to this question seems to be— No. Kal-El does not go through any particular transsubstantiation of losing his status as the occupier of a transcendent beyond, no designification to "nothing but the Holy Spirit of the community of believers" (Žižek 2004a). There is no dialectical synthesis here. Kal-El's experiences are more like Nietzsche's "eternal return;" he is constantly being symbolically born and reborn in a cycle of differences. Like Buffy, each time he dies and is resurrected, he introduces a difference, but remains conflicted, torn between transcendence and humanity, grounded by the trauma of each. Unfortunately, in keeping with my thesis, it is the perfection of a transcendental moral order that *SV* upholds, as I explain in the next chapter.

Stamping Out Alien-Human Freaks: *Smallville*'s Moral Duty

The symbolic death of Clark (Christ) would be to sacrifice his superpowers in such a way that they can be put to use to help overcome the "sins" of humankind—to negotiate the transcendental and secular worlds. The voice from the Real, Jor-El, never entirely leaves him. He is still "heard" in the seventh season (702, "Kara"; 708, "Blue"; 710, "Persona"). Psychoanalytically, all this simply means is that Jor-El is none other than Clark's superego. The superego "is nothing other than . . . *jouissance* at the core of being—which we encounter in anxiety, *in an altered form* [as a power]" (Copjec 2006, 108, author's emphasis). Clark's ad(hear)ance or disobedience to this Voice in "Solitude" is all related to how, what, and why he is able to enjoy (*jouissance*); here I signal this affectivity as the entwinement of both joy and suffering—painful pleasure/pleasurable pain.

This is complicated further by the *fundamental puritan* Voice of Jonathan that did not entirely fade away, restaging Clark's fundamental symptom (*sinthome*), the impossible decision between heaven and earth. Jonathan was riddled with guilt for having sold out to Lionel Luthor—in exchange for help with the adoption papers for Clark (207, "Lineage")— by convincing Pete Ross's family to sell their land so that LuthorCorp could build a fertilizer plant. As a result, he exhibited a self-imposed penance through isolation and self-reliance, refusing financial support of any sort, not only from Lex and Lionel, but also from Martha's dad. Engagement in heroic labor to save the family farm transfers (in the psychoanalytic sense of transference) to Kent's heroic labor to save the Earth—just slightly more meteoric Freak territory to cover! The guilt in Clark's case is doubled. To escape his imprisonment by Zod in The Phantom Zone (522, "Vessel" and 601, "Zod"), a place his father created for intergalactic criminals, he releases a number of phantoms that make it through the porthole back with him to Earth. These "Zoners" are, in effect, after revenge for what had been done to them by his father. So Kal-El feels guilty for having released them, undoing what his father had already done. The Kryptonian Freaks and the Phantom Zoners address these two levels of guilt—material (the Freaks) and transcendental (the Phantoms). Their heterogeneity is maintained by the logic of both/and: Clark is both an Earth alien and Kal-El, a cosmic, "intergalactic traveler," the latter a name that Clark gives himself in episode 610 ("Hydro").

It's Raining Mutants

Kryptonite is obviously a very fruitful substance—psychoanalytically speaking. As the Freudian uncanny (*unheimlich*) substance, it is the seat of trauma; as the Deleuzian molecular substance, it changes the BwO. It lies scattered beneath Smallville's county, waiting for its victims, emitting its radioactive rays, comparable to the unearthly noise of insects heard under the well-manicured lawns of Lumberville in David Lynch's opening sequence of *Blue Velvet*. In the original *Superman* series of 1938, green kryptonite weakened Superman as an alien immigrant, because it reminded him of home. The mourning for the loss of one's homeland and culture could lead to the pathology of melancholia, so one had better assimilate and become an American. It was from the yellow sun (the sunrise of the new homeland as iconically presented by the stock photo shot of the Kent farm bathed in sunlight) that Superman drew his strength. Getting too close to *objet a* is the cause of the anxiety of loss. But in *SV*, the trauma of home has come down to Earth—by way of a meteor shower, bringing with it the pestilence of a mutant freak show. Kryptonite is the material "cause" of humanity's sins. One xenophobic reading would suggest that the Freaks are the alien invaders from other countries who are crossing U.S. borders and who do not want to assimilate, or they are indeed terrorists, but this is more the preserve of *The X-Files*. Despite the politically incorrect (PC) stance of *SV*, the anxieties are directed toward adolescent bodies.

In a globalized world, *SV* becomes a glocal microcosm for the anxieties of the age, and on this level Clark feels responsible for having brought this pestilence with him. *He must quell the moral panic that has hit the Midwest.* This is what makes this narrative so appealing to Christians. On this level of guilt, their humanoid mutant powers as posthumans parade a variety of possible neurological and physical enhancements. Becoming-animal (D+G) is treated negatively. Beginning with episode 102 ("Metamorphosis"), where kryptonite causes Greg Arkin to become a powerful insect, the string of (generally adolescent) freaks are rolled out season after season to serve as cautionary tales to remind the audience that "normal" is the zero-degree of monstrosity. The inhuman power of the drives (*Triebe*)—as the excesses of enjoyment that these mutants suffer from—are moralized throughout the series through various hyper-exaggerated examples. An overweight girl drinks smoothies laced with kryptonite dust, which cause her to lose weight so rapidly that she ends up killing and eating people around her to sustain herself! (107, "Craving"). Then there is the promiscuous football player who becomes meteorically infected; he freezes his victims to death as he sucks out their body heat to stay warm (105, "Cool"). Having been exposed to green meteorites, Coach Arnold will do anything to win a football game by using his ability to start fires (103, "Hothead"). This is a warning about the evils of winning at all costs. Steroid-like use is explored in other episodes, when even the Green Arrow shoots up an experimental potion to heal himself, causing a personality change (607, "Rage"). There is even an attack on lesbianism—not once, but twice. In episode 104 ("X-Ray"), Tina Greer is a meteor-rock mutant teenager who is able to transform into the shape and face of whomever she wants—but she wants to become Lana and steal her identity; while in episode 211 ("Visage"), she shape-shifts to become Whitney so that she can be close to Lana.

Such incidents are too numerous to continue to list, but in all cases the Freaks are breaking community standards or the Law (Pizzino 2002). Normal becomes a prescriptive moral demand that echoes Clark demanding a "normal life." In these paranoid structures, any radical externalization of alienation—Earth Freaks or Intergalactic Phantoms—serve momentarily to sooth the discomfort caused by the instabilities of identity. The mutant is a locus of a double negative identifica-tion: on the one hand there is a threat, and on the other hand that very threat con-firms that there was something to be threatened by. As a self-referential loop, this simply confirms an imaginary psychic boundary. However, an endgame of sorts is reached in season six (615, "Freak"), when Chloe turns out to be a Freak as well. Might this be the beginning of a shift toward advocating their place as a minority in future episodes? For Lex's paranoiac purposes, these freak "gifts" or "curses" are to be paradoxically exploited. They may be used to benefit humanity or to destroy it via wetware genetic technology to produce super soldiers (as Project Ares, 621, "Prototype"), developed in Lex's laboratory to protect against metahuman crimi-nals and aliens invading America and humanity in general (in this case to be read as illegal aliens and terrorists).

At first, one wants to immediately compare *SV* to *The X-Files* because of the string of freaky incidents and strange events that are continually taking place, and of course there is Chloe's character that was modeled after Scully of *X-Files* fame. However, in *SV* not only have the alien(s) landed (we are not "looking" for them), but the conspiracy theories and anxieties are directed in just the opposite direction—toward the Freak's struggle with the world of the inner self. The stan-dard way a fantasy frame works as ideology is that it obfuscates the "true" horror of a situation, which in turn intensifies the BwO to a point of traumatization. In the cultural paranoia of *The X-Files*, the fear of aliens was directed toward eth-nic and racial assimilation; to illegal aliens crossing borders, working without green cards, and creating "mutant" children through miscegenation (Dean, 1998; Burns 2001; jagodzinski and Hipfl 2001). In *SV*, at least in one episode (609, "Subterranean"), Clark actually befriends a young Mexican illegal immigrant and defies Senator Kent's wishes to turn the young man in. This is surprisingly liberal. The meteor-infected farmer who knowingly hires illegal immigrants, and kills them when they try to escape from their labor, is trying to save his farm.

The anxiety of the age today is directed at the manipulation of the genetic structures of life itelf. The brain, in particular has become the site of experimen-tation through the manipulation of its neurology by using a varieity of prosthetic nanotechnological implants, and, of course through the pharmacopoeia of avail-able drugs to change its chemistry. Humans are but one species of many that are subject to direct manipulation of the genetic code that may lead to more gifted-ness, mutations, and cloning. The extraordinary scene in *Aliens 3*, when Ripley sees the previously failed mutations of herself has become the classic image in this regard. There are two heterogeneous anxieties at work that *SV* tackles. Clark is haunted on two levels. *First*, the Kyrptonian mutant Freaks speak to the material-ization of the body—special gifts and powers through which the posthuman body is enhanced, green kryptonite being iconic for genetic molecular research, prosthetic brain research, steroid use, and the like. Green kryptonite alters the molecular structure at the level of the BwO. *Second*, the Phantoms that escape from Krypton's prison are of course the transcendental haunts of the mind that Kal-El has accidentally unleashed. The Phantoms are haunts capable of possessing others. This psychic dimension can only be controlled with *crystals*—the memories that need to be overcome and faced, the traumas of the self. Physical power can overcome the mutant freaks, but to overcome a phantom requires another level of mental ingenuity. Body and mind appear split.

This is the narratological reason for the various kryptonite substances (besides further "humanizing" Clark) and the various *crystals* and magic stones that come into play—to cope with anxieties and overcome the Enlightenment division of body/mind. The Phantoms possess the body that is affecting the mind (e.g., Bizarro), while kryptonite affects the mind through the body. This enables a self-refleXivity to emerge by exposing the virtual Real. Red kryptonite is the most obvious. Clark as "Kal" cannot control the Real of his drives under its influence. All his repressions are lifted. It is an unpredictable substance, since it never works the same way twice. His red, yellow, and blue clothes are exchanged for black T-shirts and a black leather jacket. Kal becomes the rebel—unlimited *jouissance* is available to him as a devil, theologically speaking. The exposure of his Real self reveals the "truth" of his unconscious. Viewers quickly relate to the repressed feelings that are released. The clearest expression of this is in episode 613 ("Crimson"), when he crashes Lex and Lana's engagement party with Lois in tow. His speech to the dinner guests exposes every repressed desire he has. It should be noted that previously in the narrative red kryptonite was used to feminize Superman, to soften up his armor; now it is used to make Clark more phallic—but *not* Kal-El since doing so would unleash the inhuman within him—the very paranoia Clark fears—the potential to conquer Earth and become Lex (more below).

Silver kryptonite is a synthetic extract used on Clark by Brainiac (507, "Splinter") that makes him paranoid delusional. He becomes convinced that his friends and family are out to destroy him. As Lacan puts it, all subjects suffer from an internal alienation—a fissure between the ego and superego. The paranoiac, however, is unable to come to terms with the realization that all of us are defined by such internal ambivalence that lies at the core of our being. It is coming to terms precisely with that core impossibility that enables us to deal ethically with the *jouissance* of our drives—the joys and sufferings that surround the question of existence, externalized through our laughing and crying bodies. Black kryptonite is precisely the substance that tears asunder that "internal ambivalence." The schizoid split of the self exposes the X of our inhumanity: Kal-El/Clark split in episode 401 ("Crusade") when Kent "kills" Kal-El with a crystal. In episode 417 ("Onyx"), it is Lex's turn to split into a "good" and "bad" self. Blue kryptonite is also introduced in episode 708 ("Blue"); it temporarily strips Kal-El of all his powers.

In contrast to kryptonite are the Stones of Power, known also as the Elements that allude to Aristotelian ontology. There are three "stones" or "crystals:" the Crystals of Fire, Air, and Water. United, they transform into the one Crystal of

Knowledge, which contains the knowledge of Krypton's civilization. Each stone/crystal has a power associated with it. The Crystal of Fire is capable of healing; the Crystal of Air is capable of killing, while the Crystal of Water can cause an exchange of personas—Lionel and Clark change places in episode 406 ("Transference"). Such an impossible exchange is made to occupy the difference in the Other and to open up secrets and intrigue for further developments in the plot.

The mind games that the Phantoms play further expose self-refleXivity. The wraiths require special crystals to entrap them and a special mental effort to get rid of them. This is especially the case in episode 612 ("Labyrinth"), the episode with which I conclude this chapter. The last phantom to be dealt with appears at the end of season six (622, "Phantom"). Known as Bizarro, it is Kal-El's Doppelgänger, his inverted double figure in the mirror. Too much blue kryptonite and he can become overloaded with power, whereas green kryptonite gives him strength,while the sun weakens him. All these various types of kryptonite, stones, and crystals are like a computer game, in that they enable the writers to play in this *SV* universe with Clark/Kal-El and the viewer's psyche. The only kryptonite not introduced in the series is gold kryptonite, which does not kill Kryptonians but removes their superpowers permanently. Given that gold is symbolic of money, this leads me to the next section, for its use would end the conflict.

$ <> S : Or Why Do Lex and Clark Not Laugh at Themselves?

At the heart of *SV*, besides all of the love interests, business intrigues, freaks, phantoms, and so on, is the enigma of Lex and Clark's relationship, enfolded with each other as friend (*Freund*) and enemy (*Fiend*) alike. A number of commentators have remarked on their queer, homoerotic relationship (Kustritz 2005; Battis 2006), which has spawned a large slash fan base. Andy Warhol also famously queered Superman (Collins and Cowart 1996). This homoerotic relationship between the two bodies might also be theorized as a profound question of an ethical relationship that emerges when facing the madness within oneself. In other words, Lex/Clark explore self-refleXivity in its most extreme form. It is to face (in the Levinasian sense) the inhuman difference within us. They are two sides of each other. I am first suggesting that Lex and Clark are the *extimate* opposites of each other; as a paranoid, what Lex unconsciously feels in Clark is precisely the need to establish the limits of his narcissism. As he famously says to Clark, "There's a darkness in me that I can't always control. . . . I can feel [it] creeping over the corners. Your friendship helps keep it at bay" (404, "Devoted"). What Clark unconsciously sees in Lex is the very fear of what he might become if he let his superpowers—the Real of his drives (*Triebe*)— dominate him, to be overwhelmed by *jouissance*. As in the *Lord of the Rings*, he doesn't want to be seduced by power—to become corrupt like Gollum, who was once Sméagol. Lex is a refined Gollum. Under the influence of red kryptonite, however, Clark effectively is Lex, but only as the human Kal. On the other hand, when Lex is possessed by Zod, he effectively is the alien Kal-El on red kryptonite with unrestricted *jouissance* to seize power and dominate the Earth. So while Lex desires to dominate the world in good totalitarian fashion, Kal-El fears that he could dominate the Earth as his superego (Jor-El) demands—Enjoy! What is a fearful paranoia for Kal-El—to rule the world—is precisely the Machiavellian paranoid fantasy that Lex wants to make happen.

This reversal separates ethics from politics. Lex practices politics. Tyranny, as Hannah Arendt said, is politics at its purest. Clark, on the other hand, practices ethics, an ethics of agape,[1] the Judaic call to the face of the Other, most forcefully articulated by Levinas, setting up an asymmetrical and nonreciprocal relationship where the responsibility to the Other must be infinite, the other's face being helpless, vulnerable, and issuing an unconditional command.[2] Clark, as much as he hates Lex, can't "really" give up on him, even if "moral" redemption seems impossible. This agape love is best articulated by a short exchange between Martha and Clark near the end of an appropriately named episode (619, "Nemesis"), where Clark and Lex have been trapped in a labyrinth of underground tunnels, but both manage to escape before an explosion destroys the entire network.

> CLARK: "Mom, what if part of what Lex is . . . is because of me? What if I gave up on him too soon?
> MARTHA: "You'll never give up on anyone Clark . . . because your greatest strength might also be your greatest weakness . . . your hope."

The separation of politics from ethics is not quite the same as the separation of church and state as the compromise position: render to Caesar what belongs to Caesar and to God what belongs to God. In other words, the church looks after morality (not ethics), and the state looks after maintaining Law (not politics). The difference between ethics and politics as against morality and the Law is that the former are realms of becoming; politics being the process by which to achieve equality and distributive justice, while ethics is the process of mutual recognition. Morality and the Law are fait accompli, rules already in place.

To break the deadlock between Lex (politics) and Clark (ethics) requires the intervention of a third party: Justice, which lies outside the Law. In episode 611 ("Justice"), Kal-El refuses to join the League of Justice. He wants to remain an independent agent; he is even reluctant to take part in their planned action to blow up Lex's plant unless he is assured that no one will be in the plant at the time. In other words, a choice must be made. The Green Arrow has made it; El-Kal has not; or rather, he is incapable of doing so, since it would be an act that violates his "infinite" responsibility to the Other. He would be committing an act of evil. As Slavoj Žižek (1997) put it, a choice has to be made, for the logic that structures the primordial couple (here taken as Lex/Clark) is not active-passive but active-neutral. A choice has to be made that disturbs the neural balance. "I love you all" is only possible if there is an exception: "There is at least one person whom I hate." The universal love for humanity that Clark professes is only possible through the brutal hatred of an existing exception who is the enemy of such a possibility—Lex. Thus, the "truth" of universal love is the hatred of an exception. This very premise prevents Clark from loving Lana and telling her his secret. True love can only emerge from the background of universal indifference. Lana would have to be that unique person who stands out against that very totality that must have been neutralized. Neither Kal-El (nor Oliver, as the Green Arrow with Lois[3]) is capable of love in this sense. As Žižek points out, love and hatred are asymmetrical. "Love emerges out of the universal indifference, while hated emerges out of universal love."[4] And what of Lana in light of this reading? The script writers have her waver back and forth as a femme fatale when she is with Lex or "pure of heart" when she is with Clark, depending on which one she loves—it's her "choice!" She even falls for Bizarro more so than she does for Clark (710, "Persona"), even after she learns that she has "slept with the enemy." In her heart of hearts, Lana likes "bad men." Clark is too much the mama's boy. Besides, Bizarro was better at the "night moves," if one catches the pun.

Clark sacrifices love for Lana and eventually Lois for "humanity." His destiny should be to serve Justice, which would break the separate ethical and political spheres. Here the so-called infinite depth of the face disappears, for justice must be blind to free it from the confinement of particularity so that it can search for that space "beyond" the Law. It is because of the depthless abyss of the subject in the first place, one's inability to truly "know" the Other, that Justice comes into being to enable some regulations to be made between us. This then is the ethical and political gesture. But Lex, for Clark, is not just another criminal, just as the Joker is not just another criminal for Batman. He is his flaw, the very X of his identity that he struggles against, precisely as the episode has it, his "nemesis" (episode 619). As long as Lex and Clark remain in recurring arcs of love/hate; friend/enemy, in a vicious self-refleXive circle, no Justice will be served. They are too busy seeing each other's face in a structure of paranoia. The matheme $ <> S of the subtitle speaks to this relationship between Lex <> Clark. The split subject of wealth that is Lex ($) is in a complex relationship with the Imaginary full subject that is Clark (S). Lex demands unconditional love and recognition, while Clark demands unconditional truth and honestly. Neither can give what the other demands. They are symbolic inversions of each other. Each is the other's paranoid fantasy formation.

Egghead Paranoia

One of the unspoken mysteries of *SV* is "Just how was Lex affected by the meteor shower?" "What kind of Freak is he?" We are misdirected to raise the full implications of this question by being reassured that Lex "only" gained a super-immune system—his asthma was cured, but that's all. But, of course, this is a geek turned freak; it is his baldness that is the sign of his having a brilliant freak brain as his superpower (like Professor Xavier), raising the question of whether this paranoid-schizophrenic genius is indeed mad, or whether such madness always accompanies the new and strange that "it" creates, which we fear. He does suffer bouts of madness (308, "Asylum"). Lex's brilliance is shown in his ability to speak other languages (e.g., German in 317, "Legacy"); he is a Renaissance man; he quotes Rilke, fences, plays classical piano, and as the chief executive officer (CEO) of LuthorCorp, he is like the brilliance of schizophrenic capitalism itself. As an egghead, his imaginative capacity represents the ambiguity of today's mutant technologies. The alien technologies that he tries to harness are already posthuman in their integration of the organic and inorganic at the level of information. His best talent, through the alacrity of his self-expression, is to both lie and tell the truth; as Lacan (S XI, *Four Fundamentals*) shows in the "Lair paradox," it is impossible to tell which is which. So, another inversion presents itself: the brawn of Superman to the brains of Lex, a theme that all of Hollywood's hit *Superman* movies have played out. Christopher Reeve, who became recognized for his role as Superman in these films, performed yet another reversal both in the *SV* series and outside of it. As a paraplegic he played Dr. Swann, an expert on Kryptonian culture who helps Kal-El; and, of course, with his wife, Dana, he endeavored to help develop institutionalized cybernetic research that would explore spinal cord injuries and disorders.

Lex's paranoia is all about the need to protect himself—evidenced by the extraordinary security and surveillance of his mansion that we see on every episode—on the pretense that he is a rich billionaire who is hounded by the press and disgruntled ex-partners (CEOs and females alike). He desires to develop an army of invincible soldiers—Project Ares—which he thinks would seal global security. The parallels to the post–9/11 era are worrying in this regard—the Bush administration's unilateral approach in its global actions and in the war in Iraq; the building of fences along the U.S.-Mexican border, the talk of reviving the Reagan Star Wars fantasy to protect Americans from missile attacks.[5] As François Roustang (1987) succinctly puts it:

> I would say that the paranoiac is someone who, paradoxically, is threatened with losing his own limits. That is why he needs to provoke the other into becoming his persecutor. The other will thus protect him from the threat of dissipating like a liquid; he will set a border that the paranoiac must constantly confront in order to reestablish the certainty of his existence in a circumscribed physical or psychic space (715).

The paranoid Lex cannot recognize his own limits. They are uncertain given his inventive brain (gift/curse) and money. One might say that his primary narcissism was not curbed in his infant years to initiate the first psychic division. His totalitarian tendencies become a way to position himself as a guarantor of truth. Both of Lex's parents withdrew their love—his postpartum-depressed mother smothered the infant Julian, and to defend her, Lex took the blame. Lionel, thinking that Lex had truly done the deed, withdrew his love and put him in situations in which he had to fend for himself, with no support. "[T]he paranoid suffers from not having established at the proper time the limits of his own individuality. He is forced to invent a set of hallucinated or delirious limits, by imagining a group of persecutors" (Roustang, 716). Of course, Lionel is foremost on his list as his persecutor. "Paranoia is the illness which *surmounts the absence of individuality*; it is, therefore, a *hatred of individuation*, and that is why it is the *model of all power*" (717, emphasis added).

As a paranoid personality, Lex symptomatically insists on his individuality and perceives a world of conspiracy that helps him consolidate his imaginary psychic boundaries. He must always purify himself as "good" by repeatedly dissolving boundaries and disrupting the consolidation of identity to keep the Other at bay. Lex has no friends; he sadistically schemes to take away the *objet a* of Clark's desire—Lana Lang. Clark could never be anything but an enemy and friend to Lex; the two poles flip back and forth almost effortlessly. The trick with Lex as a character in *SV* is to continue to make him morally redeemable, for him to show some remorse for what he has done to Lana, who once trusted him and set limits to his paranoia. Such acts as his willingness to go to jail to clear himself of Lana's death (701, "Bizarro") keep viewers believing that schizoid capitalism can be contained and redeemed.

One can never laugh at Clark's *sinthome*, to which he is blind; it is the source of his suffering, of his "singular unhappiness of his singular existence" (Roustange 1987, 713). And in no episode does Lex laugh—at himself. The paranoaic is incapable of laughter, says Roustang, because he is overwhelingly convinced that his certitudes are true. In the business world, "only the paranoid survive," as Andrew S. Grove (1996) seems to think. Laughter is capable of holding suffering at a distance. It is "the smallest conceivable unit of detatchment" (711). If both Lex and Clark are incapable of laughing at themselves—to be comic rather than co[s]mic—then the next best thing is to achieve this distance through love; Lex, through his failed attempt with Lana, simply ensures his paranoid state, and Clark, through his failed attempt with Lana, ensures his paranoia by transfering his love to humanity so as to set his limit.

Between Fantasy and Delusion—Is a Very Thin Line

I end this chapter with the same "move" I made in chapter 7 concerning Buffy's psychic state. Episode 612 ("Labyrinth") has Clark caught in his unconscious, a rather brilliant piece of writing, which in effect riffs on Buffy's own psychiatric experience in the same season six and around the same "serial time," as a psychotic breakdown in episode 6017 ("Normal Again"). The doctor says, "Think about it Buffy, what is more likely? That you are a superhero killing all these fantastic creatures or that you are a poor sick girl who has created this exciting imaginary world." Clark awakens after being hit by "something" near his barn, and finds himself in a ward in a mental asylum, Fairview Mental Health Hospital. He is told by Dr. Huddson, a gentle and patient Freud look-alike—but without the cigar and glasses!—that he had a psychotic break five and a half years ago and that he is a paranoid-schizophrenic. He is further told that during the Smallville meteor storm, his biological parents had been killed and that the Kents had adopted him. He was all right for a while, but when it came to his freshman year in high school, the trauma of losing his parents got the best of him, and he had a psychotic break. He had become delusional.

All the mental patients around Clark are tired of hearing him spout about having superpowers, about Lex being his arch enemy, about creatures from the Phantom Zone, about the fact that he comes from another planet, and so on. They know the Smallville verse by heart and call him a Krypto-Freak. The asylum, although meant to be practicing up-to-date psychiatric methods, is a throw-back to the 1950's stereotype of a snake-pit: the holding cells are jail cells, the ward is like the one famously seen in *One Flew Over the Cuckoos Nest,* and the warden-like-orderlies wear white uniforms with black bow ties. One of the patients tells him that he believes him, and that he knows because he himself is from Mars! He looks exactly like the Martian Manhunter.

Clark manages to escape only to find that Lana has bought the Kent farm and taken over his bedroom in the barn. She has been patiently waiting all this time for him to receive "the" cure, which might cause some amnesia. She thinks that Clark has been cured, but he tells her that he has escaped. She reassures him that it's possible to pull through this together. Clark leaves to search for his mother at the Luthor mansion, only to find that she knows about his escape from Fairview and that she has called on the house guards to "help" him. She tells him that she had married Lionel, who had made it all possible for Clark to get the help he needed. He escapes from the house guards aided by Chloe, who has a getaway car. Chloe believes in Clark's superpowers, but it turns out that she, too, is an inmate at the same hospital. He uses her car to pay a visit to Lex, who is sitting behind his desk and is surprised at the audacity of Clark to come to visit him. It turns out that it was Clark who had caused the car accident on the bridge (series' pilot) that had left Lex a paraplegic, ruining his life. Clark goes back to Chloe, but Lana is there as well. Chloe says they have to leave because the police are out to get them, but Clark hesitates as he hears Lana pleading for him to stay and take the cure. As the police come to take both of them back to the hospital, Chloe pulls out a gun and is shot to death. Clark ends up back at the hospital in a straightjacket, talking to Dr. Huddson, who believes he has a cure for his paranoia.

In a rather brilliant bit of writing, the environment that surrounds Clark in Dr. Huddson's office has been carefully incorporated into his psychotic fantasy dream—not unlike the famous case of Judge Schreber. Jor-El turns out to be an antibacterial soap product, Jor-el; he hears Dr. Milton Fine (a.k.a. Brainiac) being called on the intercom; books are lying around with the titles *Fortress of Solitude: A Prisoner's Memoir; Labyrinth;* and *The Crystal Ship;* there is a magazine called *The Phantom Zone: Exploring the Recesses of the Human Mind.* A picture of the Employee of the Month, Oliver Queen, hangs on the wall. One of the nurses is called Raya (601, "Zod"). And the kicker is that 33.1, Lex Luthor's secret lab, is actually the number 331, a sign of the building capacity with a smudge between the 3 and 1 digit. The "good" doctor says:

> When the human mind is faced with tremendous emotional pain, it has no choice but to protect itself. You have taken bits and piece of your surroundings and created an alternate universe where you feel safe and secure. Clark . . . [I]n a world where you truly had no power, you chose to give yourself superpowers.

So, to conclude: The psychotic narrative that Clark constructs in the mental hospital (like the Freudian case of Dr. Schreber) is precisely what is required to cope with and live in the "real" world of schizophrenic capitalism, its psychotic manifestations as represented by his inverted extimate Other—the brilliantly "mad" and evil technocratic, Lex, who remains apocalyptically both the savior and destroyer of the planet.

Afterword—A Self-RefleXive Moment

I have nothing brilliant to say. Yet, I feel compelled to say something. What follows are random thoughts that I gathered up as I considered what I should put in this final section.

It is no secret that this trilogy of books was written with my son Jeremy in mind. He's in his late twenties now, and my bet is that there are many boomer dads who are trying to figure out what's up with their sons and daughters. This book, unlike the other two, took a long time in coming. I wrote the *Buffy* chapters in 2003, while my ideas regarding self-refleXivity emerged in 2006. My guess is that I was just too ambitious, just one of the many things I am cursed with.

I wonder if all those hours spent watching so much television were worth it. I mean it all seemed so trivial at times. I now know why academics are reluctant to look at television series. Six seasons of *Dawson's Creek*, seven seasons of *Buffy*, seven seasons of *Smallville*, three seasons of *Roswell*, and one season of *Freaks and Geeks* added up to a hell of a lot of hours of viewing. Stacked on top is all that "high-falutin'" theory, which I am sure I never got quite right.

I am really not sure if I have successfully articulated the concept of self-refleXivity. I thought I was being rather clever, but probably not clever enough. Eventually, I'll figure out what it *really* means.

One of the amazing things, of course, is how utterly easy it was for me to become immersed in the worlds of the Buffyverse and the Smallville-verse, to suffer with the Dawson crowd, and laugh with the Freaks and Geeks. This experience was made even more intense with the DVD boxed sets that I eagerly and seemingly endlessly devoured. I even had two boxed sets of *Roswell*, one in Edmonton and the other in Klagenfurt, my two "homes." Without them, this "research" would not have been possible. It is extraordinarily easy to see how an entire industry of commodification surrounds each "hit" series, and how easy it is to become a fan(addict), a concept I developed in *Music in Youth Culture*. The escape into video online worlds is very much a similar story, a form of protection against a world that is so uncertain in terms of where one should be in it, so dependent on one's own skills and marketing capabilities.

My immersion in these televised worlds is not that different from my immersion into the worlds of Lacan, Deleuze, Guattari, and Žižek. I am caught in the same way, and the academy is full of fan(addicts) as well. Each philosopher has a cottage industry built around him or her. Just like youth who find meaning and sustenance in these televised series, academics convince themselves that they have found the key to grasping the world. We can't escape our fantasies, and such fantasies have material consequences, so they can't be so easily dismissed as "simply" entertainment. This is precisely where our *jouissance* reveals itself. The Academy and popular culture are indeed strange bedfellows, a queer couple.

One of the most amazing aspects of writing this book has been the realization of how the "Freaks" and "Geeks" have been able to find a way to explore their anxieties through these co(s)mic narratives. I have a new respect for the writers, be they conservative or pushing edges; the arcs are just so clever. The gay sensibility of many episodes should be celebrated.

"Youth undercover" as developed in the introduction remains an apt metaphor for what I have presented. It is the freaks and the misfits, who need to see the light of day. The cover design by Gayle Gorman, a still from *Freaks and Geeks*, seems most appropriate. Sam's expression and body comportment have affinities with Edvard Munch's *Scream*, while Neill hugs the wall and braces himself for the "hit." In Canada suicide is the second leading cause of death among adolescents, while in the United States it remains the third leading cause of teenage deaths. Teen and youth suicide have tripled since the 1970s. Does that tell you something? For every successful suicide death in the United States, the National Institute for Mental Health (NIMH) estimates that in any given year there are ten failed attempts; other statistics boost that estimate to 30 to 50 unsuccessful attempts (Centers for Disease Control and Prevention, CDC). The suicide rate is even higher among lesbian, gay, bisexual and transgender/transsexual youth (LGBT). The contemplation of suicide in high schools is much more prevalent than parents, administrators, and teachers think. Conservatively speaking, one in 20 teens and adolescents is clinically depressed. The pharmaceutical fix through antidepressant drugs obviously ignores the social reality of a competitive capitalist system that has lost its social compass. The huge turnouts of youth who are supporting Barak Obama's bid for the U.S. presidency is an indication of the longing and need for change. Should it be a wonder why the post-gothic narrative form is so appealing and so relieving?

I am always struck by how fleeting what one writes is, especially when dealing with popular culture, and why the "present-ness" and immediacy of blogs have made them so popular. Books, especially academic books, seem to be a dying art. Yet they continue to emerge. Their denseness is perhaps another form of a "wall" that has to be scaled before we see the wonders on the other side. Much like I argued that the "fluff" of the Buffyverse was a wall for many adults.

It is easy to forget about all those anxieties one has growing up, the fear of approaching the opposite sex, worrying whether you have a sexually transmitted disease (STD), worrying whether you have impregnated your girlfriend (so your life is about to change drastically), your first sexual experience, the turgid love affairs, and so on. There are many dark and black days, which seem never to go away. Such anxieties were made present to me again. The array of characters available on this televised landscape present similar resonances in the Real of their desires. Today, we are all *transsexuals*, as Baudrillard once said.

As can been seen, most of the television series that I wrote about have two chapters devoted to them (the exception is *Roswell*). It seems that's how the

writing emerged for me. It was necessary to frame the larger context of each series before I could "get into it," to open up its world composed of countless episodes in order to map and manage them, cross-referencing my hunches, and so on. The analogy of finding my way around a video game comes to mind. In the end, I had to come to terms with my own affective resonances with each series: *Dawson's Creek*'s hyper-self-reflexivity, *Freaks and Geeks'* ethical dilemmas, and the paranoid schizophrenic narratives of the three post-gothic worlds of *Roswell*, *Buffy*, and *Smallville*.

That's it. I'm done.

Notes

Introduction

1. As posted on Jodi Dean's blog, July 17, 2006. http://jdeanicite.typepad.com/.
2. I remain convinced that the series of books that Arthur and Marilouise Kroker initiated through their own press efforts (New World Perspectives) during the 1990s, written in a delirious style that matched Deleuze and Guattari's efforts in *Anti-Oedipus* and *Thousand Plateaus*, were a forewarning of what has come to pass—global capitalism in full bloom continues to decenter identity into various assemblages as a means to increase profit margins through the rhetoric of digitalized technology as freedom. Paul Virilio's technology as pure speed, Jean Baudrillard's technology as simulation, Roland Barthes technology as rhetoric, Jean François Lyotard's technology of aesthetics, Foucault's technologies of the self, and Deleuze and Guattari's technology as a desiring machine present an idealized landscape of total mutability where an Enlightened subjectivity seems to be a quaint idea of the past.
3. This was the same criticism leveled at Judith Butler's performativity thesis when it was first developed in the early 1990s, with its bold claims of resistance to patriarchy despite her attempt to ward off her detractors in *Bodies that Matter*. Her thesis still remains problematic, unsolved, and strongly critiqued (see Tim Dean (2000), although her work has become progressively more psychoanalytic as she continually changes her position (see Layton, 2004, 207–240 for an assessment). By 2004, Butler had already moved on through yet another self-critique in *Undoing Gender*.
4. Difficult in this context not to think of the 1988–90 television series *Alien Nation*, where the story line enabled the exploration of issues of racial difference.
5. The East/West globalized paranoia (Al-Qaeda/Bush) is what Michael Rogin 1987 would term political "demonology": "The demonologist splits the world in two, attributing magical, pervasive power to a conspiratorial center of evil" (40). It doesn't take much foresight to see how loudly this claim is ringing on both sides.
6. Todd McGowan (2003) has written an excellent exposé of authority's loss, rehearsing Žižek's general claim that superegoic "enjoyment" has emerged due to its decentering. Jon Lewis's (1992) study of "teen anomie" in teen films and youth culture in the early 1990s had adumbrated this loss of authority as well. He expressed a rather pessimistic outlook, for although youth under capitalism are privileged beyond measure, the issue of the increase in teen suicide and depression does not go away.
7. For instance, the philosophical reflections of Giorgio Agamben (2004) and Eric Santner's (2006) magnificent study of Rilke, Benjamin, and Sebald as to the "open" of our animal nature.
8. Here I am simply referring to the "spiritualization" of artificial intelligence as discussed by Ray Kurzweil (1999) for instance, and the writings of Marvin Minsky (1986), Daniel Dennett (1991), and Patricia Churchland (1989).

9. I have Gayle Gorman to thank for getting me started watching this series about the posthuman future.

10. The same applies to the collapse of psychoanalysis with cognitive science and neuroscience. See Wilma Bucci (1997) for the former development and Mark Solms (2003) for the latter.

11. This insight concerning xenomoney comes from Brian Rotman (1987). When read carefully, Rotman does an excellent job of showing the genealogy of how the missing center of capitalism—its transcendental void that keeps it as a system open in the way profit is continually used to make more profit—develops from the notion of "zero" as it becomes adopted economically as part of the Western consciousness incorporated from its Arabic roots. As Lyotard (1993) put it, credit is "the advance of wealth which does not exist. Made in order that it comes to exist" (225).

12. This is rather well-known territory for feminists who support Irigaray's own "hysterical" writings in which she tries to establish a counternarrative to Lacan's edifice. See Lacan's (1998) "God and Woman's *Jouissance*'" in S XX, *Encore,* and Irigaray's (1985) reply in her essay, "Cosí Fan Tutti." See also Tom Hayes (1999).

13. This topological distinction of the Real I have maintained throughout my work. Sight has been reserved for the Imaginary, while cite belongs to the Symbolic register.

14. Here the entire problematics between reason and madness emerge. Foucault's (1965) historicizing of madness, as supported and praised by both Deleuze and Guattari, was severely critiqued by Jacques Derrida (1978) on the grounds that he had inadvertently set up a binary between madness and reason, which repeats the very "objective" discourses of psychiatry and the medical profession that frame madness in the first place. It seems that Descartes' method of "doubt" has a paranoiac dimension to it in the form of the *malin genie,* which is precisely where madness that underlies reason hides for Derrida. Descartes imagines that there is an all-powerful malicious demon that is controlling his perceptions, making him hallucinate or dream that he is in the world. For Derrida, the dividing line between madness and reason disappears in this case in such a way that a particular philosophy may be a form of madness itself. Madness is never excluded—the restricted economy of reason functions only in the general economy of madness. Derrida maintains that by virtue of speech, madness is staved off. It always remains the "other" of speech, as silence, but not thought (Cogito). Madness inside of thought can only be evoked through fiction (Felman 1975, 219). Yet, both present the deadlock of the role of literature as a buffer zone between madness and thought. For Derrida the fiction of madness orientates philosophy as a form of protection from it; for Foucault, it undermines and disorientates thought. The *malin genie* and madness are opposed, introducing radical doubt in Foucault's account. The binary is maintained. "The philosopher is also orientated, but in his [sic] own fiction so as to abandon it, while the madman remains engulfed by it" (220–221). In this debate we are really no closer in making any easy distinctions between being mad (as thought) and being mad (as silence). As Lee (2004) put it, "madness is part of reason, and vice versa; what remains stupid is our inability to distinguish between the two" (63).

Chapter 1

1. See Stevie Schmiedel (2004) for an important analysis of the differences between Deleuze and Lacan within the context of feminist theorizing of becoming-woman.

2. In none of the televised serials that are discussed can it be said that "the deficient paternal ego [given that it is under attack, missing, or simply weak in paranoiac plot lines]

makes the law 'regress' toward a ferocious maternal superego, affecting sexual enjoy-ment [as in Alfred Hitchcock's *Psycho* or *The Birds*]" (Žižek 1991, 99; see Buchanan 2002). Not even in the most Oedipal-looking plot, *Dawson's Creek*. When Dawson's father dies in a car accident, his mother does not begin to interfere or dominate his love life. She almost disappears from the story line for the rest of the seasons. Dawson's guilt is transferred over to Jen who is made to feel guilty for the cause of the accident. When it comes to Hitchcock films, the maternal superego is a Žižekian formulation, not a Lacanian one. However, this maternal superego becomes more and more prevalent as the Oedipal Father recedes.

3. This is where I part company with Buchanan's (2002, 112) mistaken claim that somehow the Lacanian Real is categorically separated from reality, when Lacan's claim is just the opposite: the Real is always present, but is revealed as nonsense, which "may" profoundly change one's perspective if it is encountered. Buchanan maintains that for Deleuze and Guattari, "the [R]eal and reality are one and the same thing" (112). If this is the case, then Lacan would say this is psychosis—that "other" form of madness. Buchanan maintains that "schizoanalysis begins where psychoanalysis leaves off, namely, the point where real-ity collapses into the [R]eal—the crack" (ibid.), then schizoanalysis is simply another name for psychosis. To maintain, as Buchanan does, that schizoanalysis is the moment of the crack when "it becomes clear that even though nothing has actually happened, everything has changed" (ibid.) is either to be read humorously as a psychotic break-down that is permanent, or quite comfortably Lacanian as an encounter with the Real. Again, there seems to be no way to distinguish the mad from the *truly* mad in schizo-analysis. Both are cracked, yes—but when is a delusion so great that it engulfs the sub-ject totally in the Real, despite being a "pragmatic" way of dealing with the unbearable horror of the symbolic order?

4. In *The Logic of Sense* (1990, 224–33), Deleuze discusses Lacan's phallic signifier of excess and lack and attempts to make the case that the heterogeneity of the pregenital and Oedipal series can be maintained through a disjunctive synthesis (229) rather than being ensured convergence and regulation by the phallus as object=x.

5. I make this case especially when it comes to "queering" the phallus (jagodzinski 2006a). Jan Campbell's (2000) "Queering the Phallus" covers some of this ground, as does Bergoffen (1996).

6. Perversion and hysteria are explored in *Youth Fantasies* (2004, 92, 127) and developed in *Music in Youth Culture*.

7. For example, the string of American political scandals and corruptions such as the Bay of Pigs, the assassinations of John F. Kennedy and Martin Luther King Jr., the Kent State shootings, the Federal Bureau of Investigation (FBI) involvement in the Iran-Contra Affair, the FBI's targeting of the Black Panthers, the Watergate affair, the Waco fiasco, the Oklahoma City bombing, the anthrax scares, the Columbine shootings, and of course 9/11. This list can be profiled for many postindustrial countries where similar scandals and corruptions are covered up.

8. I have tried to show this development and backdrop as it is manifested in video game culture today (see jagodzinski, 2006b).

9. While many have written about the paranoid climate since 9/11, where homeland secu-rity ironically spies on American citizens in the name of security; where America's eco-nomic resources are spent on the military to further an ill-founded hypothesis that American-style democracy should be exported to every country on the planet, especially to Islamic countries to ensure "world peace" and stamp out terrorism; where civil liber-ties and the Geneva conventions have been suspended in what Giorgio Agamben (1998) has called "zones of abandonment" (e.g., Guantánamo Bay and Abu Ghraib); and where

vote-rigging in the past presidential elections and appointments to the Supreme Court seem part of Bush's White House strategy, I am particularly drawn to Emily Apter's analysis of this situation, especially her concept of supranational "oneworldedness" (2006). Her concept goes beyond the paradigms of world systems, planetarity, and transnationalism. She claims that "oneworldedness" envisages "the planet as an extension of paranoid subjectivity vulnerable to persecutory fantasy, catastrophism, and monomania" (366). "This is a globalism in which there is no front lines in war, in which civilian and military cultures are interchangeable, in which quotidian gestures and words invite *surcodage* . . . , and in which 'thinking like the enemy' . . . locks the mind into a loop of intersubjective projection that brooks no outside world" (370, original emphasis).

10. For a similar assessment see jan jagodzinski (2006c, 2007).
11. Flieger is referring to the famous reference made to the Hans Holbein painting *The Ambassadors* by Lacan in his S XI (*Four Fundamentals*), where the anamorphic projection of the skull becomes a way of splitting the space of the picture in two. By perceiving the alien object anamorphically, the viewer adopts a paranoid subjectivity of knowing that the world is looking back at him/her as an object of relentless surveillance.
12. I note here Fred C. Alford's (2004) essay on "Levinas and Paranoia: When the Other is too Other," in which he surprisingly takes Levinas to task for his racist remarks concerning Asians, and his warning against the "Levinas Effect" where Levinas's text seems to accommodate a wide range of possible interpretations.
13. Evangelical Christian and jihadic Islamists must update their ideological ground so as to retain their fundamentalism's relevance in a contemporary society. This requires new euphemisms and redefinitions—for example, creation theory now becomes Intelligent Design, while jihad no longer becomes a spiritual struggle directed against a self within to emulate the way of prophet Mohammed, but a religious war directed outward to annihilate a designated enemy.
14. The reality television series *Survivor* and *Big Brother* are perhaps the apotheosis of a haecceity. Not only is this a self-contained unit—an island or a "container" allowing a limited range of movement that is constantly surveyed by cameras; each day seems like a repetition of the one before where changes in affect mark subtle and less dramatic differences.
15. There is an upside to artificial intelligence (AI) if Hansen's (2004, 127–60) argument is accepted: the interaction with "digital facial imagery" (DFI) offers an affective bodily experience, dispelling the currently predominant model of the human-computer interface (HCI), which is maintained to be nihilistic by theorists such as Friedrich Kittler and Lev Manovich.

Chapter 2

1. I quote the footnote with added emphasis on p. 27 (*A-O*) at length, because it seems to be glossed over by so many of Lacan's detractors. "Lacan's admirable theory of desire appears to us to have two poles: one related to 'the object small *a*' *as a desiring-machine*, which defines desire in terms of real production, thus going beyond both any idea of need and any idea of fantasy; and the other related to the 'great Other' as a signifier, which reintroduces a notion of lack." *Objet a*, like Deleuze's virtual, operates as an immanent causality. It is not transcendent and cannot be abstracted from its actualizations.

2. It is no "secret" why Rhonda Byrne's (2006) self-published New Age book *The Secret* has become the rage of neoliberal desire. It provides the illusion that success in riches and life is but an attitude, a perception of "affirmative thinking." It's all up to individuals to take responsibility for their health, finances, and emotional life—all wrapped up and delivered through the spiritualism of universal cosmic laws.

3. As Lacan puts it: "the human ego is the other and[. . .]in the beginning the subject is closer to the form of the other than to the emergence of his own tendency. He is originally an inchoate collection of desires—there you have the true sense of the expressive *fragmented body*—, and the initial synthesis of the *ego* is essentially an *alter ego*, it is alienated. The desiring human subject is constructed around a center which is the other insofar as he gives the subject his unity, and the first encounter with the object is with the object as object of the other's desire. . . . This rivalrous and competitive ground for the foundation of the object is precisely what is overcome in speech insofar as this involves a third party" (*Psychoses* III, 39, original emphasis).

4. I will be accused (should someone care) of misreading the Real as virtual in the Deleuzian system of thought. I came across at least one warning in this regard (Widder 2000, 118). Their difference is, however, not explained, since it might be said that the *virtual* Real as I am conceiving it also "presents a synthesis of difference that cannot be reinscribed either within an oppositional logic or as a mere disruption of its schema" (ibid.). These latter two operations belong to the symbolic and Imaginary, respectively.

5. One clear example of this is presented by the oeuvre of Deleuzian film enthusiast Patricia Pisters (2003), who trashes Lacan's failure to address the affective dimension of life that Deleuze is said to fulfill. This stereotype of Lacan that she employs repeats the stereotype of Freud sketched by Deleuze and Guattari's *Anti-Oedipus* book that Flieger exposes in her "Up the Ante, Oedipus! Deleuze in Oz" (2005, 90–115).

6. The appendices of Bruce Fink's *The Lacanian Subject* (1995) list all the mathematical attempts by Lacan to work out the possible logic that is operating in the unconscious.

7. To see just how easily the argument can be inverted from Deleuze's BwO to OwB, see my rebuttal to Steven Shaviro's (2002) reading of Chris Cunningham/Björk's music video "All is Full of Love" in jagodzinski (2005, chap. 16).

Chapter 3

1. In her chapter, "From Psychoanalysis to Schizoanalysis," Powell (2005) sets up the usual opposition between desire as productive and lacking, surface and depth. The contrasted readings of Hitchcock's *Psycho* that she provides along both these lines do not cancel each other out, nor does one suddenly appear to be superior to the other; rather, they coalesce as complementary readings, each enriching the other. This is the strategy of complementarity I follow.

Chapter 4

1. The target audience for these teen dramas is 12–34 years of age. Being psychically "orphaned" (like E.T.) is a theme that runs throughout many of the teen melodramas reviewed here: Jen is estranged from her parents, Jack has a father who refuses to accept his queerness, Clark Kent has a demanding biological Father, while Max and Isabel Evans on *Roswell* have no idea who their parents are. Max even "abandons" his son twice in the series, the first time when Tess, his predestined, pregnant girlfriend/wife, leaves

earth to return to the home planet, Antar, and then yet again at the end of the series when she returns from Antar with his son, and Max must give him up for adoption.

Chapter 5

1. The theme song of *Freaks and Geeks* is by bad grrrl Joan Jett and the Blackhearts, "Bad Reputation."
2. Similarly, *My So-Called Life* (1994–95), which aired on ABC, also had a cult following, but was cancelled after 19 episodes due to poor Nielsen ratings.
3. I have not provided the actors' names in this chapter, treating these fictional characters as if they were empirical people in order to develop a thought experiment.
4. The "smart-girl" phenomenon will be explored later under a section that explores the ethics of this series. Sandra B. Conaway's (2007) dissertation explores the "smart-girl" phenomenon in a number of teen television series, including *Beverly Hills, 90210* (Andrea); *My So-Called Life* (Angela Chase); *Buffy* (Willow); *The Gilmore Girls* (Rory and Paris); and *Freak and Geeks* (Lindsay).
5. Mille is the mandatory naïve girl like Donna Martin on *Beverly Hills, 90210* and the Korean American Lane Kim on *Gilmore Girls,* whose mother is a Seventh Day Adventist. They are all virginal (at least in the beginning of the series), due to their religious upbringing. Mille's sidekick status (like Willow's relationship to Buffy) becomes compromised as Lindsay moves over to the Freaks, only to act as an anchor in times of trouble (13, "Chokin' and Tokin'").
6. Alan Sepinwall does a blog that sensitively reviews all of the *Freaks and Geeks* episodes, running a column about Judd Apatow with his collaboration (see "What's Alan Watching?" sepinwall.blogspot.com).
7. The distinction between crowds and cliques is common in the sociological literature on youth studies. Crowds represent different "identity prototypes" that reflect "different lifestyles and value systems," while the term *clique* refers to a small group that hangs together because the members "share similar attitudes and behavior patterns" (Bishop et al. 2004, 236–37). The boundary as to where one stops and the other begins is never made entirely clear. Crowds swallow up cliques. In *F&G* the cliques are representative of crowds. However, sometimes a solitary character can represent a crowd: Todd is the jock, Vicky and Cindy are the cheerleaders, and Alan is the bully, while Harris Trinsky is the nerd.
8. David A. Kinney's (1993) research indicates that bright students go "undercover." He notes that "bright students in several high schools used strategies, like clowning or underachieving, to avoid the negative labels of brain and nerd" (24). In his review of adolescents who were involved in school shootings, Jesse Klein (2006) notes that a large number of them were academic achievers. Both Eric Harris and Dylan Klebold, who staged the Columbine massacre in Colorado, were good students. Harris was considered one of the smartest students in his class, writing computer programs for Doom and Quake (62).
9. I develop the psychic issues surrounding the Columbine shootings in *Music in Youth Culture* 2005, 146–50.
10. His case study is based on the Woodrow Wilson High School (WWHS), which has a large population, and it is supplemented by detailed information from other high schools scattered throughout the United States (100).
11. James Messerschmidt (2000) presents the thesis of "oppositional masculinity" where boys who are unable to acquire the traditional masculinity status of being a prep or a

jock for any number of reasons (e.g., socioeconomic class, athletic ability) may differentiate themselves by utilizing the same social markers of status—leadership, violence, and sexual prowess. Daniel would fit such a possible description—a "dark jock" as it were. It's not surprising that Daniel turns to the Goth scene, attracted by Goth store clerk Jenna Zank after he has another reoccurring spat with his girlfriend, Kim (15, "Noshing and Moshing"). The Goths accentuate the oppositional aesthetic to jocks and preps.

12. David A. Kinney (1993) maps out two distinct processes that facilitate the change of identity from nerd to normal in the transition from middle school to high school. One path is to embrace behaviors and appearances that are respected by high-status peers, while the other hinges on an emancipation from popular peers' expectations and invidious comparisons by forming intimate friendships. These paths are roughly gendered with boys taking the first direction, girls taking the second. Kinney is silent on queer youth, who would have remained invisible and undercover at the time. *F&G* skirts this issue as well.

13. Mladen Dolar's critique of Althusser is already established in 1993, where he shows that Althusser's notion of the Imaginary cannot be annexed to ideology. What is foreclosed in the symbolic returns in the Real as a remainder. In this case, Neal's "puppet" speaks as if it had intentionality of its own.

14. Robert Pfaller (1995) takes a different tack. He rereads Althusser as recognizing Spinoza's ethics, whereby ideology is taken as positive knowledge with the void of the subject not necessarily being one of negation, but where such a void, what Pfaller refers to as "nobody," can have real effects within the of ideology itself. Pfaller calls on Klaus Heinrich's discussion of Homer's Odysseus, who tricks the giant Polyphem into telling him that his name is Nobody, and Bertolt Brecht's Herrn Keuner, who alludes to the German *keiner* (nobody). In brief, for Pfaller the void of the subject (as nonidentity) turns out to be yet another Imaginary, another mask. In the Foucauldian sense, this would amount to a "doubling," a mise en abîme effect that has "real" transformative effects in the symbolic.

15. The full scope of D+G's influence on music theory is rather daunting. Timothy S. Murphy and W. Daniel Smith (2001) provide a turgid and detailed analysis of Deleuze's theory as applied to "pop" interpreted in its Spinozian sense as "that which affords the greatest potential for further connection and ramification." A more accessible approach can be found in Ian Buchanan and Marcel Swiboda (2004), especially in Buchanan's introductory essay. I draw from Buchanan's (1997) musing about applying Deleuze to pop music.

16. Lawrence Grossberg's (1992) notion of "mattering maps" is derivative of D+G's refrain theory. He defines them as "a socially determined structure of affect which defines the things that do and can matter to those living within the map" (398).

Chapter 6

1. Some examples would include Caroline Evans (1997), Lauraine Leblanc (2002), Jesse Klein (2006), and especially Stephen Frosh et al. (2002), given the influence of Frosh's own psychoanalytic background.

2. Youth sociologists would include Ben Malbon (1999) and Andy Bennett (1999, 2000).

3. For a review of the "what should be retained" and "what should be rejected" concerning the concept of hegemonic masculinity, see R. W. Connell and James Messerschmidt (2005). "The fundamental feature of the concept [hegemonic masculinity] remains the combination of the plurality of masculinities and the hierarchy of masculinities" (846).

4. Slavoj Žižek and Simon Critchley (2002) are the two most notable instances of those who question Laclau's social democratic proposal. See Brett Levinson's (2008) online article for an overview of the Laclau/Žižek disagreement.

5. I cull this possibility from Žižek's (2007) online article, "Deleuze and the Lacanian Real." The relevant passage is a quote from Hallward: "If 'individuation is a relation conceived as a pure or absolute between, a between understood as fully independent of or external to its terms—and thus a between that can just as well be described as 'between' nothing at all'(Hallward 2006, 154), *its status is then that of a pure antagonism*" (emphasis added).

6. Laclau (2002) tries to deflect this possibility by raising the question of the mysticism of Meister Eckhart. Also see Sue Golding ("On the Names of God") where she engages Ernesto Laclau with Eckhart to consider the signification of the absolute, mysticism, politics, and ethics.

7. In 1998 Lawrence Grossberg called on D+G's theoretical edifice in a tantalizingly brief statement (76–77) as to the possibility of reorientating the field of cultural studies in their direction. Apparently, Stuart Hall in 1997 had already made a gesture to Deleuze in this regard, but never took it as a paradigm shift (1997, 25; in Seigworth 2006, 108). Grossberg (2005) still maintains in an interview that he intends to bring Antonio Gramsci, Deleuze, and Foucault into dialogue, but that has yet to be seen. Gregory J. Seigworth's (2006) "Cultural Studies and Gilles Deleuze" is not an application but a comparison between Raymond Williams, Walter Benjamin, and Gilles Deleuze response to Kant's understanding of experience, coming up with their own alternative conceptions of "structure of feeling," "non-sensuous similarity," and "virtual." The direction of my personal study differs from these directions, since my interest is more in the psychoanalytic kernel of their work—where *jouissance* and affect have a similar thrust.

8. One and its multiples refer to hierarchical systems that D+G critique through the concept of multiplicity where the distribution is nomadic, nonhierarchical, and irreducible to identifiable unities. In the former, identification proceeds by virtue of a One or its multiple that transcends them.

9. I would risk saying that the formation of a fantasy frame that emerges as the cause of *objet a* is perhaps the transpositional concept to Deleuze's notion of "differenciator" (1994, 207), whereby there is a produced change in the states between a series and substances as a result of prior intensity. Deleuze uses the word "differentiation" for the virtuality of differences that have yet to be selected and given form—the potential state or content. The virtual is then the coexistence of the totality of differential relations. A particular imaginary frame of fantasy is already an actualization of some potential difference; hence, it would be a differenciator (see also *Logic of Sense*, 51). The imaginary frame "holds" a particular fantasy in place. As for differences in the realm of sameness, these would already be at the level of the signifiers, and hence the symbolic order. Just as Lacan maintains that the Imaginary is a mis(recognition), Deleuze equally speaks of the illusionary nature of identity. However, as in Lacan, identity is not produced by a mind; it is produced by fantasy; whereas in Deleuze, the illusion is produced in and through being itself in the course of actualization. We could say that Deleuze's concept of different/ciation that doubly articulates every object is precisely the psychic Imaginary framed by the stain in the Real (the *a*). The *a* is the "virtual differentiation," while the frame of fantasy it creates is the actualized image.

10. Lacan in *The Family Complexes in the Formation of the Individual* (2003) identifies neurosis as emerging when the Imaginary father and the symbolic father occupy one and the same position within the social structure. Oedipalization is therefore a specifically

historical formation producing particular psychic structures. There is no invariant human essence. As Paul Verhaeghe (1999) has shown, this structural overlap is no longer the case, as the symbolic father has decentered and the Imaginary Father emerges in many mediated forms via the multiple societal screens.

11. This summative statement was greatly helped by reading Chrysanthl Nigianni (2005), whose work is in the area of lesbian desire and the lesbian body. However, truth-functional propositional logic rolls out a similar vocabulary with the opposite aim of trying to grasp paradoxes analytically.

12. This concept is troublesome for anyone who struggles with D+G, since it is as rich as it is confusing. Haecceity has two forms, the second of which is forwarded by D+G. The first comes from the thirteenth century theologian, John Duns Scotus as a finite principle of individuation—the becoming whole of a person or a self. Self-knowledge is achieved through a rational or empirical process of discovery. The self as a self-transcendent quality is a common model. The Deleuzian haecceity works on the form of an assemblage, elements that come together in a moment of becoming as a point on a trajectory. The "logic of sense" that informs it attempts to grasp individuation as a constant condition of flux where multiple connections and changes occur between internal and external influences. This makes intuitive sense, given that becoming is always a process as the infinitives of verbs suggest.

13. Many examples appear in the commentary tracks by the writers, directors, and actors commenting on various episodes One quickly realizes how "little" control any one of these players has once the camera starts rolling: lines are often ad-libbed, other lines added in, camera shots at times miscued but "work," and little quirks are put in by the actors themselves. There are just so many takes before a director lets it go.

14. This has been a central concern in many philosophical circles, the Judaic theological influences of Emmanuel Lévinas's (1969) celebrated discussion of the "Face of the Other," which raises just how far the unknowable kernel of the Other is to be befriended. As the globe shrinks, this is an unavoidable question. In the Lacanian debates, it circles around the concept of *extimité,* the coincidence of intimacy with Otherness. It presents the relationship much like a Deleuzian fold. The concept of extimacy places *objet a* within the Other, a move from intersubjectivity (spatial) to intra-subjectivity (time), thus avoiding the usual spatial distinction of "us" and "others." The intimate and the extimate are implicated, enfolded in each other. The Other is an embedded alien that occupies the most intimate place, the "X" in self-refleXivity. The question of the Other's Face has been raised by Žižek (1997) in his polemic against Lévinas and his discussion concerning Freud and Lacan's own stance against the neighbor (*Nachbar*). See Žižek et al. (2006) and Fred C. Alford (2004).

15. Chris Wood (2000) provides a rather insightful psychoanalytic reading of this film that shows its homoerotic transferences between the actors and their characters within the filmic narrative, given that James Dean was gay and Nicholas Ray was said to be bisexual.

16. "What is realized in my history is not the past definite of what was, since it is no more, or even the present perfect of what has been in what I am, but the future anterior of what I shall have been for what I am in the process of becoming" (Lacan 1981, 63). The historicity of the subject is never closed, memory being a major part of the misrecognition that constitutes the mirror stage that masks the fragmented body. The affinity of this as yet organized body to BwO should be apparent.

17. This can be given a Hegelian spin as the move from the in-itself (*An-sich*) to for-itself (*Für-sich*), the in-itself being the affirmative preconditioned desire often presented as a question of hope and an expectation of a future yet to come. When it becomes

Für-Alle (for-All) we have reached a state of ideology, be it totalitarian or hegemonic. The system is closed, end of the dialectic.

18. Individuation is elaborately worked out by Deleuze in *Difference and Repetition* based on his readings of Gilbert Simondon (1992).

19. Inna Semetsky (2004) has discussed the difference between a Deleuzian ethics and that of Charles Taylor (1991) who develops an "authentic" self-referentiality that is unique to the specific individual, a "subjectivation of manner" rather than a "subjectivation of matter" that belongs "exclusively [to] an expression of the self" (88). Semetsky dismantles this hierarchical way of thinking, showing how Deleuze presents an alternative that speaks to self-refleXion when she writes: when it comes to a Deleuzian line of flight "each fold—in its function as a repetition of the different—add[s] up to the totality of the whole autopoietic process" (323).

20. "In a dream he is a butterfly.... When Choang-tsu wakes up, he may ask himself whether it is not the butterfly who dreams that he is Choang-tsu. Indeed he is right, and doubly so, first because it proves he is not mad, he does not regard himself as fully identical with Choang-tsu and, secondly, because he doesn't fully understand how right he is. In fact, it is when he was the butterfly that he apprehended one of the roots of his identity—that he was, and is, in his essence, that butterfly who paints himself with his own colors—and it is because of this that, in the last resort, he is Choang-tsu" (76).

21. The dog/god is a key unconscious knot in Lindsay's life. Kim accidentally runs over Mille's dog, Goliath, with her car with Lindsay as her passenger (14, "Dead Dogs and Gym Teachers"). The guilt is almost unbearable until Kim comes across and admits it at Lindsay's constant coaxing.

22. Millie, in particular, sets up her asceticism against the way students are meant to "enjoy." Her belief in God and modest dress is meant to differentiate herself from the crowd. On entering the party (2, "Beer and Weirs"), she immediately tells Lindsay that she will be the one who has the most fun. "I prefer to get high on life. I am going to have more fun than any of you . . . sober."

23. The question of judgment, how it can be rethought, is tackled by Deleuze in "To Have Done with Judgment" (1997) where he explores the attempts made by Nietzsche, D. H. Lawrence, Kafka, and Antonin Artaud, each of which had singularly suffered from judgment. Alexandre Lefebvre (2007) also attempts such a proposition through the figure of "the law without organs" (LwO), attempting to rethink judgment as developed by Kant and Ronald Dworkin's *Law's Empire* (1986).

24. In the episode on Halloween (3, "Tricks and Treats"), the costumes the Weirs wear are revealing in this regard. Jean is dressed as a cowboy hostess who bakes cookies to give out to the ghosts and goblins that come to the door, only to find out that they are throwing them on her lawn, not eating them, because they are not wrapped. The "good" hostess is being "dumped" on. The paranoia of having the cookies spiked with marijuana comes out. Harold, in contrast, is Dracula, a throwaway tag to the Count Dracula shtick he regularly did on SCTV. His fangs are "truly" showing.

25. The term "modality" is specific to the Spinozian system that Deleuze adopts and modifies through a Nietzschean reading of an eternal return. Baruch Spinoza's three basic ontological distinctions are Substance, Attribute, and Mode. In a nutshell, Substance is the univocity of being that is God/Nature, an immanent vital force that only emerges through the other two categories: Attributes are the infinite ways this Substance is expressed, while Modes are expressions within the Attributes. These modes are qualitative intensities whose existences are constantly becoming in relation to increases or decreases in power. This, then, is an atheistic notion of God brought "down to Earth" if I can put it this way, as a practical ethical philosophy.

26. It seems that such acts can "still" be staged in "reality." Six years latter (14, "Little Things") was aired on July 8, 2000. George W. Bush spoke at Kansas State University on January 23, 2006, to an ideologically groomed crowd. A student asked about the pending legislation to cut $12.7 billion in student loan programs. Bush pretended not to hear the question, and then claimed ignorance of the matter. Later, Senator Ron Wyden (D-Oregon) pointed out that this cut in spending was the precise amount of money that would be used to seal the tax cuts for the super-rich that Bush had promoted earlier (Kleinhans et al. 2006).

27. "The diagram is . . . the operative set of a-signifying and nonrepresentative lines and zones, line-strokes and color-patches" (2003, 101).

Chapter 7

1. To identify particular episodes throughout this essay, the following standard designation will be used: seasons will be represented by integers of 10's: For example, first season 10, second season 20 . . . followed by the particular episode starting with 01. Hence 4003 indicates the fourth season, third episode.

2. I develop this neologism, fan(addict), in chapter 15, "The Fan(addict): The *Sinthome* of Believing in the Multiples of ONE" in *Music in Youth Culture*.

3. The first conference, entitled "Blood, Text and Fears: Reading Around Buffy the Vampire Slayer," was sponsored by the School of English and American Studies and the School of Language, Linguistics, and Translation Studies at the University of East Anglia, and was held in October 2002. (I didn't attend.)

4. In 1998, the magazine *George* (see Stoller 1998) contrasted Buffy to the self-esteem troubles of Pipher's (1994) *Reviving Ophelia*. I discuss this development in chapter 12, "The Dilemma of Gurlz' Desires: Perverting the Post-Patriarchal Order," in *Music in Youth Cultures*.

5. I want to signal here that I am not being an apologist for the blatant consumerism of *Buffy*. However, the question of anticonsumerism is much more complex than presented by the stance of Naomi Klein's bestseller, *No Logo*. Jo Litter (2005) has shown the limitations of this approach, as well as that of *Body Shop* founder Anita Roddick, and of the counter-advertising of *Adbusters* and Reverend Billy's "Church of Stop Shopping." In a nutshell, Jo Litter makes the point that there are two forms of self-reflexivity. "[F]irst, a relatively narcissistic form of reflexivity that acts to shore up a romantic anti-consumerist activist self [Naomi Klein and company], and second, an understanding of reflexivity as a more relational and dispersed process [Scott Lash, Donna Haraway, Judith Butler, and Bruno Latour]" (229). I am advocating another self-refleXivity that addresses the fantasy space that both Lacan and Deleuze provide.

6. See Fudge's (1999) sarcastic and witty assessment in, "The *Buffy* Effect: Or, a Tale of Cleavage and Marketing." She beats up on Buffy like Courtney Love beat up on Kathleen Hanna of Bikini Kill for her immature "teen" rebellion. "This is style over substance, baby teens over action. . . . the fine line between girl-power schlock and feminist wish-fulfillment." See also Vint (2000).

7. The Parents Television Council (PTC) in 2002 ranked *Buffy* number one on their top worst shows on television from a moral standpoint.

8. Joseph Campbell's classic monomyth is developed in *The Hero with a Thousand Faces*. The hero first gets the Call. If it is first refused he becomes a victim; if the challenge is taken up, then supernatural help is given (weapons, magic rings, amulets . . .), a protective guardian is provided (Gandalf, a Jedi Knight like Yoda, Morpheus . . .). He then

faces the first threshold challenge and suffers a subjective destitution. Caught in the "belly of the whale," a womb image where an initiation struggle takes place: the hero "dies" and reemerges in a rebirth (resurrection) so that a departure can take place for the trials and tribulations that will follow. Such a tale can be read as a myth of growing up, a rite of passage. It is repeated in countless video games, *The Harry Potter* series, *The Matrix,* and so on (Irwin 2002).

9. The full synopsis of the episode that I am using can be found online: http://www.sunnydale-slayers.com/episodes/enormal.html

10. In *Youth Fantasies* I discuss how irritated fans became when such BBC programs as *Panorama, Ghostwatch,* and the famous Orson Welles *War of the Worlds* incident fooled them. At the end of season five, Buffy "dies" (yes, again!). The program ended with a camera shot of Buffy's tombstone, which read: "She saved the universe a lot." The image faded, credits ran, and then a message appeared: "Five great years. We thank you." Fans were upset. This really looked like THE END. The WB network, owned by AOL Time Warner and the Tribune Company, had staged the stunt as a (not so sincere) thank you. In the fall, the program was moving to the UPN network, which was owned by Viacom, a rival. Buffy would have to rise from the dead next season. (The pun is directed at Steven King's well-known story and film about a crazed fan holding a fiction writer captive.)

11. "Previously on *Buffy the Vampire Slayer . . . ,*" which opens each episode, plays a role similar to the one Jacques Derrida (1996) uses to explore the notion of *exergue.* It creates a space or gap between the main text and what lies outside the text. Such a gap enables a remarkable playfulness of time and space, what I have referred to in the past as a "warpage," the occurrence of a short circuit in time/space. Episode 3018 ("Earshot"), which was not shown in the United States because of the Columbine shootings, but was broadcast in Canada, presents a narrative where Jonathan is wrongly suspected of wanting to commit mass homicide at Sunnydale High. Jonathan is an insider-joke, a camera-shy outsider who appears for three seasons but is never given front and center attention. In "Earshot" the episode is presented as if Jonathan actually occupies "real" time, relating to the episode both as a character and as a fan. In episode 4017 ("Superstar"), Jonathan actually creates the episode, inverting all the roles as if the *Buffy* series is watching itself with a schizophrenic gaze. Buffy eventually breaks his spell, but leaves Jonathan's character as a splintered holograph throughout the series. In the end, viewers are not sure just what influence Jonathan truly had. Both are fine examples of the virtual Real as an exploration of self-refleXivity in the same way "Earshot" made its point on the Columbine shooting by way of its repetition.

12. As famously developed in his second volume (Cinema 2): hyalosigns (crystals of time), chronosigns (the order of time), noosigns (imagined thought), and lectosigns (sight and sound).

13. Virtual Real is my Deleuzian-Lacanian construction and is not to be confused with "virtual reality" of cyberspace. This is a virtual memory construction of the unconscious.

14. Cynthia Bowers (2000) makes this explicitly clear by reading three episodes that focus on the adults charged with Buffy's welfare: episode 2008 ("The Dark Age"), episode 2011 ("Ted"), episode 3006 ("Band Candy").

15. I borrow this phrase from Rodolphe Gasché (1986), whose book title is an exploration of Derridean deconstruction. The tain is the tinfoil used to coat clear glass so that a mirror is formed.

16. Zoe-Jane Playdon (2001 paragraph, 27) stretches this to a Greek reference. Buffy is Artemis the hunter, with the "scoobies" acting as the dogs that traditionally accompany her.

17. Terry Spaise's (2005) "Necrophilia and SM: The Deviant Side of Buffy the Vampire Slayer" does a great job of revealing its sadomasochistic subtext and the presentation of necrophilia within the range of normal sexual expression. Spaise explores this in detail, concentrating on season six through Buffy's relationship with Spike. An entire issue of the *European Journal of Cultural Studies* 2005, 8(3) was dedicated to exploring Spike. Of interest here is Dee Amy-Chinn (2005), who reads Spike as a queer transsexual character.

18. I discuss this hysterical development of "dirty virgins" in chapter 10, "Postmodern Hysterics: Playing with the Virginity Card," in *Musical Fantasies of Youth Cultures*.

19. As argued in "The Paradox of the Dirty Virgin Divas," Chapter 11 in *Music in Youth Culture*. Although this phase for many young musical stars has now been largely forgotten—since Britney fell into her own forms of excessive enjoyment—playing the "virginity card" was a clever strategy to push back an overbearing media.

20. In *Critique of Practical Reason*, Immanuel Kant (2002) argues that the libertine is willing to renounce the satisfaction of his passion if he learns that the price he must pay is the gallows. Žižek calls up the example of Mozart's Don Giovanni as a libertine who chooses death, and thereby commits an act of "evil" by choosing not to give up on his principles (Žižek 1993, 95–96). Angel knows full well that sleeping with Buffy is his death. His first kiss with her left a burning cross on his skin as a reminder of the price he will eventually pay. Sexual relations with an HIV-positive partner or spouse present the same contemporary ethical dilemma. We can also point to athletes who are willing to "die" so that they might win Olympic gold by taking massive doses of steroids. Their drive cannot be sublimated by this possible threat of death. Here, of course, the consequences of sleeping with anyone can always constitute a symbolic death—one's world changes should a pregnancy occur, for instance, or you are now branded a slut, and so on.

21. The cyborg-vampire coupling is explored brilliantly by Rob Latham's *Consuming Youth* (2002), another succinct title for its ethical implications: necromancer joins neuromancer, so to speak.

22. This is the interpretation provided by Wilcox (2002) from a Jungian viewpoint. See "'Every Night I Save You': Buffy. Spike, Sex and Redemption."

23. The Big Bad is used in the Buffyverse to identify a chief adversary or villain in a particular season. In season one it's the Master, Spike in season two, Mayor Richard Wilkins in season three, Adam in season four, Glorificus (Glory) in season five, The Trio in season six, and The First (The First Evil) in season seven.

24. http://www.whedon.info/article.php3?id_article=1784&img=

25. These categories are developed in *Music in Youth Culture*.

26. See the chapters in the section "Perversions of the Music Scene: The Boyz/Bois/Boys" in *Musical Fantasies of Youth Cultures* for the complex play of these masculinities. For discussion more specifically on the boy as a "Castrati-like" figure, see chapter ten, "The New Castrati: Men II Boys."

27. I develop this is in chapter 12, "The Dilemma of Gurlz' Desires: Perverting the Post-Patriarchal Order," in *Musical Fantasies of Youth Cultures*.

28. A Lacanian term that attempts to confuse boundaries as dichotomizations of inside/outsid.

29. The complexities of grrrl power are presented in chapter 12, "The Good Witch-Bitch: Grrrl Power as the Desublimated Ugly Aesthetic," in *Musical Fantasies of Youth Cultures*.

30. The ambivalence of the death drive should not go unnoticed. The death drive, while it is destructive in this case, is an affirmation of life as well, the force of survival. The next chapter explains this further.

31. For an attempt to apply a Greimasian semiotic square to postmodern female bodies, see jagodzinski (2003a).

Chapter 8

1. Derrida's writings on ethics are scattered throughout his oeuvre. Simon Critchley's (1992) *The Ethics of Deconstruction: Derrida and Levinas* is perhaps the best introduction to what I am attempting to develop here. Derrida develops three aporias concerning justice, about what its impassable points or double binds are. *Singularity* of the law raises the question of what goes "beyond" its general rules. There is always a case that retroactively changes the Law because it sets a precedent. *Undecidability* requires a hermeneutic interpretation by a judge as to what laws apply in a specific case. Lastly, there is *urgency* because justice cannot wait. Each aporia points to a realm that is beyond the Law.

2. Stacey Abbott (2000) interprets this meeting with the first slayer at the end of season four as the end or break with the gothic tradition that continues to cull an ecofeminist (Goddess) worship from the *Buffy* series as argued by Zoe-Jane Playdon (2001) and A. Susan Owen (1999). For Abbott, Buffy cuts her ties with the past by dispersing the ONE into a group of friends. She denies being "alone" in her task. In terms of my own argumentation, the ONE refers to the hysterical resolution for knowledge, the decentering of the Symbolic Order into many competing ONEs, but still caught by One and its Multiple (Kendra and Faith). Multiplicity, however, can be attributed to Buffy at the end of season seven, where her power is dispersed globally, empowering all would be Slayers.

3. This is developed in their tenth plateau in *A Thousand Plateaus*. This most difficult but rich conceptualization requires some struggle. They insist that becoming-animal has nothing to do with resemblance, identification, or imitation. It is also not an act of imagination, or a dream or a fantasy. What is it then? It is an effort to become the other and requires being "copresent" with the other in a zone of closeness (272–75); such proximity can yield a shared transformation. The idea is to approximate patterns of movement, rest, and speed at the molecular level. D+G believe that such a zone is possible to create because the human body has within it "an objective zone of indetermination or uncertainty, something shared or indiscernible," a proximity "that makes it impossible to say where the boundary between the human and animal lies . . . "(273). While D+G draw from literature to present this possibility, the life of Timothy Treadwell as the Grizzly Man is perhaps a graspable example. Werner Herzog's (2005) film by the same name gives a sense of what becoming-grizzly is like. In *Buffy* I take the extimate exchanges between beasts and humans to be an exemplar of becoming-animal.

4. This is where Derrida's (2002) "The Animal That Therefore I Am (More to Follow) and Santner's 2006) "On Creaturely Life" join in the Deleuzian attempt to rethink the human/nature divide.

5. The orthodox interpretation of Freud's death drive is as a dualism between Eros and Thanatos. They appear as two types of repetitions that are governed by an entropic closed system. Thanatos becomes an urge to return to an inorganic state (to die), while Eros becomes a drive to earlier states of conservation and peace. In response, D+G state "But when the dualism passed into a death instinct against Eros, this was no longer a simple limitation, it was a liquidation of the libido" (*A-O*, 331).

6. The reference is to Emmanuel Levinas's well-known notion of the "face." Our very existence is in response to the Other's Call, to the demand that the Other places on me.

7. See discussion in jagodzinski (2002a).

8. Gregory Stevenson (2003) has examined *Buffy*'s morality from a Christian perspective in his *Televised Morality: The Case of Buffy the Vampire Slayer*. The distinction between ethics and morality is not made, although it is clear that Stevenson recognizes the play of the "exception to the rule" that suspends easy decision making. What is remarkable is that Whedon is an avowed atheist; along with his writers, he attempted to avoid any sort of transcendentalism. The Buffyverse is absent of a Christian God and a single transcendent value. Its pagan allusions are obvious. Yet, despite this Stevenson is able to recuperate *Buffy* under a Christian framework. "*Buffy* employs Christian teachings as a vital piece of its moral foundation. The cross of Christ in particular strongly influences the presentation of certain characters and gives definition to themes of sacrifice, love, redemption and forgiveness" (260).

9. This is my homology for the three Lacanian registers.

10. The kicker was a 42-page report three weeks after 9/11 on *Buffy* as an antiterrorist strategy to think through biological terrorism. See Anthony H. Cordesman, "Biological Warfare and the 'Buffy Paradigm,'" Washington, D.C.: Center for Strategic and International Studies, September 29, 2001. Available at www.csis.org.

Chapter 9

1. An absolutely intriguing investigation that examined the possible interpretation of the "Ramey Memo" in order to put closure to the case was carried out by a team of scientific researchers (see Houran et al., 2002). Brigadier General Roger M. Ramey had been photographed holding a "readable" memo, which was not part of the report by the combined 509th Bomb Group and the RAAF (Roswell Army Air Field). The mystery of its message kept the question of the UFO crash open to debate.

2. In a very sophisticated argument, Nathan Widder (2000) argues that even Ernesto Laclau's celebrated attempt to escape the humanism of identity by forging a theory of difference for future socialist movements that attempts to go "beyond" the Hegelian master/slave dialectic by positing a "constitutional outside" of a fundamental antagonism to explain how hegemony works, fails in the end by inadvertently reinstating the Hegelian dialectic. In a nutshell "meaning requires identity; identity requires totality; totality requires exclusion" (123).

Chapter 10

1. Some would say little has changed. In 2000 the U.S. Army's eleventh Psychological Operations Battalion ("Psy-ops") hired DC Comics to produce special versions of *Superman* and *Wonder Woman* comic books in the languages of the Balkans, Central America, Africa, and Southeast Asia to educate locals on the dangers of land mines. The initiative failed.

2. The memoirs of the members of the German *Freikorps* (German paramilitary units) show an ego that is severed from the weaknesses and frailties of the body, strengthened only through pain. Killing what threatens the ego fortifies and stops it from dissolving. Body and psyche are united when the subject becomes a weapon, with the monstrous feminine being the ultimate threat of having this armor liquidated, since women are perceived to be the seat of irrationality.

3. I found Aaron Pevey's (2007) brief but succinct master's thesis on the background of the *Superman* comic books to be very helpful when thinking through this chapter.

4. To signal the first irony of this being a quintessentially American myth: Joe Shuster was born in Toronto, Ontario, before moving to Cleveland, Ohio, to team up with Jerry Siegel to write the first Superman comic book. Joe Shuster was the brother of Wayne; together they formed a famous Canadian comedy team—*Wayne and Shuster*, the name of their television hit on CBC in the 1960s. Jerry and Joe came from Jewish households, which plays a significant role in this myth as will be shown. The naïve young men sold the rights of what turned out to be a billion-dollar juggernaut for $130. Worse, both lived in near poverty most of their lives! (Brod 1999). Another tidbit: The "S" on Superman's shirt stands for the last name of its creators as well as for Super-Jew (in answer to Hitler)—bookish on the outside but raging warriors on the inside

5. John Byrne did away with Superman's childhood/teenage career as Superboy, which was a mistake that he later regretted. Clark Kent does not don a costume and become a super-hero until he is an adult. Byrne also significantly reduced Superman's powers and eliminated the Fortress of Solitude and Krypto, the superdog.

6. Waid in *Superman's Birthright* turns things around somewhat. Kal-El embraces his difference as a Kryptonian and the distinctiveness of his homeland, thus appealing to the postmodern proliferation of identity politics. Yet, this difference takes on a distinctive neoliberalist rhetoric of excellence, where Superman's selfish acts celebrate his "true self," thereby helping the larger community and society as a whole. Waid embraces the ideology of Marianne Williamson's (1992) work on love and spirituality. If you can just get over your fears, the "inner light" begins to shine through, for you are indeed a "child of God" who then "automatically liberates others." Superman now begins an inner spiritual practice. The principles of Hell, God, You, Surrender, and Miracles, which are the foundation of this ideology, are put to work.

7. See my "Postmetaphysical Vision: (A Mondofesto)" (2008) that works all this out along Foucauldian and Deleuzian lines.

8. This distinction is best known from the work of Giorgio Agamben (1998). *Zoë* is "bare life," deprived of the rights by the state; Bios, in contrast, is qualified life under the state. The teratological freaks would be seen as the "coming community" in his terms (1993), opposed to the sovereignty of the state.

9. In the words of Professor Xavier, "The Sentinels had been created to destroy the X-Men—and yet, it was necessary for *us* to smash *them* in order to save humanity—the humanity that *hated* us!" (Bukatman 2003, 70, original emphasis).

10. The Bronze Age X-men in the 1970s were international and multicultural. "Sunfire, Nightcrawler, and Colossus were, respectively, Japanese, German, and Russian youths; Thunderbird was a male Native American, and Storm an African American woman; and the Canadian Wolverine and Irish Banshee were middle-aged men" (Trushell 2004, 156).

11. Cary M. Jones (2006) reviews in three separate sections of "Jump Cut" the way WB has marketed *SV* to establish its market grip of the 12–34 demographic.

12. As many critics have pointed out, this fits the expected tradition of family-orientated Warner Brothers programming that has included *Dawson's Creek* and *Buffy* (but not *Freaks and Geeks*—NBC). *Rolling Stone* mentioned that a typical episode of *SV* has twice the amount of music found on most TV youth series (Jones 2006).

13. The marriage between Marxism and Christianity against consumerism is precisely the thesis Slavoj Žižek (2001) explores in his *Fragile Absolute*, maintaining that its "subversive core" can be recovered from its "fundamentalist" variants. His solution points directly to the question of self-refleXivity. The Pauline concept of agape, commonly known as Christian love, provides a way "to liberate [ourselves] from the grip of existing social reality [capitalist psyche]" by "renounc[ing] the transgressive supplement that attaches us to it" (149). This transformative renunciation takes the form of "the

radical gesture of 'striking at oneself'" (150). The aim is directed at the object of desire that grounds subjective and ideological stability. While this sounds anti-Deleuzian, it is not, as this quote seems to indicate: "[W]hile it is easy to enjoy acting in an egoistic way *against* one's duty [transgression], it is, perhaps, only as the result of psychoanalytic treatment that one can acquire the capacity to *enjoy* doing one's duty" (114, original emphasis). So this is agape with a psychoanalytic twist.

14. I am following the importance of Frank's thesis to the ideology of *SV* as developed by Anne Kustritz (2005).

15. As I write this, Senator Barack Obama—in a tight race with Hilary Clinton for the democratic nominee for president—seems to have clinched the victory. There is now a strong chance that America will have its first African-American president, rather than its first woman president. On the Republican side, it appears that John McCain is the clear winner, but he is not without his problems; the Republican base is unhappy with his "liberal" leanings. The story of this election march to the White House so far has been the mobilization of young people by Obama, and in light of this chapter, the call for a sea change is in the direction of the freaks.

16. It doesn't get more "homey" than the Thanksgiving meal on the Kent farm in season six (607, "Rage") where Kent is now representing his late father and is carving up the turkey. Every one of the main characters is there in a candle-lit scene that is strikingly reminiscent of Norman Rockwell's 1943 Thanksgiving painting, *Freedom from Want*. Josh Kelly's "Cain and Able" (*Just Say the Word*) forms the background music to make it look like a perfect, harmonious picture with all the secrets and lies lying just barely below the surface, ready to erupt at any time, just as in David Lynch's Lumbervillle setting in *Blue Velvet*. The stock shots of the Kent farm work the same way. All is tranquil and calm just before and after the storm that is always brewing.

17. Mark 6:3 as cited in www.hollywoodjesus.com/superman.htm.

18. Season four develops an arc beginning with episode 402 ("Gone"), when Lana becomes a witch as a tattoo appears on her lower back (The Mark of Transference); the same sign is also found on the walls of the Kawatche cave. She is resurrected as the evil countess Margaret Isobel Thoreaux (408, "Spell"). The haunt of this ghost is avenged when Lana (possessed by Isobel) kills Genevieve Teague, who was a descendant of Duchess Gertrude. The duchess was responsible for having her burned as a witch in the seventeenth century (422, "Commencement"). The tattoo then disappears. There is also the tongue-in-cheek episode 620 ("Noir"), where she orchestrates the murder of her tycoon husband, Lex, by using Jimmy as the "fall guy" or patsy. All this adumbrates season seven, when Lana gets revenge against Lex by staging the murder of her clone whom Lex had created (701, "Bizarro").

19. To continue the ironic jabs: Erica Durance, who plays Lois, was born in Calgary, Alberta, Canada. While I am at it, Kristin Kreuk (Lana) was born in Vancouver, British Columbia, Canada. The Canadians have infiltrated *Superman* and America!

20. The smallville Wikia.com (http://smallville.wikia.com/wiki/Smallville_Wiki) is an amazing site for virtually any detail one would wish to learn about this series.

21. Is this perhaps is yet another Canadian allusion by Jerry Siegel? "The North" is the place of the Real—foreboding, uncivilized, desolate—an empty abyss in the popular Canadian psyche.

22. This is the tip of the proverbial iceberg of the Christian infused narratives in so many Hollywood films. Anton Karl Kozlovic seems to have carved out this territory for exploration. Many of his essays can be found online.

23. John Schneider plays Jonathan on *SV*. A generation of television viewers would recall him as "Bo Duke" from the TV series *Dukes of Hazzard*. The choice of Schneider for

the role was more than just fortuitous. Giving moral advice to Clark seems appropriate for someone who had explored his own youth so wildly (on "television land").

24. "Lacanian theory of forename and family name; the first name designates the ideal ego, the point of imaginary identification, while the family name comes from the father it designates, as the Name-of-the-father, the point of symbolic identification, the agency through which we observe and judge ourselves. The facet that should not be overlooked in this distinction is that i(o) is always already subordinated to I(O); it is the symbolic identification (the point from which we are observed) which dominates and determines the image, the imaginary from in which we appear to ourselves likeable. On the level of formal functioning, this subordination is attested [to] by the fact that the nickname [that] marks i(o) also functions as a rigid designator, not as simple description" (Žižek 1989, 108).

25. First Nation's mysticism seems to be a gesture of recognition that plays out on *The X-Files* and on *Roswell* as well. However, here the caves are invaded by LuthorCorp, and not respected.

26. The story has it that Lex smothered his baby brother Julian in his crib out of jealousy; Lionel's hatred for Lex stems from this. It turns out that his wife, Lillian, smothered the boy, a case of postpartum depression brought on by Lionel's insistence on encouraging competition between the two brothers, and her not desiring yet another child.

27. The Citizens Networks.org (http://www.citizenworks.org/enron/corp-scandal.php) compiles a scandal sheet on the number of CEOs and their companies that have committed corruption of one sort or another. They provide links to articles, investigative information, and stock reports. My count was 42, including such well-known companies as Xerox, WorldCom Inc, Tyco Intl. Ltd., Merrill Lynch & Co., Halliburton, Bristol Myers, Martha Stewart Living Omnimedia, Kmart . . . you get the point. This is "overground" not underground crime.

28. As defined in the glossary of Gilles Deleuze's *Cinema 2* (1989), "the uniting of an actual image and a virtual image to the point where they can no longer be distinguished" (p. 335).

29. I follow Žižek (2004a) in his analysis here of the dilemma for theologians. "Christ's act is repeatedly designated as 'ransom,' by the words of Christ himself, by other biblical texts, as well as by the most prominent commentators of the Bible. Jesus himself says that he came 'to give his life as a ransom for many' (Mark 10:45); Timothy 2:5–6 speaks of Christ as the 'mediator between God and humanity [. . .] who gave his life as a ransom for all'; St Paul himself, when he states that Christians are slaves who have been 'bought at a price' (1 Corinthians 6:20), implies the notion that the death of Christ should be conceived as purchasing our freedom."

Chapter 11

1. This is not the same agape Slavoj Žižek develops in *The Fragile Absolute* as a way out of this bind of inverted paranoid opposites. It is much more radical, a self-destructive act of renunciation. The examples he uses are Lacan's dissolution of the *École freudienne*, Keyser Soze's decision to shoot his wife and daughter when they are held hostage in the *Usual Suspects*, Oskar LaFontaine's resignation from the SPD (Sozialdemokratische Partei Deutschlands), and Sethe's slaughter of her child in Toni Morrison's *Beloved*. In these examples, the gesture is twofold. On the one hand, what is sacrificed is saved from a worse fate (Sethe's child would end up in slavery, LaFontaine would always compromise his political position, Keyser Soze's wife and daughter would be killed anyway, and

Lacan's school would have continued to deteriorate in quality). On the other hand, giving up what is most precious enables the coordinates of the situation to entirely change. To cut lose from the precious object in whose possession the enemy is able to psychically keep one hostage is an act of freedom. Only then does the subject gain a space of free action. In this way of thinking, Superman would have to give up his powers by intentionally coming into contact with gold kryptonite, to relieve the burden of his gifts that are his curse.

2. Žižek objects to Levinas's ethics, arguing that ultimately this stance privileges the Jew as having the correct universal stance. It becomes a "Jewish man's (ethical) burden." The Judeo-Christian roots of Superman, beginning with its original writers, seem to be unconsciously furthered by the contemporary team of Hollywood script writers. Of course, the standard anti-Semitic joke about Hollywood is that it is a "Jewish town."

3. When Lois finds out his secret (711, "Siren"), she refuses to be with him. It's as though her desire has been drained. She now realizes that she would not be able to share him with the world, and would always play second fiddle. As Oliver says to Clark, "Some of us sacrifice being with the people that we really care about so that we can go make a difference. What do you do?"

4. For this section I have drawn on Žižek's (2006) essay "Neighbors and Other Monsters: A Plea for Ethical Violence."

5. Lionel mentions Operation Starhawk to Clark. The program was developed by the Department of Domestic Security, whose mission is to deal with threats from beyond the stars (716, "Lara").

References

Abbott, Stacey. 2000. A Little Less Ritual and a Little More Fun: The Modern Vampire in Buffy the Vampire Slayer. *Slayage: On-Line International Journal of Buffy Studies.* Available at http://www.slayage.tv/essays/slayage3/sabbott.htm.

Adams, Michael. 1999a. Slayer Slang. Part 1. *Verbatim* 24 Summer 3: 1–6.

———. (1999b. Slayer Slang. Part 2. *Verbatim* 24 Autumn 4: 1–6.

Adams, Parveen. 1991. Per Os(cillation). In *Male Trouble,* ed. Constance Penley and Sharon Willis, pp. 3–26. London and Minneapolis, MN: University of Minneapolis Press.

Agamben, Giorgio. 1993. *The Coming Community.* Trans. Michael Hardt. Minneapolis: University of Minnesota Press.

———. 1998. *Homo Sacer: Sovereign Power and Bare Life.* Trans. Daniel Heller-Roazen. Stanford, CA: Stanford University Press.

———. 2004. *The Open: Man and Animal.* Trans. Kevin Attell. Stanford, CA: Stanford University Press.

Alford, Fred C. 2004. Levinas & Paranoia: When the Other is Too Other. Paper presented at the annual meeting of the American Political Science Association, Hilton Chicago and the Palmer House Hilton, September 2, 2004, Chicago. Available at *http://www.allacademic. com/meta/p59331_index.html.*

Alter, Nora. 1996. The Political Im/perceptible in the Essay Film: Farocki's "Images of the World and the Inscription of War." *New German Critique* 68: 165–92.

Althusser, Louis. 1971. *Lenin and Philosophy.* Trans. Ben Brewster. New York: Monthly Review Press.

Amy-Chinn, Dee. 2005. Queering the Bitch: Spike, Transgression and Erotic Empowerment. *European Journal of Cultural Studies* 8 (3): 313–28.

Apter, Emily. 2006. On Oneworldness: Or Paranoia as a World System. *American Literary History* 18: 365–89.

Attali, Jacques. 1985. *Noise: The Political Economy of Music.* Trans. Brian Massumi. Minneapolis: University of Minnesota Press.

Badiou, Alain. 2002. One Divides into Two. *Culture Machine* 4. Available at *http://culture machine.tees.ac.uk/Cmach/Backissues/j004/Articles/Badiou.htm.*

———. 2005. *Being and Event.* Trans. Oliver Feltham. London; New York: Continuum.

Badmington, Neil. 2001. Pod Almighty!; or Humanis, Posthumanism, and the Strange Case of Invasion of the Body Snatchers. *Textual Practice* 15 (1): 5–22.

———. 2004a. *Alien Chic: Posthumanism and the Other Within.* London and New York: Routledge.

———. 2004b. Roswell High, Alien Chic and the In/Human. In *Teen TV: Genre, Consumption and Identity,* ed. Glyn Davis and Kay Dickinson, pp.166–75. London: British Film Institute.

Balibar, Etienne. 1991. Is There a "Neo-Racism"? In *Race, Nation, Class: Ambiguous Identities,* ed. Etienne Balibar and Immanual Wallerstein, pp.17–28. London and New York: Verso.

Banks, Miranda J. 2004. A Boy for All Planets: Roswell, Smallville and the Teen Male Melodrama. In *Teen TV: Genre, Consumption and Identity*, ed. Glynn Davis and Kay Dickinson, pp. 17–28. London: British Film Institute.

Barbaccia, Holly G. 2000. Buffy in the "Terrible House." *Slayage: On-Line International Journal of Buffy Studies*. Available at http://www.slayage.tv/essays/slayage4/barbaccia.htm.

Barthes, Roland. 1974. *S/Z*. Trans. Richard Miller. New York: Hill and Wang.

Battis, Jes. 2006. The Kryptonite Closet: Silence and Queer Secrecy in *Smallville*. *Jump Cut: A Review of Contemporary Media* 48: (Winter). Available at http://www.ejumpcut.org/archive/jc48.2006/gaySmallville/index.html.

Battles, Kathleen, and Wendy Hilton-Morrow. 2002. "Gay Characters in Conventional Spaces" Will and Grace and the Situation Comedy Genre. *Critical Studies in Media Communication* 19 (1): 87–105.

Baudrillard, Jean. 1983. *Simulations*. Trans. Paul Foss, Paul Patton, and Philip Beitchman. New York: Semiotext(e).

———. 1991. L'Amérique, ou l a pensée de l'espace. In *Citoyenneté et Urbanité*, ed. Y. Dauge, pp. 155–64. Paris: Éditions Espirit.

———. 1993. *The Transparency of Evil: Essays on Extreme Phenomena*. Trans. James Benedict. London and New York: Verso.

Bauman, Zygmund. 1996. From Pilgrim to Tourist—or a Short History of Identity. In *Questions of Cultural Identity*, ed. Stuart Hall and Paul du Gay. London: Sage.

Baxter, L. A., and B. M. Montgomery. 1996. *Relating: Dialogues & Dialectics*. New York: Guilford Press.

Beck, Ulrich. 1992. *Risk Society: Towards a New Modernity*. Trans. Mark Ritter. London and Newbury Park, CA: Sage.

Beck, Ulrich, and Johannes Willms. 2004. *Conversations with Ulrich Beck*. Trans. Michael Pollak. Oxford: Blackwell; Cambridge: Polity Press.

Beck, Ulrich, Anthony Giddens, and Scott Lash, eds. 1994. *Reflexive Modernization: Politics, Tradition and Aesthetics in the Modern Social Order*. Cambridge: Polity Press.

Bell, Clive. 1958. *Art*. London and New York: Capricorn Books.

Bell, Jeffrey, A. 2003. Between Individualism and Socialism: Deleuze's Micropolitics of Desire. Available at http://www2.selu.edu/Academics/Faculty/jbell/micropolitics.pdf.

Bennett, Andy. 1999. Subcultures or Neo-tribes?: Rethinking the Relationship between Youth, Style and Musical Taste. *Sociology* 33 (3): 599–617.

———. 2000. *Popular Music and Youth Culture: Music, Identity and Place*. Basingstoke, UK: Macmillan.

———. 2005. In Defense of Neo-Tribes: A Response to Blackman and Hesmondhalgh. *Journal of Youth Studies* 8 (2): 255–59.

Bergoffen, Debra. 1996. Queering the Phallus. In *Disseminating Lacan*, ed. David Pettigrew and François Raffoul, pp. 273–94. Albany: State University of New York Press.

Berlowitz, Marvin J., and A. Nathan Lang. 2003. The Proliferation of JROTC: Educational Reform or Militarization? In *Education as Enforcement*, ed. Kenneth J. Saltman and David A. Gabbard, pp. 163–76. New York: Routledge.

Berman, Morris. 1981. *The Reenchantment of the World*. Ithaca, NY: Cornell University Press.

Bersani, Leo. 1989. Pynchon, Paranoia, and Literature. *Representations* 25 (Winter): 99–118.

Bhabha, Homi. 1994. Signs Taken for Wonders: Questions of Ambivalence and Authority Under a Tree Outside Delhi, May 1817. In *The Location of Culture*, Homi Bhabha, pp.102–22. London and New York: Routledge.

Birchall, Clare. 2004. "Feels Like Home": Dawson's Creek, Nostalgia and the Young Adult Viewer. In *Teen TV: Genre, Consumption and Identity*, ed. Glynn Davis and Kay Dickinson, pp. 176–90. London: British Film Institute.

Bishop, John H., Mathew Bishop, Michael Bishop, Lara Gelbwasser, Shana Green, and Andrew Zuckerman. 2003. Nerds and Freaks: A Theory of Student Culture and Norms. *Brookings Papers on Education Policy*, pp. 141–213.

Bishop, John H., Mathew Bishop, Michael Bishop, Lara Gelbwasser, Shanna Green, Erica Peterson, Anna Rubinsztaj, and Andrew Zuckerman. 2004. Why We Harass Nerds and Freaks: A Formal Theory of Student Culture and Norms. *Journal of School Health* 74 (7): 235–51.

Blackman, Shane. 2005. Youth Subcultural Theory: A Critical Engagement with the Concept, Its Origins and Politics, from the Chicago School of Postmodernism. *Journal of Youth Studies* 8 (1): 1–20.

Bloustein, Geraldine. 2002. Fans with a Lot at Stake: Serious Play and Mimetic Excess in *Buffy the Vampire Slayer*. *European Journal of Cultural Studies* 5 (4): 427–49.

Booker, Will. 2001. Living on *Dawson's Creek*: Teen Viewers, Cultural Convergence, and Television Overflow. *International Journal of Cultural Studies* 4 (4): 456–72.

Botting, Fred. 2004. Fcuk Speed. *Culture and Organization* 10 (1): 37–52.

Boucher, Geoff. 2000. Hegel and Postmodern Discourse Theory. Available at *http://www. ethicalpolitics.org/geoff-boucher/2000/postmodernism.htm*.

Bowers, Cynthia. 2000. Generation Lapse: Problematic Parenting of Joyce Summers and Rupert Giles. *Slayage: On-Line International Journal of Buffy Studies*. Available at http:// www.slayage.tv/essays/slayage2/bowers.htm.

Bracher. Mark. 1993. *Lacan, Discourse, and Social Change: A Psychoanalytic Cultural Criticism*. Ithaca, NY and London: Cornell University Press.

Braidotti, Rosi. 2000. Teratologies. In *Deleuze and Feminist Theory*, ed. Claire Colebrook and Ian Buchanan, pp. 156–72. Edinburgh, UK: Edinburgh University Press.

———. 2002. *Metamorphoses: Towards a Materialist Theory of Becoming*. Cambridge: Polity Press.

Brockman, John. 1995. *The Third Culture*. New York: Simon and Schuster.

———, ed. 2003. *The New Humanists: Science at the Edge*. New York: Barnes and Noble.

Brod, Harry. 1999. Did You Know Superman is Jewish? *Tattoo Jew* 3. Available at http:// web.archive.org/web/20010411074229/http://www.tattoojew.com/supermensch.html.

Brothers, Joyce. 1981. *What Every Woman Should Know About Men*. New York: Ballantine.

Bucci, Wilma. 1997. *Psychoanalysis and Cognitive Science: A Multiple Code Theory*. New York: Guilford.

Buchanan, Ian. 1997. Deleuze and Pop Music. *Australian Humanities Review*. Available at www.australianhumanitiesreview.org/archive/Issue-August-1997/buchanan.html.

———. 2002. Schizoanalysis and Hitchcock: Deleuze and the Birds. *Strategies: Journal of Theory, Society & Culture* 15 (1): 105–18.

Buchanan, Ian, and Marcel Swiboda. 2004. *Deleuze and Music*. Edinburgh, UK: Edinburgh University Press.

Bucholtz, Mary. 2002. Youth and Cultural Practice. *Annual Review of Anthropology* 31: 525–52.

Bukatman, Scott. 2003. X-Bodies: The Torment of the Mutant Superhero (1994). In *Matters of Gravity: Special Effects and Superman in the 20th Century*, pp. 48–78. Durham and London: Duke University Press.

Burns, Christy L. 2001. Erasure: Alienation, Paranoia, and the Loss of Memory in *The X-Files*. *Camera Obscura* 15 (3): 194–225.

Butler, Judith. 1990. *Gender Trouble*. London and New York: Routledge.

———. 1993. *Bodies That Matter: On The Discursive Limits of "Sex"*. New York: Routledge.

———. 2004. *Undoing Gender*. London and New York: Routledge.

Byrne, Rhonda, ed. (2006). *The Secret*. Hillsboro, OR: Beyond Words Publishing.

Callander, Michelle. 1999. Bram Stoker's Buffy: Traditional Gothic and Contemporary Culture. *Slayage: On-Line International Journal of Buffy Studies.* Available at *http://www. slayage.tv/essays/slayage3/callander.htm.*

Campbell, Jan. 2000. *Queering the Phallus. In Arguing With the Phallus: Feminist, Queer and Postcolonial Theory: A Psychoanalytic Contribution,* pp. 131–58. London: Zed Books.

Campbell, Joseph. 1973. *The Hero with a Thousand Faces.* Princeton, NJ: Princeton University Press.

Castells, Manuel. 1989. *The Informational City.* Oxford: Blackwell.

Chun, Wendy Hui Kyong. 2006. *Control and Freedom: Power and Paranoia in the Age of Fiber Optics.* Cambridge, MA: MIT Press.

Churchland, Patricia. 1989. *Neurophilosophy: Toward a Unified Science of the Mind-brain.* Cambridge, MA: MIT Press.

Clover, Carol. 1987. Her Body, Himself: Gender in Slasher Films. *Representations* 20 (Fall): 187–228.

———. 1992. *Men, Women and Chainsaws: Gender in the Modern Horror Film.* Princeton, NJ: Princeton University Press.

Collins, Bradford R., and David Cowart. 1996. Through the Looking-Glass: Reading Warhol's Superman. *American Imago* 53 (2): 107–37.

Conaway, Sandra. 2007. Girls Who (Don't) Wear Glasses: The Performativity of Smart Girls on Teen Television. Unpublished PhD dissertation. Bowling Green, OH: Bowling Green State University.

Connell, R.W., and James Messerschmidt. 2005. Hegemonic Masculinity: Rethinking the Concept. *Gender & Society* 19 (6): 829–59.

Copjec, Joan. 1999. The Tomb of Perseverance: On Antigone. In *Giving Ground: The Politics of Propinquity,* ed. Joan Copjec and Michael Sorkin, pp. 233–66. London and New York: Verso.

———. 2006. May '68, the Emotional Month. In *Lacan: The Silent Partners,* ed. Slavoj Žižek, pp. 90–114. London and New York: Verso.

Cordesman, Anthony H. 2001. Biological Warfare and the Buffy Paradigm. *Center for Strategic and International Studies,* Washington, D.C., September 29, 2001. Available at www.csis.org.

Critchley, Simon. 1992. *The Ethics of Deconstruction: Derrida and Levinas.* London: Blackwell.

———. 1999. Comedy and Finitude: Displacing the Tragic-Heroic Paradigm in Philosophy and Psychoanalysis. In *Ethics, Politics, Subjectivity,* pp. 217–38. London and New York: Verso.

———. 2002. Ethics, Politics and Radical Democracy: The History of a Disagreement. *Culture Machine* 4 (the ethico-political issue). Available at http://culturemachine.tees. ac.uk/Cmach/Backissues/j004/Articles/critchley.htm.

Currie, Dawn H., Deirdre M. Kelly, and Shauna Pomerantz. 2006. "The Geeks Shall Inherit the Earth": Girls' Agency, Subjectivity and Empowerment. *Journal of Youth Studies* 9 (4): 419–36.

Danesi, Marcel. 1999. *Cool: The Signs and Meanings of Adolescence.* Toronto: University of Toronto Press.

Dean, Creasy Kenda. 2004. Somebody Save Me: Passion, Salvation, and the Smallville Effect. Available at http://www.ptsem.edu/iym/lectures/2004/Dean-Somebody.pdf.

Dean, Jodi. 1998. *Aliens in America: Conspiracy Cultures from Outerspace to Cyberspace.* New York: Cornell University Press.

———. July 17, 2006. Deleuze and Lacan. Blog, I cite. Retrieved January 14, 2008. Available at http://jdeanicite.typepad.com/i_cite/2006/07/deleuze_and_lac.html.

Dean, Tim. 2000. Bodies That Mutter. In *Beyond Sexuality*, pp. 174–214. Chicago: University of Chicago Press.

———. 2000. *Beyond Sexuality*. Chicago: University of Chicago Press.

DeAngelis, Barbara. 1990. *Secrets about Men Every Woman Should Know*. New York: Dell.

De Certeau, Michel. 1984. *"Making Do": Uses and Tactics. The Practice of Everyday Life*. Trans. Steven F. Rendail, pp. 29–42. Berkeley: University of California Press.

De La Rosa, Manuela. 2000. Buffy the Vampire Slayer, the Girl Power Movement, and HEROISM Available at www.hometown.aol.com/mdelar9493.

Deleuze, Gilles. 1983. *Nietzsche & Philosophy*. Trans. Hugh Tomlinson. New York: Columbia University Press.

———. 1988a. *Bergsonism*. Trans. H. Tomlinson and B. Habberjam. New York: Zone Books.

———. 1988b. *Foucault*. Trans. Seán Hand. London: Athlone.

———. 1989. *Cinema 2: The Time-Image*. Trans. Hugh Tomlinson and Robert Galeta. Minneapolis: Minnesota Press.

———. 1990. *The Logic of Sense*. Trans. Mark Lester with Charles Stivale and ed. Constantin Boundas. New York: Columbia University Press. Original 1969.

———. 1990. Plato and the Simulacrum. In *The Logic of Sense*. Trans. Mark Lester with Charles Stivale and ed. Constantin Boundas, pp. 253–63. New York: Columbia University Press. Original 1969.

———. 1992a. *Expressionism in Philosophy: Spinoza*. Trans. M Joughin. New York: Zone Books.

———. 1992b. Mediators. In *Incorporations*. Trans. Martin Joughin and ed. Jonathan Crary and Stanford Kwinter, pp. 281–94. New York: Zone Books.

———. 1993. *The Fold: Leibniz and the Baroque*. Trans. Tom Conley. Minneapolis: University of Minnesota Press.

———. 1994. *Difference and Repetition*. Trans. Paul Patton. New York: Columbia University Press. Cited as *DR*.

———. 1997. *Essays Critical and Clinical*. Trans. Daniel W. Smith and Michael A. Greco. Minneapolis, MN: University of Minneapolis Press.

———. 1997. To Be Done with Judgment. In *Essays Critical and Clinical*. Trans. Daniel W. Smith and Michael A. Greco and ed. Daniel W. Smith, pp.126–35. London and New York: Verso.

———. 2001. *Pure Immanence: Essays on A Life*. Trans. Anne Boyman. New York: Zone Books.

———. 2003. *Francis Bacon: The Logic of Sensation*. Trans. D. W. Smith. London: Continuum.

——— and Félix Guattari. 1983. *Anti-Oedipus: Capitalism and Schizophrenia*. Vol. 1. Trans. Robert Hurley, Mark Seem, and Helen R. Lane. London: Minneapolis: University of Minnesota. Cited as *A-O*.

———and Félix Guattari. 1986. *Kafka: Toward a Minor Literature*. Trans. Dana Polan. Minneapolis: University of Minnesota Press. Cited as *K*.

——— and Félix Guattari. 1987. *A Thousand Plateaus: Capitalism and Schizophrenia*, vol. 2. Trans by Brian Massumi. Minneapolis: University of Minnesota Press. Cited as *TP*.

——— and Félix Guattari. 1994. *What is Philosophy?* Trans. Hugh Tomlinson and Graham Brurchell, New York: Columbia University Press. Cited as *WP*.

Dennett, Daniel. 1991. *Consciousness Explained*. Boston: Little, Brown.

Derrida, Jacques. 1978. Cogito and the History of Madness. In *Writing and Difference*. Trans, A. Bass. Chicago: University of Chicago Press. Original 1967.

———. 1996. Exergue. In *Archive Fever: A Freudian Impression*. Trans. Eric Prenowitz and ed. Archive Fever. Chicago and London: University of Chicago Press.

———. 1997. *Politics of Friendship.* Trans. George Collins. London and New York: Verso.

———. 2002. The Animal That Therefore I Am (More to Follow). Trans. David Wills. *Critical Inquiry* Winter 28 (2): 369–418.

———. 2003. Autoimmunity: Real and Symbolic Suicide. In *Philosophy in a Time of Terror: Dialogues with Jürgen Habermas and Jacques Derrida,* ed. G. Borradori. Chicago: University of Chicago Press.

Deutsche, Rosalyn. 1996. *Evictions: Art and Spatial Politics.* Cambridge, MA: MIT Press.

Dickinson, Kay. 2004. "My Generation": Popular Music, Age and Influence in Teen Dram of the 1990s. In *Teen TV: Genre, Consumption and Identity,* ed. Gylyn Davis and Kay Dickinson, pp.99–111. London: BFI.

Dolar, Mladen. 1993. "Beyond Interpellation." *Qui Parlé* 6 (2): 73–96.

———. 2006. *The Voice and Nothing More.* Cambridge, MA, and London: MIT Press.

Dorr, Aimée, and Sandra Irlen. 2002. Teen Television as a Stimulus for Moral Dilemma Discussions: Adolescent Girls' Conversations about *Dawson's Creek, Freaks and Geeks, Get Real,* and *7th Heaven.* ERIC # ED465686.

Dow, B. J. 2001. Ellen, Television, and the Politics of Gay and Lesbian Visibility. *Critical Studies in Media Communication* 18 (2): 123–40.

Dreisinger, Baz. 2000. The Queen in Shining Armor: Safe Eroticism and the Gay Friend. *Journal of Popular Film and Television* 28 (1): 2–11.

Driver, Susan. 2005. Intersubjective Openings: Rethinking Feminist Psychoanalysis of Desire beyond Heteronormative Ambivalence. *Feminist Theory* 6 (1): 5–24.

Durham, Scott. 1998. *Phantom Communities: The Simulacrum and the Limits of Postmodernism.* Stanford, CA: Stanford University Press.

Dworkin, Ronald. 1986. *Law's Empire.* Cambridge, Mass.: Harvard University Press.

Eagan, Patrick L. 1987. Flag with a Human Face. In *The Persistence of a Legend,* ed. Dennis Dooley and Gary Engle, pp. 88–102. Cleveland, OH: Octavia.

Early, Frances. 2001. Staking Her Claim: Buffy the Vampire Slayer as Transgressive Woman Warrior. *Journal of Popular Culture* 35 (3): 11–27.

Eco, Umberto. 1972. The Myth of Superman. Trans. Natalie Chilton. *Diacritics* 2 (1): 14–22.

———. 1979. The Poetics of the Open Work (1959). In *The Role of the Reader: Explorations in the Semiotics of Texts,* pp. 47–66. Bloomington: Indiana University Press.

Edwards, Lynne. 2002. Slaying in Black and White: Kendra as Tragic Mulatta in *Buffy.* In *Fighting the Forces: What's at Stake in* Buffy the Vampire Slayer, ed., Rhonda V. Wilcox and David Lavery, pp. 85–97. Lanham, MD: Rowman and Littlefield.

Engle, Gary. 1987. What Makes Superman so Darned American? In *The Persistence of a Legend,* ed. Dennis Dooley and Gary Engle, pp. 79–87. Cleveland, OH: Octavia.

Evans, Caroline. 1997. Dreams that only Money Can Buy . . . or, The Shy Tribe in Flight from Discourse. *Fashion Theory: The Journal of Dress, Body & Culture* 1 (2): 169–88.

Feasey, Rebecca. 2006. Charmed: Why Teen Television Appeals to Women. *Journal of Popular Film and Television* 34 (1): 2–9.

Feig, Paul. 2002. *Kick Me: Adventures in Adolescence.* New York: Three Rivers.

Fein, Ellen, and Sherrie Schnieder. 1995. *The Rules: Time-Tested Secrets for Capturing the Heart of Mr. Right.* New York: Warner Books.

Felman, Shoshana. 1975. Madness and Philosophy or Literature's Reason. *Yale French Studies* 52: 206–28.

Felski, Rita. 1996. Fin de siècle, Fin de sexe: Transsexuality, Postmodernism, and the Death of History. *New Literary History* 27 (2): 337–49.

Fink, Bruce. 1995. *The Lacanian Subject: Between Subject and Jouissance.* Princeton, NJ: Princeton University Press.

Fiske, John. 1987. *Television Culture.* London and New York: Routledge.

Flieger, Jerry Aline. 1991. *The Purloined Punch Line: Freud's Comic Theory and the Postmodern Text.* Baltimore: Johns Hopkins University Press.

———. 2000. Becoming-Woman: Deleuze, Scheber and Molecular Identification. In *Deleuze and Feminist Theory,* ed. Ian Buchanan and Claire Colebrook, pp. 38–63. Edinburgh, UK: Edinburgh University Press.

———. 2005. *Is Oedipus Online? Siting Freud After Freud.* Cambridge, MA: MIT Press.

Foucault, Michel. 1965. *Madness and Civilization; A History of Insanity in the Age of Reason.* Trans. Richard Howard. New York: Pantheon Books. Original 1961.

———. 1983. *This is Not a Pipe: With Illustrations and Letters by René Magritte.* Trans. and ed. James Harkness. Berkeley: University of California Press. Original *Ceci n'est pas une pipe.* Montpellier: Fata Morgana, 1973.

———. 1985. *The Use of Pleasure.* Trans. Robert Hurley. New York: Vintage Books.

———. 1988. Technologies of the Self. In *Technologies of the Self: A Seminar With Michel Foucault,* eds. Luther H. Martin, H. Gutman, and Patrick H. Hutton, pp.16–49. Amherst: University of Massachusetts.

Frank, Thomas. 2004. *What's the Matter with Kansas: How Conservatives Won the Heart of America.* London: Metropolitan Books.

Freud, Sigmund. 1953–74. *The Standard Edition of the Complete Psychological Works of Sigmund Freud,* 24 vols. London: Hogarth Press. Cited as *SE.*

Frith, Simon. 1978. *The Sociology of Rock.* London: Constable.

Frith, Simon. 2004. Afterward. In *After Subculture: Critical Studies in Contemporary Youth Culture,* ed. Andy Bennett and Keith Kahn-Harris, pp.173–78. Houndmills, Basingstoke, UK: Palgrave Macmillan.

Frosh, Stephen, Ann Phoenix, and Rob Patman. 2002. *Young Masculinities: Understanding Boys in Contemporary Society.* Basingstoke, UK: Palgrave Macmillan.

Frost, Liz. 2003. Doing Bodies Differently? Gender, Youth, Appearance and Damage. *Journal of Youth Studies* 6 (1): 53–70.

Fudge, Rachel. 1999. The Buffy Effect: Or, a Tale of Cleavage and Marketing. *Bitch Magazine* 10 (Summer). Available at *http://www.bitchmagazine.com/buffy1.htm.*

Garfinkle, Harry. 2002. Assessing Lacan's Teaching Within Historical Intellectual Achievements; Or, Was Lacan a Scientific Educator? In *Pedagogical Desire: Authority, Seduction, Transference, and the Question of Ethics,* ed. jan jagodzinski, pp. 181–98. Westport, CT: Bergin and Garvey.

Gasché, Rodolphe. 1986. *The Tain of the Mirror: Derrida and the Philosophy of Reflection.* Cambridge, MA: Harvard University Press.

Giddens, Anthony. 1984. *The Constitution of Society: Outline of the Theory of Structuration.* Stanford: University of California Press.

———. 1991. *Modernity and Self-Identity: Self and Society in the Late Modern Age.* Cambridge: Polity Press.

———. 1992. *The Transformation of Intimacy.* Stanford, CA: Stanford University Press.

Gilbert, Sandra, and Susan Gubar. 1979. *The Madwoman in the Attic: The Woman Writer and the Nineteenth-Century Literary Imagination.* New Haven, CT: Yale University Press.

Gill, Rosalind. 2003. From Sexual Objectification to Sexual Subjectification: The Resexualization of Women's Bodies in the Media. *Feminist Media Studies* 3 (1): 99–106.

Gill, Rosalind, and Elena Herdieckerhoff. 2006. Rewriting the Romance: New Feminities in Chick Lit? *Feminist Media Studies* 6 (4): 487–504.

Godfrey, Richard, Jack Gavin, and Jones Campbell. 2004. Sucking, Bleeding, Breaking: On the Dialectics of Vampirism, Capital, and Time. *Culture and Organization* 10 (1): 25–36.

Golden, Christopher, and Namcy Holder. 1998. *Buffy the Vampire Slayer: The Watcher's Guide*. New York and London: Pocket Books.

Golding, Sue. 1997. *The Eight Technologies of Otherness*. New York: Routledge.

Goldmann, Lucien. 1964. *The Hidden God: A Study of Tragic Vision in the Pensées of Pascal and the Tragedies of Racine*. Trans. Philip Thody. New York: Routledge and K. Paul.

Goldsmith, Scott J. 2001. Oedipus or Orestes? Homosexual Men, Their Mothers, and Other Women Revisited. *Journal of the American Psychoanalytic Association* 49 (4): 1269–87.

Goodchild, Philip. 1997. Deleuzean Ethics. *Theory, Culture & Society* 14 (2): 39–50.

Graham, Helen. 2007. Representations, Ideologies and Affects of a Newly Post-9/11 Feminist Icon. *Feminist Media Studies* 7 (1): 1–16.

Graham, Paula. 2001. Buffy Wars: The Next Generation. *Rhizomes: Cultural Studies in Emerging Knowledge* 4. Available at *http://www.rhizomes.net/issue4/graham.html*.

Grass, Günter. 1962. *The Tin Drum*. Trans. Ralph Mannheim. London: Secker & Warburg.

Gray, John. 1993. *Men Are from Mars, Women Are from Venus: A Practical Guide for Improving Communication and Getting What You Want in Your Relationships*. New York: HarperCollins.

Grigg, Russell. 2006. Beyond the Oedipus Complex. In *Jacques Lacan and the Other Side of Psychoanalysis*, ed. Justin Clemens and Russell Grigg, pp.50–68. Durham, NC and London: Duke University Press.

Grinker, Richard. 2007. *Unstrange Minds: Remapping the World of Autism*. New York: Basic Books.

Grist, Leighton. 2003. "It's Only a Piece of Meat": Gender Ambiguity, Sexuality, and Politics in *The Crying Game* and *M. Butterfly*. *Cinema Journal* 42 (4): 3–28.

Gross, Neil, and Solon Simmons. 2002. Intimacy as a Double-Edged Phenomenon? An Empirical Test of Giddens. *Social Forces* 81 (2): 531–55.

Grossberg, Lawrence. 1992. *We Gotta Get Out of This Place: Popular Conservatism and Postmodern Culture*. London: Routledge.

———. 1997. *Dancing in Spite of Myself*. London and Durham, NC: Duke University Press.

———. 1998. The Cultural Studies' Crossroads Blues. *European Journal of Cultural Studies* 1 (1): 65–82.

———. 2005. Being Young Sucks: An Interview With Lawrence Grossberg. Interview and Introduction by Jonathan Sterne. *Bad Subjects*, no. 74, December. Available at Grossberghttp://bad.eserver.org/issues/2006/74/grossberg.html.

Grove, Andrew S. 1996. *Only the Paranoid Survive: How to Exploit the Crisis Points that Challenge Every Company and Career*. New York: Currency Doubleday.

Habermas, Jürgen. 1978. *Knowledge and Human Interests*. Trans. Jeremy J. Shapiro. London: Heinemann. Original 1972.

———. 1984. *The Theory of Communicative Action*. Trans. T. McCarthy. Boston: Beacon Press. Original 1981.

Halberstam, Judith. 2006. Popular Culture "Conceives" the Transbiological. Lecture, The Center for the Study of Women, University of Alberta, Edmonton, Alberta, Canada, presented on October 24, 2006.

Hall, Stuart. 1997. Culture and Power. *Radical Philosophy* 86 (November–December): 24–41.

Hallward, Peter. 2006. *Out of This World*. London: Verso.

Hansen, Mark B. N. 2004. *New Philosophy for New Media*. Cambridge, MA: MIT Press.

Hardt, Michael, and Antonio Negri. 2000. *Empire*. Cambridge, MA: Harvard University Press.

Hayes, Tom. 1999. A Jouissance beyond the Phallus: Juno, Saint Teresa, Bernini, Lacan. *American Imago* 56 (4): 331–55.

Hebdige, Dick. 1979. *Subculture: The Meaning of Style*. London: Methuen.

Hesmondhalgh, David. 2005. Subcultures, Scenes or Tribes? None of the Above. *Journal of Youth Studies* 8 (1): 21–40.

Hetherington, P. 1998. *Expressions of Identity: Space, Performance, Politics*. London: Sage.

Heywood, Leslie, and Jennifer Drake, eds. 1997. *Third Wave Agenda: Being Feminist, Doing Feminism*. Minneapolis: University of Minnesota Press.

Hills, Matt. 2003. Whose "Postmodern" Horror? Alejandro Amenábar's Tesis (thesis, 1996). *Kinoeye* 3 (5). Available at www.kinoeye.org/03/05/hills05.php.

———. 2004. *Dawson's Creek*: "Quality Teen TV" and "Mainstream Cult"? In *Teen TV: Genre, Consumption and Identity*, ed. Glynn Davis and Kay Dickinson, pp. 54–70. London: British Film Institute.

Hillman, James. 1988. *On Paranoia* (Eranos Lectures Series, 8). Dallas, TX: Spring Publishers.

Hirsch, Robert. 2005. The Strange Case of Steve Kurtz: Critical Art Ensemble and the Price of Freedom. *Afterimage* 32, no. 6 (May/June): 22–31.

Hodkinson, Paul. 2003. "Net.Goth": Internet Communities and (Sub)Cultural Boundaries. In *The Post-Subcultures Reader*, ed. David Muggleton and Rupert Weinzierl, pp. 285–98. New York and Oxford: Berg.

Hodkinson, Paul, and Wolfgang Deicke, eds. 2007. *Youth Cultures: Scenes, Subcultures and Tribes*. New York: Routledge.

Holland, S. 2004. *Alternative Femininities: Body, Age and Identity*. Oxford and New York: Berg.

Houran, James, and Kevin D. Randle. 2002. "A Message in a Bottle": Confounds in Deciphering the Ramey Memo from Roswell UFO Case. *Journal of Scientific Exploration* 16 (1): 45–66.

Irigaray, Luce. 1985. *This Sex Which Is Not One*. Trans. Catherine Porter. Ithaca, NY: Cornell University Press.

———. 1996. *I Love to You: Sketch of a Possible Felicity in History*. Trans. Alison Martin. New York: Routledge.

———. 2001. *To Be Two*. Trans. Monique M. Rhodes and Marco F. Cocito-Monoc. New York: Routledge.

Irwin, William. 2002. *The Matrix and Philosophy: Welcome to the Desert of the Real*. Chicago, IL: Open Court.

Jaanus, Marie. 1997. The Ethics of the Real in Lacan's Seminar VII. *Literature and Psychology* 43 (1–2, Spring): 1–18.

jagodzinski, jan. 2001. Recuperating the Flaccid Phallus: The Hysteria of Post-Oedipal Masculine Representation and the Return of the Anal Father. *Journal for the Psychoanalysis of Culture & Society* 6 (1): 29–39.

———. 2002a. A Strange Introduction: My Apple Thing. In *Pedagogical Desire: Authority, Seduction, Transference, and the Question of Ethics*, ed. jan jagodzinski, pp. xiii–lx. Westport, CT: Bergin and Garvey.

———. 2002b. The Drive toward Piercing & Tattooing: Postmodern Bodies of Performative Excess. *JPCS: Journal for the Psychoanalysis of Culture & Society* 7 (2): 251–62.

———. 2003a. Women's Bodies of Performative Excess: Miming, Feigning, Refusing, and Rejecting the Phallus. *Journal for Psychoanalysis for Society & Culture* 8 (1): 23—41.

———. 2003b. Unromancing the Stone of "Resistance": In Defense of a Continued Radical Politics in Visual Cultural Studies. *Journal of Social Theory in Art Education* 23: 104–39.

———. 2004. *Youth Fantasies: The Perverse Landscape of the Media*. New York: Palgrave Press.

————. 2005. *Music in Youth Culture: A Lacanian Approach.* New York: Palgrave Macmillan.

————. 2006a. Jacque Lacan as Queer Theorist: Is There a "Beyond" to Identification Politics in Education? *Journal of Curriculum Theorizing* 22 (3): 55–70.

————. 2006b.Video Game Cybersubjects, Violence and Addiction: A Psychoanalytic Approach. *Psychoanalysis, Culture, & Society* 11 (3): 282–303.

————. 2006c. The Trauma of the Image: Prisoner "Abuse" in Abu Ghraib Prison. *SIMILE: Studies in Media and Information Literacy Education* 6 (1). University of Toronto Press e-journal. Available at *https://webmail.ualberta.ca/horde/index.php?url=https%3A%2F%2Fwebmail.ualberta.ca%2Fhorde%2F.*

————. 2007. Revisiting and Reviewing the Media Spin Surrounding the Gulf Wars. *SMILIE: Studies in Media & Information* 7 (4). University of Toronto Press e-journal. Available at http://utpjournals.metapress.com/content/fwx6l86941721218/.

————. 2008. Postmetaphysical Vision: Art Education's Challenge In an Age of Globalized Aesthetics (A Mondofesto). *Studies in Art Education: A Journal of Issues and Research* 49 (2): 147–60.

jagodzinski, jan, and B. Hipfl. 2001. Youth Fantasies: Reading "The X-Files" Psychoanalytically. *SIMILE, Studies in Media & Information Literacy Education* 1 (2). University of Toronto Press e-journal. Available at http://www.utpjournals.com/jour.ihtml?lp=simile/issue2/jag1.html.

Jameson, Fredric. 1983. Postmodernism and Consumer Society. In *The Anti-Aesthetic: Essays on Postmodern Culture,* ed. Hal Foster, pp.111–25. Washington: Bay Press.

————. 1984. "Postmodernism or the Cultural Logic of Late Capitalism." *New Left Review* 146: 53–92.

————. 1991. *Postmodernism or, The Cultural Logic of Late Capitalism.* London and New York: Verso.

————. 1992. *The Geopolitical Aesthetic: Cinema and Space in the World System.* Bloomington: Indiana University Press.

————. 1999. Cognitive Mapping. In *Poetics/Politics: Radical Aesthetics for the Classroom,* ed. Amitava Kumar, pp. 155–67. New York: University Press.

————. 2003. The End of Temporality. *Critical Inquiry* 29 (4): 695–718.

Jasper, Karl. 1953. *The Origin and Goal of History.* Trans. Michael Bullock. New Haven: Yale University Press.

Johnson, James. 1991. Habermas on Strategic and Communicative Action. *Political Theory* 19 (2): 181–201.

Jones, Cary M. 2006. Smallville and New Media Mythmaking: Twenty-First Century Superman. *Jump Cut: A Review of Contemporary Media* 48 (Winter). Available at www.ejumpcut.org/archive/jc48.2006/SmallvilleFans/index.html.

Kahn, Richard, and Douglas Kellner. 2003. Internet Subcultures and Oppositional Politics. In *The Post-Subcultures Reader,* ed. David Muggleton & Rupert Weinzierl, pp. 299–314. New York and Oxford: Berg.

Kant, Immanuel. 2002. *Critique of Practical Reason.* Intro. Stephen Engstrom. Trans. Werner S. Pluhar. Indianapolis, IN: Hackett. Original 1788.

Kantrowitz, Barbara, and Julie Scelfo. 2006. What Happens When They Grow Up. *Newsweek,* November 27, 2006. Available at *www.msnbc.msn.com/id/15792805/site/newsweek/.*

Karlyn, Kathleen Rowe. 2003. Scream, Popular Culture, and Feminism's Third Wave: "I'm not my Mother." *Genders* 38. Available at *http://www.genders.org/g38/g38_rowe_karlyn.html.*

Katti, Christian. 2002. "Systematically" Observing Surveillance: Paradoxes of Observation according to Niklas Luhmann's Systems Theory. In *Ctrl [space]: Rhetorics of*

Surveillance: From Bentham to Big Brother, ed. Thomas Y. Levin, Ursula Frohne, and Peter Weibel, pp. 534–55. Karlsruhe, Germany :ZKM Center for Art and Media; Cambridge, MA: MIT Press.

Kinney, David. A. 1993. From Nerds to Normals: The Recovery of Identity among Adolescents from Middle School to High School. *Sociology of Education* 66 (1): 21–40.

Klein, Jesse. 2006. Cultural Capital and High School Bullies: How Social Inequality Impacts School Violence. *Men and Masculinities* 9 (1): 53–75.

Klein, Naomi. 2001. Reclaiming the Commons. *New Left Review* 9 (May–June): 81–89.

Kleinhans, Chuck, John Hess, and Julia Lesage. 2006. The Last Word: Education Under Attack. *Jump Cut: A Review of Contemporary Media* 48 (Winter). Available at *http://www.ejumpcut.org/archive/jc48.2006/lastword/index.html.*

Kozlovic, Anton Karl. 2002. Superman as Christ-Figure: The American Pop Culture Movie Messiah. *Journal of Religion and Film* 6 (1): 1–25. Available at http://www.unomaha.edu/jrf/superman.htm.

———. 2006. Spider-Man, Superman—What's the Difference?" *Kritikos: An International and Interdisciplinary Journal of Postmodern Cultural Sound, Text and Image* 3 (July). Available at http://garnet.acns.fsu.edu/~nr03/spiderman-superman.htm.

Kramer, Roderick. 2004. *The Power of Paranoia* [videorecording]. Stanford, CA: Stanford Video; Mill Valley, CA: Kantola Productions.

Kristeva, Julia. 1991. *Strangers to Ourselves.* Trans. Leon S. Roudiez. New York: Columbia University Press.

Kroker, Arthur. 1992. *The Possessed Individual: Technology and the French Modernism.* New York: St. Martin's Press.

Küchler, Tilman. 1994. *Postmodern Gaming: Heidegger, Duchamp, Derrida.* New York: Peter Lang.

Kurzweil, Ray. 1999. *The Age of Spiritual Machines: When Computers Exceed Human Intelligence.* New York: Viking.

Kustritz, Anne. 2005. Smallville's Sexual Symbolism: From Queer Repression to Fans' Queered Expressions. *Refractory: A Journal of Entertainment Media* 8. Available at http://www.refractory.unimelb.edu.au/journalissues/vol8/kustritz.html.

Lacan, Jacques. 1962–63. *The Seminar of Jacques Lacan.* Book 10, 1962–1963. Trans. Cormac Gallagher. Unpublished. Cited as *S* X, Anxiety.

———. 1966–67. *The Seminar of Jacques Lacan.* Book 14, The Logic of Phantasy [in French], 1966—1967. Trans. Cormac Gallagher. Unpublished. Cited as *S* XIV, Logic of Phantasy.

———. 1975–76. *The Seminar of Jacques Lacan.* Book 23. Joyce and the Sinthome [in French], 1975—1976. Trans. Cormac Gallagher. Unpublished. Cited as *S* XXII, Sinthome.

———. 1979. *The Seminar of Jacques Lacan.* Book 11, The Four Fundamental Concepts of Psycho-Analysis [in French], 1964. Ed. Jacques-Alain Miller. (Trans. Alan Sheridan. Harmondsworth, UK: Penguin Books. Cited as *S XI,* Four Fundamentals.

———. 1981. *The Language of the Self: The Function of Language in Psychoanalysis.* Trans. Anthony Wilden. Baltimore: John Hopkins University Press.

———. 1993. *The Seminar of Jacques Lacan.* Book 3, The Psychoses [in French], 1955—1956. Ed. Jacques-Alain Miller. Trans. Russell Grigg. New York: W.W. Norton. Cited as *S III,* Psychoses.

———. 1997. *The Seminar of Jacques Lacan.* Book 12, The Ethics of Psychoanalysis [in French], 1959—1960. Ed. Jacques Alain-Miller. Trans. Dennis Porter. New York: W. W. Norton. Cited as *S VII,* Ethics.

———. 1998. *The Seminar of Jacques Lacan.* , Book 20, Encore, On Feminine Sexuality: The Limits of Love and Knowledge [in French], 1972—1973. Ed. Jacques-Alain Miller. Trans. Bruce Fink. New York: Norton. Cited as *S XX,* Encore.

————. 2002. The Direction of the Treatment and the Principles of its Power (1958). In *Écrits: A Selection*. Trans. Bruce Fink. New York: W. W. Norton.

————. 2003 *Family Complexes in the Formation of the Individual* (1938) Trans. Cormac Gallagher. Unpublished. London: Karnac Books.

————. 2007. *The Seminar of Jacques Lacan*, Book 17, The Other Side of Psychoanalysis [in French], 1969–1970. Trans. with notes Russell Grigg. New York: W.W. Norton and Co. Cited as S XVII, Envers.

Laclau, Ernesto. 1988. "Politics and the Limits of Modernity." In *Universal Abandon? The Politics of Postmodernism*, ed. Andrew Ross, pp. 63–82. Minneapolis: University of Minnesota Press.

————. 2002. Ethics, Politics and Radical Democracy: A Response to Simon Critchley. *Culture Machine* 4 (the ethico-political issue). Available at *http://culturemachine.tees. ac.uk/Cmach/Backissues/j004/Articles/laclau.htm*.

Laclau, Ernesto, and Chantal Mouffe. 1985. *Hegemony and Socialist Strategy: Towards a Radical Democratic Politics*. Trans. Winston Moore and Paul Cammack. London: Verso.

Lash, Scott. 1990. *Sociology of Postmodernism*. London and New York: Routledge.

————. 1994. Refexivity and Its Doubles: Structure, Aesthetics, Community. In *Reflexive Modernization: Politics, Tradition and Aesthetics in the Modern Social Order*, ed. Ulrich Beck, Anthony Giddens, and Scott Lash, pp. 110–73. Stanford, CA: Stanford University Press.

————. 2003. Reflexivity as Non-Linearity. *Theory, Culture & Society* 20 (2): 49–57.

Lash, Scott, and Jonathan Friedman, eds. 1992. *Modernity and Identity*. Oxford and Cambridge, MA: Blackwell.

Latham, Rob. 2002. *Consuming Youth: Vampires, Cyborgs, and the Culture of Consumption*. Chicago: University of Chicago Press.

Latour, Bruno. 1993. *We Have Never Been Modern*. Cambridge, MA: Harvard University Press.

————. 2003. Is *Re*-modernization Occurring—And if So, How to Prove It? A Commentary on Ulrich Beck. *Theory, Culture & Society* 20 (2): 35–48.

Layton, Lynne. 2004. *Who's That Girl? Who's That Boy? Clinical Practice Meets Postmodern Gender Theory*. London and Hillsdale, NJ: Analytic Press.

Leblanc, Lauraine. 2002. *Pretty in Punk: Girls' Gender Resistance in a Boys' Subculture*. New Brunswick, NJ and London: Rutgers University Press.

Lee, Kyoo. 2004. The Madness of Measuring Madness: Revisiting Foucault vs. Derrida on Descartes's Madmen. *Naked Punch* 4: 53–65. Available at *http://www.nakedpunch.com/ nakedpunch4.html*.

Lefebvre, Alexandre. 2007. Critique of Teleology in Kant and Dworkin: The Law Without Organs (LwO). *Philosophy & Social Criticism* 33 (2): 179–201.

Levinas, Emmanuel. 1969. *Totality and Infinity: An Essay on Exteriority*. Trans. Alphonso Lingis. Pittsburgh, PA: Duquesne University Press.

Levine, Judith. 2002. *Harmful to Minor: The Perils of Protecting Children from Sex*. Minneapolis: University of Minnesota Press.

Levinson, Brett. 2008. *In Theory, Politics Does Not Exist*. Available at http://abdn.ac.uk/ modernthought/archive/publications/levinson1.doc.

Lewis, Jon. 1992. *The Road to Romance and Ruin: Teen Films and Youth Culture*. New York: Routledge.

Litter, Jo. 2005. "Beyond the Boycott: Anti-Consumerism, Cultural Change and the Limits of Reflexivity." *Cultural Studies* 19 (2): 227–52.

Lupen, Deborah. 1999. *Risk*. London: Routledge.

Lyotard, Jean François. 1971. *Discours, Figure*. Paris: Klincksleck.

————. 1993. *Libidinal Economy*. Trans. Iain Hamilton Grant. Bloomington: Indiana University Press.

MacCormack, Patricia. 2004. Perversion: Transgressive Sexuality and Becoming Monster. *thirdspace* 3(2): 27–40.

MacNeil, William. 2007. "You Slay Me!" *Buffy* as Jurisprudence of Desire. In *Lex Populi: The Jurisprudence of Popular Culture*, pp. 28–43. Stanford, CA: Stanford University press.

Maffesoli, Michel. 1996. *The Time of the Tribes: The Decline of Individualism in Mass Society.* Trans. D. Smith. London: Sage.

Malbon, Ben. 1999. *Clubbing: Dancing, Ecstasy and Vitality.* London: Routledge.

Malik, Suhail. 2002. Between Bodies without Organs and Machines without Desire: Deleuze-Guattari's Elision of Prosthetic Actuality. *New Formation* 46 (Spring): 34–47.

Mangels, Andy. 2000. *From "Scream" to "Dawson's Creek": An Unauthorized Take on the Phenomenal Career of Kevin Williamson.* Los Angeles: Renaissance Books.

Marchant, Oliver. 2003. Bridging the Micro-Macro Gap: Is There Such a Thing as a Post-Subcultural Politics? In *The Post-Subcultures Reader,* ed. David Muggleton and Rupert Weinzierl, pp. 83–97. New York and Oxford: Berg.

Markula, Pirkko. 2003. The Technologies of Self: Sport, Feminism, and Foucault. *Sociology of Sport Journal* 20 (2): 87–107.

Massumi, Brian. 1993. *A User's Guide to Capitalism and Schizophrenia: Deviations from Deleuze and Guattari.* Cambridge, MA: MIT Press.

Maturana, Humberto, and Francisco J. Valera. 1980. *Autopoiesis and Cognition: The Realization of the Living.* Dordrecht, Holland and Boston: D. Reidel.

McCulloch, Stewart, Alexis and Nick Lovegreen. 2006. "We Just Hang Out Together": Youth Cultures and Social Class. *Journal of Youth Studies* 9 (5): 539–56.

McClelland, Bruce. 1999. By Whose Authority? The Magical Tradition, Violence and the Legitimation of the Vampire Slayer. *Slayage: On-Line International Journal of Buffy Studies.* Available at http://www.slayage.tv/essays/slayage1/bmcclelland.htm.

McGowan, Todd. 2003. *The End of Dissatisfaction: Jacques Lacan and the Emerging Society of Enjoyment.* New York: State University of New York Press.

McRobbie, Angela. 2004. "Post-Feminism and Popular Culture." *Feminist Media Studies* 4 (3): 255–64.

Melley, Timothy. 2000. *Empire of Conspiracy: The Culture of Paranoia in Post-War America.* Ithaca, NY: Cornell University Press.

Mendlesohn, Farah. 2002. "Surpassing the Love of Vampires: Or Why (and How) We Are Denied a Queer Reading of Buffy/Willow." In *Fighting the Forces: What's at Stake in Buffy the Vampire Slayer,* ed. Rhonda V. Wilcox and David Lavery, pp. 45–60. Lanham, MD: Rowan and Littlefield.

Messerschmidt, James. 2000. *Nine Lives: Adolescent Masculinities, the Body, and Violence.* Boulder, CO: Westview.

Mestrovic, Stepan. 1998. *Anthony Giddens: The Last Modernist.* London: Routledge.

Meyer, Michaela D. E. 2003. "It's Me. I'm It": Defining Adolescent Sexual Identity through Relational Dialectics in Dawson's Creek. *Communication Quarterly* 51 (3): 262–76.

Milner, Murray, Jr. 2004. *Freaks, Geeks, and Cool Kids: American Teenagers, Schools, and the Culture of Consumption.* New York: Routledge.

Minsky, Marvin. 1986. *The Society of Mind.* New York: Simon and Schuster.

Montgomery, B. M., and L. A. Baxter. 1998. *Dialectical Approaches to Studying Personal Relationships.* Mahwah, NJ: Lawrence Erlbaum.

Muggleton, David, and Rupert Weinzierl, eds. 2003. *Post-Subculturalist Reader.* London: Berg.

Murphy, Keith, and Jonathan David Tankel. 1998. Collecting Comic Books: A Study of Fan and Curatorial Consumption. In *Theorizing Fandom: Fans, Subculture and Identity,* ed. Cheryl Harris and Alison Alexander, pp. 55–68. Cresskill, NJ: Hampton.

Murphy, Timothy S., and W. Daniel Smith. 2001. What I Hear Is Thinking Too: Deleuze and Guattari Go Pop. *ECHO: A Music-centered Journal* 3 (1). Available at www.humnet. ucla.edu/echo.

Newman, Kim. 1999. *Millennium Movies.* London: Titan Books.

Newman, Michael Z. 2006. From Beats to Arcs: Toward a Poetics of Television Narrative. *Velvet Light Trap* 58 (1): 16–28.

Nietzsche, Friedrich Wilhelm. 1994. *On the Genealogy of Morals.* Trans. Carol Diethe and ed. Keith Ansell-Pearson. Cambridge: Cambridge University Press. Original 1887.

Nigianni, Chrysanthl. 2005. Narrative (Schizo)analysis: Moving Away from Representational Thought. Available at http://www.uel.ac.uk/cnr/documents/Nigianni.doc.

Norwood, Robin. 1985. *Women Who Love Too Much.* New York: Putman.

Owen, A. Susan. 1999. Vampires, Postmodernity and Postfeminism: *Buffy the Vampire Slayer. Journal of Popular Film and Television* 27 (2): 24–31.

O'Donnell, Patrick. 2000. *Latent Destinies: Cultural Paranoia and Contemporary U.S. Narrative.* Durham, NC, and London: Duke University Press.

Parenti, Michael. 2004. *Superpatriotism.* San Francisco: City Lights Books.

Peebles, Gustav. 2003. Jesus Hates New York. *Believer,* February. 8. Available at http://www. believermag.com/issues/200311/?read=article_peebles.

Pender, Patricia. 2004. "Kicking Ass is Comfort Food": Buffy as Third Wave Feminist Icon. In *Third Wave Feminism: A Critical Exploration,* ed. Stacey Gills, Gillian Howie, and Rebecca Munford, pp. 175–84. Basingstoke, UK: Palgrave Macmillan.

Pevey, Aaron. 2007. From Superman to Superbland: The Man of Steel's Popular Decline Among Postmodern Youth. Unpublished Master of Arts thesis, Georgia State University. Available at *http://etd.gsu.edu/theses/available/etd-04172007-133407/.*

Pfaller, Robert. 1995. Negation and its Reliabilities: An Empty Subject for Ideology? Available at Phafhttp://www.lacan.com/pfaller.htm#1.

Philips, Maxine. 2003. The "Buffy Paradigm" Revisited. *Dissent Magazine.* Available at http://www.dissentmagazine.org/article/?article=511.

Pipher, Mary. 1994. *Reviving Ophelia: Saving the Selves of Adolescent Girls.* New York: Ballantine Books.

Pisters, Patricia. 2003. *The Matrix of Visual Culture: Working with Deleuze in Film Theory.* Stanford, CA: Stanford University Press.

Pizzino, Christopher. 2002. A Legacy of Freaks. *Postmodern Culture* 12 (2). Available at *http://www.iath.virginia.edu/pmc/textonly/issue.102/12.2contents.html.*

Playdon, Zoe-Jane. 2001. "The Outsiders' Society": Religious Imagery in *Buffy the Vampire Slayer. Slayage: On-Line International Journal of Buffy Studies.* Available at *www.slayage. tv/essays/slayage5/playdon.htm.*

Plessner, Helmuth. 1970. *Laughing and Crying: A Study of the Limits of Human Behavior.* Evanston, IL: Northwestern University Press.

Powell, Anna. 2005. *Deleuze and the Horror Film.* Edinburgh: Edinburgh University Press.

Rich, E. 2005. Young Women, Feminist Identities and Neo-Liberalism. *Women's Studies International Forum* 28 (5): 495–508.

Riviere, Joan. 1929. Womanliness as a Masquerade. *International Journal of Psychoanalysis* 10. Available at www.ncf.edu/hassold/WomenArtists/riviere_womanliness_as_masquerade. htm.

Rogin, Michael. 1987. *Ronald Reagan, the Movie and Other Episodes in Political Demonology.* Berkeley: University of California Press.

Romanyshyn, Robert D. 1989. *Technology as Symptom and Dream.* London and New York: Routledge.

Rotman, Brian. 1987. *Signifying Nothing: The Semiotics of Zero.* New York: St. Martin's Press.

Roudinesco, Elisabeth. 1997. *Jacques Lacan.* Trans. Barbara Bray. New York: Columbia University Press.

Roustang, François. 1987. How Do You Make a Paranoiac Laugh? *MLN* 102 (4): 707–18.

Santner, Eric L. 1996. *My Own Private Germany: Daniel Paul Schreber's Secret History of Modernity.* Princeton, NJ: Princeton University Press.

———. 2006. *On Creaturely Life: Rilke, Benjamin, Sebald.* Chicago: University of Chicago Press.

Scharff, Christina. 2007. Perspectives on Feminist (Dis-)identification in the British and German Contexts: A Performative Approach. Paper presented at New Femininities: An International Conference, London, UK, January 26, 2007. Available at www.lse.ac.uk/collections/newFemininities/Perspectives.

Schefer, Jean-Louis. 1995. *The Enigmatic Body: Essays on the Arts.* Trans. Paul Smith. Cambridge and New York: Cambridge University Press.

Schefer, Jean Louis. 1976. Split color/blur. *Twentieth Century Studies* 15/16: 82–100.

Schmiedel, Stevie Meriel. 2004. *Contesting the Oedipal Legacy: Deleuzean vs. Psychoanalytic Feminist Critical Theory.* Piscataway, NJ; M LIT.

Schneider, Jay Steven. 2000a. Kevin Williamson and the Rise of the Neo-Stalker. *Post Script: Essays in Film and the Humanities* 19 (2): 73–87.

———. 2000b. A Tale of Two Psychos (Prelude to a Future Reassessment). *Senses of Cinema.* Available at *http://www.sensesofcinema.com/contents/00/10/psychos.html.*

Seem, Mark. 1983. Introduction. In *Anti-Oedipus: Capitalism and Schizophrenia.* Vol. 1, ed. Gilles Deleuze and Félix Guattari and trans. Robert Hurley, Mark Seem, and Helen R. Lane, pp. xv–xxiv. London and Minneapolis: University of Minnesota.

Seigworth, Gregory J. 2006. Cultural Studies and Giles Deleuze. In *New Cultural Studies: Adventures in Theory,* ed. Gary Hall and Claire Birchall, pp. 107–27. Edinburgh, UK: Edinburgh University Press.

Semetsky, Inna. 2004. Becoming-Language/Becoming Other: Whence Ethics? *Educational Philosophy and Theory* 36 (3): 313–25.

Sennett, Richard. 1998. *The Corrosion of Character: The Personal Consequences of Work in the New Capitalism.* New York: W. W. Norton.

Shalit, Wendy. 2000. *A Return to Modesty.* Touchstone, New York.

Shank, Barry. 1994. *Dissonant Identities: The Rock'n'roll Scene in Austin, Texas.* Hanover, NH: University Press of New England.

Sharpe, S. 2001. Going for It: Young Women Face the Future. *Feminism and Psychology* 11 (2): 177–88.

Shaviro, Steve. 2002. The Erotic Life of Machines." *Parallax* 8 (4): 21–32.

Shields, Robert. 1992. The Individual, Consumption Cultures and the Fate of Community. In *Lifestyle Shopping,* ed. Robert Shields, pp. 99–113. London: Routledge.

Siegel, Don. 1993. *A Siegel Film: An Autobiography.* London and Boston: Faber and Faber.

Silverman, Kaja. 1993. What Is a Camera? or: History in the Field of Vision. *Discourse* 15 (Spring): 3–56.

Simondon, Gilbert. 1992. The Genesis of the Individual. In *Incorporations,* ed. Jonathan Crary and Sanford Kwinter, pp. 297–319. New York: Zone.

Sloterdijk, Peter (1983). *Erster Band.* Vol. 1 of *Kritik der Zynischen Vernunft.* Frankfurt: Suhrkamp Verlag.

———. 1987. *Critique of Cynical Reason.* Trans. Michael Eldred. Minneapolis: University of Minnesota Press.

Smith, Daniel W. 2004. The Inverse Side of the Structure: Žižek on Deleuze on Lacan. *Criticism* 46 (4): 635–50.

Smith, Paul. 1988. *Discerning the Subject*. Minneapolis: University of Minnesota Press.

Smith, Richard G. 2003. Baudrillard's Nonrepresentational Theory: Burn the Signs and Journey without Maps. *Environment and Planning D: Society and Space* 21:67–84.

Solms, Mark. 2003. *The Brain and the Inner World: An Introduction to the Neuroscience of Subjective Experience*. New York: Other Press.

Spah, Victoria. 2000. "'Aint Love Grand?" Spike and Courtly Love. *Slayage: On-Line International Journal of Buffy Studies*. Available at *http://www.slayage.tv/essays/slayage5/vint.htm*.

Spaise, Terry. 2005. Necrophilia and SM: The Deviant Side of Buffy the Vampire Slayer. *Journal of Popular Culture* 38 (4): 744–62.

Spicer, Arwen. 2004. "It's Bloody Brilliant!" The Undermining of Metanarrative Feminism in the Season Seven Arc Narrative of Buffy. *Slayage: On-Line International Journal of Buffy Studies* 4 (December 15). Available at *http://slayageonline.com/essays/slayage15/Spicer.htm*.

Spillers, Hortense. 1996. "All the Things You Could Be by Now, If Sigmund Freud's Wife Was Your Mother": Psychoanalysis and Race. *boundary 2* 23 (3): 75–141.

Stern, Daniel. 1985. *The Interpersonal World of the Infant: A View from Psychoanalysis and Developmental Psychology*. New York: Basic Books.

Storr, Meryl. 2003. *Latex and Lingerie: Shopping for Pleasure at Ann Summers Parties*. Oxford and New York: Berg.

Straw, Will. 1991. Systems of Articulation, Logics of Change: Communities and Scenes in Popular Music. *Cultural Studies* 5 (3): 368–88.

———. 2001. Scenes and Sensibilities. Available at *www.arts.mcgill.ca/ahcs/html/Pubscene.pdf*.

Stengel, Wendy A. F. G. 2000. Synergy and Smut: The Brand in Official and Unofficial Buffy the Vampire Slayer Communities of Interest. *Slayage: On-Line International Journal of Buffy Studies*. Available at *http://www.slayage.tv/essays/slayage4/stengel.htm*.

Stevenson, Gregory. 2003. *Televised Morality: The Case of Buffy the Vampire Slayer*. New York and Oxford: Hamilton Books.

Stoller, Debbie. 1998. The 20 Most Fascinating Women in Politics: Fresh Blood. *George*, September: 110–13.

Sweetman, Paul. 2004. Tourists and Travellers? "Subcultures," Reflexive Identities and Neo-Tribal Sociality. In *After Subculture: Critical Studies in Contemporary Youth Culture*, ed. Andy Bennett and Keith Kahn-Harris, pp. 79–93. New York and Houndmills, Basingstoke, UK: Palgrave Macmillan.

Taylor, Aaron. 2007. "He's Gotta Be Strong, and He's Gotta Be Fast, and He's Gotta Be Larger Than Life": Investigating the Engendered Superhero Body. *Journal of Popular Culture* 40 (2): 344–60.

Taylor, Charles. 1991. *The Ethics of Authenticity*. Cambridge, MA and London: Harvard University Press.

Theweleit, Klaus. 1977–78. *Male Fantasies*. Trans. S. Conway, E. Carter, and C. Turner. 2 vols. Minneapolis: University of Minnesota Press.

Thompson, J. B. and David Held, eds. 1982. *Habermas: Critical Debates*. Cambridge, MA: MIT Press.

Topping, Keith. 2001. *Slayer*. London: Virgin.

Trushell, John M. 2004. American Dreams of Mutants: The X-Men—"Pulp" Fiction, Science Fiction and Super Heroes. *Journal of Popular Culture* 38 (1): 149–68.

Tudor, Andrew. 1995. Unruly Bodies, Unquiet Minds. *Body & Society* 1 (1): 25–41.

Tyler, Imogen. 2005. "Who Put the 'Me' in Feminism?" The Sexual Politics of Narcissism. *Feminist Theory* 6 (1): 25–44.

Udovitch, Mim. 2000. What Makes Buffy Slay? *Rolling Stone*, May 11: 62–66.

Varela, Francisco, Evan Thompson, and Eleanor Rosch. 1991. *The Embodied Mind: Cognitive Science and Human Experience.* Cambridge: MIT Press.

Verhaeghe, Paul. 1999. *Love in a Time of Loneliness: Three Essays on Drives and Desires.* New York: Other Press.

Vint, Sherryl. 2000. "Killing us Softly"? A Feminist Search for the "Real" Buffy. *Slayage: On-Line International Journal of Buffy Studies.* Available at http://www.slayage.tv/essays/slayage5/vint.htm.

Vollum, Scott, and Cary D. Adkinson. 2003. The Portrayal of Crime and Justice in the Comic Book Superhero Mythos. *Journal of Criminal Justice and Popular Culture* 10 (2): 96–108.

Waid, Mark. 2005. The Real Truth about Superman: And the Rest of Us, Too. In *Superheroes and Philosophy*, ed. Tom Morris and Matt Morris, pp. 3–10. Chicago: Open Court.

Whedon, Joss. 2003. Slayonara Buffy. Interview, *SFX* 106 (July): 49–56.

Widder, Nathan. 2000. What's Lacking in the Lack: A Comment on the Virtual. *Angelaki* 5 (3): 117–38.

Wilcox, Rhonda V. 1998. There Will Never Be a "Very Special Buffy": Buffy and the Monsters of Teen Life. *Slayage: On-Line International Journal of Buffy Studies.* Available at http://www.slayage.tv/essays/slayage2/wilcox.htm.

———. 2002. "Every Night I Save You": Buffy. Spike, Sex and Redemption. *Slayage: On-Line International Journal of Buffy Studies.* Available at http://www.slayage.tv/essays/slayage5/wilcox.htm.

Wilcox, Rhonda V., and David Lavery. 2002. *Fighting the Forces: What's at Stake in Buffy the Vampire Slayer.* Lanham, MD: Rowan and Littlefield.

Williamson, Marianne. 1992. *Reflections on the Principles of a Course in Miracles.* New York: HarperCollins.

Wilson, Scott. 2000. Schizocapital and the Branding of American Psychosis. *Cultural Values* 4 (4): 474–96.

Winslade, J. Lawton. 2000. Teen Witches, Wiccans, and "Wanna-Blessed-Be's": Pop-culture Magic in Buffy the Vampire Slayer. *Slayage: On-Line International Journal of Buffy Studies.* Available at http://www.slayage.tv/essays/slayage1/winslade.htm.

Witse, Ed. 2004. Fans, Geeks and Nerds, and the Politics of Online Communities. Proceedings of the Media Ecology Association 5:1–7.

Wittkower, Rudolf, and Margot Wittkower. 1963. *Born under Saturn: The Character and Conduct of Artists: A Documented History from Antiquity to the French Revolution.* New York: Random House.

Wood, Chris. 2000. Finding the Father: A Psychoanalytic Study of Rebel without a Cause. *Senses of Cinema.* Available at http://www.sensesofcinema.com/contents/00/5/finding.html.

Zalloua, Zahi. 2004. Foucault as Educator: The Question of Technology and Learning How to Read Differently. *symploke* 12 (1–2): 232–47.

Žižek, Slavoj. 1989. *The Sublime Object of Ideology.* London and New York: Verso.

———. 1991. *Looking Awry: An Introduction to Jacques Lacan Through Popular Culture.* Cambridge, MA and London: MIT Press.

———. 1993. *Tarrying with the Negative: Kant, Hegel, and the Critique of Ideology.* Durham, NC: Duke University Press.

———. 1994. *For They Know What They Do: Enjoyment as a Political Factor.* New York and London: Verso.

———. 1996. "I Hear You with My Eyes": or, The Invisible Master. In *Gaze and Voice as Love Objects*, eds. Renata Salecl and Slavoj Žižek, pp. 90–126. Durham, NC: Duke University Press.

———. 1997. Smashing the Neighbor's Face. Available at *http://www.lacan.com/zizsmash. htm.*

———. 1998. The Cartesian Subject Versus the Cartesian Theatre. In *Cogito and the Unconscious Sic 2,* ed. Slavoj Žižek, pp. 247–74. Durham, NC: Duke University Press.

———. 1999a. The Undergrowth of Enjoyment: How Popular Culture can Serve as an Introduction to Lacan . In *The Žižek Reader,* ed. Elizabeth Wright and Edmond Wright, pp.11–36. Oxford: Blackwell Publishers.

———. 1999b. *The Ticklish Subject; The Absent Centre of Political Ontology.* London and New York: Verso.

———. 2001. *The Fragile Absolute, or, Why is the Christian Legacy Worth Fighting For?* New York: Verso.

———. 2004a. Death's Merciless Love. *Lacanian Ink.* May 9, 2004. Available at http://www. lacan.com/zizek-love.htm.

———. (2004b. *Organs without Bodies: On Deleuze and Consequences.* New York and London: Routledge.

———. 2004c. On Divine Self-Limitation and Revolutionary Love (with Joshua Delpech-Ramey). *Journal of Philosophy & Scripture,* Spring. Available at http://www.lacan.com/ zizekscripture.htm.

———. 2006. Neighbors and Other Monsters: A Plea for Ethical Violence. In *The Neighbor: Three Inquiries in Political Theology,* ed. Slavoj Žižek, Eric L. Santner, and Kenneth Reinhard, pp.134–90. Chicago: University of Chicago Press.

———. 2007. Deleuze and the Lacanian Real. Available at http://www.lacan.com/zizrealac. htm.

Žižek, Slavoj, Eric L. Santner, and Kenneth Reinhard. 2006. *The Neighbor: Three Inquiries in Political Theology.* Chicago: University of Chicago Press.

Zupančič, Alenka. 2000. *The Ethics of the Real.* London and New York: Verso.

Index